MESSAGES

Free expression is in trouble.
It can no longer be certain of its best protection – 'the general spirit of the people' – as Alexander Hamilton, one of the founders of the United States, put it over two centuries ago.

Today, the public, faced with the excesses of tabloid journalism and explicitness of all kinds in other media, appears no longer to be convinced that free expression is a crucial foundation of civil society.

Yet, for all its faults, free expression under the law has, as Churchill once said of democracy, to be better than any alternative system.

Messages is a search for the origins of media forms, from print and stage through photography to film and broadcasting. With a wealth of illuminating anecdotes and quotations, Brian Winston clearly and forcefully argues, in accessible jargon-free language, the case for the media's central importance as an essential engine underpinning all human rights and driving the Western concept of the individual.

This is essential and entertaining reading for anyone concerned about the protection of liberty of expression.

Brian Winston, currently a Pro-Vice Chancellor at the University of Lincoln, worked in the 1960s on Granada TV's *World in Action*; then for the BBC and WNET (New York) where he won an Emmy for documentary script writing in 1985, as a columnist on *Ink*, *The Soho* (New York) *Weekly News* and *The Listener*, as a co-producer of a Canadian feature film and a governor of the BFI. He has taught at Universities on both sides of the Atlantic and at Britain's National Film School. *Messages* is his thirteenth book.

Messages

Free Expression, Media and the West from Gutenberg to Google

Brian Winston

LONDON AND NEW YORK

First published in 2005
by Routledge
2 Park Square, Milton Park, Abingdon, Oxon OX14 4RN

Simultaneously published in the USA and Canada
by Routledge
270 Madison Ave, New York, NY 10016

Routledge is an imprint of the Taylor & Francis Group

Typeset in Galliard by M Rules
Printed and bound in Great Britain by
Antony Rowe Ltd, Chippenham, Wiltshire

British Library Cataloguing in Publication Data
A catalogue record for this book is available from
the British Library

Library of Congress Cataloguing in Publication Data
Winston, Brian
Messages / Brian Winston.
p. cm.
Includes biographical references and index.
1. Mass media—History. I. Title.
P90. W496 2005
302.23'09—dc22   2005007301

ISBN10: 0-415-23222-8 (hbk)
1SBN10: 0-415-36457–4 (pbk)

ISBN13: 9-78-0-415-23222-7 (hbk)
ISBN13: 9-78-0-415-36457-7 (pbk)

For
The University of Lincoln

CONTENTS

CONTENTS

CONTENTS

CONVERGENCE

PREAMBLE

What we obtain too cheap, we esteem too lightly – Tis dearness
only that gives everything its value. Heaven knows how to put
a proper price upon its goods; and it would be strange indeed
if so celestial an article as FREEDOM should not be highly rated.

Thomas Paine, radical, writer and failed corset-maker, wrote those words
on Christmas Eve 1776, amidst George Washington's defeated army
camped at Fort Lee, New Jersey. This book, designed for the general
reader, is dedicated to the proposition that Paine was right about this; and
that the freedom for which he and many fought across the intervening
centuries and bequeathed so cheaply to us, we do indeed esteem too
lightly. In fact, we have allowed the very word to become tainted in the
mouths of modern braggadacios, to stand more for the unbridled exercise
of power and repression than as a right constraining such abuses.

This book is also predicated on the belief that, of those freedoms which
progressives of Paine's time deemed 'celestial', none is greater than the
individual's freedom of expression. This is especially so when it is used to
address others in the mass and therefore 'the liberty of the press is the palladium of all civil, political and religious rights' (as the eighteenth-century
radical who wrote under the pen-name 'Junius' put it). As we enter a third
century since Paine's and Junius's day, when no freedom is treated so cav-
alierly, if not quite in practice then certainly as a principle, it is perhaps time
to attempt to reanimate their language, cleansing it of its Enlightenment
taints of paternalism, élitism and hypocrisy. This book seeks to do this, in
a small way, by retelling the story of how we have come to this point via
the media. Yet this is no chronicle of repression and censorship offered in
the name of uncontrolled media libertarianism. Rather, by recounting

the origins of media forms, it offers a narrative about individual and collective human creativity as it has been expressed through the last six centuries in Europe and its outreaches by the means of mass communication – from press and stage through photography to screen and loudspeaker.

Space and understanding have necessarily limited this account. As a sketch of the origins of media forms and practices, it is perforce abrupt in determining those points when originality gives way to more routine mature activity outside the scope of the book. The book's limitations would have been even more severe, of course, without the help and advice I have received from many friends and colleagues, but especially from Anthony Smith, who has most generously shared his vast stock of knowledge with me. Robert Franklin made an equally crucial contribution by helping me to focus my argument and Richard Keeble not only did that but also expended much effort on closely fact-checking my text. (Wrong dates are assuredly not his fault.) Other parts of the manuscript were read and much improved by Roberta Pearson, Michelle Hilmes, Liz Wells, David Bate, Annabel Leventon and Michael Early. Needless to say, any errors and confusions have nothing to do with them. At an earlier stage, I benefited from initial conversations with Richard Barbrook, help from Jane Chapman, Mike Mason, Erin Bell, Julian Petley, Alan Schneider, Maud Tyler and Harry Zeigler; and the whole thrust of my argument reflects, I hope not too inaccurately, an agenda determined by Nicholas Garnham. My daughter and son have been a massive encouragement by hearing me out and cheering me on; and my wife, as ever, has provided essential corrections.

This is, almost exclusively, a meditation on media histories written by others. It has been specifically designed for the non-specialist. It is, therefore, enormously and extensively (and repetitively) indebted to those I acknowledge too inadequately in the list of sources. I have tried to do nothing but make what I hope is an accessible, uncluttered (albeit picaresque) narrative pattern of their work in the name of an argument about media freedom and individual expression – an argument which I believe now needs urgently to be put.

PRINT

Prologue I

'THE LIBERTY TO KNOW':
PRINT FROM 1455

'The work of the books'

Mainz, the Rhineland: some time in 1455.

The men slid the inked forme under the platen and screwed it down, as they had done, modern scholars calculate, 237,169 times before. The printer, Peter Drach of Speyer, Clas Wolff, Jans von Koblenz – we just do not know who was at work that day – heaved the press-bar. Another heave and the forme was released. The 1282nd and final sheet of that copy of the Bible, the last of the edition, slid from the press, its black letters glistening.

'The work of the books' involved using four (or maybe six) presses upon which the men could produce between eight and 16 impressions an hour. Six compositors and 12 printers had taken almost a year to finish the run of 180 copies and, in the course of their labours, they had worn down four cases of type (both upper and lower). The type – Gothic Textura – aped the style of writing used by monks. Six centuries later, ten copies survive, the ink – soot, varnish, urine and egg white – still gleams.

The men were employed by a 55-year-old goldsmith and entrepreneur, Johnny Gooseflesh – Henne (Johann) Gensfleisch zu Gutenberg. Johann was eventually awarded the title 'Chevalier', but the 'zu' in his name did not denote aristocracy, merely that his family had lived in a house in Mainz called 'Gutenberg'. For more than a century, the Gensfleisch had been 'house retainers' of the master of the Bishop of Mainz's mint. Johann Gutenberg was just the latest of a long line of metal artificers, a member of the Goldsmiths' Guild, who also had skills as a diamond cutter and polisher. The Gutenberg family, because of their episcopal connections, tended to the more patrician party among the burghers who ruled the city.

The ordered hierarchy of the feudal world – from serf to yeoman to noble to king or bishop, and from kings and bishops in their turn to the Emperor and Pope – had been much battered in the calamitous previous century. Plague was a repeated disaster. The worst outbreak lasted from 1333 for 19 years, taking a third of Europe's people and eventually writing itself upon European consciousness as the 'Black Death'. The labour shortage it created severely undercut the traditional bonds tying each man to the man above him, leading to such outbreaks of unrest as the English Peasants Revolt of 1381 as authority attempted to impose the old restrictions on a much-depleted work force.[1]

In the small urban concentrations such as Mainz, although deference remained powerful, the unbroken chain of fealty was severely weakened. A less feudal and hidebound urban world was establishing itself. In that environment, developments such as double-entry book keeping introduced in Genoa at the beginning of the thirteenth century laid the foundations of mercantilist capitalism. Being able to strike a balance of debt against credit on an ongoing basis was to be as important to European civilisation as any technological advance.

Politically, too, the town was a place of innovation and experiment. Urban government stood between the citizen and the overlord. A collective, the burghers, was bound communally to a lord but their relationships, one to another, loomed as large as did their joint responsibility. Nowhere was this more the case than in southern Germany, where the hand of the Holy Roman Emperor was barely felt and the local lord had often seen his powers progressively curtailed by the growing independence of the burghers. For serfs still tied to their lord in the countryside, it was a truth of the day that '*stadluft macht frei*' – town air made you free.

Gutenberg was an urbanite, in his own day a comparatively rare figure, almost an outsider to the feudal structures which governed his world. He was still, of course, of that medieval world but his career also reveals a certain modernity, most importantly in what seems to have been a somewhat entrepreneurial spirit. Having been forced to flee from Mainz to Strasbourg in some municipal political upheaval, by 1437 he was immersed in a scheme to produce some 20,000 small mirrors mounted as brooches. These were to be sold to the swarms attending the Shrine Pilgrimage to see Aachen Cathedral's four most sacred 'Great Relics', which were exposed only once every seven years.[2] It was believed that if a mirror caught the image of the relics, it would itself be touched by the relics' beneficent strengths – a curious spiritualised echo of the photograph's power and attractiveness.[3] Gutenberg persuaded some other merchants to back him and set about making the mirrors – probably using a press to stamp out the brooches. Presses were a by no means uncommon machine of the day, important not only for making wine and oil but also for use in paper manufacture and in metal work. The only problem with the mirror money-making scheme was that the pilgrimage took placed in 1439, not 1438 as Gutenberg and his partners had erroneously calculated. This created a serious cash-flow problem and, inevitably, they finished up in court suing each other. Out of the legal records of this fiasco come the earliest hints indicating that Gutenberg thought the press might be put to other uses.

Gutenberg returned to Mainz in 1444 and by 1448 he was pursuing in earnest what subsequent court records refer to as 'Werk der Bücher' – the work of the books. He needed to 'invent' nothing for this new enterprise. Not only was the press to hand but so was the book. Handwritten on parchment, it had been around for 1,000 years, an alternative to the scroll. Paper was being produced by specialised manufacturers and by Gutenberg's time it was generally available, although production remained centred in Italy. The town of Fabriano was noted as making the best, but rivals were to be found further north. There were enough papermakers in Paris by 1398 for them to form a guild. Nevertheless, parchment continued to be used and was available in bulk, ready cut. Gutenberg printed 30 copies of the Bible on vellum, using the skins of about 170 sheep for each copy.

Different facets of the trade in texts had become specialised. To reduce the possibility of scribal error, for example, there was a business in hiring authoritative manuscripts, *exemplaria*, to copyists, normally quire by quire so that many hands could work simultaneously on the same book. Text copiers were distinct from illustrators. Illustrators were organised into workshops and used a form of tracing paper to make copies from master designs, 'cartoons'. Getting an image from a wood block in a press, xylography, was well established. They had been doing this in the East for 600 years at least. Pictures of the Virgin and the saints were particularly popular in Gutenberg's part of the world and in Burgundy. They were bought as talismans for the home. At first such prints bore handwritten legends but these became part of the engraving. Complete books of whole blocks – blockbooks – had begun to appear in the 1440s and *The Poor Man's Bible* (*Biblia Pauperum*) and *The Art of Dying* (*Ars Moriendi*) were particularly popular in this form. On the other hand, xylography also produced tools for the Devil's work in the form of playing cards.

Gathering all these elements together – paper or parchment, ink and wood block, putting copyists or xylographers to work, selling or hiring manuscripts for reading as well as copying – became the job of stationers, an ancient term which had been revived by the Italian universities. From the last quarter of the thirteenth century on, stationers were to be found in towns housing courts or universities, increasingly replacing monastic scriptoria as the source of manuscripts. The idea of the book, handwritten but as a set of identical multiple copies, was firmly established. Over 2,000 manuscript copies of Aristotle survive from the two centuries before Gutenberg. Some 250 copies of Sir John Mandeville's fantastical *Travels* (1356) survive in ten languages, including Irish. It was possible to be an avid collector. In 1346, the poet Petrarch had written: 'I cannot get enough books. It may be that I have already more than I need, but it is with books as it is with other things: success in acquisition spurs the desire to get still more.' Petrarch's was a passion which would not go away and feeding it remained profitable for many. Ninety years later Cosimo di Medici, *de facto* ruler of the Florentine

Republic, acquired what was probably the largest private collection in the West, the 800 books gathered by the early humanist scholar Niccolo Niccoli, and in 1444 he had them housed in Europe's first public library. It is no wonder that one successful stationer in the city, Vespiano di Bisticci, had enough work to employ 50 copyists on a permanent basis.

Gutenberg seems to have made two original technical contributions to the 'work of the books'. He concocted a new ink base, a variant on the recent Flemish development of oil-based paints. As his ink was better for vellum than paper, this improvement was not so critical, given paper was anyway replacing vellum. On the other hand, his refinement of the type-casting process was an essential advance. Gutenberg seems to have developed a little hand-held mould, a type-founder's tool, into which the liquid metal could be poured. It enabled individual letters – sorts (or even, perhaps, subdivided elements of individual letters) – to be made which could be assembled into texts, printed and taken down to be reused. The mould was also reusable, producing up to four sorts a minute, and could be easily disassembled. As many sorts were needed for every page of text and wore out quickly with repeated use, the mould was a critical development.

The recipe for ink and the creation of the little mould aside, Gutenberg was otherwise what we would today think of as a systems engineer, putting together machines and techniques readily available from parallel practical purposes, rather than the 'Eureka' inventor of popular imagination. Perhaps the surest claim he has to such a title rests on the idea of reusability rather than the creation of any particular device; it is the type-case, overflowing with letters, spaces and symbols, rather than the sorts or types themselves, which is the most radical new thing. *Reusability* of individual letters is the breakthrough, a concept which perhaps would come more readily into the mind of a metal worker than to a stationer surrounded by the paraphernalia of mass manuscript production. Otherwise, the skills Gutenberg needed to engrave the reversed letter in the mould would have been part of his stock-in-trade as a goldsmith. The concept of the metal punch had been known in antiquity and was the basis of the minting of money, also something with which Gutenberg would have been most familiar. Over the two centuries before the introduction of movable type, die stamps were being used in Europe for an increasing number of purposes, from inscribing crests to marking pewter. And presses were everywhere. That he was not alone in the 1440s in realising the potential of a system of printing using individual types is a proof that the 'invention of printing' is not the unexpected and inexplicable product of a single person's genius.

Metal workers, who were to be found in every European town and city, were all familiar with the tools and techniques necessary for printing. In 1444, the year Gutenberg quit Strasbourg, Procopius Waldvogel, a silversmith of Prague, was in Avignon, at work using a steel fount and press. In contracts dated from that year and 1446, there are clear references to the art of artificial writing (*ars artificialiter scribendi*) and to Latin and Hebrew letters, but no examples exist of his work. It must also be said that nothing that Gutenberg might have printed before 1448, despite veiled references, exists either. Given how little Gutenberg and Waldvogel had that was new, there might well have been other 'inventors'. Let Laurens Janszoon Coster of Haarlem, a rhetorician, stand for these putative lost others. At the same time as Johann and Procopius, this Laurens, according to a story published a century after his death, reputedly brought together punches to make metal letters, presses, formes and paper. None of his printing work, if there was any, survives either, although his writing does.

And then there is the problem of the East's influence. The earliest surviving blockbook is in Chinese and dates from 868 AD and type had been well known in China since the eleventh century AD at the latest. A major Korean treatise on etiquette had been produced with individual metal types in 1234. Yet Marco Polo, who said he was in China in the 1270s, made no mention of printing techniques – but he might never have actually travelled to the East. On the other hand, visitors who indubitably reached the Orient – emissaries of the Pope on recurrent visits to the Great Khan, or Catholic bishops sojourning in Beijing continuously between 1307 and 1368 – produced no records to show that the idea of movable type printing was ever transmitted to Europe – to Mainz – to the Hof zum Gutenberg – either. Against this, early that century Rashi ed-Din had noted the existence of type in Iran. The influence of the East is clear in the matter of paper, which the Chinese had made from rags from antiquity. It had been introduced to Europe via the Arab world in the twelfth century (although initially it gained little favour because it lacked the durability of vellum). With printing, the case for Europe merely imitating the Orient is far less clear-cut.

'Without the help of reed, stylus or pen'

The real question is why nobody in the West was moved to 'invent' printing before this time, not whether, when they did so, they were inspired by the East or by other unknown Europeans. Every element needed was to all intents and purposes lying around; even if knowledge came from the East, then it too must have arrived the previous century. There was simply no technological reason, in the form of a fundamental breakthrough without which it could not be made to work, to account for the emergence of printing from movable type in the 1440s. On the other hand, its simultaneous appearance in widely distanced towns within years of each other does speak to a shared set of social pressures, a level of demand for written texts which the old scriptorium system could not meet.

It is no accident that these men all worked in thriving urban environments of which the lords, one way and another, were removed beyond the walls. The seat of the Bishop of Mainz, an elector of the Holy Roman Emperor and Primate of the German-speaking lands, had moved some 10 kilometres downstream, across the river to Eltville. The burghers were left as much to their own devices as was anybody in that period. Strasbourg had closed its gates to an imperial army sent by the Emperor to bring its burghers back into line in 1391. Haarlem (if indeed it is involved) was one of a number of Dutch towns which had long enjoyed exceptional municipal rights guaranteed by charter. Avignon had a history of defiance to its overlord in the twelfth century and was, throughout most of the fourteenth century, home to the schismatic French popes in exile from Rome. The presence of the popes brought a host of merchants and bankers to the town. By Wandvogel's time, the popes had returned to Rome but Avignon was still a thriving centre of commerce, ruled by the Pontiff, it is true, but at a considerable distance.

Whatever the structure of urban control, all over Europe the burghers constituted an ever-expanding market for the written word. In the town, many were necessarily and increasingly literate – lawyers, scholars and doctors as well as merchants. They needed the paraphernalia of urban life – calendars for example. Gutenberg's earliest surviving production was a calendar for 1448. Secular literacy required grammars and encyclopaedias. These too were among Gutenberg's earliest productions – Donatus's *Ars Minor*, a standard Latin grammar, and the *Catholicon*, an encyclopaedia. There were three editions of the *Donatus* in 1458 and Gutenberg issued it no less than 23 times; 40 per cent of the output of William Caxton's successor in London, Wynkyn de Worde, was schoolbooks.

This is not to say that the universities, then purely ecclesiastical institutions, as well as the Church proper were neither interested in, nor of interest to, the printers. Priests, too, needed calendars. Gutenberg clearly understood the needs of the Church and among the first pages to issue from his press in the late 1440s were printed indulgences, a certificate sold by the Church as a means of raising revenue in return for the remission of sin. The major driver, though, was the critical importance of accuracy in the Holy Writ and other sacred texts. For churchmen worried about the spiritual health of their flocks, uncorrupted texts were essential. For example, at a local south German council in the 1420s in Basle, Nicholas of Cues exhorted abbots and bishops to ensure they had, at a minimum, clean copies of both the Bible and the missal.[4] This was not merely a matter of accuracy in Holy Writ; for Nicholas it was a central element in the reforms Church corruption necessitated. Gutenberg had put himself in the business of meeting that need; hence the Bible of 1455 and the Psalter of 1457. Within the Church, there was a rising demand for such accuracy grounded in the growing belief that individual salvation required uncorrupted scripture and prayer. This was a demand that could never be satisfied by the copyists.

Social needs, in the shape of the reform of the Church as well as the edification and entertainment requirements of educated townsfolk, were widespread by the mid-fifteenth century. If a 'cause' for the printing press is sought, here is where it is to be found. This explains the phenomenon of simultaneity in the 'invention' of printing from movable type in the 1440s. The curious 'accident' of different individuals putting together pre-existing technological systems for a new purpose at more or less the same moment is not uncommon. Because technologists exist and work in society like everybody else, it is scarcely surprising that they are affected by, and respond to, the same social forces – as happened in this instance and was to happen repeatedly in the history of communication technology. Very often, as in this case, the technological advance involved in what is commonly thought of as the 'invention' is minimal. It is the focusing of social needs which really acts as the driver pushing more than one individual 'inventor' onward.

Scholarly clergy, both conservative and reformist, were enthusiastic about the press: 'What an ascent towards God!' cried one bishop. 'What ecstatic devotion must we feel on reading the many books printing has given us.' As early as 1466, Cardinal Torquemada invited Ulrich Hahn of Ingelstadt to print the *Meditations* he had written. Torquemada was not alone in such an initiative. Major monasteries, such as Cluny and Citeaux, established print shops. Nor was the Church itself unique in its demand for accuracy. Within the universities, there was a growing thirst for accurate classical texts. Lawyers, too, were prominent among the urbanites demanding faultless printed matter.

In the half-century before 1500, between 15 and 20 million volumes were published: 77 per cent were in Latin; 45 per cent were religious. Religious texts took precedence over secular and within secular, Latin took precedence over the vernacular. One in three books were reprints of classic texts and one in ten were either scientific/medical or legal. The *Imitation of Christ* of Thomas à Kempis was the second most printed title after the Bible, followed by St Augustine's *Civitatis Dei* and handbooks for priests. Latin grammars, for the first time using the vernacular as the language of instruction, were the most printed secular texts, followed by the classics. There were many editions of popular works, including Aesop's *Fables* and Cato's *Distichia*, both often used as beginners' readers. In the vernacular, poets such as François Villon and Geoffrey Chaucer were deemed 'vendible'. There were 15 editions of Dante and 11 of Boccaccio. What were termed in the middle ages the 'Matters' of 'Rome' (classical stories from Homer on), of France (Roland) and of Britain (Arthur and the Round Table) were all printed. The popularity of bawdy was early established. Two hundred books were printed in Hebrew, including rabbinical commentaries as well as Holy Scriptures.

These common social needs ensured that presses spread quickly. Aided by the sacking of Mainz in 1462 by one of two rival claimants to the bishopric, Gutenberg's printers fanned out across Europe, sharing their craft as they went. By 1480, 110 towns had printing shops, the majority in Germany and Italy but also in France, Spain, England, Bohemia and Poland. Presses were set up to the south and east before 1500. Printers were in business in Montenegro and Gorazde by 1490. By 1515, there was a press in Abyssinia. The Bishop of Mexico imported the New World's first press in 1539 to produce ABCs, devotional manuals and law books. Moscow's first press dates from 1563. By the end of the century, the technology had returned in Western form to Nagasaki, via Goa (1557) and Macao (1588).

Initially, editions tended to match the maximum that the manuscript system could produce. John of Speyer, who brought the art of artificial writing to Venice, printed only 100 copies of Cicero's *Letters* in 1469, but this was quickly seen to be unnecessarily limited. A thousand-copies edition of the *Decretals* – papal letters on disciplinary matters – was printed in the same city two years later, while 930 copies of the Bible were made in Hamburg in 1478. In 1490, 700 copies of the Catalan epic romance, *Tirant Lo Blanc*, were printed. Although Erasmus's *In Praise of Folly* had an initial print run of 1800 in 1515, only the best-selling humanist texts could hope to exceed 1500, which remained the upper limit for many books throughout the sixteenth century. Religious titles were normally limited to runs of 2,000, but Luther's German vernacular translation of the New Testament, the so-called 'September Bible' of 1522, was issued in an edition of 4,000 and sold out in ten weeks.[5] It was reprinted 80 times in his lifetime.

From the beginning, the book began to distance itself from the manuscript and to assume its modern form, but it did so quite slowly over the better part of two centuries. First the old metal clasps and nail-studded covers produced in the monastic binderies gave way to leather-covered cardboard, made from old paper. Books were no longer designed to rest on desk or pulpit but to be stored upright on shelves. Although binding was very much a separate business from printing, the great printer Aldo Manuzio (better known by his latinised name Aldus Manutius), used 'morocco' leather from Cordova and introduced gold tooling for decoration and titling. Because of weight, though, the usual practice was for books to be shipped unbound to be finished by a local binder in a style ordered by a buyer.

To help binders, printers added a letter to the bottom of the page to identify a book's sections as determined by the printing process. These sections were soon themselves numbered by leaf for the same reason and then, in 1499, Aldus paginated a book right through. Page numbers allowed for more accurate citation. Previously, this had not been easy because of variations in the manuscript editions. A handwritten text needed to be broken down into chapter and verse if it was to be accurately quoted. Nevertheless, pagination in printed works only became common a century later at the turn of the 1600s. By that time, all the other elements and aspects of the modern book it facilitated were being regularly used, such as cross-referencing and tables of contents.

The names of the publisher and the author and the title of the work moved from a colophon, a final mark made by the scribe on the last page of a manuscript to form a title page, something seldom seen in handwritten texts. Manuscript titles tended to be the first words of the text, the 'incipit'. Thus the first book of the Bible in Hebrew is entitled

Beresheth, 'In the beginning . . .'. This system was still vibrant enough in the sixteenth century for the first printed book in Welsh to be called, *Yny Lhyvyr hwnn*, 'In this book . . .'. In print, titles replaced the incipit and were often set in ornate engraved frames such as those Hans Holbein was already making by 1510; the colophon stating the printer and his mark, however, remained at the back of the book. In early practice, colophons could be quite wordy explanations of a book's production history. The Gutenberg *Catholicon*'s colophon reads:

> With the help of the Most High . . . this noble book *Catholicon* has been printed and accomplished without the help of reed, stylus or pen but by the wondrous agreement, proportion and harmony of punches and types, in the year of the Lord's incarnation 1460 in the noble city of Mainz of the renowned German nation . . .

Titles may have been more efficient than incipits but they too were very long by modern standards. A century after the *Catholicon*, an English best seller's title page reads:

> Acts and Monuments of these latter and perilous days, touching matters of the Church, wherein are comprehended and described the great persecutions and horrible troubles, that hath been wrought and practised by the Romanish prelates, especially in this realm of England and Scotland, from the year of our Lord a thousand, unto the time now present.

Known more commonly as *Foxe's Book of Martyrs*, this was a hit in 1563. By then, the title page was as much an advertisement for a book's contents as a means of identifying the text. A century later, titling convention was settling down but the advertising function was still prominent:

> The Pilgrim's Progress FROM THIS WORLD TO That which is to come: Delivered under the Similitude of a DREAM Wherein is

Discovered, the manner of his setting out, His Dangerous Journey; and safe Arrival at the Desired Country. I have used Similitudes, Hos. 12.10. By John Bunyan.

The colophon eventually became an optional feature but the place and year of printing as well as the names of printer and/or publisher (and often his device or symbol) immigrated to the front of the book and were found on the title page or its reverse. The title page of *The Pilgrim's Progress* concludes: 'Licensed and Entered according to Order. LONDON, Printed for Nath. Ponder at the Peacock in the Poultrey near Cornhill, 1678'.

Aldus's influence was more quickly felt in other innovations. Since the compositor had less trouble than did the scribe in maintaining a straight line, Aldus set the print across the entire page instead of in scribal columns. He also realised that printing reduced the rarity of books and that, because print was more legible than handwriting, it could be smaller, allowing for reduced page sizes. Aldus exploited these insights by producing works a quarter or even an eighth the size of the folio and thereby liberated the book from the pulpit and library. Quarto and octavo volumes – devotional, professional or entertaining – were specifically designed to be easily carried.

But Aldus's most important influence was in popularising the 'roman' family of typefaces. Gutenberg had aped scribal 'gothic' black and the convention was quickly established that his textura face was appropriate for the Bible and other holy books. In a smaller variant, bastarda, this 'black-face' could be used for other works. The earliest editions of Francois Rabelais' knock-about parody of Arthurian epics, *Gargantua* and *Pantagruel*, were first printed in Lyons in the 1530s using this face. Aldus, on the other hand, was moved to mimic the writing engraved in the stone of ancient Roman monuments for the classics he was printing, such as Cicero's letters. These were in use from 1495. Aldus's designer, Francesco Griffo, copied the cursive minuscule writing used in the papal chancery to create a more informal type which became known as italic. The art of typography suggested the use of conventions. For example, multi-lingual sixteenth-century books might assign typeface by language: Italian in italic, French and English in roman, Flemish and German in black-face. Eventually, half a millennium later, roman finally overcame black-face even in its Teutonic homelands.

Given the centrality of the woodblock to the idea of printing from movable type, it is no wonder that printing was illustrated from the very outset. Engraving on copper much improved the definition of the image and the durability of plate over block was another advantage. It was a century, however, before an engraved image could be set into a page of text with the ease of a woodcut. Woodcuts therefore continued in use in books even as the old business of religious prints, the previous main application of the technology, was failing. The old religious wood-block print was transformed into best-selling books such as *Images of the Bible*, published in 1540 and illustrated with vignettes drawn by Holbein. By the end of the sixteenth century, the hawkers who sold such things town-to-town and village-to-village were a thing of the past, although they were to be reborn in many places the following century selling the news in various printed forms.

Throughout most of the 1500s, engravings were printed separately and then bound into learned scientific or medical treatises. Otto Brunfels published the first book of plant engravings in Strasbourg in 1530. In the same year as Copernicus's *On the Revolution of Heavenly Bodies*, 1543, Vesalius produced his treatise about the structure of the human body with extremely detailed woodcuts (and labels in italic) which had already served in another manual of anatomy in 1538. The first modern atlas, *The Theatre of the World*, with 53 maps engraved by Abraham Wortels (Ortelius), appeared in 1570, in Antwerp. Equally influential, but less weighty, types of publication also began appearing. For example, pattern-books, especially of Spanish fashions, emerged making it possible for tailors everywhere to make copies of clothes in the most modish styles. Jean Thevet brought out a collection of engravings, *Portraicts de hommes illustres* (1574), feeding a taste for images of the famous that has never been satiated.

In 1450, an extensive library meant 15 to 20 manuscript volumes. A century later privately held collections of 500 printed books were not uncommon. This exponential growth was despite the fact that books were not cheap – a bound *Canterbury Tales* cost a hefty 5/- – but even at this sort of price they were cheaper than manuscript texts. These last could not survive the onslaught. Decades after Gutenberg's innovation, the old-fashioned bookseller Vespiano di Bisticci self-interestedly reported that one of his customers, the Duke of Urbino, had such a wonderful manuscript library, 'written with the pen', that a printed book 'would have been ashamed in such company'. Yet the Duke did have printed books in good number and Vespiano paid for his hostility to the new by losing his business. He closed his doors in 1478. The impact of the press was of extreme importance, but nevertheless, it is easy to exaggerate its revolutionary significance.

For instance, because a corrector oversaw the compositor's proofs and errors were easily emended, the press was certainly more accurate than the scriptoria. Indeed, the author – when contemporary work was being printed – was often present to ensure accuracy. Nevertheless the result was not invariably error-free and inaccuracies were never to become entirely a thing of the past. A 'wicked' seventeenth-century Bible appeared with the commandment 'Thou shalt commit adultery'. Another had, 'The lord hath shewed us his glory and his great asse'. A third confused Judas and Jesus. The compositor can make a mistake as easily as can a scribe; and the compositor's error is much more widely diffused than was a scribe's. The lonely scribe, though, if sufficiently hedged about with, for example, sacred rules and regulations, could keep himself from error, as did Jewish penmen for centuries when copying Torah scrolls.

It is also true that engraving fixed labels, an important factor especially for the scientific accuracy of illustrations, but again this brought no automatic guarantees. Images could be wrongly titled, either by accident or mendaciously, as easily in print as they could be by hand. Labelling the same engraving with captions identifying different towns or, in portraits, different individuals was not uncommon. Copperplates wore out just as the woodblocks – which of course had also fixed labels – had done, albeit more slowly. Print did not solve these difficulties and, indeed, could exacerbate them because of more extensive duplication.

As with manuscript production, the print shop's workforce was specialised. Under the master printer, the head compositor oversaw the work of a team. A crew of pressmen serviced the press itself, five men to a machine normally. Five presses in a shop were not unusual. Supplies would be secured from the paper-mill by the bookseller; workshops of illustrators would prepare blocks and, later, plates. Binders would be on hand to finish the work. In the print shop, 12-hour days were not unusual, with a couple of hours for a midday break and meal. A day off every two weeks and four holidays a year were established as the norm in Frankfurt in 1563. Other local practices could allow half-days off beyond these limited agreed allowances. This harsh regime, lacking the variety of the old feudal agricultural cycle, was softened by the fact that printers were notorious for their fondness for drink, unauthorised holidays and, in general, a somewhat lackadaisical approach to attendance.

The master printers, together with publishers and booksellers, began joining Guilds of St John the Evangelist in 1401. In England the stationers were members of scribes' guilds by 1403. In the next century these guilds metamorphosed into more modern companies of stationers. All persons involved in a trade ought to have been admitted but in practice journeymen and, certainly, apprentices were excluded and only their masters allowed. In response, the workers banded together in brotherhoods or chapels. A primary object was to establish welfare systems, money for a mass or a banquet or to help widows and sick colleagues. Printers were among the first urban workers to follow the miners of south Germany in forming such fraternal organisations. These print unions were either town-wide or based on one large establishment. For instance, Christoffel Plantijn, one of Antwerp's most successful publisher/printers in the middle decades of the sixteenth century, acknowledged a workers' leader, a father-of-the-chapel, within his shop and paid money into the chapel fund.

There were strikes over conditions in Lyons and Paris as early as 1539 and 1542. In Geneva in 1561, men struck to establish a uniform afternoon off on Wednesdays which some shops allowed and others did not. The half-day was agreed by the masters for all. Despite the proprietor's support of the chapel, Plantijn's firm was hit by strikes three times between 1569 and 1573. In 1571, French printers struck to restrict their masters' ability to take on unlimited numbers of apprentices, who could be used to undercut their terms and be potential strike-breakers. The men won their point and legislation limiting apprenticeships was passed in 1573.

Print had occasioned legal moves to protect the business arising from the early exploitation of the technology. For example, John of Speyer, who brought the press to Venice, was awarded one of the first European patents for it. This was designed to protect his investment and ensured the republic a flow of printed matter. Other laws were passed to encourage printing. In England, the first books at Oxford and Cambridge had been printed by Theodorich Rood of Cologne and his fellow-countryman John Siberch. Wynkyn de Worde, Caxton's assistant who inherited his business, was a native of Alsace, from the town of Worth. Such immigration was welcomed, thanks to the enlightened view of Richard III, who, in 1484, removed printers and booksellers, 'of whatever nation he be', from the general restriction on foreign workers. Half a century later, Henry VIII felt that local talent had become so well-established that this liberality was damaging 'our subjectes who . . . have the sufficient art, feate and treade of printing and imprinting', and the act was repealed in 1534.

'The Donkey Pope' and 'Lutheran Maniacs'

On the last day of October 1517, Martin Luther, a monk and university lecturer, nailed *95 Theses* (handwritten in Latin) to a church door in Wittenberg, essentially denouncing the sale of the very indulgences Gutenberg and others had freely printed. He also sent a copy to his bishop – in Mainz.

Print and the Reformation are inextricably intertwined but it is a simplification to say that the former 'causes' the latter. In fact, the opposite case can be made. It was the reformist impulse of men like Nicolas of Cusa in the fifteenth century that created the social need which Gutenberg, Waldvogel and their successors rushed to fill. Nevertheless, few technological advances are deemed to have had a greater impact than movable type. That type is the essential conditioning factor determining the *mentalité* of the West is typical of a dominant nineteenth- and twentieth-century way of thinking about the world. Technology, by those who hold this view, has, supposedly, an all-powerful effect on our society. The machines *determine* the way we live and are often deemed to be the agents of extensive social change. Some technicists, or technological determinists, are positive, believing changes usually mark progress and the betterment of the human condition. Others, equally technicist, believe the opposite: that the effects of innovation can be very negative and are seldom fully anticipated. Either way, both agree on the central importance of technological innovation as an agent of – often totally unexpected – social change. Yet closer readings of the historical record suggest that this is to put the cart before the horse. It is social pressure that conditions the development of technology and controls its diffusion, not the other way about. The results therefore 'fit' society, however much some effects are not fully articulated before the device or technique is diffused. Technologies figure prominently in the ceaseless development of society but as expressions of that development, not as determinants. The horse pulling society is named 'social (including military) need' while the cart behind it is called 'technology'.

More temperate assessments of the effects of print illustrate the problem of disentangling technological 'causes' and social effects. For example, in the age of the manuscript and authority, the concept of the original writer was apparently obscured. St Bonaventura in the thirteenth century itemised four sorts of writers: the copyist, the compiler, the commentator and the *auctor*. The *auctor* or author, though, was only a commentator who put his own thoughts first. He still used the words of others to sustain his argument. For the saint, the wholly original author was of no apparent importance. These come into their own in the age of print. It is seductive, therefore, to see the press as the agent that creates the modern author; but it would be wrong. Sole authors of texts beneath saintly attention, the poets Chaucer and Villon for example, did appear in manuscript copies before 1450. If such writers proliferate after the introduction of print, this is more the result of the changing circumstances of economic life in general and urban life in particular than it is a function directly of the press. As with the Reformation, the same pressures produce both press and author.

Or take travel books. Sole original authors who sold very well in print included the writers of travellers' tales. These quickly became a publisher's staple in this age of exploration; but there had also been extensive manuscript editions of Manderville and Polo. These were frequently reprinted at the same time as contemporary books such as Lopez de Gomara's *History of the Indians and the Conquest of New Spain.* Printing cannot be said to have 'caused' the search for new lands any more than it created the modern author, or the Reformation. Print publicised exploration and thereby encouraged it. It did not instigate it.

For all that the Church was an early enthusiast for printing, the schism which developed between those who were to become Protestants and those who remained Catholic produced a deluge of anti-Catholic materials and equally raucous pro-Catholic responses. The centrality of Holy Writ and the taste for religious prints and popular literary forms, such as lives of the saints, had accustomed the broad mass of the public to associate written matter and faith, even before movable type was introduced. This partiality for sacred texts continued into the print era and embraced the intemperate language of religious controversy. Vernacular Bibles, books, treatises and pamphlets flooded from the press. Pamphlets were often especially offensive to one side or the other. *The Donkey Pope* or *Lutheran Maniacs*, not untypical titles, suggest that these lacked the sophistication of Luther's famous argument *To the Christian Nobility of the German Nation* – 4,000 copies of which were printed and distributed within three weeks of its appearance on 18 August 1520. It ran to 13 editions over the next two years. In

21

1534, a most effective and widely distributed printed placard attacked the practice of the mass itself.

Protestants were prominent among printers and seemed to constitute a majority of buyers. *Lutheran Maniacs*, for example, was not the best seller that some Protestant attacks on the Pope were, but then printers and readers were both more likely to be urban than rural; progressive, in terms of the time, rather than conservative. The very substance of a more personal protestation of faith, coupled with the earliest demands for freedom of religious conscience, meshes seamlessly with the more individual, less deferential quality of urban life. The fact of printing is of a piece with such social realities, not a cause of them. So, while it is true the press spread the word of revolt and reform, it is equally true that the other side's press failed to build resistance to it across large swathes of Europe.

Nevertheless, it is also argued that the press was the one significant factor differentiating Luther's attack on the Church from its predecessor heresies. All these had been defeated and, it is claimed, in the success of Protestantism is a proof of the power of print. Certainly the press ensured the widespread dissemination of the Protestant leaders' ideas at every level from complex theological dispute to low, scatological abuse. The result was defiance at a scale unlike the national difficulties caused by the Albigensians in southern France in the twelfth century, or the English Lollards in the fourteenth, or Jan Hus in Bohemia in the early fifteenth. On the other hand, though, these centuries of persistent attempts to break or reform the Church demonstrate that there was continuous and widespread dissatisfaction which antedated print and often erupted into schism without it. Lutherism without the press is easily conceivable.

'If it's banned in Rome ...'

A press without censors is far harder to envisage. Certainly the flood of print in the sixteenth century occasioned everything from uneasiness to panic among the more authoritarian elements in the society. In the centuries that have followed, the discomfort caused by printing's in-built bias towards free expression has never been assuaged. The authorities attacked and, in addition to patents and licences, they were quite quick to establish systems of direct censorship.

The University of Cologne petitioned the Pope to be empowered to censor liturgical texts in 1475. The request was granted. Berhold, the conservative Archbishop of Mainz, appointed his own censorship offi-cials in 1486. Two years later the Pope, Innocent VIII, demanded prior approval for the first time. By 1496, the Papal Legate at Venice was requiring that all religious works be subject to his approval. In 1501, Pope Alexander VI insisted that all books, religious or not, be approved prior to printing in Germany. This was extended to all Western lands by the Lateran Council of 1515. In 1543, Cardinal Caraffa, who had revived the Inquisition, ordered that no book could be printed or sold without its authorisation. In 1559, Caraffa, now elected Pope as Paul IV, issued a general *Index Librorum Prohibitorum*, banning, among much else, a number of texts written or sponsored by his cardinals. In the 'M' section of authors totally banned – *libri & scripta omnia* – is to be found 'Martinus Lutherus'.[6] The Jesuits, working as imperial cen-sors, arrived at Frankfurt in 1579. As a free imperial city, it had become a refuge for printers driven hither and yon by the religious conflicts of the early sixteenth century. Its book fair had become the major market for the publishing trade. It took the Jesuits nearly two centuries but eventually their interference closed it down.[7]

The publishers and printers facilitated this official involvement by seeking to protect their investment from pirating and competition in general. This had become a more pressing need as the trade added new, contemporary titles to the sacred and classical texts that had at the outset constituted its main business. From 1481 on, publishers fre-quently sought a copyright in the form of a licence to print a specific work. In 1483, the Duke of Milan had granted a five-year licence specif-ically for the printing of the humanist Francesco Filelfo's *Convivium*. Either at the behest of printers or on the initiative of the authorities, similar specific licences were given to individual publishers for specific works in Venice, France and parts of Germany. More general licences created official printers who were encouraged to establish monopolies within the territories controlled by the licensor. The Pope licensed Paulus Manutius as an official printer for 30 years on this basis. Plantijn made his first fortune exploiting a licence from the King of Spain, then suzerain of the Netherlands, granted to him for the printing of liturgical texts, all as approved by the Council of Trent.

Licensing and prohibition were the two faces of censorship, closely intertwined. Charles IX assumed a monopoly of licensing in France and created a system for this in 1563 that required his chancellor's seal on every work prior to publication. The English crown published a list of prohibited books in 1529 and created a licensing system in 1530. In 1557, Mary Tudor granted a Royal Charter to the Stationers' Company, transforming this medieval guild to which scribes and pressmen had belonged for over a century. They were charged with monitoring the pirating of any works which had been registered with them. Registration created a *de facto* copyright for publishers but the price of this royal acknowledgement and the commercial advantage it brought was the strict control of content. To obtain protection, works had to be registered at Stationers' Hall and master printers were appointed to the company by the Archbishop of Canterbury and the Bishop of London.

Elizabeth, like her father, Henry VIII, endeavoured to ban the importation of all Catholic books and tried to control production by licensing the physical presses themselves, rather than the products of the press. In 1586, she strengthened the Stationers' Company's monopoly but gave the Court of the Star Chamber oversight over its activities; yet, unlike in France, in England the printers were expected to police themselves. Even when the French emulated the Stationers' Company by transforming an old-fashioned guild structure into a Chambre des Syndicats in 1618, Louis XIII insisted it met in the presence of royal officials. It was, therefore, an overt system of direct control, with the Chambre being seen as a state institution in a way in which the

Stationers' Hall was not. Either way, licensing on this scale easily merged with direct censorship. The number of English, largely London, presses was fixed at 25, as had been done in France, but that was reduced in 1662 to 20. Here it remained until the post-Civil War attempt to re-establish Tudor censorship structures finally began to crumble when Parliament refused to renew formal censorship in 1695. It took until 1725 before presses were common to all the major English cities.

The prison house of censorship, though, was built on sand. It was widely understood from the outset that *Notabitur Romae, legetur ergo* – if it is banned in Rome, then it is bound to be read. Samuel Pepys had to pay 30/- (£1.50) for a second-hand copy of Hobbes's *Leviathan* that was originally published for 8/- (40p) after the book was banned in 1668. This was because, as he noted, illegality made it 'mightily in demand'. It is possible to argue for measures of general control for various reasons from state security to the protection of endangered sections of society, but it has never made much sense specifically to censor expression in one medium or another. Who, after all, remembers the officials who caused the works of Montesquieu and Rousseau to be printed in Holland and Voltaire's in London and Berlin, except as nameless fools, dupes, bigots and philistines – just trying to do their jobs, of course?

More than that, the early censorship system could not work because it was extremely leaky. While it is true that a proper printing house was an easily recognisable capital-intensive mini-factory, it was equally the case that the press itself was a comparatively small and moderately movable device. Taken down, it was a mere cartload. Erected it could fit in many rooms and most barns or stables. Yet, in the censor's eyes, a single sheet from a single press operated by one person was just as dangerous as the products of a large publishing operation. Any sheet was potentially (to use the word Lenin was to adopt centuries later for his newsletter) a 'spark' that the censor needed obsessively to snuff out. Given the policing resources to hand even in the most despotic state, looking for a press in a teeming town or city could be fairly futile.

The problem was exacerbated because nowhere was an outright ban contemplated. This was the peculiar difficulty printing presented to authority – on the one hand, a challenging threat but on the other, a valuable tool of government. Its usefulness was quickly, and widely, noticed. The King of Hungary, for example, in early 1485, issued the *Dracola Waida* (*The Devil Prince*), a propaganda piece about atrocities in neighbouring Rumania suitably illustrated with a woodcut of Vlad having his lunch, impaled corpses arrayed behind him. Henry VII of England had the papal bull confirming his usurpation of the throne and his marriage to Elizabeth of York printed in broadsheet and distributed in 1486, the year after the Battle of Bosworth.

His son, Henry VIII, was a prolific user of the press to sway public opinion against Rome both internally within England and externally across the rest of Europe in favour of his marital adventures. In 1531, for instance, he had reprinted: *The determination of the universities of Italy and Fraunce, that it is so unlafull for a man to marie his brothers wyfe, that the pope hath no power to dispence therewith*. He was always ready to combat treason and rebellion with print. In 1536 he issued: *Answer made by the Kynges hyghnes to the Petition of the rebelles in Yorkshire*. In 1549, faced with yet another rebellion, it was *A Message sent by the kynges Maiestie, to certain of his people, assembled in Deuonshire*. Nor was 'spin' beyond him. For example, another 1549 publication, anonymous and extremely damaging to the West Country rebels' case, appeared looking suspiciously as if it too were from the press of the royal printer, Richard Grafton. More positively, Henry's reign was also marked by published news releases (as it were), from a *Joyfull medytacyon of the coronacyon of Henry the eyght*, through *The noble tryumphaunt Coronation of Quene Anne* (Boylen). The last was a notice of his death.

The French crown was assiduous in its use of print for the dissemination of official information. The texts of treaties with Austria (1482), Franche-Comté (1483) and England (1492) were published. Official leaflets appeared about Charles VIII's progresses and even, in nine separate reports, his death. The French government also began announcing regulations – ordinances – in this form. These *occasionnels* came to appear at the rate of as many as six or seven a year. Official communications, printed on broadsheet, eventually appeared quite regularly all over Europe. For instance, in 1540 Hans Singriener was licensed in Vienna to publish them under the title *Novitäten*.

Arguably much of this had nothing to do with the arrival of print since, propaganda aside, there was really no reason for official announcements to be printed. Proclamations were not only handwritten after the coming of print, they were still being inscribed on parchment for durability. In 1489, for example, four parchment-makers continued producing vellum in Paris as against 11 *paupelars* manufacturing paper. Nevertheless, it was widely believed that nothing, except the pulpit, matched the press's effectiveness as a voice within the civil sphere (insofar as that could be said to exist in the modern sense). These two were the primary tools by which public opinion, it was believed, could be swayed. By the seventeenth century, those in power believed, as the philosopher Hobbes put it: 'the Common-peoples minds, unless they be tainted . . . are like clean paper, fit to receive whatsoever by Publique Authority shall be imprinted in them'.

Rival powers were ever ready to encourage printers to export supposedly incendiary materials even as they endeavoured to exercise internal control. Pockets of liberality undermined the entire censorship structures of Western Europe. For example, in the Netherlands, civil disorders had turned into a full-scale revolt against Spanish Hapsburg rule. Complicated by an internal civil conflict between the (essentially) Catholic south and the (essentially) Protestant north, the Flemish and the Dutch took decades of revolt to escape the Spanish yoke. Nevertheless, once *de facto* independent, the pioneering pre-eminence of Antwerp and Amsterdam as printing centres was confirmed and they became an uncontrollable source of publications in many languages. This was why many French classics were first printed in the Low Countries. Such factors, coupled with the difficulty of catching native unlicensed, illegal printers within the borders, eventually caused some states to give up the whole idea of direct prior censorship, in England as early as 1695 and elsewhere before the end of the eighteenth century.

Authority never discovered how to exploit the press's benefits while at the same time containing what it saw (and, in many places, yet sees) as its disadvantages.

'Crowding free consciences'

Against this semi-paralysis was mounted an onslaught in the name of liberty of conscience. It was the demand for this freedom that came to underlie the call for religious reform. Of course, it was hedged about with contradictions because the freedom sought did not mean those demanding it were ready to give it to others. Certainties about revealed truth were prone to lead all groups of true believers into thinking that their best course of action was to extirpate, by sword or stake if all else failed, the errors of non-believers. The freedom envisaged was still a long way from the modern concept of tolerance, much less of rights; but it was also equidistant from the ancient principle that the religion of the prince was automatically the religion of the people. However lacking in practice, the concept was potent.

Freedom of conscience suggested the concept of a 'natural right' and, under this rubric, a progression from a right to choose a religion to, for instance, a right to choose, by vote, one's leader. It also encouraged the thought that these were necessarily expressions and that expression, including expression uttered or printed, ought also to be free. Indeed, unless expression were free then all these other freedoms were moot. This was a revolutionary new position. In 1513, Machiavelli, for example, had acknowledged in *Il Principe* that citizens might have a right to 'think all things, speak all things, write all things', but insisted that the prince was always equally entitled to deny them this privilege. A century later, the Scottish (and English) 'prince', James VI and I, took Machiavelli's position and in a proclamation inveighed against 'freedome of speech'. But many others now disagreed and rows about such advanced ideas of freedom were added to the fuel firing up the Civil War in England in the 1640s which was to cost James's son Charles his head.

The press was positioned as an engine of liberty early in this conflict. In August 1643, the poet John Milton, his marriage to a much younger woman in ruins, published an anonymous pamphlet in favour of divorce: *The Doctrine and Discipline of Divorce, Restored to the good of both sexes from the Bondage of Canon Law and other Mistakes*. A signed and expanded version appeared in February 1644. In July, he struck again: *The Judgement of Martin Bucer concerning Divorce*. On the technicality that his work was unregistered at Stationers' Hall, he was hauled before Commons and Lords because in 1643 Parliament had reaffirmed the Tudor licensing system through the Stationers' Company.

His defence, whatever the self-interest that originally moved him, remains, after three and a half centuries and more, a most eloquent expression of the principle of freedom of conscience as it applies to the concept of free speech. He called the pamphlet he wrote to explain himself simply, if eruditely, *Areopagitica*, after the hill upon which sat the highest tribunal in ancient Athens. It was published, deliberately unlicensed, on 25 November 1644, subtitled 'A speech of Mr. John Milton for the Liberty of VNLICENC'D PRINTING, to the PARLIAMENT OF ENGLAND':

> If we think to regulate printing, thereby to rectify manners, we must regulate all recreations and pastimes, all that is delightful to man . . . A little generous prudence, a little forbearance of one another, and some grain of charity might win all these diligences to join, and unite in one general and brotherly search after Truth; could we but forego this prelatical tradition of crowding free consciences and Christian liberties into canons and precepts of men . . . Believe it, Lords and Commons, they who counsel ye to such suppressing, do as good as bid ye suppress yourselves.

For Milton, he was merely restating an ancient truth. As Euripides had written (and as was translated from the Greek for the title page of the pamphlet), 'This is true liberty when free born men having to advise the public may speak free'. For Milton, the Greek idea became a plea: 'Give

me the liberty to know, to utter, and to argue freely according to consciences, above all liberties'. And a famous warning: 'As good almost kill
a man as kill a good book'. Yet just as Euripides could not contemplate
this right of expression for slaves, so Milton was rather unwilling to
grant it to Catholics; and it was to be ever thus. The idealism of the concept and the frequently contradictory and hypocritical exercise of free
speech were at odds at the outset and they have remained so ever since.

King Charles I was defeated at the Battle of Naseby and Milton's royalist wife (for politics as well as age and temperament had divided them)
returned to him. The tide of his rhetoric on divorce and on press freedom slacked. As Latin Secretary to the English republic, he even became
for a time Cromwell's censor, himself a licensor of the press. Only the
rhetoric of the *Areopagitica* remained, a monument to modern Europe's
concept of free and individual expression that neither the cracks in its
foundation nor the buffets of time have as yet overthrown.

Sources

Paul Bennett (1962), *Book and Printing*, Cleveland: World Publishing
   Elizabeth.
Einstein (1979), *The Printing Press as an Agent of Change*, Cambridge:
   Cambridge University Press.
Lucien Febvre and Henri Jean Martin (1976), *The Coming of the Book: The
   Impact of Printing 1480–1800* London: Verso.
P. M. Handover (1960), *Printing in London: from 1446 to Modern Times*,
   London: George Allen & Unwin.
Janet Ing (1988), *Johann Gutenberg and his Bible*, New York: The Typophiles.
Albert Kapr (1996), *Johann Gutenberg: The Man and His Invention* (trans.
   Douglas Martin), Aldershot, Hants: Ashgate.
John Milton (1644, 1951), *Areopagitica* and *Of Education*, Northbrook, Ill.:
   AHM.
Herman Plleij (2001), *Dreaming of Cockaigne: Medieval Fantasies of the Perfect
   Life* (trans. Diane Webb), New York: Columbia University Press.
S. H. Steinberg (1955), *500 Years of Printing*, Harmondsworth: Penguin.
Robert Temple (1986), *The Genius of China: 300 Years of Science, Discovery and
   Invention*, New York: Simon & Schuster.

1

'TAKING OFF VIZARDS AND VAILES AND DISGUISES': NEWSPAPERS FROM 1566

'Prodigious and admirable stories'

The earliest *printed* news-sheets began to appear in Venice in 1566, in the form of letters about single events. They carried such news to all who could afford the small coin, a gazzetta, worth a fraction of an old English penny, which it cost either to buy or, more probably, to hear the story read out.[1] The cost of the product became its name – *Gazzetta de la novita* – the Gazette. Another term, the *aviso*, notice, described the same thing, a news-sheet, but referred more to the nature of the contents than to the cost of the product.

The arrival of the news-sheet was not surprising as, from the first, printers had been quick to exploit any market niche. As well as the Bible, religious literature and the classics, a host of other works, from atlases through medical texts to 'lewd ballads', flowed from the press. What remains hard to explain is that none, apparently, thought to write up, print and sell the news for a century after the development of the printing press. Even then, nothing emerged that could be considered newspapers proper – that is, regular, unbound, timely, printed independent public reports and comments on all the events of the day, foreign and domestic, serious and sensational. In the world of print, news was like chocolate chips in a cookie. Newspapers needed not only entrepreneurial printers, of whom there were plenty, but ones with insatiable curiosity, writing talent, a feel for popular interests and, in the face of almost certain official harassment, steady nerves. They would

31

also need an understanding of the curious fact that the printed news and commentary being sold in the market place are more like perishable fruit than like ageless works of literature. They would have to be as quick as they could and their work would never be done. It would take another century after the *Gazzetta*, a full 200 years from Gutenberg's 'work of the books', for such people to conceive of the first daily newspaper. (Apart from anything else, then, to claim that technology engendered the newspaper is to stretch the concept of historical causality to breaking point.)

Decades before the first *Gazzetta*, in 1536, sheets had appeared in Vienna written by hand to chronicle the advance of the Turks towards the gates of the city. As late as at the outset of the English Civil War in the 1640s, hundreds of copies of speeches were still being written out by hand and distributed. It is simply the case that the 'who, what, why, when, where'[2] of journalism does not require a printing press at all and, in fact, traces of what we might call the journalistic impulse can be found many centuries before the arrival of print:

> In the year one thousand one hundred and twenty-seven, on the sixth day before the Nones of March, on the second day that is, after the beginning of the same month . . . about dawn, the count at Bruges was kneeling in prayer in order to hear the early Mass in the church of Saint Donatian. The office of the first hour was completed . . . and when the count, according to custom, was praying . . . those wretched traitors, already murderers at heart, slew the count, who was struck down with swords and run through again and again . . .

Good Count Charles of Flanders was murdered in Bruges by a group of his disaffected followers on 2 March 1127 in the early morning. Galbert of Bruges witnessed the event.

Galbert's account fully explains the causes of this crime but it is silent as to why Galbert himself was moved to write down what he saw as quickly as he could: 'I, Galbert, a notary, though I had no suitable place for writing, set down on tablets a summary of events . . . I had to wait for moments of peace during the night or day to set down in order the present account of events as they happened.' A lawyer, probably a clerk in minor orders, he felt that his response to the civil commotion around him – making notes and writing them up – was strange. He had no clear audience in mind and, indeed, his manuscript did not become widely known at the time. He was following no obvious models except that he knew that whatever it was he was writing, it was not proper history, being in the style neither of the ancients nor of his contemporaries, the chroniclers. For the latter, although they did sometimes establish their source ('I will speak of all that was done from the information I had at the time . . .'), speed was not a factor ('In this year . . .'). Nor did Galbert's profession offer then the example that it would today. In twelfth-century Europe, eyewitness was not unknown but it was far from proof.[3] Galbert was, in short, being a journalist; but, as that figure did not finally emerge for another 500 years or so, he could not have known this.

Nevertheless, like the Reformation, journalism is often deemed to be a child of the printing press, despite much of a newspaper's characteristic contents long existing in handwritten form – proclamations, intelligence gathering – or even orally, as in that strand of the ballad tradition which made a recent event its subject. The minstrel Laurence Minot, for example, wrote eleven timely ballads celebrating the victories of Edward III in the fourteenth century Hundred Year War between England and France. News, in all these forms, continued either in writing as intelligences or was easily transferred to print as, for instance, proclamations. Poetic news ballads spawned a prose alternative and both forms appeared in print. Kings used the press for propaganda and others found in the printer an ally who could publicise their arguments in the novel form of a pamphlet.

All this kept the printers busy and, in part, contained any enthusiasm they might have had to publish their own accounts of events regularly and more comprehensively; but the official little propaganda reports of royal triumphs did demonstrate that a public appetite for such news existed. The occasional 'newsbook', in effect an expression of the Minot ballad tradition, began to appear. The earliest surviving one in English details the *Trewe Encounter* between the English and the Scots at the Battle of Flodden Field and was published in 1513 by Richard Faques in London. Throughout the sixteenth century, printers slowly expanded the range of reports on the doings of the great and the good outside the court and, increasingly, they covered anything of a significant, titillating or sensational nature – but still not with any systematic sense of what constituted 'the news' nor on a regular basis.

The claim of these books to be news was grounded in their reflection of actual (or supposedly actual) occurrences. In 1541, for example, in Mexico City, a lawyer, Juan Rodríquez, wrote a *Relación* about a terrifying earthquake 'which has occurred in the Indies in a city called Guatamala'. Driven by credulity, as the century progressed the newsbooks became ever more fanciful: *Strange Signes seene in the Aire, strange Monsters behelld on the Lande, and wonderful Prodegies both by Land and Sea, over, in and about the Citie of Rosenberge in high Germany* . . . Truly translated out of the high Dutch Copie.' This typical example from 1594 includes the almost obligatory woman giving birth to monstrous children. The shock, horror sensation was that after she and her four awful offspring had died, the coffin in which they were laid could not be raised, although when it was opened only three drops of blood were found. Such time-honoured titillations persisted into the next century in newsbook form. In 1601, an English example luxuriated in the mutilating tortures of a German witch, her sons and her five companions: 'This being done, the woman had six stripes given her with a Whip of twisted Wier: and after, had both her arms broken with a Wheel: her body was immediately burnt.'

The popular taste that made such publications readily 'vendible' everywhere took a particular form in France. Parallel to the official *occasionnels* throughout the sixteenth and seventeenth centuries, unofficial *canards* were published, little six- or eight-page pamphlets often as crudely illustrated as the English newsbooks and some as small as

80 mm × 120 mm. These also dealt with miracles, disasters, crimes and celestial phenomena. In 1567, a dragon appeared in the sky above Paris and earned its place in a *canard*. In 1619, in Lyon, a child dead for 24 hours was resuscitated *par l'intercession de la Vierge* – indeed a 'prodigious and admirable' story (*l'histoire prodigieuse et admirable*) of the sort that sold well. The word *veritable* frequently appeared in the titles of the *canards* to reassure their readers that the report being retailed was just unembellished fact. (The dragon, though, has not been seen again.)

In England, such populist material escaped the authorities' ban on all reporting of local events apart from sycophantic accounts of court life. Newsbooks on natural disasters, for instance, avoided this prohibition: *Lamentable newes out of Monmouthshire in Wales* contained an account of

> the wonderfull and most fearefull accidents of the great ouerflowing waters in the saide Countye, drowning infinite numbers of Cattell of all kinds, as Sheepe, Oxen, Kine and horses: together with the losse of many men, women and Children, and the submersion of xxvi Parishes in Inauary last 1607.

The frontispiece has a vivid woodcut of folk clinging to trees, sitting on roofs and sinking beneath the waters. Sensationalism sustained the newsbook well into the seventeenth century: *The Crying Murther: Contayning the cruell and most horrible Butcher of Mr. Tate* appeared in 1624, for example, with a gruesome crude woodcut of the murderers wandering about, each holding a different bit of the unfortunate Mr Tate.

The popularity of gore was of great value in the Reformation's war of print. Apart from posters, handbills and pamphlets, learned or libellous or both, newsbooks made a telling contribution along these lines. Sixteenth- and seventeenth-century stories about Catholic and Protestant atrocities, often lamentably true even if exaggerated, were

35

not unique, standing as they do between fictitious medieval horror reports of Saracens murdering babies and more modern ones, such as Huns raping Belgian nuns in 1914. Shock reports persistently appeared for decade after decade.

Religious atrocities aside, the effectiveness of sensational news, fancied dragons or real murders, in the market place is time-honoured and most certainly not a twentieth-century tabloid discovery. Moreover, given authorities' basic suspicion of the press and their ever-changing sensitivities because of political and religious uncertainties, portents, miracles, disasters and the death of witches were safer for the printer or author than was more overtly political – 'serious' – coverage. It is therefore the case that the popular newspaper agenda antedates the politics and economics of the quality one and acts in part, as did the official proclamation and *occasionnel* and the opinionated pamphlet, to inhibit the independent appearance of the latter.

Politics and economics were dangerous topics, if not entirely secret then certainly not considered to be suitable matters for the public at large. Traditionally the state alone was allowed to acquire political and economic intelligence and it did so confidentially, via its ambassadors. As the banking system had developed in southern Germany and northern Italy in the fourteenth century, however, the gathering of 'intelligences' became vital to the merchant as well. The earliest surviving image in European art of a filing cabinet appears in the background of a painting of a Fugger, one of the most prominent south German banking dynasties based in Augsburg. Its drawers are marked with the names of towns where the commercial equivalent of the regal ambassador, the factor, was placed. Like the ambassador, one of a factor's functions was to keep the home office informed.

Knowledge was obviously power. It was as crucial for a merchant in the West to know how threatened by the Turk a venture to the East was likely to be as it was for a prince to glean information about the steadfastness of his allies and the machinations of his enemies. The merchant class grew with the towns, and the intermittent and haphazard exchange of information, for example at the periodic great fairs, was no longer enough for business. The rising complexity of economic structures within and between the nation states then emerging to the west of Europe, the statelets of the rest of the continent as well as the powers to the east involved more and more decision-makers. Slowly economic pressures ensured that the information originally indispensable only to princes had to be shared more widely – and on an ever more timely basis.

Hence the newsletter: by the first half of the sixteenth century, the Fuggers were copying the reports of their corresponding factors, still in manuscript, to the most privileged of their clients. Eventually these were printed but the circulation was limited to those who banked with them. The move to print, though, did not kill off the handwritten newsletter. Still in the later seventeenth century, a newsman like Henry Muddiman, closely tied to the restored royal government in England, was producing officially sanctioned printed news publications while he issued subscribers, for some as often as three times a week, a private hand-copied newsletter. This was made valuable by his astute use of spies, postmasters, clergy and customs and he charged accordingly – £5 per annum. His readers were also his correspondents: 'Sir. In your last you desired me acquaint you what non-conformists, papists and others were indicted at quarter sessions . . .'

Handwritten newsletters continued to circulate until the early eighteenth century, as was sometimes echoed by the use, in their printed alternatives, of italic fonts resembling manuscript and the opening salutation, 'Sʳ'. The private printed version also still persisted and, in an extremely high-priced variety written for particular commercial and industrial sectors, they are with us yet, albeit now electronically transmitted; but in the early sixteenth century their existence continued to absorb much of the need for more public newspapers. The newspaper is, entertaining sensationalism aside, a capitalist tool; but for the limited number of merchants involved, there was no reason to make the news public. On the contrary. It is the handwritten, private newsletter that could ultimately account for the slowness of the development of the newspaper between 1450 and 1650.

The anomalous occurrence of a printed publication retailing such intelligence very precociously on the periphery of the mercantilist world is the exception that proves the rule. The Polish authorities published a *Neu Zeitung*, a digest of 'News from Lithuania and concerning the Muscovites', in 1513. What was private and commercial in Western Europe needed to be public and official in the East to encourage the development of the mercantilist system. The printers in the West, however, were themselves also merchants and the same pressures to turn a profit that motivated their fellow traders, causing an ever more general demand for private intelligence, eventually pushed them into selling information to the public.

'You may balance . . . and accordingly beleeve'

The exploitation of the public possibilities of news publication involved a move towards ever more regular issues of the sheets. Numbered printed pages, following the Venetian model, were appearing at Basle, Strasbourg and Augsburg by 1570. This then opened up another possibility. The enterprising printer could collect the sheets from various places and reprint them all in digest form. At first this happened irregularly, for example *News Lately come on the last day of Februarie* (1591) or *Certen newes written towardes London from Italye Fraunce Hungarie and other places* (1602). The move to regular publication was an obvious one.

In Cologne, between 1588 and 1593, Michael von Aitzing had prepared six-monthly summaries of ecclesiastical and political news, the *Relatio Historica* or *Messrelationen* to be sold at the twice-yearly Frankfurt book fairs.[4] In 1597, Samuel Dilbaum, picking up on the success of von Aitzing's biennial publication, began a monthly periodical digest dealing with the great powers of the day in editions of between six and 12 pages in newsbook format. Printed in Rorschach on the Swiss shore of Lake Constance, it was entitled: *Historical Relation or Narrative of the most important and noteworthy actions and events which took place here and there almost in the whole of Europe in the month of*— —, 1597. As in Poland at the beginning of the sixteenth century, the public provision of timely news was now being considered, especially in the great German-speaking trading cities, as much as a municipal function as a printer's opportunity to make a profit. By the first decade of the seventeenth century, imitations of Dilbaum's relations were appearing in a number of places at the behest of city fathers. *Relation of Select and Noteworthy Happenings*, published by the authorities in Strasbourg, for example, noted, in the edition published 4 September 1609, that a professor of mathematics named Galileo at the University of Padua had constructed a telescope. The Wolfenbüttel *Avisa-Relation oder Zeitung*, which also started in 1609, was produced to argue a case in a proto-form of what today would be described as 'civic journalism'. It was edited in Prague by Duke Heinrich Julius, an imperial councillor, and was designed to highlight news that could reconcile Protestant and Catholic. It was not emulated. The Strasbourg model, however, was copied the following year by Basle's city fathers who produced a weekly, the *Ordinari-Zeitung*. That title, *Zeitung* – tidings – became the common one for these municipal publications.

The German municipal weekly was copied by printers in the Netherlands. For example, Abraham Verhoeven had started his *Nieuwe Tydinghe* in 1605. Verhoven was initially protected by the upheavals and confusions of the Dutch revolt against Spain, which included the defeats of his licensers. By 1617 he was publishing weekly and, in the 1620s, even sometimes as much as thrice weekly and his product was being described as a *coranto* rather than a relation. *Nieuwe Tydinghe* contained elaborate engravings and maps, better than the crude illustrations in the *canards* and newsbooks but not to be much emulated before the nineteenth century.

Without immediately wiping out the gazettes, *avisos*, *canards*, relations and newsbooks, *corantos* were a great success. The first to be published regularly from the outset in the Dutch language was Caspar van Hilten's *Courante uyt Italien, Duytslant &c*, which he started in 1618. *Corantos* on this model appeared in Spain in 1621 and, at the instigation of a German printer, in Denmark from 1634, but many more were simply direct translations. Verhoeven's was translated into French from 1610 on and Hilten's was translated into both French and English. By 1620, *corantos* were being published in English in the Netherlands specifically for export. The first of these, one double-sided sheet, was printed in Amsterdam by George Veseler and written by Peter van der Keere (Petrus Kerius), a mapmaker and engraver. The *coranto*, in its small format, was imported into England without hindrance and appeared in 15 editions between 2 December 1620 and 18 September 1621.

In the midst of this run, an English printer, Thomas Archer, started a *coranto* in London itself but by August 1621 he was in prison for publishing an unlicensed work on the continental war. Official hostility, though, was not maintained and he and two others, Nathaniel Bourne and Nathaniel Butter, the latter a freeman of the Stationers' Company since 1604, were allowed to try again. On 24 September 1621 they published a '*Corante, or, news from Italy, Germany, Hungarie, Spaine and France . . . out of the Hie Dutch Coppy printed at Franckford . . .*'. After some folio editions and a gap of a few months, their *coranto* became a quarto pamphlet of between eight and 24 pages.

Archer left after two years to join the growing band of rival publications. Butter and Bourne continued, with the usual high level of caution then necessary to the business of journalism, rigorously eschewing any mention of English or Scottish news. Publication was not entirely regular and on occasion there could be a wait of as long as 17 days between editions; but, on the other hand, these *corantos* also sometimes appeared as often as twice a week and 'continuations' of a previous edition were not unknown. The title changed to announce the contents ('News from . . .'), thus serving a little like a headline. It was regularly on sale, numbered and dated, 'at the sign of the Pied Bull at St. Austin's Gate' and, for a period, it was printed not for Butter and Bourne but for *Mercury's Britannicus*, a sort of brand-name they invented borrowing the term 'mercurius' from mainland Europe.

In that learned age, the classical reference to the messenger of the gods had been used in the name of news publications on the continent for some time. An occasional Latin digest of events in central Europe, specially prepared for sale at the great fairs following the model of von Aitzing's *Relatio*, had appeared under the title *Mercurius* from the late 1580s. The *Mercurius Gallobelgicus*, also in Latin, began in Cologne in 1594 with an edition covering the previous six years. Thereafter, its author, Michael ap Isselt, produced two a year covering mainly events in France and Belgium but also in Spain, Italy, England, Germany and Poland. It ceased publication in 1635 but was of great importance to the development of English journalism as it had preceded the Dutch *corantos* as the first regular news publication to circulate widely in England. An annual chronicle, digesting both *ocassionnels* and *canards*, appeared in France from 1611 called the *Mercure française*. By the time of the English Civil War, *Mercurius* was a common term, as was 'mercurist' for the men who wrote them. The name was also something of an insurance policy since it proclaimed the authors to be mere messengers who, implicitly, were not responsible for the news itself.

This was reinforced as readers were promised not the truth but only that the authors had sought their material 'Out of the best Informations of Letters and other'. News sources were as important as the news itself. Consider this report from the first edition of Veseler's *coranto* written on the Battle of the White Mountain. This, the first major encounter of the Thirty Years' War, had taken place in November 1620. The following month, van der Keere reported that:

> Letters out of Nuremberg make mention that they had advice from the borders of Bohemia, that there had been a very great Battle by Prage, between the King and the Duke of Beyeren and many 1000 slaine on both sides, but that the Duke of Beyeren should have any folks with in Prage is yet uncertaine.

Of the 56 words in this story only 25, some 45 per cent, lay claim to be fact: '. . . there had been a very great Battle by Prage, between the

King and the Duke of Beyeren and many 1000 slaine on both sides . . .'.
Twenty-eight per cent of this report is supposition in the form of a rev-
elation to the reader of the writer's ignorance of the state of the
Protestant Duke of Bavaria's army after its defeat at the hands of the
Emperor's forces and his most effective general, Johannes Tserclaes,
Count of Tilly: '. . . but that the Duke of Beyeren should have any
folks . . .'. No less than 27 per cent is given over to provenance, the
modern equivalent of which is merely the date- and by-line. The detail
that information had come, not from the capital but from the borders
of Bohemia, to Nuremberg and thence to the West is as important as
the news of the battle itself. As the mercurist promised only accurate
reprinting, without any other earnests for the underlying truth of a
report, such elaborate accounts of provenance were crucial if any judgement of veracity was to be made.

All reports began with full statements of their provenance and the
appeal to the readers' judgment of the trustworthiness of such sources
was often explicit. Butter and Bourne used direct address to their readers if they had doubts about their stories:

> Indifferent Reader, we promised you (in the front of our last
> Aviso) the Death and Interment of Monsieur Tilly, which we
> now performe; notwithstanding that the last Antwerpian
> Post hath ruemored the contrary, against which you may
> balance each other, and accordingly beleeve.

Tilly still had sixth months to live when they ran this report of his
death on 20 October 1631. The offer was almost certainly rather spurious, because how could the *coranto* buyer be expected to gauge the
credibility of, say, the 'last Antwerpian Post'? This editorial ploy, nevertheless, proclaims the report as being something more than mere
opinion. It had been warrantised, as it were, by prior publication elsewhere. Other *coranto* editors were not above using the personal voice to
explain difficulties, excusing the lack of date-line, for example, because
of deficiency in the original; or complaining of the failings of rivals,

'those who would have out any falsitie if they were but perswaded that the novelty will sell it'.

The *corantos* were not always entirely serious and the news agenda of the *canards* and the more sensational newsbooks seeped through a little. Butter and Bourne were not above finding space for '. . . certaine prodigies seene in the Empire' as well as important commercial matters such as 'The Turkish Pyracies'. For the most part, the mercurist, although a seventeenth-century person when it came to superstition, was a model of sobriety, an objective messenger who eschewed comment and emotive language while concentrating on a hard core of weighty political reports from abroad. Despite this, they worried the authorities. Reporting the hostilities between Catholic and Protestant princes was always, if only potentially, vexatious. By 1632, the Court of the Star Chamber had decided that even foreign intelligences were too threatening to the King's peace. The Thirty Years' War was into its second decade and the crown had long been uneasy because of reports of the victories of the Catholic League army under Tilly (which had begun at the White Mountain in 1620). Now, as the tide turned a little, it was jealous of the Protestant successes of Gustavus Adolphus, King of Sweden, Tilly's nemesis. Moreover, the Spanish ambassador did not welcome reports about the Hapsburgs and complained loudly. Given the prohibition on printing any local news, such sensitivities found receptive ears and all *corantos* were banned; but, with 500 copies an edition being sold, the business was too profitable (and the war too interminable) to let the matter be. After successful petitioning, Butter and Bourne were allowed to recommence publication in 1638.

The English *coranto* writers had long known enough of their market to feature the doings of 'some gentlemen of our nation', the few English and Scots enlisted on the continent, in their 'forraine avisoes', much as modern television sports commentators highlight minor national individual performance at international events at the cost of balanced reporting. This was increasingly inadequate, however, as crown and parliament headed towards violent confrontation: 'And now by strange alteration and vicissitude of times we talke of nothing else but what is done in England'. Publicising the 'talke . . . of what was done in England' was aided by the early collapse of the Star Chamber in the crisis, abolished by the Long Parliament in June 1641. The Stationers' Company also had its privileges removed. The first news publication dealing with national events appeared in November 1641, but, quite suddenly as the flood of handwritten material attested, more news was being created than could be consumed even in newsbooks focused on domestic politics.

News was coming to be understood as a daily occurrence and to have occurred in the very recent past so that regular weekly publications dealing with not more than the previous seven days were the way to deal with it. The first of the weeklies, *The Diurnall, or The heads of all the Proceedings in Parliament*, appeared in December 1641. At last, Galbert's curious impulse to note down what was happening as it happened was being brought into the public arena on a regular basis. Dozens of other uncontrolled news publications appeared, stealing each other's titles and stories. Parliament banned all unlicensed news publications in March 1642 but by May a large number had reappeared. The rents in the political fabric frustrated authority's attempts to assert traditional control. On 22 August 1642, King Charles I raised his standard at Nottingham, effectively marking the start of the English Civil War. The upheavals that followed created a confused independence for the press. Although its freedom was periodically removed, always treated with suspicion and eventually partially contained, the liberty journalism then gained was never again entirely destroyed by the authorities.

The concept of the diurnal speaks to the growth of the idea of news as a perishable commodity. Purveyors of *canards* had known that the more recent local events were, crimes especially, the better they sold, but most news was not yet news merely because of its recency, especially that arriving with distant date-lines. Rather news was news because the readership had not read about it before. It followed that corrections were news and a seventeenth-century scoop could legitimately consist of 'late intelligences' which put right the erroneous information already published by rival *corantos*.

These regular dated and numbered periodical publications now had fixed titles, and the old function of announcing content in the name was passed to a brief list of the stories within published on the front page, sometimes above the title. They were often printed in verse, exhibiting a taste for word play that persists in the contemporary British fondness for punning headlines. For example, the twelfth edition of the *Mercurius Civicus*, which proclaimed itself LONDONS INTELLIGENCER OR, *Truth impartially related from thence to the whole Kingdome, to prevent mis-information* for the week Friday 11 August to Thursday 17 August 1643 contained reports on:

> The London Malignants disarmed,
> Fifty thousand pounts to be raised,
> The Lord Capels Forces dispersed,
> The Cavaliers from Gloucester repulsed.

Most were more prosaic: 'A testimonial of the valiant acts of the Plimouth Regiment. The King moves not towards Oxford. Four Northern Counties entering into Association. Crowland Abbey said to be lost. Two Popes of Rome chosen . . .'.[5]

The tone remained sober in all of these papers, however earth-shattering the news. Although the mercurists were writers originating material, their pre-Civil War experience was largely as translators and editors merely preparing foreign sources for English publication; and perhaps this conditioned their careful approach to their new function. Samuel Pecke's *A Perfect Diurnall of the Passages in Parliament*, published in the first week of February 1649, is the perfect example of this detachment:

> Tuesday Ianuary 30. This day the King was beheaded, over against the Banquetting house by White-Hall. The manner of Execution, and what passed before his death take thus. He was brought from Saint James about ten in the morning, walking on foot through the Park, with a Regiment of Foot

for his guard, with Colours fflying, Drums beating . . . After which the King, stooping down, laid his necke upon the blocke, and after a very little pause, stretching forth his hands, the executioner at one blow severed his head from his body. Then his body was put in a coffin covered with black velvet; and removed to his lodging chamber in Whitehall.

Pecke's next paragraph begins: 'The House of Commons this day, according to given orders, sat early, and the Dutch Ambassadors, having sent them a transcript of their Embassie in English, the House spent much time in hearing the same read . . .'. The paper was organised as a diary (*A Perfect Diurnal*) and the King's death no more disturbed its pattern than it altered Parliament's business. Pecke ran the story on page 3.

Yet Pecke's tone did not hurt sales and, in these tumultuous times, his circulation was reaching up to 3,000 a week. The press itself had recently acquired the only significant modification it was to undergo between Gutenberg and the coming of the all-metal machine in the late eighteenth century. A counter-weight to automatically raise the pattern had been introduced in the 1620s, increasing speeds from Gutenberg's 15 impressions per hour (iph) to 150 or even more. Given the long days worked by printers, even allowing for type-founding and setting, an average shop with two presses could produce 2,500 sheets a day – more than enough for a weekly publication. News publications were anyway seen as a profitable sideline to the main business of book-production, a way of maximising the use of the presses.

The *coranto* might have been the ancestral voice of the broadsheet but it was not the only influence on English journalistic practice. Liberated by the collapse of central authority in the Civil War, the sensationalism of some newsbooks and the raucous tone of many a pamphlet also found its way into English journalism. Take the *Mercurius Britannicus, Communicating the affaires of great Britaine: For the better Information of the People: From Monday the 28. Of July, to Monday the 4. Of August, 1645*:

Where is King Charles? What's become of him? The strange variety of opinions leaves nothing certain: for some say, when he saw the Storm coming after him as far as Bridgewater, he ran away to his dearly beloved in Ireland; yes, they say he ran away out of his own Kingdome very Majestically . . . Because there is such a deale of uncertainty; and therefore (for the satisfaction of my Countrymen) it were best to send a Hue and Cry after him. If any man can bring tale or tiding of a wilfull King, which hath gone astray these foure years from his Parliament, with a guilty Conscience, bloody Hands, a Heart full of broken Vowes and Protestations . . . Then give notice to Britannicus, and you shall be well paid for your paines: So God save the Parliament.

Marchamont Nedham, the author of this squib, revived the old Butter and Bourne trademark as a title and made the *Britannicus* into Parliament's most important newspaper and propaganda tool in the first phase of the Civil War. His style echoed that of the first professional writers, pamphleteers such as Thomas Nashe, who had tried to live by their pens alone half a century before in Elizabeth's day. Nashe wrote plays and the first novel in English as well as pamphlets. He has the same vivid colloquial quality as Nedham: 'Hee fumde, hee stampt, hee buffeted himself about the face, beat his head against the walls, and was ready to byte the flesh off his armes if they had not hindred him.' By Nedham's time, there was also a general violence of the language in contemporary pamphlets, especially the radical religious ones:

All my strength, my forces were utterly routed, my house I dwelt in fired; my father and mother forsook me, the wife of my bosome loathed me, mine old name rotted, perished; and I was utterly plagued, consumed, damned, rammed, and sunke into nothing.

47

It is not for nothing that the sect founded by Abiezer Coppe, the writer of this broadside *A Fiery Flying Roll*, was known as the Ranters. Adding this voice to the business of the news is what distinguishes Nedham and his royalist rival, Sir John Berkenhead.

In fact, it was Berkenhead, described by the gossip John Aubrey as 'exceedingly bold, confident . . . Great goggli eies, not of a sweet aspect', who had introduced it. In the first years of the War, Sir John had produced for the King, whose court had removed to Oxford, the *Mercurius Aulicus* – the *Court Mercury* – which had a suitably conservative book-like design but had deliberately broken the boundary between news and comment. Although the *Aulicus* was subtitled *a diurnall, Communicating the intelligence and affaires of the Court to the rest of the* KINGDOME, yet it included jibes and biting comments as well as reports about Puritan atrocities and human-interest stories on the royal family. Berkenhead produced 118 editions, deliberately publishing on Sunday to offend the Puritans. He greeted the arrival of Nedham's *Mercurius Britannicus* in typically robust fashion: 'All other Newes (I mean Lyes) you must expect from a fine new thing borne this week called *Mercurius Britannicus*'. Nedham responded in kind, publishing Berkenhead's obituary once when the weekly *Aulicus* failed to appear.

Their enthusiasm, partisanship and wit came to condition the English newspaper. What they added, crucially, to the *corantos*' sober reporting tradition was the verve and combative vigour of pamphlet and debate. The mix was new, unique and explosive and, arguably, the English press has never moved far from the legacy of that historic Civil War moment. As this crucial rupture between authority and the periodical press occurred, although the latter's independence was initially deeply compromised by it being politically and religiously highly partisan, and although other forces have continued to undercut its liberties one way or another ever since, a tradition of press freedom was established at the beginning of the 1640s. English journalism began, and has remained, obstreperous, argumentative, entertaining and vehemently competitive. Happy as it was (and is) to sell itself as purveying truth, it was (and is) none too constrained by the *corantos*' limiting notions of objectivity. Their original objective tone was never re-established as English journalism's only tone of voice, while on the other hand passionate partisanship and vivid colloquialism were never to disappear from the pages of English newspapers.

Nor were its writers too restrained by ties of conviction and conscience. Berkenhead, it is true, remained a Royalist through thick and thin but others were more flexible, especially Nedham. Although his 'Hue and Cry' for Charles was radically anti-Royalist enough to get him into trouble even with the Lords still sitting in Parliament, he nevertheless changed sides in the summer of 1647, going over to the Royalists to start the *Mercurius Pragmaticus*. This was not perhaps the smartest of moves as the King was about to be captured, but, after five years of commotion, Nedham had despaired of Parliament's ability to control Cromwell: 'For Mr Crumwell hath them in the Mill and grind they must, seeing they are at his Beck who holds a Whip and a Bell over their guilty heads'.

The War made no difference to authority's usual dilemma, on both sides. As had become usual over the previous century, central power appreciated the usefulness of its own publications but deplored any it did not control. For all that Cromwell and, later, the restored Stuarts tried to maintain a censoring function, in the long term the task was impossible. The genie of unlicensed free journalism, for good or ill, was out of the bottle and in England it would never be fully stopped up again for long by overt governmental control. Not that the politicians did not try. Despite the liberal-like sentiments of some republicans, such as Milton, even before the establishment of the Commonwealth, the Parliament attempted to reassert the sort of control once exercised by the otherwise hated Court of the Star Chamber. It moved to do so in 1643 but to no effect. The year following, a news-addicted Londoner could still buy 12 papers a week, three on Monday and Friday, two on Wednesday and Thursday and one each on Tuesday and Saturday. These included the *Aulicus*, published on the Sabbath in Oxford but readily available on Mondays in Parliamentary London. Cromwell tried again in 1645 to restrict the flow but to no avail. Even after the King was executed, the Royalist press continued its harassment of the victorious republicans: 'Hugh Peters [a close confidant of Cromwell's] . . . Is turn'd one of Venus Souldiers, for he hath got a Wench with Child'. The King's cause was finally extinguished by the defeat of Royalist forces at the Battle of Worcester in 1651. The presses were closed down and in 1655, and again in 1659, the Commonwealth asserted its right to a monopoly on news by banning all but its own authorised publications. These included, from 1650 on, the *Mercurius Politicus* edited by Nedham, once more a Parliament man.

Nedham's turncoat antics earned him a reputation, with his contemporaries, of being like a cat, always falling on his feet. He, of course, claimed he was always consistent and it was those above him who veered and tacked. He had been arrested and imprisoned when Charles I was executed but had escaped. Now, once more, he landed on his feet, by returning to the Republican fold, rewarded with £100 a year for editing the *Politicus*. The slippery Marchamont was licensed in his activities, somewhat curiously, by the apostle of an unlicensed press, John Milton. Nedham, despite the controls on him, maintained the independent tone of the mercuries of the 1640s, promising that although the 1650s were 'a ticklish time to write Intelligence', he would be resolute. The *Politicus*, he boasted, was 'the only State-Almanack to tell what Weather is in the Commonwealth'. It was a *coranto*-like digest of the news that included extremely well-informed dispatches from abroad (as might be expected given his access to Cromwell's Council of State). But the editor could also be as biting as ever: Charles II was regularly referred to as 'young Tarquin'. However, in the peace, he returned to the comparatively safe ground of the original mercantilist news agenda and regularly published lists of 'Ships this week arrived in the Port of London' with details of their cargoes. Port news of this kind was to remain a newspaper staple – as was the sensational: 'Christian Mathie, convict of severall Adulteries with marryed men, she herself being a marryed Woman . . . she was ordered to be hanged on Wednesday May 8'. Despite Puritan oppression, the press as a whole continued to titillate.

John Crouch, a Royalist who in 1649 had pioneered the scurrilous, smutty, penny mercury, *The Man in the Moon*, survived the censorious temper of Commonwealth times. In and out of hiding, with a £50 price on his head, he was captured in 1650 but was released from prison in 1652 and, with the *Mercurius Democraticus*, consolidated his position as the British father of what would become known, centuries later, as 'the yellow press'. The *Democraticus* was not a diurnal but a 'Perfect Nocturnall' with 'Wonderfull News Out of the World in the Moon, The Antipodes, Tenebris, Faery-Land, Egypt, Green-land and other adjacent Countries'. The title became the *Mercurius Fumigosus* but the smut and parody were unchanged – jokes about giant farts and lost maidenheads; careful use of 'facts' (173,000 witches mustered on Salisbury Plain); satire at the expense of politicians and sects; even pornographic woodcuts. The *Fumigosus* carried a mere half-page of 'diurnall' news while the rest was devoted to the 'Nocturnall' which yielded little to today's offerings in 'adult' explicitness:

> She offered to lend the Taylors man as much haire from her
> Innoncency as would make him a beard, and moreover, That
> if his Masters bald crown did want Hairs to cover it, she
> would spare as much from the noodle of her Gate-house to
> make him a Night-cap against Winter.

Crouch constantly complained of poverty but the fact that he had emulators suggests a living was to be made from satisfying the lowest of tastes, even under the rule of Cromwell's austere major-generals. Nedham himself was certainly well rewarded for his less scurrilous publications, eventually earning, as the Protector's major apologist, £500 a year. But there were risks: prison for Crouch and political upheavals for Nedham. Having jumped twice, Nedham did not quite make the third leap at the Restoration of Charles II. The Council of State dismissed him in March 1660 and he fled to Holland. He died, once again in England, in 1678.

'An Act for the restraint of printing'

Charles II arrived in London in triumph in May 1660. By June the Commons decided that 'no person whatsoever do presume, at his peril, to print any votes or proceedings of this House without special leave of this House'. Since the order was specific about 'printing', it encouraged the persistence of the handwritten newsletter, but reports of parliamentary debates, a staple of the diurnals before the Commonwealth, ceased. Henry Muddiman, described by Samuel Pepys as both 'a good scholar' and 'an arch rogue', replaced Nedham as the favoured newsman. He shared with Nedham an easy command of language and a flexible sense of his own integrity. Although he was running the *Parliamentary Intelligencer*, Pepys noted that Muddiman 'declared that he did it only to get money; and did talk very basely of many of them', that is, his political paymasters. As an early supporter of the restored throne, his newsbook, which became the *Kingdom's Intelligencer* in January 1661, and another of his titles, the *Mercurius Publicus*, alone were licensed, by the old cavalier and newly appointed licenser, Berkenhead. 'Published by Order', they declared.

The throne's full-scale attempt to roll back the clock began in 1662 with a positively Tudor-style Licensing Act, 'for preventing the frequent Abuses in printing seditious, treasonable, and unlicensed Books and Pamphlets, for the regulating of Printing and printing Presses'. A restored Stationers' Company would have its membership limited by this statute to the 59 master printers then in business in London. Their number was to fall to 20 before any new members could be admitted. Apart from members of the Company, only Oxford and Cambridge Universities and the Archbishop of York were licensed to run presses. A Surveyor of the Press was to be appointed with a monopoly on news publications as well as responsibility as a censor on all other output. Censorship was to be enforced by General Warrant, which allowed the Surveyor and his men 'to search all houses and shops where they shall know, or upon some probable reason suspect any books and papers to be printed, bound or stitched, especially printing houses, booksellers shops and warehouses, and bookbinders' houses and shops'. The job went to Sir Roger L'Estrange, who immediately ousted both Muddiman and the loyal Berkenhead. Sir John retired from the press to become a spymaster.

Sir Roger, a fervent Royalist, was appointed because he had written a pamphlet of impeccable repressive opinion: *Considerations and Proposals In Order to the Regulation* OF THE PRESS TOGETHER WITH *Diverse Instances of Treassonous, and Seditious Pamphlets, Proving the Necessity thereof.* For L'Estrange, the news element in all this flood of what the Act described as 'heretical, schismatical, blasphemous, and treasonable books, pamphlets and papers' was threatening because it 'makes the multitude too familiar with the actions and counsels of their superiors, too pragmatical, too censorious'. L'Estrange and official opinion were too convinced of the Hobbesian view of the power of the press over 'the Common-peoples' minds' to essay an outright ban on print in general or news in particular. They thought to exercise that supposed power themselves even while preventing others from doing so. Sir Roger therefore proposed a monopoly on news publications and that was put in place. His two journals, the *Intelligencer. Published for the Satisfaction of the People* and the *Newes*, were both priced 2d and identified as being published 'With Privilege'. In a subsequent publication, the *Observator*, Sir Roger explained his journalistic philosophy: 'it is the *Press* that has made'um *Mad*, and the *Press* must set 'um *Right* again'.

But he did not quite manage to do this, although his 'Messengers to the Press' (or King's Messengers) were an active police. Armed with general warrants and the threat of prison, the stocks or even, in the case of sedition or treason, the gallows, they were able to re-establish a good measure of control. Sir Roger was a better censor, however, than he was journalist. As a writer he was too much the amateur to fulfil the function of official mercurist and during the plague year of 1665, with the court returned (with Parliament) to Oxford, his enemies there re-employed Muddiman. Muddiman produced the *Oxford Gazette*, 'By Authority'. It looked far more like a modern newspaper than did its predecessors – two pages, double columns, printed on a half-sheet in folio, price 1d. That year, 1665, saw the first appearance of the term 'journalist' for one who writes such publications. Only the name, 'newspaper', was not yet to hand – but it was to be coined by 1670.

L'Estrange, who had bravely remained in London during the plague, was bought out, placated with the promise of £100 a year from the sales of the *Gazette* and other money. On 5 February 1666, the court being once more in the capital, Muddiman's new paper became the *London Gazette*. It missed one issue because of the Great Fire but then carried 'this short, but true Accompt of it':

> On the second instant, at one of clock in the Morning, there hapned to break out, a sad and deplorable Fire in Pudding-lane, neer New Fish-street, which falling out at that hour of the night, and in a quarter of the town so close built with wooden pitched houses spread itself before day and with such distraction to the inhabitants and Neighbours that care was not taken for the timely preventing of further diffusion of it.

The *London Gazette*, still the official government paper, is Britain's oldest news title, but today it contains only specialist details of laws and regulations.

The old system of hawking broadside ballads and popular prints had been adapted to market the news. News-hawkers, often women, cried their wares on the street. For example, in the year of the Great Fire, a Mrs Andrews using this method was distributing 3,000 to 5,000 copies of the *London Gazette* per issue. L'Estrange had a troop of 'book women' who were allowed 100 free copies a month to sell on their own account. News publications, including newsletters, were also being distributed through the coffee-houses which had been proliferating since the first was opened in 1652. These were becoming key to establishing and sustaining a paper. Printers and writers sent them free copies of new titles and they themselves advertised the provision of news as a selling point:

> The Plot and Counter-plot Coffee-House . . . Invites all
> people, as not only having the best Coffee, Chocolate and
> Tee sold there but also all sorts of News Pamphlets, lying
> ready on the Table, for any Person to read that will spend
> their penny.

The real difficulty now lay more in political will than in the logistics of suppression. Too much water had passed under the bridge for it any longer to be axiomatic that the provision of news was a royal prerogative. Nor was there agreement either in political theory or in practice that L'Estrange's role as licenser/censor was legitimate. Against the pessimistic Hobbes, the Restoration generation produced John Locke, an apologist for the necessity of revolution when 'the prince or legislative act contrary to their trust'. The ultimate judge of when this trust was broken, argued John Locke, was the people who have 'a right to act as supreme' rather than have all power relinquished to Hobbes's 'great leviathan'. Charles II was no god-like leviathan, much as he might have longed to be. The country was certainly war-weary and party and faction were no longer in arms against one another; but they were not so exhausted as to have disappeared and all were unwilling to yield a monopoly of print to the crown. One measure of Charles's limited prerogative can perhaps be seen in the fact that his draconian Printing Act of 1662 had to be presented as a temporary measure, renewable every two years. It had therefore lapsed in 1679 in the confusions caused when MPs threatened to bar Charles's brother James, a Catholic, from the succession and Charles prorogued Parliament in response. The renewal of the Act was among the business that had fallen by the wayside. Like indestructible weeds, unlicensed journalism immediately appeared and smut also sprouted amongst the plethora of anti-Catholic, anti-Royalist (and anti-Dissenting) information and propaganda. For example, the three-a-bed romp, a story beloved of the late twentieth-century British tabloid, enlivened the *Loyal Protestant* of 2 September 1682. An unnamed Dissenting minister reportedly 'laid with two Wenches ten Nights at a Guinny a Night: That he exercised one whilst the other raised his inclination'.

The format 'Printed for . . .' came to indicate the writers of a journal, and 'To be sold by . . .', to signify the publisher/printer. Apart from the prior printing of matter translated by other, usually foreign, journals and the material supplied by correspondents (literally readers in touch with the paper by private letter), the printers were now more systematically seeking material, perusing the daily lists of the dead, the Bills of Mortality, for instance. Also, fitfully emerging from the shadows was a new figure, the 'news-gatherer' or 'intelligencer'. News-gatherers, really a species of spy, were not acknowledged by name in print although they were rewarded for their efforts. One, William Bond, was earning 7/- a week 'spectating for hire' as a hostile pamphlet described his sort of occupation. These 'spectators' were sometimes women, 'she-intelli-gencers'. 'Persons are employed (One or Two for each Paper) at so much a Week, to haunt Coffee-Houses, and thrust themselves into Companies where they are not known'. Nathaniel Thompson accused his rival Benjamin Harris in print of paying one William Beckett '2s. 6d. for every paragraph of news bought him, true or false'. Whether this itself was true or false cannot be known but it does attest to the existence of reporters although it was to be another 140 years before that term would be used.

The spirit of Civil War mercurist competition survived the Restoration and occasionally appeared in the more modern form of the scoop rather than correcting or simply plagiarising from rivals. In 1681, for example, Thomas Benskin, who alone published on Thursday in London, held his first column to print news of a verdict in a treason trial being held on a Wednesday in August at Oxford. It was not his fault that the defence delayed the outcome and his Oxford correspondent was reduced to the prediction that the defendant 'would be cast for his life'.

In 1683, the Printing Act being still in abeyance, the King prohibited unlicensed printing of news by proclamation and these more independent papers were once again closed down. In 1688, James II managed to have Parliament reimpose the Act for five years. The journalists, however, seized the moment again when his Protestant daughter

Mary and her husband William grabbed the throne in the bloodless Glorious Revolution of 1689. The papers flourished as before but so did the King's Messengers. The crown again moved to have Parliament renew the Licensing Act. But specific control was no longer an agreed objective:

> we do in a manner Libel our own Truth when by Licensing and Prohibiting, fearing each Book, and the shaking of each Leaf, we distrust her own strength: Let her and Falsehood grapple; who ever knew Truth put to the worst in free and open Encounter?

Such rhetoric, echoing the *Aereopagitica*, was very much in play. Moreover, in 1694, with the death of Queen Mary, the concept of the divine right of the crown was abandoned and with its passing died many royal prerogatives, including the right to license the press.

But of equally great long-term significance, in 1695, Edward Clarke MP, using arguments drafted by his friend John Locke, successfully pleaded in the House of Commons that, royal prerogative aside, the laws of sedition and libel, blasphemy and treason meant that publishers were anyway accountable. The weight of existing law 'makes', he claimed, 'this or any other Act for the restraint of printing very needless'. This was not to enact the principle of a free press but it was a major step forward towards that position. The Printing Act was not renewed. On the other hand, the power of the general warrant was left in place. Neither was the prohibition on reporting Parliament lifted and, soon, specific taxes as a form of control were imposed – nevertheless, a crucial stage had been reached in the development of the idea that what was soon to be called 'prior constraint' was illegal under the common law. In 1695, with the final removal of a general prior constraint, once more papers flooded the streets, the coffee-houses and the inefficient mails.

'Was it for me to examine the deeds of the government?'

Tobias Peucer defended his media studies doctoral thesis on the nature of news reporting, *De relationibus novellis*, at the University of Leipzig in 1690. Although he suffered obscurity, as most scholars in his field were to do thereafter, it seemed that he was not burdened by the animosity of colleagues, unlike some of his modern successors. His supervisor, Professor Adam Rechenberg, was no less a figure than the university's rector. Serious analysis of journalistic practice started to appear in German as early as 1676 and by the time Peucer wrote, many assumptions about the nature of the news were being articulated. Peucer, for instance, noted that the 'six familiar elements' of journalism were character, events, cause, place, time and manner – already almost exactly Kipling's 'who, what, why, where, when'. Peucer understood the importance of timeliness and argued that every story 'gives more pleasure if the place, if the famous personages, at whose instance a particular deed was performed . . . are known to us'. These are exactly today's notions of the need for speed and the attractions of celebrity, localism and relevance in a news story.

Peucer was not entirely happy with much of the German press of his day, disliking its taste for trivial information about the famous and titillating reports of criminal activity. He was already basically arguing for a 'quality' news agenda, denying the legitimacy of lighter story genres. Nor did he have much sense of a need for free expression, although demands for this were not unknown among the English and the Dutch. Peucer did, though, understand the roots of journalism, seeing newspapers as having a specific utilitarian value for merchants, but the range of legitimate news did not, for him, include 'the affairs of princes'. Anything 'they do not want printed should not be bandied about'. He was quite clear 'that news should not appear in type before approval by censors'.

Peucer stands in a continental European tradition which, although twin to that conditioning journalism in English, is nevertheless significantly different. The established continental view was, as Machiavelli had put it, that the prince controlled the flow of public information. Only in England and in the recently liberated Protestant provinces of the Spanish Netherlands had this been challenged, and even in these two countries, the press could not be called free in practice. Nevertheless there was a sense of the legitimacy of press freedom as an ideal, for all that achieving it was to be an ongoing struggle. Almost everywhere else on the continent, few individuals, much less a majority of a royal council or an assembly, would have disagreed with Machiavelli and Peucer.

Take France. As in the British Isles, but in contrast to the German lands, the conflict between Protestant and Catholic was not the central domestic issue in the seventeenth century. France had undermined Protestant power within its borders during the previous century. It had experienced the same pressures as did England to limit the power of the throne, but its internal political upheaval, the so-called War of the Fronde and the unsuccessful revolt by some nobles which followed it (1648–53), had seen the royal party and the boy-king, Louis XIV, emerge completely victorious. No further challenge to authority occurred to allow the machinery of control to slip. The French throne was, by the measure of the English royal disaster, secure, with its pre-rogatives untouched, and by 1660 Louis had grown into the perfect model of the autocratic *Grande Monarque*, exercising an extreme form of personal government.

The press, which the French crown had early exploited with its *occasionnels*, never became an effective tool in the hands of the powerful, politically disaffected as it did in London. Despite this contrast, the central need for news as a source of information about foreign affairs was as clear in mercantilist France as it was in England, the Netherlands or the German lands. The Dutch *corantos* were being translated into French by 1610 just as they were rendered into English. The *Mercure français* followed a year later.

In the midst of the Thirty Years' War the royal physician, Dr Théophraste Renaudot, a Protestant who converted to Catholicism in 1628, found himself the possessor of a sole licence from the King 'to have printed and sold by those appropriate, news, gazettes and accounts of all that has happened and is happening inside and outside the Kingdom'. The *Gazette de France* began in 1631 with Renaudot as its editor. It was a four-page weekly, 23 cm × 15 cm, so successful that it doubled in size within a year, printing the usual foreign stories but also covering some domestic events – the health of the Duchesse of Longueville, for example, or the establishment of a charity for the poor in Reims.

Parodies of the *Gazette* appeared, such as the *AntiGazette* or *News from the Four Quarters of the Other World*; but its dominance was not seriously challenged except in the years of the Fronde. As in England, the upheaval loosened controls and between 1649 and 1652 there was a vogue for vigorous printed political versifying. Some 4,300-plus *mazarinades*, little verse pamphlets, were published.[6] Even Renaudot's two doctor sons produced a paper, the *Courrier française*, in the *Parlement*'s interest – but only for 12 editions. The thirteenth was suppressed by their father, and, with the triumph of Louis XIV, the *Gazette*'s monopoly was re-established.

Exactly the same factors had influenced both French and English journalism. Both societies had published sensationalist newsbooks and *canards*; both knew of newsletters and *gazeta*; both had received translated *corantos* from the Dutch; both produced low parodies of news publications: the English *Nocturnals* had in fact been nothing but a copy of *Nouvelles . . . de l'autre monde*. The crucial difference between the countries was the fall-out from the internal power struggle with the crown. In England, against a background of the defeat of absolutism as a principle of government, direct control of editorial material slipped for more than a decade and then faltered again and again until it was abandoned. In France, the five years of the Fronde were an aberration. The idea that news was a royal monopoly was not abandoned – just as the concept of the divine right of the French throne was not abandoned either.

Louis XIV was as fond of official *occasionnels* proclaiming his victories as his fifteenth-century ancestors had been. The *Gazette* was constantly privately informed by the throne. The very idea of a free press in Miltonic or Lockean terms was scarcely mooted. The King, Renaudot wrote, was in touch 'almost regularly': 'Was it for me to examine the deeds of the government? My pen was only the grafting tool.' Contrast Nedham: 'I tooke up my pen for disabusing his Majesty, and for disbishoping and dispoping his good subjects, and for taking off vizards and vailes and disguises.' It is not surprising that the *Gazette*, editorship of which had been confirmed by letters patent to Renaudot's son Eusèbe in 1679, did little to advance the European journalistic enterprise. Eusèbe tinkered with the paper's presentation but in essence it remained unchanged. In 1685 it looked just as it had in 1631. Its conservatism allowed the common idea that 'the affairs of princes . . . should not be bandied about' another century in which to deepen its roots in France.

These secret royal matters, however, were not deemed to include business, which was to be encouraged, and Renaudot's contribution in confirming the press's role as a crucial handmaiden of commerce was of lasting significance for the whole of Europe. He had come to journalism because he had been persuaded by his patron Cardinal Richelieu to accept the role of Commissioner-General for the Poor. In that capacity he introduced an idea of the philosopher Montaigne, which he in turn had heard about from his father, for a sort of glorified labour exchange and swap-shop. 'In all cities', the philosopher had written in 1580,

> there should be a certain appointed place to which whosoever should have need of anything should come and cause his business to be registered by some officer appointed for that purpose; as for examples, if one have pearls to sell, he should say, I seek to sell some pearls; and another, I seek to buy some pearls.

In the thinking of both Montaigne and Renaudot, such a facility would reduce beggary and create work for the poor by providing a place where the rich could find what they needed, from wet-nurses to dancing masters.

61

In Paris, in 1630, Renaudot made Montaigne's 'appointed place' a reality by opening the *Bureau d'Adresses et de Rencontre*. Goods and services were advertised by notices on the *Bureau's* walls. It also functioned as a pawn-shop, an Italian idea that Renaudot hereby introduced into France. In 1639, all Parisian unemployed had to register at the *Bureau*. Clearly, printing the advertisements that adorned the walls of the *Bureau d'Adresses* would be even more efficient than just displaying them in one place. Renaudot began to do this from time to time. The idea of the *Bureau* was copied in London, where an Office of Public Advice was established along French lines. Nedham had an interest in it since, like Renaudot, he also saw the relationship between such exchanges and printed advertising booklets.

Signs, advertisements and public notices had always been a part of the townscape, even ancient Rome's. By the end of the sixteenth century, single leaves printed on one side, broadsides or broadsheets, were being used for all sorts of advertisements in many countries. In 1593, for example, in London one H. Platte announced a number of inventions including 'a New Kinde of Fire and a Portable Pumpe'. In James I's day, lotteries to raise funds for the Virginia colony were publicised in this way. Broadsheet bills were soon advertising everything from goods ('Notice by the Masters, Wardens, Assistants and Companie of Pin-Makers . . . the Companie have in readiness all sorts of Pinnes' – 1619) to rewards ('Those that can bring any newes of the Robberie shall have one hundred crowns given them to drink' – 1630).

In England, the placing of advertisements within other publications rather than as single sheets, no great leap forward after all, had already occurred. News journals commonly used their own space to promote themselves. For example, the *Weekly Relations of Newes* dated 23 August 1622 contained a note announcing that the title's two back numbers were still available for sale and the contents of future issues could, on occasion, be trailed. During the Civil War ads for books began to appear in news publications. Diurnalist Samuel Pecke, for instance, was soon pilloried for this practice in one of the mock newsbooks: 'Peck the Perfect Diurnall maker, the last page of which most commonly he lets out to the Stationers for sixpence a piece to place therein the titles of their books'. Land was also advertised: 'Those that intend to buy, delay no time'.

Nedham began publishing the *Publick Adviser*, a 16-page weekly pamphlet consisting entirely of advertisements, in May 1657. It was designed for 'Communicating unto the whole Nation the several Occasions of all persons that are in any way concerned in the matter of Buying and Selling, or in any kind of Imployment or dealings whatso-ever'. As with Renaudot's printed advertising sheets and the Paris *Bureau*, this London publication was the Office of Public Advice trans-lated into print. Its most serious matter put ships' masters in touch with merchants with cargo but there were many other 'Advices', all classified and headed e.g. 'Artificers', 'Physitians', and so on. The first news of chocolate came in the *Publick Adviser* for 16 June 1657: 'In Bishopsgate-Street in Queens-Head Alley, at a Frenchman's House is an Excellent West India drink, called Chocolate, to be sold, where you may have it ready made at any time, and also unmade at reasonable rates.' Tea was announced in Nedham's other proper newspaper, the *Mercurius Politicus*, the following year as 'That Excellent, and by all Physitians approved China drink, called by the Chineans, Tcha, by other nations Tay *alias* Tee'. The most significant of these new exotic bever-ages was coffee, which had been introduced on a broadside sheet in 1652 leading to a fashion for coffee-houses. By 1700 there were hun-dreds of these in London and the fad had become a prominent feature of the city.

Many goods and services were publicised in the *Publick Adviser*: 'At the King's Head in Southwerk goeth a Wagon every Monday and Thursday from thence to Dover'; 'There is a Gentleman lately come to London, who hath invented and found a way for amending all sort of chimnies'. Thomas Shelton's son, a proto-Pitman, offered to teach the 'new Art of Short-writing by a more easie and speedy way' in 'Boars-head Court, next door to the crown near Cripplegate'. The descriptor 'advices' gave way to 'advertisements', which had been infrequently used in this sense since the late sixteenth century, as the preferred term in English. The French stuck with 'Adresse'. Some were quick to take offence at these notices, whatever they were called, characterising them as 'impertinences' or, in another term that came to stick, 'puffs'.

In this way, the intemperate English turncoat hack Nedham came to produce, albeit in different publications and, often, in very different tone, the same range of advertising and editorial material as the cautious French royal physician, Renaudot. The crucial difference between them was the political environment in which they worked. Advertising was safe everywhere and their approach was similar, which is not surprising given the shared economic system.[7] Political assumptions and realities, on the other hand, were somewhat distinct – producing a chasm in journalistic practice. Nedham, for all his rank opportunism, had a sense of free expression which Renaudot did not. Nedham's lack of principle demonstrates that, unlike all the other entitlements which were to become categorised as human rights, the liberty of free expression did not remotely result in unambiguous public good. The struggle for freedom of expression, despite all the high-minded Miltonic rhetoric it occasioned, was never simply (and therefore conveniently) a laudable question of civic virtue, like the right to due legal process or the right to shelter. The right of free speech was from the beginning a matter of looking at the stars while lying in the gutter. That is exactly why, although it is less central to the maintenance of life than the other rights, it is the crucial measure of liberty and the engine of freedom.

Sources

Roy Atwood and Arnold de Beer (2001), 'The Roots of Academic News Research: Tobias Peucer's *De relationibus novellis* (1690)', *Journalism Studies* 2.4. November.

C. Bellanger (1969), *Histoire général de la presse française*, Paris: Presses Universitaires de France.

Jeremy Black (2001), *The English Press 1621–1861*, Stroud, Glos.: Sutton.

George Boyce, James Curran and Pauline Wingate (eds) (1978), *Newspaper History from the 17th Century to the Present Day*, London: Constable.

Jerôme Carcopino (1941, 1957), *Daily Life in Ancient Rome*, Harmondsworth: Penguin.

Abiezer Coppe (1649, 1973), *A Fiery Flying Roll*, London: Imprint Academic.

G. A. Cranfield (1978), *The Press and Society: from Caxton to Northcliffe*, London: Longman.

Blanche Elliot (1962), *History of English Advertising*, London: Business Publications.

Joseph Frank (1961), *The Beginnings of the English Newspaper 1620–1660*, Cambridge, Mass.: Harvard University Press.

Galbert of Bruges (1967), *The Murder of Charles, the Good Count of Flanders*, New York: Harper Row.

Christopher Hampton (ed.) (1984), *A Radical Reader: The Struggle for Change in England 1381–1914*, Harmondsworth: Penguin.

Michael Harris and Alan Lee (eds) (1986), *The Press in English Society from the Seventeenth to the Nineteenth Centuries*, Rutherford, NJ: Fairleigh Dickinson University Press.

A. Hyatt Mayor (1971), *Print and People*, Princeton: Princeton University Press.

Steve Knowlton and Patrick Parsons (ed.) (1995), *The Journalist's Moral Compass: Basic Principles*, Westport, Conn.: Praeger.

Michael Leapman (ed.) (n.d.), *The Book of London*, London: Weidenfeld & Nicholson.

Thomas Nashe (J.B. Steane (ed.)) (1596, 1972), *The Unfortunate Traveller and Other Works*, Harmondsworth: Penguin.

T. R. Nevett (1982), *Advertising in Britain*, London: Heinemann.

Joad Raymond (1996), *The Invention of the Newspaper: English Newsbooks 1641–1649*, Oxford: Oxford University Press.

M. A. Shaaber (1929, 1966), *Some Forerunners of the Newspaper in England*, London: Frank Cass & Co. (repr. of Philadelphia: University of Pennsylvania Press).

Anthony Smith (1979), *The Newspaper: An International History*, London: Thames & Hudson.

Keith Williams (1977), *The English Newspaper*, London: Springwood.

2

'CONGRESS SHALL MAKE NO LAW': JOURNALISM FROM 1702

'Giants to write it'

In the upheavals of Commonwealth, Restoration and Glorious Revolution, no notice had been taken in England of one crucial continental advance, the daily newspaper. Nobody in England had thought to do this, although dailies had begun in Germany half a century earlier. In Leipzig, the first daily paper, the *Einkommende Zeitung*, had appeared in 1650.[1] It was only after Queen Anne came to the throne in 1702 that a London printer, Samuel Buckley, took advantage of the rising numbers of cross-Channel packets, always a crucial determinant of newspaper frequency, to publish the *Daily Courant*.

Buckley's *Daily Courant* was revolutionary only in the fact that it appeared daily (that is Mondays through Saturdays), which it did from 11 March 1702 until 1728. Otherwise it was very old-fashioned in that it echoed the objective tone of the *corantos* of Butter and Bourne 80 years earlier. It was a two-column single foolscap sheet printed on one side and Buckley made much of its slimness:

> This Courant (as the Title shews) will be Publish'd Daily: being design'd to give all the Material News as soon as every Post arrives; and is confin'd to half the Compass, to save the publick at least half the Impertinences of ordinary Newspapers.

Buckley had a big continental story to sustain him – the War of Spanish

Succession, the obscure conflict that gave the British Gibraltar and gave John Churchill, Duke of Marlborough, Blenheim Palace, built by a grateful nation in thanks for his victory at the battle of that name.

The first *Daily Courant* carried stories from the Harlem and Amsterdam *Courants* and the *Paris Gazette*, all published a mere four days before.[2] Of course, these continental papers themselves had deadlines, all carefully reproduced in the *Daily Courant*. The news from Naples about the arrival of French troops there had taken three weeks to reach the streets of Paris and Harlem. Another report in the *Paris Gazette* on the dispatch of more French troops for Italy from Toulon had taken 13 days to cross France.[3]

Its daily publication was the most radical feature of the *Daily Courant*. In old *coranto*-style, no context was provided for the readers, who were expected to supply this themselves. In consequence detailed information stood alone. Here in its entirety is the report from Rome picked up by Buckley from the Paris paper:

> We have Advice by an express from Rome of the 18th of February, That notwithstanding the pressing Instances of the Imperial Embassadour, the Pope had Condemn'd the Marquis de Vasto to lose his Head and his Estate to be confiscated, for not appearing to Answer the Charge against him of Publickly Scandalizing Cardinal Janlon.

This is not, on its face, material for new readers, yet despite the unfriendly, austere approach, the *Daily Courant* was soon selling 800 copies a day. The title was probably owned not by Buckley alone but by a consortium of booksellers – certainly the case after 1708. A daily newspaper was, obviously, a good item to stock since it brought customers into shops on a regular basis. Other sales were handled by 'E. Mallet', printer Elizabeth Mallet, one of a number of women involved in the trade after the Restoration.

The coming of the daily newspaper indicated that the press could produce materials on a speedy basis and, obviously, that it could publish with equal regularity on a longer cycle. As daily publication began to take hold, so too did a new species of periodical publication which had extended intervals between appearances. In part, these filled the space created as the endless flow of religious pamphleteering began to abate. Pamphlets, licit and illicit, continued to be the main format for theological and, where possible, political debate. In contrast to these, the earliest of the new journals concentrated on, and in fact facilitated, information about the rise of science. Unlike the pamphlet, and indeed unlike many newspapers at this time, the journals, usually appearing monthly, could have multiple authors and, therefore, something much more akin to the modern editor. The first, the *Monatsgespräche*, devoted to philosophy and general scholarship, surfaced in 1663.

All the learned societies were to publish journals in the form of transactions. The Royal Society started theirs, *Philosophical Transactions*, in 1665. In the same year, in France, Mazarin's successor, Colbert, thought that French philosophy and science also deserved such a showcase and encouraged Denis de Salo to launch the *Journal des sçavants*. Francesco Nazzari produced *Giornale de'letterati* in Rome in 1668. What was possible for learned societies was also available to other learned institutions. The University of Halle began producing a weekly carrying scholarly articles and advertisements for books (but no politics) in 1727, an innovation that was emulated by universities in the Italian states where, for instance, Apostolos Zenos of the University of Venice established a periodical. The official *St. Petersburg Journal* (*Petersburgskiye vedomosti*) began in 1727 but it contained a supplement on cultural and scientific matters which became the model for the *Moscow Journal*. Science and literature were not entirely safe in such regimes – nothing printed was – but they were a lot safer than politics. The journal, *Moskovskiye vedomosti*, began publishing in 1755.

In countries under autocratic rule, a tradition of intellectual, apolitical journalism was established. These publications existed in parallel with the stunted political coverage of the official or closely monitored but privately owned *Zeitung* which were allowed to continue in many places, as long as domestic politics were avoided. General foreign news could be published, *coranto*-style, but to do even this required great caution from the printer, given the fears and suspicions of most authorities. At its worst, in Russia, the entire idea of newspaper was alien and only arrived when Peter the Great inaugurated an official handwritten newsletter. Freedom of expression was unthinkable.

On the European continent, outside of the universities, less academic collections of book reviews and the advertisements to accompany them had been identified by printers as another new sort of journal, the literary review. These had been made even more attractive as commercial publications by the addition of (non-political) gossip and some original writing. In 1672 the *Mercure galante* (which became the *Mercure de France* 22 years later) appeared along these lines. Its editor, Donneau de Vizé, applied the form of the learned journal specifically to the trivial and the entertaining, publishing everything from court news to poems, songs (both lyrics and music) and puzzles as well as a digest of the month's events. It was widely copied, in Holland (1686), Germany (1688) and Britain in 1690, when the *Athenian Mercury* came out. The attractiveness of a monthly to a female readership was quickly noticed. The *Ladies' Mercury* was being dispatched to (presumably) female readers all over town and country from 1693 on.

In an age that increasingly focused on the refinement and fashionability of the capital city, these cousins of the newspaper became a vital source of information on taste and behaviour, especially for provincial readers. The *Athenian Mercury* introduced the advice column:

> I have lately courted a young gentlewoman and she is now
> in mind to marry me. Lately died a relative and left me £100
> a year, on condition moreover, that I never would marry the
> aforementioned lady. Query, whether to take the lady and
> leave the money or take the money and leave the lady.

This seems so pat and succinct that one can perhaps wonder if it is not only an early example of the advice column but also of the practice of originating correspondence to fill space. Be that as it may, the press's function as a source of personal advice certainly begins at this time. ('Take the lady', advised the *Mercury*.) Richard Steele and Joseph Addison were more subtle in the guidance offered thrice-weekly in their 'observations on life and manners' published in their *Tatler* between 1709 and 1711. Under Steele, the subject matter closely followed the French model, that is, reviews of new plays and books, original poetry, trivia and advertisements. It was Addison's contribution, essays on manners, which quickly came to mark the *Tatler* out.

The *Spectator*, which followed it, was a daily published by Sam Buckley from 1711 to 1714 but it was, like the *Tatler*, not in any sense a newspaper. Rather, as Addison and Steele put it, it was 'a sheetful of thoughts every morning' chief among them the observations of 'Mr. Spectator'. He had things to say about everything from the education of girls to shop-signs to coffee-house culture:

> Sometimes I am seen thrusting my head into a round of politicians at Will's and listening with great attention to the narratives that are made in these little circular audiences . . .
> I appear on Sunday nights at St. James's coffee-house, and sometimes join the little committee of politicians in the inner room, as one who comes to hear and improve . . .

At its height the *Spectator* was selling 3,000 copies a day but could reach as many as 20,000 copies for some issues. For the first time such occasional writing was collected into more permanent book form. Bound essays from the *Spectator* sold 9,000 copies and were reprinted ten times in 20 years.

In 1731, Edward Cave, a printer, cleverly lit upon a title for his new printed miscellany from the pens of various writers, the *Gentleman's Magazine*. In his dictionary, Samuel Johnson, whom Cave had been the first to employ as a journalist, credited the printer as being the coiner of this term, 'magazine', originally meaning a store-house. 'Magazine' came in English to describe all such publications except the review and the learned transactions. By 1745 the *Gentleman's Magazine* was selling

15,000 copies a month. Cave had become rich enough to own a house in which lavish amateur theatricals could be staged.[4]

In Britain, at least, there were also political journals, often produced so regularly as to be readily confused with newspapers which were, after all, written in a now well-established politically partisan tradition. Such journals were not a substitute for otherwise forbidden political publications as they were under the continental autocracies. Both Daniel Defoe and Jonathan Swift, regular pamphleteers, also produced a considerable amount of writing in this form. (It is with much reason that journalism historian Francis Williams characterised the English press of the early eighteenth century as having 'giants to write it'.)

Daniel Defoe came to newspapering in 1704, aged 45, by founding the *Review*, a thrice-weekly political journal. He was a spy who travelled the country on behalf of Robert Harley, his patron, the leader of the governing Tory administration. After Queen Anne's death, he lived through the Whig ascendancy by becoming a spy for them. For seven years, three times a week, he wrote every word of his paper. In so doing he laid aside all rhetorical flourishes, instead melding the difference between the sober style of the *coranto* or diurnal and that of the spirited Civil War era mecuries into what would become the norm of journalistic language in English:

> If any man was to ask me what I would suppose to be the perfect style of language, I would answer, that in which a man speaking to five hundred people of all common and various capacities, idiots and lunatics excepted, should be understood by them all.

Defoe, the secret agent, and the silent loitering Mr Spectator reflect the continued consanguinity of spy and news reporter; but the reporter was also, as Addison put it, a person apart, 'rather . . . a spectator of mankind than one of the species'. Apart from the established practices of carrying the reports of intelligencers and correspondents, reprinting material from other publications and factual information from the ports about arrivals, sailings and cargoes, papers were also increasingly ready to exploit fairly tenuous sources such as 'ship news', that is, stories and rumours brought to the ears of the newspaper from the port – matters, however uncertain, of supreme interest for the merchants in the coffee-houses.

The coffee-houses were crucial to the newspapers since they had to buy copies in bulk to satisfy their customers' expectations. Outside the city, the continued backwardness of the English postal system as com-pared with continental norms was partly compensated for by a scheme for cut-price or free delivery. From the last years of the seventeenth cen-tury, the privilege of free mail was exercised by clerks to the Secretaries of State. One of these was dispatching 500 papers a week in 1711. The six Clerks of the Road, officers of the Post Office, were also allowed this privilege in the first decade of the eighteenth century and maintained it as a further source of income for their sinecures. They came to be share-holders in newspapers and magazines and were not above distorting distribution in their own interests. Cave, for example, abused his role as a Clerk by pushing his own publication. By 1764, the Clerks were taking between them £3,000–£4,000 a year from the newspaper proprietors. The investigation which revealed this also showed that in a single week the Clerks had dispatched 20,000 copies of newspapers to all corners of the kingdom. MPs had enjoyed the same privilege of free use of the royal mail and, eventually, they were allowed to share this with others. By 1771 over 1,000 persons were registered at the Post Office as agents of the MPs and 63,000 newspapers a week were being dispatched by them. The Secretaries managed only 756 and the Clerks were reduced to just under 13,000. All this was before the (belated) arrival of the mail coach on the expanding turnpike road system in 1784.

There were also specialised news carriers who delivered to the provinces in bulk. These entrepreneurs established local distribution networks for provincial newspapers as well. Despite this, the combined efforts of all these distributors meant that the London titles dominated and local papers remained marginal. Printing in any form had been for-bidden outside London until the collapse of the Printing Act, but only a few took advantage of the new situation to challenge the metropolitan product. There was space, however, for a cheap weekly round-up, largely gleaned from the London papers, and printers in Worcester and Norwich moved to exploit this niche. Fifty-five towns followed suit, but of the 130 titles which appeared in the first half of the eighteenth century, only 35 survived to 1760. Many of these, if they made it through this infancy, lived on for another 200 years and more – the *Bath Advertiser* and the *Reading Mercury*, for example.

The overall complexity of the mid-eighteenth-century press caused the emergence of another specialised journalistic figure in addition to the printer, writer, proprietor, correspondent and proto-reporter 'intelligencer'. Papers began to acquire a distributor, now called 'publisher'. By 1750, the London news marketing system had to cope with 100,000 copies a week. In London, as in Paris and other cities, the news-hawker selling on the street was a ubiquitous successor to the old print and ballad monger. In Paris such *colporteurs* had to be able to read and were licensed. In London, they were responsible for much distribution and were especially important to the survival of the unstamped farthing press. A vast range of goods and services could be picked up on the seventeenth and eighteenth-century city street but on none of these did this method of selling have a more profound effect than on newspapers. The need to 'cry the news' through the streets encourages a sensationalism that the newspaper proprietor who is secure in subscriptions can eschew. The news-hawkers had a tendency to over-dramatise their wares, the better to shift them: 'In times of war, the lyes prevail / All ears are open to the tale . . .'. News-hawking, organised by the publishers, was crucial in Britain to correct the failures of the postal system, and subscription via post was and remained a subsidiary distribution method. The result of this eighteenth-century reality is still played out in the daily war of British tabloid splashes.

The news-hawkers were well organised. At street level in London in the 1720s and 1730s they were all employed by either Mrs Nutt or Mrs Dodd. Their beats were not allowed to overlap. Anne Dodd also opened a specialised kiosk for news publications in 1721. The hawkers and their employers, like the printers and publishers, all took consider-able risks because draconian libel laws were still vigorously enforced, and the King's Messengers of the Press used the general warrant, which did not require persons to be named, against all these parties. Writers, of course, were pursued, but they were usually the hardest culprits to find. Mrs Nutt and Mrs Dodd, like all publishers and news-hawkers, sometimes had to endure prison for selling other people's words.

'No previous restraints on publications'

Indeed, too much should not be made of English press liberties despite the crucial removal of direct censorship in 1695. The challenge which the press presented to authority was not removed. Rather, political exi-gencies forced the English authorities to hobble themselves in dealing with the press by denying them only the most obvious tool of repres-sion, licensing. That left them free to impose other restrictive measures – taxation, for example.

Robert Harley's Tory administration introduced a stamp tax, specif-ically to put the Whig press, which was hostile to his attempts to bring the War of Spanish Succession to a close, out of business;[5] but the power of party and popular sentiment against the control of political communication required subterfuge. The tax had to be added to a bill also levying duties on soap, paper, linen, silk and calico. From 1 August 1712 all printed sheets, half sheets or less were taxed at 1d or ½d respec-tively. Printed advertisements attracted 1/- duty. Swift, another Tory, reported privately in his journal to Stella (Esther Johnson): 'Grubb St.[6] is dead and gone last week. The *Observator* is fallen, the *Medleys* are jumbled with the *Flying Post*, the *Examiner* is quite sick . . . No more ghosts or murders now for love or money.' Swift, though, was too quick to credit the tax with such suppressive success.

A new game between authority and, especially Whig, journalism now began. Most papers passed the charge on to their buyers, many of whom were coffee-house proprietors who had to absorb the increased

costs for the sake of their own businesses. The majority of papers survived, exploiting the loopholes in a poorly drafted law. For instance,
they published a sheet and a half when it was noticed that the tax did
not apply to this size. After this omission was corrected in revised legislation in 1725, other techniques were deployed. The usual two
columns, for example, became three or four to save space. Of course, it
was possible simply not to pay the stamp and risk the imperfect efficiency of the King's Messengers, especially outside London. Many
country papers remained unstamped. There is further evidence that
the government was not prepared to push the tax to its limits for fear of
the usual disorderly protests. The tax therefore did not halt the growth
of the newspapers and, moreover, a new species of untaxed ¼d papers
appeared.

If taxation constantly failed to achieve its purpose then the older
tools of direct suppression via the general law were still always available.
For example, John Matthews, who worked in his mother's printing
shop, published a Jacobite pamphlet arguing for the overthrow of the
Hanoverians, *Vox Populi, Vox Dei*, in 1719 but was informed on by two
of the other printers and hanged for treason. Mrs Powell, another incor-
rigible refractory pamphleteer, restarted her trade after one episode in
Newgate, but tempered her printed promise not 'to speak ill of
grandees' with the further thought that 'whosoever will speak well of
them, must tell many a lie'. In 1720 she reprinted *Vox Populi, Vox Dei*
and had to go into hiding as a consequence. Nathaniel Mist, another
partisan for the Stuart Old Pretender, was one of the most important
news publishers of the early century who suffered repeated imprisonment for his views until he fled to France in 1728.

It was not only the demand for a Stuart restoration that animated the
opposition press; the radical – or passionate liberal – political agenda
was also kept alive, continuing the transformation of the original concept of freedom of conscience ever more precisely into the idea of
freedom of expression. Take a series of articles written in 1720 by the
journalists John Trenchard and Thomas Gordon under the nom de
plume 'Cato':

> Freedom of speech . . . is the right of everyman, as far as by
> it he does not hurt or control the right of another; and this
> is the only check which it ought to suffer, the only bounds
> it ought to know . . . Whoever would overthrow the liberty
> of a nation, must begin by subduing the freedom of speech.

The Cato essays in the *London Journal* caused a sensation but its proprietor, Elizee Dobree, was not so committed to the free expression for which his essayists were arguing as to ignore the blandishments of the government. Politicians and their bureaucratic servants had a growing awareness that corrupting journalists was a far less fraught strategy than attempting outright suppression via the draconian laws of sedition or libel. Buying off the press was becoming a viable alternative to both censorship, now unavailable, and the increasingly uncertain operation of the law which could easily provoke the London mob into riot. An under-secretary entered into correspondence with Dobree about halting the Cato series. Elizee claimed that he was selling 15,000 copies of his journal to make £960 profit a year but he reckoned that 'By turning off the Strength of Expressions & thereby Lessning the sale to ab^t 7 or 8000 there would be little or no profit at all'. However, for £800 a year he was prepared to drop the column. Trenchard and Gordon moved to the *British Journal* but that too was soon sucked into government control the same way.

In 1742, the first identifiably modern prime minister, Robert Walpole, finally lost power. His private papers, made public by a Committee of Secrecy especially empanelled to investigate his official behaviour, revealed that over the previous decade alone he had passed no less than £50,077 18s 0d to news-writers, printers and proprietors. The practice of buying the press became a well-established method of subjugation, a carrot for toady journalists while the stick of the law was ever present to control any who could not be bought. Not that many resisted and by the late 1780s, seven of London's ten dailies had sold their independence to the Treasury. For example, John Walter, founder of *The Times*, had acquired the post of Printer to the Customs and his paper was taking £300 a year from Whitehall in secret subsidy. The *Observer*, the first Sunday paper which managed to establish itself, albeit as a scandal sheet, took government money well into the nineteenth century.

In this still hierarchical, deferential and corrupt society, another method of control apart from the common law and bribery was available – totally illegal exercising of power, usually by prohibiting distribution. Walpole, for example, was known to order postmasters not to distribute offensive publications, and outside London it was entirely possible for the local authorities likewise to ignore the law altogether. One incident: in 1720, Defoe, after complaining to a publican in Rochester, Kent about the lack of most London papers in his inn, reported the publican's excuses:

> Why really, Sir . . . We had Mist's Journal here and Dormer's letter; but they did so much Mischief among the Seaman and Tradesfolks, that our Magistrates and the Justices of the Peace have forbid the Publick-Houses taking them in . . . Mist has a Man came down on Horse-back every Saturday with two or three hundred Journals; however he happen'd last Week to be laid by the Heels for it.

It was not only officialdom that wanted to control the number of titles. For different reasons, the coffee-house proprietors had an interest in reducing the number of papers – so they could limit the expense of providing this attraction. This led them on occasion to support authorities' attempts to contain the press. In 1743, they pushed for a new Stamp Act which worked to kill off the farthing papers, essentially by encouraging the King's Messengers to round up the news-hawkers who peddled them. This did not work. By 1750 there were still 16 stamped papers – five dailies, five weeklies and six thrice-weeklies – as well as the journals and magazines of learned, review, political, specialist or general essay varieties and pamphlets. There was also a new collection of unstamped ¼d thrice-weeklies. The growth of the newspaper was not noticeably affected by any of these measures. Two and a half million stamps at the introduction of the tax rose steadily to 7.3 million by 1750, of which some 20 per cent were on provincial titles. By 1775, 12.6 million newspapers were being stamped.

Towards the end of the eighteenth century, some titles revived the seventeenth-century pornographic tradition but, far more significantly, English newspapers were constantly absorbing material that initially appeared under a separate guise. The contents of the magazines became part of mainstream newspapers in the form of features on 'Bons Mots', 'Theatricals' and 'Literature and Music'. In a ceaseless search for revenue, some newspapermen also aped the corrupting example of bribery. This was to lead to the most corrosive abuse of press freedom, not by the authorities but by the journalists themselves.

The *Morning Post* in 1772 melded the function of the advertising sheet and the gossip of the magazines of taste, while also echoing the raucous disrespect of the old Civil War mercuries. In doing so, the paper not only uncovered a popular taste for such a mixture; it also found a new source of revenue – blackmail. This involved accepting a bribe *not* to run stories. His highly irregular (i.e. morganatic) marriage to a Catholic widow in 1789 made the Prince of Wales himself vulnerable to this sort of attack. The *Post* blackmailed him twice, the second time taking his money to suppress just a short paragraph: 'It is confidently reported, that a certain marriage has been solemnized by a Romish Priest, who immediately quitted the kingdom.' The *Post* was not alone and the Prince at one point even offered to buy another paper outright for £4,000. It is no wonder that by 1795 journalists could be described, disgustedly, as 'bankrupts, lottery-office keepers, footmen and decayed tradesmen'. Yet the *Morning Post* also found space to publish the Lake Poets, Southey and Wordsworth. Charles Lamb turned a penny as its critic, society reporter and, admittedly, not very good wit: 'Two disputants made up to a soldier on guard the other day in the Park and asked him, when shall we arrive at the next century? Before you come to Buckingham Gate was the answer!'

This expansion of content did not mean that the essence of the 'quality' news agenda was ever completely lost. Behind the press's sala-ciousness, triviality, venality and corruption, there was still the high ideal of freedom and the serious ambition of publishing political news. For good or ill, journalists had now established that commerce, industry and government were, if not everybody's business, the business of a ruling, albeit factious, elite who needed, and would pay for, the information it carried. The more progressive within this elite demanded ever more information and, specifically, the struggle to obtain it became a campaign against the law of libel and the instrument of the general warrant.

Although the argument that the press ought not to be subject to spe-cial legal provisions had been won, nevertheless the common law of libel remained exceptional in that juries were limited to determining only if a publication had occurred. They could not find on the question of whether a matter was libellous or not. That was for the bench to decide. Many saw this as a denial of the fundamental right, guaranteed by Magna Carta, to be tried by one's peers. The general warrant was also anomalous in that it named no specific person.

John Wilkes was not only a member of the House of Commons, sit-ting for Aylesbury, a seat he bought after the fashion of the time for £7,000; he was also a well-known rake, a member of the notorious Hellfire Club. He had become a journalist, proprietor of the *North Briton*, in order to attack the Tory administration of the Earl of Bute, whom he hated. When Bute was driven from office over his tax pro-posals, Wilkes still did not give up his offensive. In the forty-fifth issue of the *North Briton*, 23 April 1763, he accused the new administration of proposing 'odious measures' which would bring the King into dis-repute: 'I wish as much as any man in the Kingdom to see the honour of the Crown maintained in a manner truly becoming royalty: I lament to see it sunk even to prostitution.'

The authorities claimed that this was an 'infamous and seditious libel tending to influence the minds and alienate the affections of the people from His Majesty and to excite them to traitorous insurrections against his Government'. A general warrant was issued for the arrest of Wilkes and, as was usual at the time, all those involved in producing and distributing the journal, and no less than 48 other persons were caught in the net. Unsurprisingly, Wilkes claimed parliamentary immunity as an MP and Chief Justice Parry agreed with him. More astonishingly, Parry went even further, to declare that the use of general warrants was illegal under the common law.

There was an inexorable judicial logic at work. Mid-eighteenth-century lawyers understood that licensing, and, by osmosis, censorship was either against the common law or against its spirit; but they remained unwilling to go further and establish a right of free expression. The great jurist William Blackstone, for example, in his extremely influential *Commentaries on the Laws of England*, published in four volumes by Oxford University Press between 1765 and 1769, acknowledged the importance of a free press yet saw this in a very limited way: 'The liberty of the press is indeed essential to the nature of a free state; but this consists in laying no *previous* restraints on publications, and not in freedom from censure for criminal matter when published.' Between this and the concept of press freedom as a right lay a considerable gap. Parry had further narrowed it, though, by indicating that, as the spirit of the common law required that the press should not be singled out by any legal process, so warrants ought to name the person or persons being sought in the usual way. The general warrant was against the spirit of the common law. Only the curious restriction of the power of the jury remained.

In 1769, 'Cato' was followed by 'Junius', another 'giant' of an essayist, one whose identity remains hidden to this day. The explosive *Junius Letters* began to appear in Henry Sampson Woodfall's *Public Advertiser* in January, raising the paper's circulation from 2,800 to 3,400. 'Junius' covered, in biting insider detail, the political events of the day. On 19 December, he wrote an open letter to the King reminding him of the consequences of absolutism, as seen in the fate of the Stuarts: 'Sire . . . The prince who imitates their conduct, should be warned by their example; and while he plumes himself upon the security of his title to the crown, should remember that as it was acquired by one revolution, it may be lost by another.' The *Public Advertiser*'s circulation topped 5,000 and the piece was reprinted in five other papers.

Junius was never named, much less arrested, but, general warrants now being illegal, four specific warrants were issued against various proprietors and printers. This resulted in two trials. The first was heard in Westminster against one of the publishers who had reprinted the piece, and a verdict of guilty was returned. The second case, against Woodfall and two others, was heard in the less controllable environs of the City. Chief Justice Mansfield put Blackstone's point directly to the jury:

> As for the liberty of the press, I will tell you what it is; the liberty of press is, that a man may print what he pleases without a licence; as long as it remains so, the liberty of the press is not restrained.

Mansfield held that the libel was proved but the jury did not agree that it had been 'published'. They found that Woodfall was guilty only of printing and distributing the letter, not of 'publishing' it. The other two they acquitted altogether. In effect, they resisted Mansfield's opinion and made an ass of the law.

'Junius' wrote:

> Let it be impressed upon your mind, let it be instilled into your children, that the liberty of the press is the palladium of all civil, political, and religious rights of an Englishman, and that the right of juries to return a general verdict, in all cases whatsoever, is an essential part of our constitution, not to be controlled or limited by judges, nor in any shape questioned by the legislature.

'Un des droits les plus précieux de l'homme'

France produced no rabid journalists, no Junius, Cato or Wilkes. Instead, the *ancien régime* maintained 120 local censors as well as the central control apparatus in Paris. All material which 'tended to attack religion, arouse feelings against . . . the authority of the Government, or undermine due order and tranquillity' was punishable by death. Such tight regulation was the norm on mainland Europe, although Locke's liberal philosophy achieved wide distribution, and did so, paradoxically, in the continent's *lingua franca*, French. Free expression yet remained a philosophical issue rather than the site of everyday journalistic uproars. Voltaire in the *Lettres philosophiques* (1734) retailed Locke's views (and Newton's science) as implicit critiques of French autocracy. Diderot, who became editor of the crucial liberal *Encyclopédie* in 1750, translated Locke. In Volume XIII of the *Encyclopédie*, he wrote: 'One asks if the liberty of the press is advantageous or prejudicial to a state. The reply is not difficult. It is of the greatest importance to keep this practice in all states founded on liberty.'

These intellectuals believed that they were living in an 'Age of Reason', an era of 'Enlightenment', and so pervasive did they make the idea of natural rights, prominent among them freedom of speech, that wherever absolutism faltered, such previously unknown freedoms might well be incorporated into law. For example, George II of Great Britain's son-in-law, Christian VII, King of Denmark and Norway, was widely considered an idiot and a rake. In 1761, in his name, Denmark abolished censorship, although the powers behind Christian's throne were still fearful enough to specifically exclude the periodical press from this provision. In Sweden, King Adolph Frederick too had been reduced to not much more than a figurehead, having failed to curb the growing power of the Swedish Estates in 1756. In 1766, the liberty of the press and the right of free expression in general, *Offentlighetsprincipen*, rather than the removal of censorship as in the English Act of 1695 or the Danish regulation of 1761, were enshrined in statute for the first time.

Conversely, where autocracy had kept (or regained) its power, such rights remained unknown or were extinguished. Adolph Frederick's successor in Stockholm, Gustav III, re-established the unfettered power of the throne in a coup and revoked the press regulation (although, it must be said, he still allowed freedom of religion – including Judaism –

and he abolished judicial torture). Or take Joseph II of Austria, who publicly fancied himself as the very model of an enlightened monarch. In 1780, after the death of his mother, Maria Theresa, with whom he had jointly ruled, he proposed a number of reforms, but his liberalism did not, of course, embrace the revolutionary idea of a free press. In Austria, in addition to the Jesuits, a civil Censorship Commission was empowered to demand the posting of money by publishers to be forfeited if the commissioners felt the printer had, despite their licence and strict prior constraint, nevertheless produced something unacceptable. All Joesph's enlightenment meant was that the only permitted paper, the *Wiener Dirarium*,[7] was allowed to acquire a number of competitors, but this experiment in competing papers did not last long and these were soon suppressed.

As Joseph lay dying in Vienna in 1789, the French provincial aristocracy and magistracy demanded, just as some courtly aristocrats had done before the Fronde 140 years earlier, that the King call an Estates-General. Faced with a financial crisis which could not be avoided and needed their approval to solve, Louis XVI yielded and the Estates met. Coming together, they had much more than his financial difficulties on their agenda and among the radical issues they wanted addressed was the question of the press. Suddenly, 150 years of French absolutist horror at the English example was turned on its head. For example, the influential Marquise de Mirabeau published a translation of the *Aereopagitica* and he ascribed Britain's astonishing prosperity, enviable richness and power specifically to its free press.

When Louis closed the Estates' meeting place, the delegates retired to the Versailles Tennis Court and, after the army refused to move against them, declared themselves to be a Constituent Assembly. This began its work, at the behest of its vice-president, La Fayette (another aristocratic but progressive marquis), by publishing *La Déclaration des droits de l'homme et du citoyen*. Article XI was passed on 24 August 1789:

> The free communication of thoughts and opinions is one of
> the most precious of the rights of man. Every citizen can

speak, write and publish freely, only to answer for an abuse
of this liberty in a scheduled action at law.[8]

Already more than 40 new newspapers had appeared. Their number was
to grow to 500 titles in the course of the next three years. There were
a dozen *Patriotes* – *française, républicaine, sincère, incorruptible.* As
many celebrated *Révolutions* – *de Paris, de France and de Brabant, de
l'Europe.* In his journal *l'Ami du Peuple,* Jean-Paul Marat, a leader of
the extremist Jacobins, deployed revolutionary language redolent of
Nedham: '*En combattant contre les ennemis d'État, j'attaquerai . . . Je
démasquerai les hypocrites, je dénoncerai les traîtres, j'écarterai des
affaires publique les hommes avides.*' Camille Desmoulins, another
extreme Jacobin, saw the journalist as the final political arbiter:
'*Aujourd'huie, les journalistes exercent un ministère public; ils dénon-
cent, décrètant, règlent à l'extraordinaire, absolvent ou condamnent.*'
Some of those who did this were not revolutionary but royalist, since
many titles supported the throne and many more were produced by
radical Constituent Assembly members whose votes and voices in print
were crucial to the more moderate majority. But the victory won in
Article XI was to prove to be as fleeting as had been newspaper competition in Vienna.

In France, behind the smoke of civil war and foreign attack, defence
of the high ideals of what had mutated into a revolution became, spu-
riously, a justification for the imposition of a state terror. Needless to
say, the principles of Article XI were soon abandoned. Already in
August 1792, the Paris Commune had halted the distribution of all royalist publications. Their action was made legal the following December
by the ruling Convention, which had replaced the Assembly that
autumn. In January 1793, Louis was guillotined. In March, a new law
was passed and advocacy of the restoration of the throne or the dissolution of the Convention became punishable by death. *Colporteurs*
were to be imprisoned for three years if they were found carrying such
printed matter. This act silenced the moderate republican Girondists.

A few months later, a new constitution was passed. Article VII simply abolished the right of free speech: '*Le droit de manifester sa pensée et ses opinions, soit par la voie de presse, soit de toute autre manière être interdit.*' This interdiction wiped the slate clean of Article XI of the *Rights of Man* and its insistence on free communication as a precious privilege. The freedom of the press had existed in France a few weeks short of three years.

Robespierre became the force behind a new Committee of Public Safety in July 1793, but after his fall a year later, the Directory was established and the pendulum of revolutionary upheaval began to swing back. For the press matters improved, although the legal right of free expression was not restored. Revolutionary publications, such as the communistic ex-manservant Françoise Babeuf's *Journal de la liberté de la presse*, which became *Tribun du Peuple*, or Ève Demaillot's *L'Orateur plébéien*, were countenanced albeit under strict surveillance. There was also a revival of royalist opposition papers; but, like the King and the Committee of Public Safety, Napoleon Bonaparte and his two colleagues in the Directory could not live with the consequences. The Directory decided to restart Renaudot's *Gazette* to rebut these opposition papers of both left and right. Babeuf was imprisoned for six months in 1795 for *provocation à la rébellion* during the so-called White Terror which rounded up the remaining radical leaders but did not execute them. The following year, Babeuf moved to planning an actual coup, for which he was arrested and guillotined in April 1797. Another attempted radical rising in September of that year exhausted the government's patience and this second more limited period of French press freedom came to an end. Forty-four papers were closed and those who produced them kept their heads but were deported. All the remaining papers were put under complete police control and a stamp tax imposed on them.

When Napoleon seized power from his Directory colleagues two months later, there was little he needed to do to flesh out this repressive structure. By the end of that November, all editors and publishers were being vetted by a Political Bureau staffed by journalists as Napoleon turned the state control apparatus from negative censorship to positive propaganda production. He told the Bureau to 'Tell the journalists that I will not judge them for the wrong which they have done, but for the lack of good which they have done'. As far as he was concerned, it was to be a maxim that 'Four hostile newspapers were more to be feared than a thousand bayonets'.

After all the flaming rhetoric, the horrifying blood-letting and the brave adventure in republican government, French journalism found itself exactly where it had begun, with the *Moniteur*, the *Journal de l'Empire* and the *Journal de Paris* all playing the same role as the official voice of the government that the *occasionnels* of Louis XI had played, admittedly on a more intermittent basis, in the 1480s. Even the *Gazette* was back in business.

'The times that try men's souls'

The struggle for free expression achieved a more durable outcome in Britain's North American colonies, where, throughout the century, there had been much talk and even a little strife over the 'rights of an Englishman'. The American colonists came rather slowly and somewhat unwillingly to put John Locke's theory of justified revolt against arbitrary power to the test. But rebel eventually they did, and in so doing made such extensive use of the press as an organising tool that it thereby gained, uniquely, a central place in a nation-making myth. This was to give it, in however flawed a manner, a more durable foundation as a vehicle of free expression than it achieved anywhere in the Old World.

It was not obvious at the outset of the English settlement of North America in the seventeenth century that this would be so. Although two of the Pilgrim Fathers were printers, no newsbook, *coranto* or diurnal appeared. *Publick Occurences, Both Foreign and Domestic*, the first colonial newspaper, was published in Massachusetts in September 1690, ignoring a 1662 ordinance which required it be licensed. It was to be issued monthly 'or if any Glut of Occurrances happen, oftener'. The work of an English newspaperman, Benjamin Harris, who had fled with his family to Boston after falling foul of the King's Messengers in London for a second time in 1686, the paper upset the Puritan religious authorities with a salacious, false story about the French king fornicating with his daughter-in-law. The secular authorities were no happier for it also to have suggested that it was a mistake to ally with favoured Native Americans tribes 'in whom we have too much confided'. This one publication constitutes the entire seventeenth-century American newspaper archive. No second edition of *Publick Occurences* ever appeared and Harris himself returned to London in 1694.

In 1700, the first official postmaster for Boston, John Campbell, who regarded the dissemination of news as one of his duties, began producing a handwritten newsletter for a number of inland correspondents. Its popularity eventually suggested to him that it be printed, and the first edition of the *Boston News-Letter* appeared on 24 April 1704, 'Published by Authority' (as it announced in black-face, perhaps to increase typographically the authority in question). Campbell had the model of the official *London Gazette* in mind as well as the old tradition of printing stories from foreign news publications *coranto*-style. He was careful to have all his material vetted by the colonial administration. His reprinted stories were, in the nature of the case, months old. The first issue led with reprints from the *London Flying-Post* dated 4 December 1703, about five months earlier. This was about average for the time lapse. Staleness, though, was no bar to publication since news still meant not just recent information but rather information new to readers. Limiting the concept of news solely to information about recent events was not to become an essential mark of journalism for a century or more, but competition between rival publications did soon encourage a rush to be first with the latest tidings from the home country. Papers would hire fast news-boats to scour the shipping lanes for incoming vessels and rush the months-old London papers they carried back to port.

Despite these cautious beginnings, the colonial press did echo metropolitan journalistic uproars; the Cato papers, for example, were reprinted from the *London Journal*, but just as typical was the emulation of non-political English journalism. In 1720, the year of Cato, 'Silence Dogood', a Mr. Spectator-like figure, made his debut in the pages of James Franklin's *New England Courant*:

> Tis true, drinking does not improve our Faculties, but it enables us to use them; and therefore I conclude that much Study and Experience, and a little Liquor, are of absolute necesity for some Tempers, in order to make them accomplish'd Orators.

'Silence Dogood' was Franklin's younger brother, Ben, then aged 15.

The elder Franklin's attacks on administrative inefficiencies caused the General Court of Massachusetts to prohibit him by name from printing 'the *New England Courant* or any Pamphlet or paper of the like Nature, Except it be first Supervised, by the secretary of this Province'. It was as if the lapsing of the Printing Act nearly 30 years earlier in England had never taken place. James defied the ban but had to run the paper from prison. Upon his release he subverted control by passing ownership of the paper over to young Ben, but Ben left for Philadelphia and the *Courant*, its sting drawn, went into a slow but steady decline. James gave up political criticism and became government printer in the Rhode Island colony. His attempt, in 1732, to start a *Gazette* there did not prosper. Young Ben, of course, was to do better but at the cost of avoiding contentious issues. By emulating Addison and Steele, he had converted the *Pennsylvania Gazette*, a paper he took over in 1729 having concluded his apprenticeship as a printer in London, into the best-selling periodical in the colonies. He also became the official printer in Pennsylvania and deputy postmaster for the colonies. Benjamin Franklin's avoidance of official censure was probably as great a monument to his much-noted sagacity as anything he ever did. Any of his peers who tried a more independent line were a lot less fortunate.

Peter Zenger, for example. In 1734, he published a crude satire against the Royal Captain General and Governor in Chief of New York and New Jersey, William Crosby, in the *New-York Weekly Journal*. The Governor snapped, not least because Zenger's paper had been specifically created a year earlier to be the mouthpiece of Crosby's political opponents and had not let up. The Governor hit back:

> A Proclamation: Whereas by the Contrivance of some evil Disposed and Disafffected Persons, divers Journals or Printed News Papers (entitled, *The New-York Weekly Journal, containing the freshest Advices, Foreign and Domestick*) have been caused to be Printed and Published by John Peter Zenger, in many of which Journals or Printed News Papers are contained divers Scandalous, Virulent, False and Seditious Reflections, not only upon the whole Legislature, in general, and upon the most considerable persons in the most distinguished Stations in this province but also upon his Majesty's lawful and rightful Government, and just Prerogative . . . Wherefore I . . . have thought fit to issue this proclamation, hereby Promising a Reward of Fifty Pounds . . .

Zenger was indicted for seditious libel by a grand jury and held in jail from November 1734 until his case was heard in August 1735. His wife, Anne, conducted the paper during his incarceration. Andrew Hamilton, a highly respected Philadelphia lawyer, appeared for his defence. Hamilton made exactly the legal argument that was to be made in the Junius case in England in 1769, that the jury must decide the fact of libel as well as the fact of publishing, but placed it unambiguously in the broader principle that had been articulated by Cato. Zinger's case was 'not the cause of a poor printer nor of New York alone'; rather it was the 'Cause of Liberty . . . That, to which Nature and the Laws of our Country have given us the Right, – the Liberty both of exposing and opposing arbitrary power . . . by speaking and writing Truth'. The New York jury acquitted. Zenger was free.

Never mind that at this time, truth did not constitute a defence against libel, either in Britain or in its colonies. For the first time in a common law jurisdiction, the right, both natural and civil, to print material was clearly put to a jury. Hamilton had in effect made Cato's point: 'Whoever would overthrow the liberty of a nation, must begin by subduing the freedom of speech.' It was an important symbolic victory for the concept of free speech, a pointer to increasing impatience with the arbitrary power of the mother country and her local representatives, a common law precedent and the first event positioning the American press as a central agent in the struggle for independence.

Over the next three decades, opposing arbitrary power led to six major slave rebellions, 40 serious riots and no less than 18 uprisings with the specific intention of overthrowing the colonial governments. The press could not but reflect this unrest. In 1752, for example, Franklin's by no means radical *Pennsylvania Gazette* published the famous cartoon snake cut into pieces with the caption 'Join, or Die', an injunction to the 13 colonies to realise that only in unity could they resist any unwelcome designs of Great Britain. One such plan, a stamp duty on paper imposed in 1776, seemed specifically fashioned to provoke two of the most vociferous, articulate groups in colonial society, the lawyers and the printers. In the protracted uproar caused by the stamp tax, the grip of firm government loosened and, as had become usual in such circumstances, a number of unlicensed papers appeared. Westminster backed down even though it continued to insist on its taxation rights.

One consequence of this confrontation was the emergence of the 'Sons of Liberty' with chapters of 'Patriots' throughout the colonies demanding, in terms made familiar by seventeenth-century English Parliamentarians, that their supposed ancient liberties, including press freedom from prior constraint, be restored and respected. After all, every self-respecting English lawyer emigrating to the colonies carried with him Blackstone's *Commentaries*.[9] The liberal legal case for an unlicensed press was widely known and, in the face of further provocation, vigorously exploited. Sam Adams, Harvard graduate, failed lawyer and tax-collector, had taken over the *Independent Advertiser* in Boston in 1748 at the age of 26. Throughout the 1750s he had also contributed to the *Boston Gazette*, even as he rose to local prominence through the democratic town meeting structures in place in the Massachusetts Bay Colony. In such formal arenas, he and his political allies, who came to constitute the 'Boston Caucus', became adept at speaking in the voice of the excluded colonial poor. Adams's critical insight was to position not only his own journalism but entire journalistic networks in the service of his cause. The press became integral to the political process rather than a critical observer of it or an occasional factor in it.

So, on the one hand, as a politician, he instigated a political campaign of 'non-importation agreements', a boycott of British goods in protest against new duties imposed by Westminster; but, on the other, when the Governor called for military reinforcements to enforce these taxes, Adams set up a network of Sons of Liberty publishers to begin in earnest a newspaper propaganda war against the British. He arranged for stories of British military abuse and rapine to appear in a *Journal of Occurrences*. These were picked up in Isaiah Thomas's *Massachusetts Spy* and Adams also passed them to another like-minded Son of Liberty, New York publisher John Holt. The rest of the network – the *Pennsylvania Chronicle*, the *Maryland Chronicle*, the *Newport Mercury* and the *Gazette of South Carolina* – all reprinted these sensationalist tales, for much of the material was almost certainly fraudulent, from Holt's paper.

In 1772, Adam took the idea of a network a stage further – from the dissemination of information to its acquisition. He established Committees of Correspondence to monitor all 'occurrences' and public opinion throughout the colonies. The Committees could also on occasion themselves become the story. The 'Boston Tea Party' was a public-relations stunt in the campaign against yet another tax imposed in the Tea Act; but the colonists who dressed up as Native Americans and dumped the tea chests in the harbour as a protest in 1773 were from the ranks of Adams's colleagues and correspondents.

It was this chain of presses which ensured that the fracas at Concord,

Massachusetts, on 19 April 1775 became the 'shot heard round the world'. The editor of the *Massachusetts Spy* in Worcester, Isaiah Thomas, printer, self-taught writer and scholar, one of Adams's most radical associates, was an eye-witness:

> The troops then set out upon the run, halloing and hus-saing, and, coming within a few roods of them, the commanding officer accosted the militia, in words to this effect, 'Disperse, you damn'd rebels – Damn you, disperse.' Upon which the troops again hussaed . . . and then there seemed to be a general discharge from the whole body. Eight of our men where killed and nine wounded . . .

In the 3 May issue of the *Massachusetts Spy*, Thomas placed the story, in traditional non-sensationalist style, inside on page 3.

By the time of this encounter, some 400 pamphlets had been published on all sides of the issues – from the 'Patriots' who wanted Britain to come to its senses in some way or another (and therefore were quite unpatriotic in reality) to the Loyalists or Tories who supported the rights of the Westminster Parliament and the local governments. Although it took six weeks for news to travel via the reprinting process from the Massachusetts papers to those in Georgia, the efforts of the Patriotic press did unify protest. Even the Loyalists who fundamentally supported the crown could not readily stomach the constant attempts at taxation without representation. A meeting of representatives from all 13 colonies assembled in Philadelphia as a Continental Congress to discuss a common response to the political crisis. The local colonial militias were also gathering to be welded into an army under George Washington. The question of independence, however, was by no means an agreed objective. Indeed it was many months before the most vociferous voices in the Congress, Sam's brother John for example, could persuade their more cautious colleagues even to discuss the matter.

In February 1776, a new more radical note was sounded when yet another pamphlet, *Common Sense*, addressed 'To the Inhabitants of America' appeared, calling quite clearly and unambiguously for independence. It was by Thomas Paine: 'Everything that is right or reasonable pleads for separation. The blood of the slain, the weeping voice of nature cries, "TIS TIME TO PART".' Paine's was a classic American success story. A self-taught failed stay-maker, customs man and bankrupt from England, in the New World he became an effective writer. His was the authentic English Defoean journalistic voice in polemical mode.

On William the Conqueror:

> A French bastard landing with an armed Banditti and establishing himself king of England against the consent of the natives, is in plain terms a very paltry rascally original. It certainly hath no divinity in it.'

On the potential of a united state in North America:

> O! ye that love mankind . . . Stand forth! Every spot of the old world is over run with oppression. Freedom been hunted round the globe. Asia and Africa have long expelled her. Europe regards her as a stranger and England hath given her warning to depart. O! receive the fugitive, and prepare in time an asylum for mankind.

Common Sense went through 25 editions in 1776 alone and must have been known to every colonist.

Within months of its appearance, the Continental Congress approved Thomas Jefferson's draft proclamation, which directly translated Locke's 1691 political theory outlined in *On Civil Government: The Second Treatise* into a practical Proclamation of Independence. The rights the colonists claimed were 'self-evident': 'Life, Liberty and the pursuit of Happiness'.[10] Not all agreed. John Dickinson of Pennsylvania, who earlier had not hesitated to argue passionately in the newspapers against the taxes, turned out to be a real 'patriot', still seeking compromise with Britain. He refused to sign for New Jersey, but too many of his countrymen and women were of a different mind. Having rejected the Loyalist position, they were also now ready to go beyond Dickinson's moderate Patriotic one. The Declaration, which took them down the road mapped by Paine, was reprinted within the month in at least 29 newspapers. It took a mere six weeks to cross the Atlantic to be copied by the *London Chronicle* and the *Daily Courant*. The French authorities foolishly printed it as a piece of anti-British propaganda but many of their citizenry, of course, read it rather as an anti-royalist tract, as pertinent to the French as to the British throne. In the absolutist German states and in the autocracies of Spain and Russia it was, perhaps more prudently, instantly banned.

Those in the Congress who supported 'independency' were divided by the question of slavery. Jefferson, although a slaveholder, by removing the Lockean right to 'estates' had prepared the ground for other more overt anti-slavery language to be used. Among the charges he originally proposed laying against George III was that the king had prevented the colonies from legislating against the 'execrable commerce' of slavery; but even this slanting reference was vetoed by the representatives of the southern colonies. Paine had written in *Common Sense*, 'We have it in our power to begin the world again'; but the world was not begun again for the one in five souls in the revolted colonies who were enslaved. The grievous wrong of slavery dimmed the light of liberty which the congressional delegates claimed they were igniting when they signed the Declaration on 4 July 1776. Their hypocrisy was quickly noticed. 'How is it', asked Dr Johnson in distant London, 'that we hear the loudest yelps for liberty from the drivers of negroes?'

Thomas Paine tramped off to join Washington at his Fort Lee headquarters that Christmastide and wrote – by candlelight on a drumhead, story has it – a handbill, *The American Crisis*:

> These are the times that try men's souls. The Summer soldier and the sunshine Patriot will, in this crisis, shrink from the service of their country . . . Tyranny, like hell, is not

easily conquered; yet we have this consolation with us, that
the harder the conflict the more glorious the triumph.

Washington had the essay read to his troops and it was printed in the
Pennsylvania Packet on 27 December and, by reprinting, was slowly distributed into the 40,000 or so homes that received the Patriot press. A
week after its initial publication, the Americans won their first major victory over the British at Trenton.

Twenty of the colonies' 35 newspapers survived the war, some being
conducted by the wives of absent printers and authors, following the
example of Anne Zenger. Holt's widow took over his *Journal* in New
York and the publisher of the *Gazette of South Carolina*, Ann Timothy,
was widow of Peter whose mother Elizabeth had founded the paper in
1738. After William Goddard quit his *Providence Gazette* in Rhode
Island to start the *Pennsylvania Chronicle* in 1767, his mother and sister
continued it.[11] Some papers professed themselves to be exceptionally
successful during the conflict. The *Connecticut Courant* claimed an
exceptional circulation of 8,000 but for most the newspaper business was
hard, with paper, ink and the presses themselves in extremely short
supply. Washington, as conscious of the usefulness of the press as many
other leaders had been over the previous three centuries, called for ladies
to gather rags to meet the newspapers' need for paper.

George Mason had inscribed a right to free expression, including
press freedom from prior constraint, in both the Virginia Constitution
and that state's Bill of Rights which he had drafted even as the
Continental Congress continued to ponder whether or not even to
debate independence. In the draft bill that was to influence, among
others, La Fayette (who, as a 19-year-old major-general, had fought
with the Americans against the British), Mason had written, 'That freedom of the Press is one of the great bulwarks of liberty, and can never
be restrained except by despotick governments'. No less than nine of
the new state constitutions adopted similar radical language and guaranteed freedom of speech; but in practice a free press was more difficult
to countenance than the theory suggested. Against the background of

what amounted to civil strife, even the most balanced anti-Patriot arguments were, perhaps not surprisingly, unacceptable. For one thing, Tory or Loyalist sentiments inflamed the mob, which could be no more countenanced by the new independent governments than contrary opinions could be by the colonial ones they had replaced.

Take the foppish Loyalist 'Jemmy' Rivington, the black sheep of the family who had for generations been official publishers to the Church of England, who conducted his *New-York Gazetteer* in the Tory cause. Somewhat surprisingly, he did keep faith with his masthead promise that his journal was a product of 'his Open and Uninfluenced Press'. His account of the Concord incident, for example, confirms Thomas's in the Patriot *Massachusetts Spy*, but this balanced approach did not protect him from the New York mob. Like other Tory journalists, he was burned in effigy and his shop attacked. Rivington had much justice on his side when he suggested that the Patriots believed in press freedom only for journalists that agreed with them.

There was never any doubt that the 13 sovereign colonies were going to be anything other than the United States of America. The Declaration had already spoken of 'these united colonies' but by 1784 the single house of Congress, with no formal powers, collapsed. Among its unfinished business was a number of questions about the press. Could it be taxed, for example? Massachusetts decided to try, in 1785, causing Isaiah Thomas to make the *Spy* a monthly, thereby avoiding the impost, whilst crying out against the sovereign republican commonwealth's action: 'Should the liberty of the press be once destroyed, farewell the remainder of our invaluable rights and privileges.' The public agreed and the tax was removed after the sort of protests that had so successfully toppled the colonial government of Massachusetts a few years before.

Eleven years after the Declaration of Independence and four years after the surrender of the British, representatives of the new states once more gathered in Philadelphia in a congress to write a constitution. It took them five months but by September 1787 it was ready to be 'proposed to the Legislatures of the several States' for ratification. It began in the spirit of 1776: 'We, the people of the United States, in order to form a more perfect union . . . do ordain and establish this Constitution for the United States of America.' But after this preamble, 'the people' only appear as voters. Although in the absolutist world of the late eighteenth century that was no small thing, even if the franchise excluded slaves, women, Native Americans and most poor men, it was not a substitute for a bill of rights which more radical opinion was expecting. The language of rights is barely heard in the Constitution and when it is, it is reserved to the privileged political class. The Senators and Representatives elected under the new system, for example, shall be privileged from civil arrest while their Houses are in session.

The political battle-lines over ratification were drawn between those in favour of the proposed arrangements – the Federalists – and their anti-Federalist opponents. The Federalists took their name from a series of articles, *The Federalist Papers*, printed in the *New York Independent Advertiser* from October 1787 to April 1788 and written by Alexander Hamilton and some of his colleagues as editorials in support of the proposed constitution. They worried about the untrammelled exercise of states' rights and the potential anarchy of 'uncontrolled democracy' (or, as it might be, democracy of the unpropertied), especially as they had the awful warning of the bloody upheaval in France under the Terror before them. Their anti-Federalist opponents were those who feared federal power as a distant and conservative force not a little like Westminster. This opposition embraced both those worried that the proposed federal government would trample over the rights of the poor and those with very different interests concerned to protect the rights of slave owners.[12] Hamilton was nevertheless prepared to compromise for the sake of the union by suggesting that further fundamental protection of personal and states' rights would be forthcoming. The several states did ratify the constitution, some – Massachusetts, for example – only because it was believed that a bill of rights would follow.

In 1791, the first Congress elected under the new federal dispensation passed ten amendments to the Constitution. Together these amount to the missing bill of rights and a curb on central power as both liberal and southern interests demanded. The first of these amendments caught up with the states' constitutions and Article XI of *les Droits de l'homme*. It took the form of a restraint – 'Congress shall make no law . . .' – on the general Enlightenment principle:

> Congress shall make no law respecting an establishment of religion, or prohibiting the free exercise thereof; or abridging the freedom of speech or of the press; or the right of the people peaceably to assemble, and to petition the Government for the redress of grievances.

This did not mean that the matter of a free press was now settled in America merely because it had been enshrined in law. In 1786, Alexander Hamilton had argued against such an amendment as being either unnecessary, or if needed, a useless parchment protection: 'whatever fine declarations may be inserted in any Constitution respecting it [Liberty of the Press] must altogether depend on public opinion, and on the general spirit of the people and of the Government'. Within years, events were to prove him right. In 1798, under a somewhat fraudulent threat of war with the French, the Federalist president John Adams and the Congress had passed a Sedition Act criminalising 'false, scandalous or malicious writing or writings against the government . . . to excite against them the hatred of the good people of the United States'. It was, of course, exactly a 'law . . . abridging the freedom of speech or of the press' which was rendered illegal by the First Amendment. Clutching their Blackstones, the Federalists argued, like the good conservative eighteenth-century English lawyers they were, that the 1798 Act did not affect prior constraint and prior constraint was all that Congress was prohibited from 'abridging'. Eighteen writs, 12 trials and ten convictions ensued but the journalists who were imprisoned were all, as it happened, anti-Federalists. Press freedom could have been as shortlived in the USA as it had been in revolutionary France but for Thomas Jefferson. He fought the next presidential election in 1800 under the slogan 'Jefferson and Liberty' and made securing the journalists' release an element in his campaign. After his victory, which he regarded as a second American revolution, they were freed and all further planned trials were abandoned. However, although the Sedition Act became a dead letter, it was not repealed. Hamilton's 'general spirit of the people', though, was to remain strong enough throughout the nineteenth and twentieth centuries for the United States government to be constrained in its use. Nevertheless, in 1917 it was revived as a war-time temporary measure. In the 'crisis of freedom' provoked by the early twenty-first-century 'War on Terror', it is still there as a potentially repressive measure, in abeyance (at the time of writing) because 'the general spirit' remains, at least in theory, as a control. The security of a free press, as Hamilton correctly surmised, ultimately depends on this sentiment alone.

Sources

Hannah Barker (1998), *Newspapers, Politics and English Society 1695–1855*, Oxford: Clarendon Press.

C. Bellanger (1969), *Histoire général de la presse française*, Paris: Presses Universitaires de France.

Jeremy Black (2001), *The English Press 1621–1861*, Stroud, Glos.: Sutton.

George Boyce, James Curran and Pauline Wingate (eds) (1978), *Newspaper History from the 17th Century to the Present Day*, London: Constable.

G. A. Cranfield (1978), *The Press and Society: from Caxton to Northcliffe*, London: Longman.

Edwin and Michael Emery (1984), *The Press and America*, Englewood Cliffs, NJ: Prentice Hall.

Eric Foner (1998), *The Story of American Freedom*, New York: Norton.

John Gray (1986), *Liberalism*, Buckingham: Open University Press.

P. M. Handover (1960), *Printing in London: from 1446 to Modern Times* London: George Allen & Unwin.

Michael Harris and Alan Lee (eds) (1986), *The Press in English Society from the Seventeenth to the Nineteenth Centuries*, Rutherford, NJ: Fairleigh Dickinson University Press.

A. Hyatt Mayor (1971), *Print and People*, Princeton: Princeton University Press.

'Junius' (John Cannon ed.) (1978), *Letters*, Oxford: Oxford University Press.

Steve Knowlton and Patrick Parsons (eds) (1995), *The Journalist's Moral Compass: Basic Principles*, Westport, Conn.: Praeger.

Frank Luther Mott (1962), *American Journalism*, New York: Macmillan.
Thomas Paine (1776, 1997), *Common Sense*, New York: Dover.
Roy Porter (2001), *The Enlightenment*, London: Macmillan.
Anthony Smith (1979), *The Newspaper: An International History*, London: Thames & Hudson.
Michael Twyman (1970), *Printing 1700–1970*, London: Eyre & Spottiswood.
Francis Williams (1957), *Dangerous Estate: The Anatomy of Newspapers*, London: Longmans, Green.
Keith Williams (1977), *The English Newspaper*, London: Springwood.
Howard Zinn (1980), *A People's History of the United States*, New York: Harper.

3

'HERE'S THE PAPERS, HERE'S THE PAPERS!': JOURNALISM FROM 1836

'He is an editor – he is on public duty'

Helen or Ellen Jewitt, a 23-year-old prostitute, was hacked to death in a fancy bordello in Manhattan on 10 April 1836. It is no surprise that this was a big story for the papers. Sensational murders had been the stuff of news since the days of the newsbooks but coverage of the Jewitt murder signalled a journalistic breakthrough that was to have ramifications beyond crime reporting.

The United States had not adopted the continental European practice of selling newspapers by subscription but, as in Britain, cried them through the streets with the usual resultant stress on sensation. By the time cheap 1c newspapers appeared, newsboys were everywhere, as the English newspaper proprietor (and novelist) Charles Dickens noted in *Martin Chuzzlewit* (1843):

> 'Here's this morning's New York *Sewer*!' cried one. 'Here's this morning's New York *Stabber*! Here's the New York *Family Spy*! Here's the New York *Private Listener*! . . . Here's all the New York papers! Here's full particulars of the patriotic locofoco movement yesterday, in which the Whigs was so chawed up; and the last Alabama gouging case; and the interesting Arkansas dooel with Bowie knives . . . Here they are! Here's the papers, here's the papers!'

Although the categories of reports had been long settled, leading to a certain overall predictability which, cynics might say, tended to turn the news into the 'olds', individual news stories were coming, under the increasing pressures of competition, to require a timely freshness. Where once correction of a rival could itself be news, by the early nineteenth century recency was emerging as a primary news value. Publishing a 'beat' – beating one's rivals to the street – became a major American journalistic objective.[1] So great was the need for them, on occasion truth could not be allowed to stand in the way.

The first 1c paper, the *New York Sun*, which had been founded in 1833, reported in August 1835 that Sir John Herschel – a real, and indeed famous, scientist – had made 'astronomical discoveries of the most wonderful description'. Follow-up stories on what his observations of the moon had revealed included sightings of a species of man-bat and 'a glimpse of a strange amphibious creature of a spherical form, which rolled with great velocity across a pebbly beach'. The paper's normal 15,000 circulation leaped to 19,000 during the publication of the series – the greatest in the world, the *Sun* was quick to claim. John Locke, the 'reporter' of this positively sixteenth-century absurdity, was soon revealed as a hoaxer but the paper was unrepentant. It had performed a public service, it claimed, 'for diverting the public mind, for a while, from that bitter apple of discord, the abolition of slavery'. Even this was something of a lie, though, since the 'reports' were, in effect, a 'spoiler'.[2] Some four months earlier, on 6 May 1835, in an already crowded field, James Gordon Bennett had founded a 1c paper, the feisty *New York Morning Herald*. Never mind 'the bitter apple of discord', the *Sun*, in effect, was 'diverting' not only the mind but also, hopefully, the money of the public away from the *Herald*.

It was to take two decades before the *Herald* outsold the *Sun*, but Gordon Bennett had joined battle from the outset, and the spoiling tactics he marshalled were superior not least because they did not involve publishing fiction as news. Starting with the second issue of the paper, he had deployed his expertise as an erstwhile student of economics by writing well-informed 'money articles' on Wall Street. Bennett was soon claiming these were read by everybody 'in business in the lower part of the city' – 'Some of the banks take half-a-dozen copies a day'. For the mass of his readership, he offered regular *frissons*: offensive words (e.g. 'legs' instead of 'limbs'), a new informality of style ('We have not had a peep at the sun for ten days past') and an innovative, more vivid approach to crime reporting.

In covering the Jewitt murder, Gordon Bennett put himself in the story in two ways. Always a flamboyant self-publicist, he was on the crime scene before the body had been removed and wrote up what he witnessed without using the conventional editorial plural – not 'we' but 'I': 'I could scarcely look at [the corpse] for a minute or two . . .'. To get a real jump on his competitors, he went beyond eyewitness, which would normally include simply reporting the case as it emerged in court. Instead, he sought out the madam, Rosina Townsend, for a private conversation:

> She sat on the sofa, talking – talking – talking of Ellen – Ellen – Ellen . . . 'I am going,' said Mrs Townsend, 'to have a funeral sermon preached next Sunday on poor Ellen. Poor thing. The Episcopals are too nice people. They wont do it.' 'By all means have a funeral sermon and let it be at Arthur Tappan's Tabernacle.' No, that would not do. Arthur Tappan is an abolitionist – and Rosina detests abolition. Oh! virtue! Oh! morals! Oh! the age of civilization!

Although very far from 'Mr. Spectator's' disengagement from the 'species', in another sense this was no great step forward. Papers on both sides of the Atlantic had regularly run reports of court interrogatories, often as a source of light relief: 'Margaret Thomas was drunk in the street – said she never would get drunk again "upon her honour". Committed, "upon honour".' On occasion, the question and answer of cross-examination was used. Gordon Bennett had himself written such stuff, but, convinced it had had its day, he refused to run these jokes in the *Herald*. Instead, he determined in effect to imitate the actions of a magistrate, which he well understood and was prepared to justify:

'. . . let us not suppose but courts and juries and justices have a right alone to examine a matter affecting our morals'. He was bolstered in this view by his treatment by the police at the murder scene. 'Why do you let that man in?', he reported one of the crowd asking an officer. 'He is an editor – he is on public duty.'

The English newspapers of the seventeenth-century Civil War had blurred the distinction between observation and intervention by melding the bald reporting of the diurnals with the editorialising of the pamphlet. Although this mixture was to be an early distinguishing mark of the English-speaking press, nevertheless, after the commotion of the war, understanding of the difference between the two activities remained. At the end of the eighteenth century, there was still a sense in which editorialising was seen as not being quite the business of a newspaper. One, the *New York Journal*, went so far as to print editorials in italics (itself an indicator of a personal hand) to make the distinction clear. In Britain, the law acknowledged the difference because pamphlets carrying opinion were not subject to the newspapers' stamp duty. The outspoken William Cobbett, whose stamped *Political Register* cost 1s 1½d (and therefore had to be read in groups by his targeted working-class readership), also published an unstamped version for 2d; but it was opinion only, entirely without news reports.

Papers, of course, carried subjective opinion in the form of letters to the editor, as well as the editor's or correspondents' opinions. Despite these 'non-reporting' (as they might be termed) precedents, and despite the model of court reporting, Bennett was intervening in the world in an unprecedented way, beating his rivals with material none of them had simply because he, in some sense, created the event being reported – the interview. The introduction of the interview marks a sort of corruption of the idea of the reporter as mere observer.

'Corruption' is perhaps an inappropriate term since the interview, whatever its differences from observational reporting, could well be a considerable source of illumination. For example, the personal experience of enduring poverty in Victorian England is nowhere more vividly to be found than in the interviews conducted by the journalist Henry

Mayhew and his collaborators Angus Beach, Charles Mackay and Shirley Brook. These were published (somewhat surprisingly) in the conservative *Morning Post* from October 1849 and throughout 1850. Mayhew's systematic studies used both interviews (conducted according to a template) and meetings of workers in various trades specially called to determine conditions.[3]

The journalist Horace Greeley, although he stood as a Liberal Republican/Democrat candidate for the American presidency in 1872 (and was overwhelmed by Grant's second victory), is best remembered for his famous advice: 'Go west, young man, go west'.[4] In 1859, he had been in the West himself, and from Salt Lake City he reported that:

> My friend Dr Berhisel, MC, took me this afternoon, by appointment, to meet Brigham Young, President of the Mormon Church, who had expressed a willingness to receive me at 2 pm . . .
>
> H.G.: What is the position of your Church with respect to Slavery?
> B.Y.: We consider it of Divine institution, and not to be abolished until the curse pronounced on Ham shall have been removed from his descendants . . .

The conversation was conducted at a stately pace but did not avoid the issue which must have been the greatest popular interest:

> H.G..: What is the largest number of wives belonging to any one man?
> B.Y.: I have 15; I know no-one who has more . . .

> Such is [Greeley concluded], as nearly as I can recollect, the substance of nearly two hours' worth of conversation, wherein much was said that would not be worth reporting . . .

105

A certain self-consciousness around the interview process long persisted. London, 1871, for *The World:*

> R. [a journalist, R. Landor]: It would seem that in this country the hoped-for solution whatever it may be, will be attained without the violent means of revolution . . .
>
> DR. M.: I am not so sanguine on that point as you. The English middle class has always shown itself willing enough to accept the verdict of the majority so long as it enjoyed the monopoly of the voting power. But, mark me, as soon as it finds itself outvoted on what it considers vital questions we shall see here a new slave owners' war.

> I have here given you as well as I can remember them the heads of my conversation with this remarkable man . . . the civilised world has a new power in its midst with which it must soon come to a reckoning for good or ill.

The 'remarkable man', 'Dr. M.', was Karl Marx.

It was not just a question of the interview itself. One of the century's most enduring news adventures was merely the story of how a meeting was achieved. The subject says but one word:

> BUNDER UJIJI, ON LAKE TANGANYIKA, CENTRAL AFRICA, NOVEMBER 23, 1871 . . .
>
> There is a group of the most respectable Arabs, and as I come nearer I see the white face of an old man among them. He has a cap with a gold band around it, his dress is a short jacket of red blanket cloth, and his pants – well, I didn't observe. I am shaking hands with him. We raise our hats, and I say:
> 'Doctor Livingstone, I presume?'
> And he says, 'Yes.'
> *Finis coronat opus.*[5]

Henry Stanley was wandering through the African interior in 1871 in search of the famous British explorer at the behest of James Gordon Bennett Junior, who had taken over the *Herald* from his father in 1867.[6] The *Herald* shared the expenses of Stanley's African exploits with the first mass-circulation London newspaper, Joseph Levy's *Daily Telegraph*.

The interview was not absorbed into everyday journalistic practice without misgivings as to its validity as news. In 1860 the *Chicago Tribune* opined: 'A portion of daily newspapers in New York are bringing the profession of journalism into contempt, so far as they can, by a kind of toadyism or flunkeyism, which they call interviewing.' In 1869, the New York *Nation* thought that the interview was 'the joint production of some humbug of a hack politician and another humbug of a newspaper reporter'. In Britain, the business was seen as yet another unfortunate American innovation and was still being treated with suspicion in the 1880s, although by that time it had become an established element in foreign reporting. As late as 1884, in the London evening daily, the *Pall Mall Gazette*, the editor W. T. Stead wrote that 'one of the superstitions of the English press – superstitions which are fortunately on the wane – is that interviewing in England is a monstrous departure from the dignity and propriety of journalism.' He was running a dozen or so a month in his paper and claimed that this was the year that saw the interview finally 'acclimatised' in Britain. Even interviews conducted in the UK – still dismissively characterised as 'Celebrity at Home' encounters – secured their place in the papers. Essentially corrupt or not, interviews pointed the way to other forms of journalistic intervention in the world.

Elizabeth Jane 'Pink' Cochran, a middle-class 27-year-old from western Pennsylvania, fast-talked her way into the office of Colonel John Cockerell, managing editor of Joseph Pulitzer's *New York World* in September 1887. Pulitzer had bought the ailing *World* four years earlier and, with a vibrant mix informed by his own immigrant sensibility of sensational reporting and graphic (but still non-photographic) illustration, had increased its circulation ten-fold. Pink Cochran had cut her teeth as a journalist at the *Pittsburgh Dispatch*. One of 15 orphaned children, unable to afford to finish her teacher training, she obtained her first journalistic job via a letter to the editor, signed 'Little Orphan Girl'. Its recipient, George Madden, thought she needed a better by-line than Pink Cochran and so re-christened her 'Nellie Bly'. Two years later, she took herself off to New York and the offices of the *World*. Bly thought to sell Cockerell a first-person piece on conditions in steerage on the transatlantic steamers. This would involve her going to Europe (not in steerage) to get the story. Cockerell had another idea, closer to home. As the single-column headlines of the day put it:

INSIDE THE MADHOUSE
Nellie Bly's Experience in the Blackwell's Island Asylum . . .
How the City's Unfortunate Wards are Fed and Treated
The Terrors of Cold Baths and Cruel, Unsympathetic Nurses
Attendants Who Harass and Abuse Patients
And Laugh at Their Miseries

Bly checked into a working women's boarding house as Nellie Brown, feigned madness and got arrested, as was reported, using her pseudonym, in Charles Dana's rival *New York Sun* – 'Who Is This Insane Girl?' That she was obviously well-spoken, educated (and, of course, strikingly good-looking) meant her unexpected situation perfectly fitted Dana's city editor, John Bogart's, famous definition of news: 'When a dog bites a man, that is not news; but when a man bites a dog, that is news.' All the city's papers ran stories on the mysterious Miss Brown but, as the only official who harboured any suspicions about her was ignored, she made it through a committal procedure into the Women's Lunatic Asylum on Blackwell's Island. 'My teeth chattered and my limbs were goose-fleshed and blue with cold. Suddenly I got, one after another, three buckets of water over my head – ice-cold water, too . . . For once I did look insane.' Ten days later, on 4 October 1887, an attorney sent by Cockerell got her released, ostensibly into the care of friends. Still in the dark, the *Sun* and the *New York Times* reported this as her recovery. Forty-eight hours after that, Bly's first sensational story appeared in the *World*. Her book, *Ten Days in a Mad House*, was out in time for Christmas. This was the 'New Journalism' (as Matthew Arnold supposedly called it) in action.

An editor ordering a reporter to gather material, even to behave fraudulently, was an assignment just like an honestly conducted interview was. Deception was justified as a morally unassailable and straightforward extension of the concept of information as a public right. Take W. T. Stead, advocate of the interview, supporter of women journalists and, all in all, a premier pioneer of Pulitzer's New Journalism in Britain who also popularised signed columns, illustrations and the use of crossheads. He was the son of a Congregationalist minister and himself a Sunday school teacher who had begun his journalistic career on the *Northern Echo* in Darlington, eventually becoming its editor. On moving to London, he was first the assistant editor of the Liberal *Pall Mall Gazette* and then, from 1883, its editor. As was expected, he took a campaigning view of the issues of the day. Among those most exercising Christian opinion, 'the Purity Lobby', was the vexed question of prostitution, a far more visible and widespread social phenomenon than it was to be in the twentieth century. Doing something about the issue, though, was somewhat fraught. Specific legislation, for example, allowed for legal prostitution in naval ports and army garrison towns, to the complete disgust of the Purity Lobby, which mounted a long, and eventually successful, campaign to have this act repealed. This, of course, did nothing about the problem in general. In 1885, a four-year-old girl was repeatedly raped in a brothel but the perpetrators walked from court free because she was too young to give evidence against them. Stead was approached to use his paper to 'rouse public opinion'.

Convinced that merely reporting actual incidents of child prostitution would not do the trick, he decided to stir up a demand for legislative action by himself buying, with the help of Mrs Josephine Butler, a leading Purity campaigner and wife of a canon of Winchester Cathedral, a 13-year-old girl. High-minded motives nevertheless did not diminish the opportunity for sensationalism. Stead explained the enterprise as 'a Special and Secret Commission of Inquiry which we appointed'. On the Saturday prior to the publication of this 'Commission's' report (which would be headlined by Stead, 'The Maiden Tribute of Modern Babylon') in July 1885, he gave 'A Frank Warning' to his readers:

> All those who are squeamish, and all those who are prudish, and all those who prefer to live in a fool's paradise of imaginary innocence and purity, selfishly oblivious of the horrible realities which torment those whose lives are passed in the London inferno, will do well not to read the Pall Mall Gazette of Monday and the following days.

He was arrested for abduction, not quite the outcome he, Mrs Butler and the Purity Lobby intended; but the 'procuress' turned out to be no such thing and the girl innocently believed she was being hired as a maid. The magistrate who committed Stead to trial was not impressed with 'The Maiden Tribute of Modern Babylon', which he described as a 'deplorable and nauseous article . . . which . . . has greatly lowered the English people in the eyes of foreign nations'. Stead's journalistic rivals – especially the other three London evenings – had a field day:

> Newspaper sensationalism had been carried very far before this present week of grace [thundered the *St. James's Gazette*], but yesterday it reached its utmost possible point in the production of the vilest parcel of obscenity that has ever yet issued from the public press . . . The man who invented the 'sensation' . . . has flung all decency aside, openly dealing with the worst abominations in the plainest and foulest language.

At trial Stead was given three months without hard labour. Upon his release he resumed the editorship, becoming 'The Man with a Muck-Rake', as a caricature put it. Although the scandal had severely damaged his reputation, he was not silenced until the night of 14 April 1912 when he died, in the words of the *Daily Mirror* report, 'the greatest man on the Titanic'.

Not all New Journalism assignments involved matters of serious moment. After she had started the fashion and followed up her adventure in the madhouse with exposés of factory conditions, employment agency fraud, reformatories for fallen women and the like, Nelly Bly's second most famous exploit had not a whiff of the right to know, or any other social value, about it. It was entertainment, a 'stunt' of the sort that was integral to Pulitzer's journalism. In 1889, for no particular reason, she set off to beat the fictional Phileas Fogg's 80-day rush round the globe.

When it was suggested in an editorial meeting at the *World* that a male reporter ought to be sent instead of her because he could travel without a chaperon and with fewer than a 'round dozen trunks', Bly told Cockerell he should start his man and she would beat him – for another paper. This was a threat he knew she was more than capable of carrying out, so it was for the *World* that she left New York on 14 November. In Paris, she interviewed Jules Verne, who thought her 'the prettiest young girl imaginable'.[7] When tedious stretches of sea voyage halted the flow of news of her progress, the *World* ran a competition to guess how long it was going to take her. The prize was a free trip to Europe. A hundred thousand entries furnished enough stories about the entrants to plug the gap. Although Bly had promised to use only public transport, in San Francisco she boarded a special train – the main line being blocked by a blizzard – to take a southern route back to the East Coast. She was in New York by Saturday, 25 January 1890 – 72 days, six hours, 11 minutes and 14 seconds after she left. 'It's not so very much for a woman to do,' she said in an interview, 'who has the pluck, energy and independence which characterise many women in this day of push and get-there.' Few publicly drew attention to the essential pointlessness of the exercise. 'A young woman sent around the world for no practical purpose will work to greater advantage in booming a newspaper than a dozen men sent after the facts', wrote Allan Forman, never a Bly fan, in the *Journalist*, a rival paper.

From editorial to interview to exposé to stunt to campaign. The New Journalism transformed the oppositional political rhetoric of earlier radical writing into structured campaigning for specific localised outcomes. This sort of journalism's most enduring monument can still be seen in New York's Lower Harbour – it is the base of the Statue of Liberty. The statue itself was a gift from the French on the occasion of the one hundredth anniversary of the Declaration of Independence. A public campaign in the United States to raise $100,000 for its base faltered – until Pulitzer took the matter in hand: '*The World* is the people's paper and it now appeals to the people to come forward and raise this money.' One hundred and twenty thousand of them did. The base was built and the statue erected, albeit a decade late, in 1886.

In 1891, the publisher of the *San Francisco Examiner* decided to try his hand on the East Coast. Pulitzer's new rival was 28, the impossibly wealthy son of the prospector who had discovered the Comstock silver lode. William Randolph Hearst had been expelled from Harvard and had begged his father for control of the *Examiner*, which had been acquired by the elder Hearst as a political platform. Having learned the newspaper business, on his father's death in 1891, Hearst inherited $7,500,000 and used $180,000 of them to pick up a failing New York scandal sheet, the *Morning Journal*. The sellers threw in the German-language edition for the same money. The *Journal* (Hearst immediately dropped 'Morning' from the title) not only campaigned but went to court to compel those it was crusading against – public utility companies, construction firms and the like – into toeing the paper's line. This was 'a new idea in journalism' and the masthead made sure everybody knew it: 'While Others Talk, the *Journal* Acts'. Hearst's staff not only interviewed witnesses to crimes, now an old-hat practice, they set about solving mysteries themselves. On one occasion *Journal* reporters, spurred on by the $1,000 bonus Hearst offered them, discovered the identity of a headless, limbless corpse found in the East River and fingered the perpetrators of the deed.

Hearst also stole stars from Pulitzer's *World*, such as the 'Yellow

Kid' cartoonist, Richard Outcault; and as a result the New Journalism began to be known as the 'yellow press', with all its implications of irresponsibility and sensationalism.[8] After Stanley's successful exploit, young Gordon Bennett had said, with no little truth, 'I *make* news'. For Hearst, this, rather than reporting the world, had become the point:

> HEARST, JOURNAL NEW YORK:
> EVERYTHING IS QUIET. THERE IS NO TROUBLE HERE. THERE WILL
> BE NO WAR.

cabled the Western painter Frederick Remington, whom Hearst had dispatched to Cuba in 1897 with the then famous writer Richard Harding Davis. Hearst replied:

> REMINGTON, HAVANA:
> PLEASE REMAIN. YOU FURNISH THE PICTURES AND I'LL FURNISH
> THE WAR.

Hearst always denied he wrote this, but whether he did or not is immaterial since Remington certainly wanted to come back and Hearst certainly wanted American military action against the Cubans.

MANILA OURS!
DEWEY'S GUNS SHELL THE CITY
PANIC IN MADRID AND REVOLUTION FEARED.

Between the murder of Helen Jewitt and Hearst's war in Cuba a transformation had taken place in journalism. Its price has perhaps been best summed up in the obituary published by the *New York Tribune* on the occasion of the elder Gordon Bennett's death in 1872: 'He developed the capacities of journalism in the most wonderful manner, but he did it by degrading its character.'

'There sat a fourth estate'

Yet 'degradation' is not quite right if only because it implies some prior state of greater grace. It is hard to see when, if ever, that might have been. Take political reporting, arguable a central journalistic task in representative democracies and certainly the site, over the centuries, of the greatest battles for a free press.

At a dinner one night more than a century before the yellow press, Samuel Johnson and some friends were bemoaning a decline in political oratory in the House of Commons. The elder Pitt was quoted, to Johnson's surprise, as evidence of the superiority of earlier days. 'That speech', he spluttered, '. . . I wrote it in a garret in Exeter Street.'

The Houses of both Commons and Lords are technically the High Court of Parliament and their decisions are recorded in their Acts. Any debates were no more to be reported and examined than were the deliberations of a jury in any other court. Not only that, members did not want the king to know what had been said; nor foreign princes or, later, disaffected North American British colonists. The printing of 'any votes or proceedings of this House without special leave of this House' was declared a breach of privilege as soon as the throne had been reoccupied in 1660. Yet, the idea that the public (however limited by property and literacy) had a right to know what its elected representatives did was not entirely alien and, more compellingly, newspaper publishers knew their readers had an appetite for reports of parliamentary debates.

Edward Cave sought to oblige them but he realised that getting information out of Westminster would require a certain amount of subterfuge. He had used members' initials rather than their full names and at one point he ran the reports as 'The Proceedings of the Senate of Lilliput'. He knew that no obvious writing would be permitted in such circumstances of, at best, technical illegality. Johnson explained to his dining companions how Cave got round the problem:

Sir, I have never been in the gallery of the House of

Commons but once. Cave had an interest with the door-keepers. He, and the persons employed by him [notably Guthrie – a man of prodigious memory but no literary style], gained admittance, they brought away the subject of discussion, the names of the speakers, the side they took, and the order in which they rose together with notes of the arguments adduced in the course of debate. The whole was afterwards communicated to me, and I composed the speeches in the form they now have in the Parliamentary Debates.

Given that the illegality of reporting the House was well-known, Johnson had assumed his words would obviously be read as fictions and was appalled to discover that, all those years before, he had been an 'accessory to the propagation of falsehood'.

Reporting the thinking of such a central organ of the state was seen everywhere as revolutionary. Even in the United States, that bastion of representative democracy, where journalism figured so heavily in the mythic narrative of the nation's birth, there was unease at the reporting of Congressional debates. It was not until 1860 that an accrediting system, initially for 75 journalists, was finally put in place. In France, at the outset of the French Revolution, the Estates General had discussed the radical possibility of allowing its debates to be reported, eventually deciding that democratic logic demanded that this be done. A *Journal de débats et décrets* appeared in 1789, published by a press entrepreneur, Baudouin, and soon had a number of rivals. Despite guaranteed accuracy through *logographie*, a new shorthand system, some deputies nevertheless accused these *comptes rendus* of bias. Part of the response to such charges was the technique of inserting reaction to a speaker in brackets, e.g. '[Laughter]'.

It was in the French National Assembly that these reporters were first given a special gallery. The front row of the public gallery of the House of Commons in Westminster was also set aside for reporters who were allowed to write in the chamber itself.[9] In 1803, Thomas Hansard, whose father had worked in the official printer's office at Westminster, began publishing reports of the debates, initially culled from newspaper accounts.[10] Thomas Carlyle remarked that 'there were three Estates in Parliament, but in the Reporters Gallery yonder, there sat a fourth Estate more important far than they all'.[11]

Hansard sought objectivity through the same means as had been developed by the *comptes rendus parlementaires* – unembellished shorthand, the key to specialised accurate reporting of speech, as well as minimal notes on reactions. Shorthand systems antedated *logographie*. Pepys, for example, had used Shelton's system and Defoe took down dying words at the foot of the scaffold, yet its potential for everyday journalism remained largely unexplored until the early nineteenth century. By 1800, the 'intelligencer' had become a reporter, a distinct and common role. The leading exponent of the craft at *The Times* (London) in the post-Napoleonic period was John Tyas. Tyas had been assigned to cover the radical Henry 'Orator' Hunt as he went around the country agitating for an expansion of the suffrage in the summer of 1819. Together with reporters from the *Leeds Mercury*, the *Liverpool Mercury*, the *Manchester Observer* and the *Manchester Chronicle* (a veritable proto-press corps), on the hot early afternoon of 16 August, Tyas waited with an expectant crowd of 20,000 'reformers' to hear Hunt – as did a cohort of the yeomanry called out by a nervous magistrate. Tyas was to relay more than 'Orator's' speech to an astounded country:

> A cry was made at the cavalry, 'Have at their flags'. In consequence, [the yeomanry] immediately dashed . . . at those which were posted among the crowd, cutting most indiscriminately to the right and to the left to get at them . . . From that moment the Manchester Yeomanry Cavalry lost all command of temper.

Within 72 hours the outcome of the mêlée on St Peter's Field was known everywhere: more than 400 wounded; 11 dead including, most shockingly, two women. A few days later, the *Manchester Observer* called the catastrophe, in a punning echo of the carnage of a real and recent battle, 'Peter-Loo'. And Peterloo it has been ever since.

The Times had been founded in 1785 by a printer, John Walter, who had no great ambitions for it. Indeed, 'he never did an honest act in his life' (according to one ex-employee) and his paper's behaviour in those early decades was exactly of a piece with that of its competitors. Rather more than a commitment to news, bribes and blackmail characterised its daily operation. Then, under the son, John Walter II, this changed. In 1817, Walter II appointed John Barnes, a Cambridge graduate who had been working in various reporting capacities and as leader writer, to be editor. Unlike many proprietors, then as now, Walter II had the good sense to leave Barnes in sole control. Under him, *The Times* initially developed a somewhat liberal agenda. Tyas had reported from Peterloo that when he had explained to a constable that, 'we merely attended to report the proceedings of the day, [the officer] replied, "Oh! Oh! You then are one of their writers – you must go before the Magistrates".' Not unnaturally, given this seemingly in-built hostility to the press, Barnes opposed the repressive Six Acts, passed in panic in the aftermath of Peterloo, which included two measures specifically directed against news-papers increasing the stamp duty, making seditious libel a transportable offence and introducing one-off deposits as security for good behaviour.

On ascending the throne in 1820, George IV attempted to divorce his estranged and scandal-ridden queen, Caroline. Barnes was con-scious, from his reporting correspondents round the country (whom he regularly quizzed on the state of local opinion), that she enjoyed wide sympathy among the mercantile class, and swung *The Times* behind her. He thereby abandoned the Establishment, but doubled the circu-lation of the paper from 7,000, a good but not far above average figure for the day, to 15,000. Its nineteenth-century dominance now began. Over the next decades, it voiced no party's or faction's line in any con-sistent way. As a result, some called it 'The Turnabout', but by 1830, it was far more widely known as 'The Thunderer' – 'a free journal', Barnes claimed perhaps a little tendentiously, 'unattached to any other cause than that of the truth, and given to speak boldly of all parties'.

Barnes died in 1841 following surgery, an event which *The Times* noted with a brief two-line announcement, the first time his name had appeared in its columns. To succeed him, Walter II appointed an Oxford graduate who was working his way up in the office, as Barnes had done. John Thaddeus Delane was 23. He was to hold the job for 36 years. Unlike Barnes, he wrote little, but, like Barnes, he did oversee every word published, spending every night at the paper. Unlike the private Barnes, who had high friends but did not flaunt his relationships, Delane was very much a public figure, arguably the most influential journalist Britain has ever seen. Barnes was of a generation of newspaper people who were still considered somewhat beyond the pale of polite society. In 1807, for instance, the benchers of Lincoln's Inn had determined never to call to the bar anybody who had published in a newspaper. Although the fact of such hostility largely remained, matters had moved on by Delane's time. The Secretary of the Admiralty in the 1850s, Sir John Crocker, observed that 'the times are gone when statesmen might safely despise the journals'.

The first murmurings about the need for a public-relations official were heard at the height of the Napoleonic Wars in vague suggestions of an innovative Government Press Bureau, which would bribe selected publications with information rather than money. Wellington had a similar idea in the 1820s, but both came to naught. Thirty years later the prescient Crocker wrote:

> The day is not far distant when you will (not *see,* or *hear*) but *know* that there is someone in the Cabinet entrusted with what will be thought one of the most important duties of the State, the regulation of public opinion.

The day turned out to be more distant, and public opinion more resistant to manipulation, than had perhaps been anticipated, but Sir John was not far off the mark. Of *The Times*, Crocker's contemporary Lord John Russell complained to Queen Victoria that: 'The degree of information possessed by *The Times* with regard to the most secret affairs of

State is mortifying, humiliating and incomprehensible' – not least because journalists were still, in theory at least, confined to their gallery.[12] In practice, some politicians were already acting to manipulate the press by controlling information. As early as 1837, Palmerston had bought a London press corps both rail tickets to Tiverton and hotel rooms there to ensure his election address would be reported to a metropolitan audience. In 1852 the Conservative Benjamin Disraeli, sending Delane his election manifesto, wrote, 'I hope you will be able to back me . . . but if you can't, we must take the fortunes of war without grumbling'. Delane chose to describe him as a 'quack doctor' and an 'inimitable illusionist'.

The Times presented a new challenge to the authorities. Here was no radical unstamped rag, as it were, designed to agitate the lower orders. This was a respectable stamped publication read by the ruling class but not necessarily on the Establishment's side.

> HEIGHTS BEFORE SEBASTOPOL OCTOBER 25 1854.
>
> [. . .]
>
> We could hardly believe the evidence of our senses! Surely that handful of men were not going to charge an army in position? Alas! It was but too true – their desperate valour knew no bounds and far indeed was it removed from its so called better part – discretion . . . At twenty-five to twelve not a British soldier, except the dead and dying, was left in front of these bloody Muscovite guns.

That a doomed, and militarily irrelevant, cavalry charge in a minor nineteenth-century war has lodged itself into the British national psyche has not a little to do with this report. Recognisable war correspondents, referred to as 'TGs' or Travelling Gentlemen, represented a further specialisation within reporting. Delane's chief TG was William Russell, whose most famous report was to be this dispatch on the charge of the Light Brigade. Russell also gave us 'the thin red line', a phrase he penned to describe the British infantry before Balaclava. His persistent exposés of

the incompetence and stupidity of the British military authorities led the
Queen to wonder why *The Times* was allowed to attack her officers and
Prince Albert to call Russell 'a miserable scribbler'. The exposés in *The
Times* were reinforced by parallel accounts in the other papers such as
those of Edwin Godkin, who had been sent to the Crimea by the *Daily
News* and had been quick to report the 'folly', 'ignorance' and 'mistakes'
of the General Staff. A mere call made in the House of Commons for a
Select Committee inquiry 'into the condition of our army before
Sebastopol' in January 1855 was sufficient to bring down the govern-
ment which had been presiding over these lethal ineptitudes. Lord John
Russell, a member of the Cabinet, exited with this complaint: 'If
England is ever to be England again, this vile tyranny of *The Times* must
be cut off.' England, though, was never 'to be England again' in terms
John Russell would understand, but the solution to the 'vile tyranny'
(and much else) was already in train, if he had had the wit to realise it.

'To secure circulation amongst both poor and rich'

Newspapers had been scaring Russell and his class for a couple of centuries. It was an enduring inheritance of the seventeenth-century Civil
War and its aftermath that they could not be easily suppressed. Take the
most famous early nineteenth-century militant journalist, William
Cobbett – 'the Contentious Man' as he was once called. He produced
the *Political Register* from 1802 until his death in 1835. He might
have needed to publish stamped and unstamped versions; he might
have been imprisoned, as he was in 1812; he might have had to flee the
country for a time, as he did in 1817 – but he was never effectively
silenced. He was more than something of a romantic, never quite losing
the conservatism of his earliest thought: 'I wish to see the poor men of
England what the poor men of England were when I was a boy'; but he
was also ever the enlightened rationalist: 'the hirelings call aloud for
sending forth penal statutes and troops to put you down, I send you the
most persuasive arguments my mind can suggest'.

The government attempted to meet such radical fire with fire, by issuing official newspapers, for instance the *Anti-Cobbett* and the *White Dwarf*, both published in 1817. This never worked. They were no more successful than L'Estrange's parallel efforts – the *Intelligencer*, the *Newes* and the *Observator* – had been during the Restoration. The *Black Dwarf*, the *Republican*, the *White Hat*, the *Cap of Liberty*, on the other hand, might have lasted for only a year or two, but there was a constant flow of titles – more than 200 of them, stamp and security deposits or no. The simple fact, which seemed always to have eluded the authorities, was that a newspaper, however expensive, could be read by more than one person. The tax encouraged group readings, bringing together exactly those articulate, informed and disaffected members of the lower orders whom the ruling class were terrified of seeing assembled. A second-hand market, at half price, in day-old issues also increased readership. You could arrange with a news-seller for a few pennies a week to 'hire' a paper for an hour. This had been made illegal in 1789 but that was no more a deterrent than any of these other measures. The circulations of individual radical titles were often very small but, by the 1830s, it has been estimated that the unstamped press collectively had two million readers, exceeding that of the stamped press. Collectively, as Henry Hetherington's unstamped *Poor Man's Guardian* cheekily announced, they were published 'Contrary to "Law" to Try the Powers of "Might" against that of "Right"'.

In 1838, political unrest was focused into a reformist set of demands outlined in 'The People's Charter', in effect a draft parliamentary reform bill. The British press was as central to Chartism, as the movement pushing to enact these proposals became known, as it had been to the independence struggles in the American colonies half a century before. Chartism was so popular that some titles had large enough circulations to cock a snook at the authorities by paying the tax, albeit at a cost to their street credibility. Fergus O'Connor, the most popular Chartist leader, MP and publisher of the major northern Chartist weekly the *Northern Star*, apologised for obeying the law in the first issue: 'Reader – Behold that little red spot, in the corner of my newspaper. That is the Stamp; the Whig *beauty* spot; your *plague* spot.' In the second half of 1839, the *Northern Star*'s circulation peaked at 30,000 a week; over the next decade it still managed an average 10,000 or so. This was enough, with a cover-price of 4½d, to allow O'Connor to meet running costs of £9 10s 0d a week – including the stamp and the luxury of paid correspondents – and still turn a handsome profit in excess of £6,000 a year; but, and here is the rub, its stable circulation was around a quarter of that achieved by the most popular of the militant papers, the *Weekly Police Gazette*. Founded in 1835 by John Cleave, the *Gazette* combined radical politics with sensational crime reporting. The other militant titles also covered non-political topics, but Cleave, a successful publisher before he had become involved in Chartism, put crime very much to the fore, as the name of his paper implied. By the end of the decade it was claiming to sell 40,000 copies a week. Sensational politics, Cleave demonstrated, could be sold by sensational crime.

In 1842 another, less prominent Chartist and publisher, Edward Lloyd, also started a weekly. He had made a fortune with 'Penny Dreadfuls', popular literature issued in cheap parts – a penny for a chapter of *Vice & Its Victim: Phoebe, the Peasant's Daughter*, for example – and he sought to exploit the market reached by the *Weekly Police Gazette* with a new Sunday publication, *Lloyd's Penny Weekly Miscellany*. Sunday digests of the news, made attractive by the high cost of the stamped dailies, had existed since Mrs E. Johnson had started her *British Gazette and Sunday Monitor* in 1779 (despite milk and mackerel being the only commodities that could legally be sold on the Lord's Day). Lloyd, unlike Cleave, was far more interested in his readers' pennies than in their politics.

A year after *Lloyd's Weekly* came the next logical step, sensation only, without the radical politics. On Sunday 1 October 1843 the *News of the World* appeared, stamped and priced 3d. Its contents echoed those of the *Weekly Police Gazette* but where politics, discussed with passion in hectoring tones, marked the Chartist papers, in the *News of the World* the opening column headlined 'The Politician: The State of the Nation' was only an advert for its editorial policy. 'A paper that will combine the attractions of the rich newspaper, and that from the smallness of price will be certain', it hopefully asserted, 'to secure circulation amongst both poor and rich'. The real point of the new publication was to be found in the next columns: 'EXTRAORDINARY CHARGE OF DRUGGING AND VIOLATION' and 'JOKES (From Punch of Yesterday)'. Inside was news of 'Sudden Death of a Gentleman of Fortune'; 'Suicide at Blackfriars Bridge'; and much more of the same but also including a weather forecast: 'October. This month will record fearful storms and earthquakes, especially in the middle of the month from the eleventh to the seventeenth'. It was soon claiming sales of 60,000 a week.

And this is the point: sensationalist populism did not necessarily equate with radicalism. This was the clue, in plain sight since the success of the *Weekly Police Gazette*, both to drawing the sting of the radical press and 'cutting off' *The Times*, that is, destroying its supremacy. Although readers were happy to live with politics if at the same time they could get crime, scandal and, increasingly, sport, the clever sugaring-the-radical-pill strategy of a militant publisher like Cleave was undercut by this taste for sensationalism alone.

Not only that, mass circulations demanded production at industrial levels. The *News of the World*, claimed its proprietors, had required 'a great outlay of capital' to launch and needed 'a very extensive circulation' to survive. This was a great change from previous centuries when newspapers had cost very little to start compared with other businesses. Until 1800, a full-scale commercially viable publication required far less than £1,000; but by the mid-nineteenth century and the *News of World*, this had become a more hefty £20,000 rising to £150,000 in the 1870s (and millions in the twentieth century). Despite printing being an early site of concentrated, structured production (and concomitant trade-union activity), printing shops themselves had remained close to their artisan roots – a few presses and a small number of pressmen per shop persisting as the dominant mode of production. This pre-industrial reality was an aid to the radical press but, as start-up costs increased and circulations expanded, it was fast becoming a thing of the past. In the

first 350 years after Gutenberg, printing speed had increased to a maximum of 400–500 impressions per hour (iph) with the only major
advance being the introduction in the seventeenth century of a counter-
weight which automatically raised the platen. The first all-metal,
cast-iron press, along the same general flat-bed design as that introduced by Gutenberg, appeared in the 1780s. Still small enough for the
back of a cart, it became an industry standard but was not much more
productive.

It is possible to define all these machines, starting with Gutenberg's,
as prototypes, responses to the social needs of Church reform and
growing urbanisation which had then been sustained in technological
stasis – except for a very gradual increase in iph – for centuries. The
widely believed claim that such prototypes, in the words of the 1960s
media guru Marshall McLuhan, 'brought in nationalism, industrialism,
mass markets, and universal literacy and education' makes a nonsense of
any idea of historical causality, given the time that separates Gutenberg
from these far more recent phenomena. If the press is defined as a
device capable of producing at least 5,000 iph, the claim makes better –
albeit still not much – sense. At least McLuhan's phenomena and
5,000+ iph press inhabit the same time frame; but the notion that
printing rather than, say, Napoleonic invasions, 'causes' modern nationalism is, as with the belief that the Reformation was a by-product of the
press, somewhat far-fetched.

What is clear, though, is that print's technological stasis was swept
aside as the burgeoning urban, literate and industrialised potential readership now necessitated, for the first time since moveable type was
introduced, a serious expansion of capacity. The concept of a polygonal
cylinder of type, a rotary press, dated back to 1660 but *The Times*
acquired its first example in 1814. The steam engine, in its modern con-
figuration, had been around since 1699 but now *The Times*'s masthead
proudly proclaimed that the paper was 'printed by steam', because
steam engines powered the new presses.[13] By 1828, the iph rate reached
4,000; by 1848, 12,000 iph – and the biggest presses, the American
Hoe for instance, needed 25 men and boys to operate it and a factory-

sized building to house it. It also cost 100 times the price of an old cast-iron flat-bed. The day of the solitary 'dangerous' Cobbett threatening the state with the aid of a few printers was passing. By 1857, speeds of 20,000 iph were possible and, of course, *The Times* achieved them. It was said that the cellars of the offices in Printing House Square had become full of discarded press machinery as the paper sought to exploit its commanding lead over its rivals.

With the fast presses came other advances. In 1803, the Fourdrinier, an industrial-scale paper-making machine capable of a tenfold increase in output over traditional artisan methods, was introduced. Paper production increased in Britain from 11,000 tons a year to 100,000 over the next half-century. The falling price of Fourdrinier paper helped the American 1c press establish itself in the 1830s. By 1866, the sheets had given way to a continuous roll of paper, a technique then nearly a century old in the textile and patterned paper industries. A web system for printing both sides of a sheet at once was introduced in 1863 at the *Philadelphia Inquirer*. By this time even higher iph speeds were possible with stereotyping, an eighteenth-century technique recovered for newspapers more or less simultaneously in London, Paris and New York. It involved making a papier-mâché mould to cast an entire typeset page as a single, curved metal plate. Stereotyping also enabled headlines to spread across more than one column for the first time and, in the US, such banners began to replace the stacked 'tombstone' style.

Content also became far more expensive to gather, involving mounting numbers of specialised editorial staff and ever more costly 'beats' and 'stunts'. Competition was not cheap. Already pricy eighteenth-century American news-boats had been matched on land by horse expresses, as titles sought to maintain an edge. Twenty-four horses in relay could take news the 227 miles from Washington to New York in less than a day but at a cost of $2,000 a week. By the 1840s some papers, both in the USA and in Europe, had supplemented the horses with carrier pigeons; *The Times* even set up a dromedary express to speed Far Eastern dispatches through a canal-less Suez region. The cost of these news-gathering systems made the concept of an agency selling news more cheaply to a number of newspapers attractive, but the first such agency, a pigeon service started by Charles Havas in Paris in 1832, was too much given to transmitting government dispatches.

Telegrams eventually became essential to both agencies and correspondents but although newspapermen figured prominently as investors in Morse's Magnetic Telegraph Company and the papers generally waxed lyrical over what the *Baltimore Sun* called the telegraph's 'mystic band', in practice they were less ecstatic over the prices charged and telegraphy's take-up by the press was slower than might have been expected.[14] For example, two decades after Havas, Paul Julius de Reuter opened a London agency still using pigeons. (Unlike Havas, Reuter aimed at Hansard-like levels of dispassionate coverage and prospered as a result.) It was not until 1866, more than 20 years after the introduction of a commercial telegraph system, that an extensive cable – a report of a speech by the King of Prussia announcing the end of the Six Weeks War between his country and Austria – was sent to a paper. It cost the *New York Herald* $6,500 in gold, which is why, in part, it still took 20 days for Russell's report of the destruction of the Light Brigade to reach London – six days to Constantinople, 12 to cross the Mediterranean, two more days to traverse France and the Channel. The process was slow enough, even with the new technology, for the report to be trailed:

11 November 1854:

THE ATTACK ON BALAKLAVA

(By Submarine and British Telegraph)

We have received from our correspondent at Marseilles the following dispatch, which had reached that port by French post steamer which left Constantinople on the 30th ult.:

'Your correspondent in the army before Sebastopol writes on the twenty-eighth that 607 light infantry were engaged in the affair of the twenty-fifth, and that only 198 returned . . .'

Nevertheless, cables were soon costing *The Times* £40,000 a year as competitiveness, which had already fetishised the freshness of news, overwhelmed the pricing barrier.

In this way, had John Russell realised it, the press was being safe-guarded for capitalism. Scores of employees in the pressroom; tens more in the newsroom; reporters with shorthand; horse expresses, carrier pigeons and telegram cables; fervid competition; and, above all, a sensationalist product for the masses, were working to control the oppositional excesses (as a John Russell would see them) of the press more effectively than any more overt censorship system ever had. Newspapers had become big business. In Britain, mid-century prosperity stifled Chartism, which had anyway always tended towards reform rather than revolution. The ever more literate work-force, made orderly by the factory and the chapel, turned away from Cleave's mixture of sensationalism and angry politics. Folks just wanted crime and scandal, which, after all, had been staples for centuries. And sport: sports coverage, which had begun with news stories about horse-racing in the eighteenth century, had long produced dedicated titles, such as the fortnightly *Historical List of Horse-Matches Run* (1733). (In the United States, some specialised titles, for instance, *The Spirit of the Times*, which lasted from 1831 to 1902, covered prize-fighting too.) Now their contents seeped into more general publications.

'The free press is the ubiquitous vigilant eye of a people's soul'

All this required funding and a third party intervened between reader and proprietor to meet the bill – the advertiser. Advertising revenues had been a supplementary source of income to cover-price, as were handouts from government in the form of bribes and also the revenue from blackmailing people who paid to keep their names from being published. By the early nineteenth century ads were becoming the preferred secondary source of revenue; by the mid-century they were as critical as circulation. In 1837, it was estimated that a London paper needed a circulation of at least 12,000 if it were to survive on cover-price alone. As only *The Times* had that, the rest of the press had to rely on ad revenue as well. It was much the same in the provinces, where 3,500 copies were thought to be necessary but in fact many titles survived on less than that.

There were as yet no audited circulation figures apart from statistics about the stamp and certainly no rate-cards listing the costing of placing ads; one in *The Times* cost more or less the same as in far smaller rival titles. Nevertheless, the business of placing advertisements was well-established. William Tayler served the country papers with news of parliament, official communications and the London markets, while also collecting advertising copy and undertaking to place it as effectively as possible. In 1812, William Lawson, who printed *The Times*, and a partner, Charles Barker, began the same way as Tayler, supplying metropolitan news to the provincial press, but soon, under Barker, concentrated on placing advertisements. Agents like Barker not only offered the possibility of ensuring coverage of a region through their contacts with a number of country titles, but because they could buy space in bulk, they also obtained advantageous rates. The power they came to wield increasingly exercised newspapers fearful for their editorial independence but they were generally seen as far less corrupting than the old system of political bribes and blackmails. Only *The Times*, safe behind (and much desired by advertisers because of) its circulation, remained immune from this threat. The combination of high circulation and strong advertising demand underpinned Barnes's editorial move to independence of party; but the centrality of the advertiser was signalled by the fact the front page each day consisted of nothing but small commercial announcements.

In New York advertising also wiped out the need for party subventions, destroying the American partisan press of the Jackson era. Gordon Bennett, with a very different readership from Barnes, nevertheless was also able to proclaim his 'independence'.[15] As in Britain, the business of placing ads created agents by the 1850s. In the 1870s, George Rowell bought space in bulk and resold it to advertisers 12 lines of copy a time – 'an-inch-of-space-a-month' – in 100 newspapers for a fee of $100, making himself handsome profits in the process. Soon agents began to offer professional copywriting and design services as well as the placement service.

Advertisements for both books and patent medicines remained staples and, in Britain, £10,000 a year was a common level of spend. The London *Morning Post* trebled its profits from this source to £12,400 between 1800 and 1819. In the late 1830s, the *Morning Chronicle* carried nearly 200 advertisements in every edition and *The Times* 480, despite the fact that the duty payable made advertising in the British stamped press about three times more expensive than it was in New York or Paris. Rothschild's advertised financial opportunities; during the 1840s boom the railway development companies advertised shares. Barker also handled ads for a wide range of less expected goods and services, the newly founded London University, for example, or election campaigns and charities.

Most significantly, amid the notices of auctions and announcements, the idea of the brand began to spread from patent medicines to all other goods. Most brands failed to establish themselves in public consciousness for long: who remembers 'CARTER'S THRIXALINE' ('TRAIN YOUR MOUSTACHE IN THE WAY IT SHOULD GO')? Others, though, are with us yet. Jacob Schweppe, who had set up a soft-drinks factory in London in 1792, began advertising the following year and by 1840 the company was using the royal arms in its copy. Packaging had much to do with the rise of branded groceries and medicines: paper bags were introduced in the 1850s and by the late 1860s could be overprinted, as could tins. Cardboard boxes followed. Wholesale manufacturers who, early in the century, had packaged their goods for retailers now began to use those retailers instead to sell those same goods, packaged and advertised with their own brand name. By 1871 there were 121 patented brands in America; within 30 years there were 10,000. All papers in the West, metropolitan and provincial, benefited from the move to brands, which were creatures, in many ways, of advertising.

In Britain, with the falling attractions of Chartism and rising mid-Victorian prosperity, it became ever clearer that advertisers and radical politics did not mix; nor did revolution appeal to the men of capital who now owned the labour-intensive, industrialised press. Populist Sundays and other weeklies threatened the circulation of radical papers and were also a proof that massive success could be achieved by others, not just *The Times*. Some sections of the Establishment now realised a cheap, distracting daily press could kill off the one and curb the other, but they confronted one main hindrance, the artificially high cover-prices caused by the newspaper taxes.

Direct censorship was long gone as a politically viable option. Bribery in Walpole's style had been washed away by advertising, which had also weaned the papers from the habit of blackmail. The taxes had not suppressed the radical press nor prevented *The Times* from pursuing whatever line it chose. These taxes were anyway absurd in their operation – that is, when they were not being ignored. For example, book reviews were not, for the purposes of the tax, 'public news, intelligences or occurrences'; theatre reviews were. In 1822, the then Home Secretary, Sir Robert Peel, halted prosecutions of tax-dodging publishers, as these trials usually caused riots; distributors, however, remained at risk.

In 1836 an Association of Working Men to Procure a Cheap and Honest Press, involving many of those who were also caught up in Chartism, had claimed that the taxes denied ordinary people 'any participation in the benefits of the readiest, the commonest, the chief vehicle of knowledge – the newspaper'. This was a brilliant spin: newspapers equalled knowledge and therefore the duties on them were 'taxes on knowledge'. An Association for the Promotion of the Repeal of the Taxes on Knowledge followed, led by the Chartists and liberal MPs who were fighting at the same time for the withdrawal of the Corn Laws.

For all that hindsight suggests that newspapers could be unfettered because a combination of low public taste and capital-intensive expenditure was making the press safe for capitalism, nevertheless the abolition of the taxes was a radical move. In France, there was not only a stamp tax, *l'impôt de timbre*, but also *le dépôt de cautionment*, a much more financially significant deposit required for both initial authorisation and, unlike Britain's one-off payment, regular reauthorisations every four months. Nevertheless, the press flourished. By the 1820s, the *Journal de Débats* was outselling *The Times*. Robert Hoe made his first European sale in Paris, to *La Patrie*; but the superior policing of the more centralised state bequeathed by Napoleon to his Bourbon and Orleanist successors had prevented the emergence of an unauthorised press on the British scale. In 1848, a year of European-wide revolutionary disorders which gave birth in France to a Second Republic, both *l'impôt* and *le dépôt* were swept away and hundreds of papers appeared in Paris, some – *L'Ami du peuple*, for example – recalling the 1790s. But, after the Republic imploded into the Second Empire four years later, the 67 press *lois, ordonnances, décrets, actes, chartes* and *Sénatus-consultes* which had been put in place since 1810 – including, of course, the financial burdens of stamp duty and authorisation deposits – were reimposed.

It was, then, no little matter for the Establishment across the Channel to nerve itself, in the name of a liberal notion of enlightenment and freedom, to lift the British duties; but lift them it did. The first abolition, significantly, was of the advertisement stamp in 1853. In 1855, the very year of the government's fall at the hands of the press over conduct of the Crimean War (at least in the opinion of the disgraced Cabinet), the liberal elements in Parliament forced through the repeal of the tax on newspapers. The tax on newsprint was abolished in 1861. By then, some 85 million copies a year were being sold, six copies for every adult in the land. By 1920, this figure was 182 copies per adult, with an annual sale of 5,604 million.

Among the flood of new titles, national and provincial, launched as the taxes were removed was a populist daily, the *Daily Telegraph and Courier*. Passing into the hands of its printer, Joseph Levy, who also published *The Sunday Times*, it lost the old-fashioned 'courier' in favour of the more up-to-date technology, and its price was halved to 1d. It was soon outselling *The Times* as Levy adopted journalistic intervention and news creation in the latest American style. (This editorial stance is the reason why the *Daily Telegraph* was the *New York Herald's* partner in underwriting Stanley's adventures in Africa.) By 1861, when the last tax on newsprint was removed, the *Daily Telegraph* was outselling *The Times* two to one. A decade later the *Telegraph*'s masthead claimed, with 240,000 copies a day, 'The Largest Circulation in the World'.[16]

In France, the same logic leading to a populist, cheap press was inescapable and slowly the duties and deposits were reduced there too. Oppositional publications managed to meet all the regulations, not just newspapers but also magazines, and reflected the diversity of political opinions, keeping alive the old tradition of the *canards*. Governments had gone beyond bribery to *amortissment*, covert ownership and the placement of their partisans as editors, but no intervention entirely bent the will of the press. As in Britain, there had to be a better way.

In February 1863 Paris saw its first tabloid, a 5-centimes paper, the *Petit Journal*. Populist and strenuously 'non-political' – that, of course, being in effect the political stance most acceptable to the authorities – the paper was an instance success. By July, its circulation was 38,000; by October, 83,000. Within two years, it was selling 259,000 (greater than the London *Daily Telegraph*) and had acquired a number of rivals. Three years after that, the authorisation requirement was abandoned in the *Loi du 11 mai 1868*. The stamp duty was lifted during the crisis of 1870, which saw the Prussians at the gates of Paris and the collapse of the Second Empire, but not until 1881 did the Third Republic finally repeal the rest of the tangled mass of previous legislation and bring in a new law. The *Loi du 29 juillet 1881 sur la liberté de la presse* begins: '*L'imprimerie et la librarie sont libres*'; and they were, more or less. The 1881 law still made it an offence to insult the President of the Republic, foreign heads of state, or the dead; or to defame public officials (including priests). Outraging public morals was also specifically *interdit*. *The Times* in London nevertheless congratulated the French on reaching this British (in fact, Whigg-ish) level of reform. It wrote, in an echo of Edward Clarke in 1695: 'a better press makes exceptional laws needless'. Experience now showed that 'better' did not actually mean a press more serious and more committed to coverage of burning social, economic and political issues. 'Better' meant better business.

By the end of the century, France could boast a

gutter press in heat, making its money out of pathological curiosity, perverting the masses . . . higher up on the scale the popular newspapers, selling for a sou [ ] inspire atrocious passions . . . [as well as] the higher so-called serious and honest press [ ] recording all with scrupulous care, whether it be true or false.

This last, at least, could also make space for Emile Zola's shattering intervention in the Dreyfus Affair. Zola, who wrote the above diatribe about the French press (in *Le Figaro*, 5 December 1897), thought to publish his attack on the French military establishment's cover-ups in the time-honoured form of a pamphlet, but changed his mind. As *Le Figaro*, where he had been placing his journalism, had decided to join the anti-Dreyfusards, he took the piece, an open letter to the President of the Republic, to *L'Aurore*. A special edition was published on 13 January 1898:

I accuse Lieutenant-Colonel du Paty de Clam of having been the diabolical artisan of judicial error . . . I accuse General Mercier . . . I accuse General Billot . . . General de Boisdeffre and General Gonse . . . General de Pellieux and Commandant Ravary . . . I accuse the three handwriting experts . . . I accuse the War Office . . . I accuse the first Court Martial . . . the second Court Martial . . . In bringing these accusations, I am not without realising that I expose myself in the process to articles 30 and 31 of the press law of 29 July, 1881 which punishes offences of libel. And it is quite willingly that I so expose myself . . . I am waiting. Rest assured, Mister President, of my deepest respect.

L'Aurore printed 300,000 copies.

The headline, *J'Accuse . . .!*, which stretched across four of the paper's six columns, was the idea of the paper's radical founder, the politician Georges Clemenceau, who at the end of his life became

133

France's implacable premier in the last years of the First World War. Clemenceau was a medical doctor by training but, as with the English radicals, when he turned to politics he saw partisan newspapers as being critical to his political project. He was far from alone in this. Continental politicians of all political hues could boast of journalism on their CVs. For example, the Hungarian nationalist Lajos Kossuth, who led the struggle in the 1840s against the Austrian Empire of which his country was then part, edited *Pesti Hirlap* and, during 1848, *Kossuth Hirlapia*.[17] Camillo Benso, the Count of Cavour, founded *Resurgence – il Risorgimento* – a daily dedicated to the unification of Italy (as the PROGRAMMA in the first edition, 15 December 1847, put it) '*dall'Alpi al mar Affrica*'. He became a conservative Piedmontese MP the following year and prime minister three years after that. He was able to bring much of the peninsula under the crown of Piedmont in a movement known to historians as *il Risorgimento*. Prince Otto von Bismarck, the parallel figure in the unification of Germany, found time to edit the *Norddeutsche Allegemeine Zeitung* in the early 1870s while also holding down the newly created job of German Imperial Chancellor. The possibility of press freedom along British or American lines was not an issue for him. After all, Germany had a long tradition of municipal publications with a heavy focus on commercial news, and the provision of public information was still seen as a legitimate government task.

This is not to say that the notion of an oppositional press along 'Anglo-Saxon' lines was unknown, but, whenever attempted, it was simply repressed. Karl Marx's first article, on 5 May 1842 for the liberal *Rheinische Zeitung für Politik*, which also carried news in the German tradition of *Handel und Gewerbe* (Trade and Commerce), was on newspaper censorship. He was 24 and the piece appeared on his birthday. Having suggested that 'You Germans can only express yourself at great length' he went on to write five more extensive pieces on the matter, concluding the series on 19 May with a quote from Heroditus which he addressed to the 'highly sage, practical bureaucrats . . . the hereditary leaseholders of political intelligence' who favoured censorship: 'You know what it means to be a slave, but you have never yet tried freedom.'

He had argued: 'The free press is the ubiquitous vigilant eye of a people's soul, the embodiment of a people's faith in itself, the eloquent link that connects the individual with the state and the world.' He started his own paper, the *Neue Rheinische Zeitung*, an *Organ der Demokratie*, in the Year of Revolutions but, by autumn of 1849, he had to keep his vigilant eye on Germany from exile in London.

For exiled militants, from the Italian nationalist Guiseppe Mazzini in the 1830s to the Marxist Russian Lenin in the 1900s, the newspaper, printed abroad and distributed illegally at home, was an essential radical tool. The authorities saw these underground publications as a spark which could ignite the flame of revolution and Lenin also hoped that this was so. He called his first such journal exactly that, *Iskra*, '*The Spark*', with the banner, 'From the spark to the flame'.

'The newspaper of the twentieth century'

In Britain and America, the spark was sensationalism and the flame a basic conformity. On both sides of the Atlantic, mass readership suggested the very style of the news should be less prolix, less hectoring than radical discourse demanded – Defoe's 'perfect style of language' accessible to all. This was somewhat at odds with the nineteenth century's usual orotund prose and much more like the tone of the first diurnals ('This day the king was beheaded . . . what passed before his death take thus'). Its lucidity gave an earnest of objectivity to the press which was reinforced by a new and extremely curious narrative style that had begun to emerge in the American papers after their Civil War. Instead of withholding information until denouement and climax in normal narrative order, reports now began to reveal all in the first paragraph. The rest of the story contained ever-greater detail and context in what came to be called an 'inverted pyramid' structure. One of the earliest examples can be found, not in a journalistic report but in what was really a press release, the cable dispatched by Lincoln's Secretary of War and *de facto* public-relations man, Edwin Stanton, to New York with news of the commander-in-chief's assassination in Washington on 14 April 1865. It was reprinted in many papers:

> This evening at about 9.30 P.M., at Ford's Theatre, the President, while sitting in his private box with Mrs. Lincoln, Mrs. Harris and Major Rathburn, was shot by an assassin, who suddenly entered the box and approached behind the President.
>
> The assassin then leaped upon the stage, brandishing a large dagger or knife, and made his escape to the rear of the theatre . . .
>
> Edwin M. Stanton
> Secretary of War

By contrast, the New York *Herald* began, admittedly under a flurry of ten single-column headlines: 'President Lincoln and his wife, with other friends, this evening visited Ford's Theatre, for the purpose of witnessing the performance of the "American Cousin".' Such chronological reports only slowly gave way to inverted pyramid stories but, reinforced by the need for concision necessitated by the telegraph, this new approach eventually created the dominant journalistic style in English which (not least because of the even greater terseness expected from broadcasting) is yet with us.

In Britain, which by the 1850s had become the first country where the majority of the population lived in towns, the extending provision of state education in the last third of the century created more and more readers for the popular press. The same pressures for mass urban entertainment that encouraged the growth of a sensational non-radical press, popular theatre and the world of 'attractions' also moved the pastimes of football and cricket to a higher level of organisation. The national football cup was first played for in 1872 and 'England' beat Australia in the first test match in 1877. Edward Hulton, a Manchester publisher, exploited this audience's interest in professionalised sport, including track and ring, by introducing a ½d local evening title with this as its primary focus. The horse-racing tipster's column became one of the most popular innovations of the ½d evening paper as Hulton's idea was widely copied in British cities (and no national evening title emerged to rival them). Seeking the same market, another Mancunian, George Newnes, a travelling salesman, had the thought that a weekly miscellany of brief stories clipped from other publications would also appeal. Within six months of its launch in October 1881, *Tit-Bits*, by then produced in London, was outselling any single daily edition of the *Daily Telegraph* three to one, at 900,000 copies a week.

In 1899, the proprietor of the successful ½d *Daily Mail* and the London *Evening News*, Alfred Harmsworth, found himself on a liner crossing the Atlantic with Joseph Pulitzer of the *New York Herald*. Harmsworth had worked on papers devoted to the main fad of the 1890s, cycling. From the editorship of *Bicycling News*, he had moved into publishing by copying *Tit-Bits* and by 1896, his *Any Answers* and a raft of sister publications – *Home Chats, Comic Cuts* – had prospered sufficiently for him to launch a national morning paper, the *Daily Mail*, billed as 'A 1d paper for ½d'. Cheapness had hitherto always indicated an intended working-class audience, but Harmsworth had himself endured a somewhat straitened childhood – his father was an unsuccessful barrister – and he always aligned himself with the lower middle classes, the clerks and shop-assistants, white-collar rather than blue. Although the *Mail* never shied from covering the sensational and luxuriated in gossip, it also had a sober-sided air which matched the respectable pretensions of this readership.

During the Atlantic crossing, Pulitzer and Harmsworth cooked up a little, mutually advantageous, 'stunt': Harmsworth would replace Pulitzer for one single edition of the *World*. Under him, on 1 January 1900, the paper appeared in a new form, 32 half-size pages. The Englishman called it a 'tabloid newspaper . . . the newspaper of the 20th century'.[18] As one of Pulitzer's rivals pointed out, '"Tabloid" journalism was successful here a hundred years ago; it is a century out of date now'; and, indeed, the 1c papers in the 1830s had saved costs by being small. Illustrated papers such as the New York *Daily Graphic*, founded in 1880 and a pioneer in the use of photographs, had also been constrained in size because of limitations on printing engraved plates. The French had long since related size to populism, exactly as Harmsworth now intended. Once the edition was published, the *World* went back to the broadsheet format and Harmsworth went back to England and the conservatively designed (and sized) *Daily Mail.*

In the early decades of the twentieth century, the *Mail*, with a circulation of some 800,000, achieved a dominance in the English newspaper marketplace matching that of the mid-nineteenth-century *Times*. This did not satisfy Harmsworth. He acquired other ailing titles, including, in 1908, a very sick and old-fashioned *Times*, its circulation shrunk to a mere 38,000. He also started new papers, notably the *Daily Mirror*, a tabloid specifically designed for women. *The Mail* had made a success of special features for women and Harmsworth insisted on at least one story of supposed female interest on every news page. Women and newspapers went together surprisingly well. They had been involved in distribution and had worked as 'she-intelligencers', and there was a well-established tradition of printers' and publishers' wives and widows keeping their imprisoned or deceased husbands' enterprises going. Specialised magazines for women had been available from the seventeenth century, and in the nineteenth century writing for the papers became one of few possible careers for a woman. It was not just Nellie Bly and not only in America. In Britain, Harriet Martineau, whose father's business collapsed after his death, was forced like Bly to earn a living. She did so by writing leaders and reviews for the *Daily News* from 1852, thereby becoming the 'she-Radical', one of the best-known figures of her day. W. T. Stead made a practice of employing women journalists from Hulda Friederichs, who disdained any special treatment as a female, to Annie Besant, the birth-control advocate. Lady Florence Dixie sent dispatches on the 1879 Zulu War to the *Morning Post*, thereby possibly becoming the first female war correspondent. In the 1890s, Rachel Beer for a time simultaneously edited both *The Sunday Times* (which she purchased in 1893) and the *Observer*.

Hearing that women journalists planning a new paper were meeting in Stead's office, Harmsworth jumped first and in 1903 founded the *Daily Mirror*, 'a daily newspaper for gentlewomen'. It was a disaster, the only one of his career. Circulation fell to 24,801 and the paper was soon losing £3,000 a week. Harmsworth reflected: 'It's taught me that women can't write and don't want to read.' This was clearly untrue, as the success of the *Daily Mail*'s women's material alone demonstrated; but the *Mirror* spoke to an absurdly limited idea of feminine interests, assuming that because some topic (fashion or cooking) attracted women, others (crime, sex and the rest of the day's events) did not. The daily for gentlewomen died in consequence, sacrificed perhaps on the altar of Harmsworth's own saccharine attachment to his mother.[19] The title survived, though. On 2 January 1904, with a war between Russia and Japan in the offing, the *Daily Mirror* appeared with a large front-page portrait of the Japanese admiral Tora Ijuin and a two-column photo of his sailors at gun-drill. Harmsworth had belatedly realised that a mirror was not only a female accoutrement, but also a reflection of the world in general. The *Mirror* was reborn as 'the first illustrated paper for ½d'.

Centuries of print making, itself an important element in the development of free expression, had fed into all the products of the letter press.[20] The development of new systems for imaging – including, in the last decades of the nineteenth century, photography – were inevitably melded with journalism. Half-tone photographic images had been successfully engraved and printed on flat-bed presses from 1880 on; by the following decade they were common. For example, the *Boston Journal* carried 21 such images for its Sunday edition, 6 May 1894, which it had printed on its Hoe presses. Printing illustrations became easier yet with the introduction of perfecting presses in 1897, and the taste for photographs had become strong enough for the appearance of the first staff photographers and photographic agencies.

On the type-setting side, development had been inhibited by the difficulties of mechanically manipulating types in an automatic device without causing jams and, just as serious, the perception that a type-setting machine would allow anybody – even women – to become compositors. The speed of the press and the needs of the market had however eventually produced a genuinely original development, the hot metal process. Created by Ottmar Mergenthaler in the 1880s, this was a keyboard-driven device which produced single lines of type in a slug. With this Lin-o-type machine, modern non-photographic printing was finally completely 'invented'. By 1895, *The Times*'s Hoes were capable of printing, cutting and folding 24,000 copies of a complete newspaper in an hour; but by then, across the Atlantic, the latest Hoe octuples were producing 48,000 16-page papers an hour. Colour presses were also introduced, so that Hearst, who was especially enthusiastic for this development, could ensure that 'The Yellow Kid' really was yellow. *Le Petit Journal* also had colour by the 1890s, but it was seen in most places as lacking seriousness, even by Britain's most popular papers, and limited to cartoons.

The newspaper as we know it had always been recognisable as such, even in its earliest newsbook form, but by the dawn of the twentieth century it was, more or less, exactly what it was to be at the dawn of the twenty-first. Columnists, initially only comedic commentators, would become serious and grow in authority. Muck-raking would be renamed investigative journalism. The (very) short story would disappear. Crosswords and horoscopes would appear. Sexual explicitness would resurface; but, in essence, it was as it was going to be. Take, entirely at random, the front page of the New York *Evening Graphic* for 18 October 1925: 'RUM FLIGHT IN BAY Liquor Valued at $100,00 Seized by Police' shared the front page with news that the ballerina Lenora Lopokova was seeking a divorce, her entire story encapsulated in a three-line caption beneath a very large photograph of the lady showing a lot of leg.[21] The genius of Western democracy had solved the 'problem' of the press at last. It functioned, apparently, as those who had cried for its liberty centuries earlier had wished; but, despite occasional offensiveness, it never really disturbed the peace. This trick was made flesh, if you will, in the persons of the press's leaders. Prince Albert might have thought William Russell of *The Times* 'a miserable scribbler', but Albert's son Edward, the Prince of Wales, made him an equerry for a royal tour of the Far East and Russell died Sir William.[22] Levy's son Edward was ennobled as Lord Burnham, and Harmsworth and his brother became the Viscounts Northcliff and Rothermere respectively, while three other brothers (from a family of 11 siblings) were knighted. Be he ne'er so vile nothing so surely gentled his condition as the ownership of a press, the more newspapers possessed the better.

In America, the crowning glory could not of course be entry into the nobility but merely the acquisition of untold wealth, largely through concentration of ownership. E. W. Scripps, for example, began moving to establish a chain of titles in the 1880s and in ten years he had 34 newspapers in 15 states. He started them up as cheaply as possible. In cities with populations of 50,000 to 100,000 he would put a man (always) with a $25,000 stake, the resources of the rest of the Scripps's group and a salary of $25 a week. The chosen one had to make the paper pay before the stake money ran out. By the time he died aged 71 in 1926, Scripps's empire contained 25 massively successful newspapers, the UPI news agency and a syndicated news service.

All this ennoblement and accumulation of capital does not quite mean that the essential purpose of the press was irrevocably lost, gone with the radical nineteenth-century papers, leaving it enchained, literally as well as metaphorically, by ownership patterns and commercial dictate. Despite these constraints, it could also, when the times demanded and the situation became desperate enough, still regain its most fundamental purpose, still fulfil its Miltonic (as it might be) function as an engine of free expression. Never so far, perhaps, in the history of the West has the press discharged that obligation with greater bravery, assiduity and effect than in Europe between 1939 and 1945. As the fascists engulfed the continent, trampling on the rights and the bodies of humanity, once again sparks from clandestine presses (and more modern duplicators) flew up. In the face of the Nazis' ubiquitous propaganda publications, such as the daily *Völkischer Beobachter*, from Greece to Denmark the underground production of alternative news and contrary opinions became a central resistance activity.

Courageous but not untypical, on the day after the German armour rolled across the Dutch border in the summer of 1940, a journalist typed a duplicator skin to produce the first edition of the *Nieuwsbreif de Pieter 't Hoen*: 'Exactly as we expected, it's happened. Without ultimatum, without declaration of war, the Germans have invaded our country . . .' The name ' 't Hoen' was, of course, a pseudonym. The newsman was F. G. Goedhart and his purpose was agitation. He wrote, more or less exactly, in the manner of the newsletters penned in Vienna as the Turks approached the city's gates just over four centuries earlier. In less than six months, seeking to break through his 7,000 circulation – a not inconsiderable number of copies to hand-crank off a duplicator regularly and in secret – he established an expanded editorial team and a broad illegal distribution system with the backing of the underground social democratic party. The sheet became *Het Parool*, 'The Word':

********************HET PAROOL********************

Vrij Onverveerd

No.1.   10 Februari 1941.

WE DON'T WANT THIS	N.S.B.[23] want a civil war!
	We'll get them!
	The Wehrmacht has given up.

The Wehrmacht had not, of course; but nor did Goedhart, his colleagues or his readers.

As the Nazis swept into northern France, the communists took their daily, *L'Humanité*, underground. The Gaullist resistance started a new clandestine paper, *Libération*. It was properly, if somewhat smudgily, printed. It proclaimed: 'Un seul chef: DE GAULLE, Une seule lutte: pour nos Libertés' and its ambition, its 'seul but', was to bring 'parole au Peuple Français'. The Gaullist resistance illegally printed and distributed 100,000 copies of each edition. But, as the bombs were falling on the other side of the Channel, the press was still free to show its alternative, equally time-honoured face. The *Daily Mirror*, for example, was serious enough for its criticism of Churchill in these early days of the war to bring the threat of a ban down on its head; yet in 1940 it could also run a headline such as 'WELL OF ALL THE LUCK' over a photograph of two young women with the caption:

> On the hottest day of the year, these two girls set out for a day's work at a film studio in Denham. And found that their job was to be photographed in their undies . . . And if that isn't luck on a blazing day, we'd like to know what is.

In the Commons debate on the proposed banning of the paper, Aneurin Bevan effectively quoshed it by demanding: 'How can we . . . speak about liberty if the Government are doing all they can to undermine it?'

On Friday 18 August 1944, with the Allies in Chartres, Dreux and Orléans, the French collaborationist press failed to appear. *L'Humanité* and *Libération* came out of hiding (as *Het Parool* was to do) to publish freely. All three still publish – as does the *Daily Mirror*.

The press system perfected in the West in the second half of the nineteenth century is one whose crucial value to human rights is, as it were, latent. In the darkness of oppression, control and terror, it can display its true worth. In (more or less) peaceful everyday Western light, the press hides this worth beneath a veneer of titillations, libels, misrepresentations, invasions of privacy and other abuses, but even in these weak piping times the traditions of an unauthorised, oppositional, fundamentally 'unstamped' press have never entirely died. In the words of H. L. Menken, one of America's greatest twentieth-century newspapermen, the duty of the journalist remains: 'to comfort the afflicted and afflict the comfortable'. But, as has always been the case, high-mindedness does not tell the whole story of journalism's functions – amusing the punters, selling snake-oil and, above all, making money are just as long-established and equally persistent. What Western press freedom really means in everyday practice has never been better summed up than it was by another great American journalist writing in the mid-twentieth century, A. J. Liebling:

Anybody in the ten-million-dollar category is free to buy or found a paper in a great city like New York or Chicago, and anybody with around a million (plus a lot of sporting blood) is free to try it in a place of mediocre size like Worcester, Mass. As to us, we are free to buy a paper or not, as we wish.

Sources

Hannah Barker (1998), *Newspapers, Politics and English Society 1695–1855*, Oxford: Clarendon Press.

C. Bellanger (1969), *Histoire général de la presse française*, Paris: Presses Universitaires de France.

Jeremy Black (2001), *The English Press 1621–1861*, Stroud: Sutton.

George Boyce, James Curran and Pauline Wingate (eds) (1978), *Newspaper History from the 17th Century to the Present Day*, London: Constable.

Jean-Denis Bredin (1986), *The Affair: The Case of Alfred Dreyfus*, New York: George Braziller.

John Carey (ed.) (1987), *Eyewitness to History*, Cambridge, Mass.: Harvard University Press.

Edward Cook (1915), *Delane of the Times*, London: Constable.

G. A. Cranfield (1978), *The Press and Society: From Caxton to Northcliffe*, London: Longman.

James Curran and Jean Seaton (2003), *Power without Responsibility*, London: Routledge.

Maurice Edelman (1966), *The Mirror: A Political History*, London: Hamish Hamilton.

Blanche Elliot (1962), *History of English Advertising*, London: Business Publications.

Edwin and Michael Emery (1984), *The Press and America*, Englewood Cliffs, NJ: Prentice Hall.

Matthew Engel (1996), *Tickle the Public: One Hundred Years of the Popular Press*, London: Victor Gollancz.

Trevor Fisher (1995), *Scandal: The Sexual Politics of Late Victorian Britain*, Stroud, Glos.: Sutton.

Michael Harris and Alan Lee (eds) (1986), *The Press in English Society from the Seventeenth to the Nineteenth Centuries*, Rutherford, NJ: Fairleigh Dickinson University Press.

Philip Knightley (1975), *The First Casualty*, New York: Harvest.

Brooke Kroeger (1994), *Nellie Bly*, New York: Random House.

A. J. Liebling (1964), *The Press*, New York: Ballantine.

David Mindich (1998), *Just the Facts*, New York: New York University Press.

Frank Luther Mott (1962), *American Journalism*, New York: Macmillan.

T. R. Nevett (1982), *Advertising in Britain*, London: Heinemann.

Barbara Onslow (2000), *Women of the Press in 19th Century Britain*, London: Macmillan.

R. G. G. Price (1957), *A History of Punch*, London: Collins.

Christopher Silvester (ed.) (1993), *The Penguin Book of Interviews*, London: Viking.

Anthony Smith (1979), *The Newspaper: An International History*, London: Thames & Hudson.

Louis Snyder and Richard Morris (eds) (1962), *A Treasury of Great Reporting*, New York: Simon & Schuster.

Susan Strasser (1989), *Satisfaction Guaranteed*, Washington, DC Smithsonian.

Dorothy Thompson (1984), *The Chartists*, New York: Pantheon.

Michael Twyman (1970), *Printing 1700–1970*, London: Eyre & Spottiswood.

Keith Waterhouse (1989), *Waterhouse on Newspaper Style*, London: Penguin/Viking.

Bernard Weisberger (1961), *The American Newspaperman*, Chicago: University of Chicago Press.

Francis Williams (1957), *Dangerous Estate: The Anatomy of Newspapers*, London: Longmans, Green.

Keith Williams (1977), *The English Newspaper*, London: Springwood.

IMAGES, SPECTACLE
AND SOUND

Prologue II

'*LEAL SOVVENIR*': IMAGING
FROM 1413

'Reflection painting'

In or before 1413, Filippo Brunelleschi, like Gutenberg a master gold-smith, entered the cathedral in Florence, turned his back on its interior and, settling in the doorway, prepared to make a painting of Giotto's Baptistery in the piazza opposite. Filippo – bald, argumentative and unkempt – was the very model of an eccentric artist of the day: a multi-talented architect, engineer and scientist who scarcely bothered with drawing and painting except as design tools for other work. The church he was in, at this date, was still in part under construction. Within a few years, he was himself to design and build its dome. Some of the doors of the building he painted were also unfinished and Lorenzo Ghiberti, another goldsmith and Filippo's great rival, was labouring on the bas-reliefs to complete them. Brunelleschi's painting, now lost, was to be the first perspective image using a single vanishing point to be recorded in the history of Western art. It was followed almost immediately by fur-ther experiments along the same lines painted by Tommaso di Ser Giovanni de Mone, known as Masaccio, Hulking Tom. Masaccio's fres-cos in the churches of Santa Maria Novella and Santa Maria del Carmine contain such startling novelties as barrel-vaulted roofs and golden halos, seemingly floating in three dimensions.

The largely illiterate medieval European world was suffused by images. In contrast to the word, decipherment of which could be accomplished by only the few, pictures and statuary illustrating Christianity's master narrative were understandable by all. Churches

149

were festooned with paintings, carvings and decoration. Yet most significantly for media development, there was no code in use in the West whereby three-dimensional space could be represented on a flat surface. Techniques for representing the human form realistically were in abeyance, the ancient mature styles of Rome and Greece apparently forgotten, never mind those that existed in the East. In the ancient Western world, the abstractions of the Attic had given way between the fifth century BC and the time of Christ to the verisimilitude of the Romans. Now, as Brunelleschi turned his back on the nave of the Florentine Duomo, the West was to succumb again to such illusionism. It was to be an addiction, this pursuit of verisimilitude; and more than half a millennium later most westerners are still in its thrall.

The reintroduction of a system for representing space on a flat surface can be seen, like printing, at least in part as a product of urbanisation. The market economy of the town required a highly developed sensitivity to space, especially to volume. Trade was conducted using unstandardised containers – sacks, barrels, bottles, crates – and the complex business of calculating how much they contained was an essential part of a burgher's education – and artists, too. For example, among the writings of Piero della Francesco, who was to be as well known as a mathematician as he was as a painter, can be found *The Short Book on the Five Regular Solids*. The conversations Brunelleschi, Masaccio and their circle were having in Florence in the early 1400s could well have taken in this everyday problem. There were also surviving examples of ancient perspective painting which, together with architectural and sculptural remains, were being increasingly carefully examined. Brunelleschi had himself travelled to Rome to make exactly such a study.

It could be that, despite this context, Brunelleschi was moved to make his image of the Baptistery as a sort of hoax. He was given to practical jokes. In 1409 he had, with the help of numerous accomplices, sought to convince a master carpenter by whom he thought himself slighted that the man was not himself but another person altogether. Brunelleschi arranged for people to call the carpenter by another name, denying that he was who he claimed to be, while Brunelleschi changed the locks on the man's house and so on. By 1413, Brunelleschi was at odds with Ghiberti, to whom he had lost the competition to make the Baptistery bas-reliefs. Brunelleschi painted the Baptistery on wood and mounted this panel on a hand-held frame facing a mirror. He drilled a hole through the wood and, on the back of the panel, affixed a funnel to this aperture. Looking through the funnel allowed the viewer to see nothing but the mirror; and the mirror reflected nothing but the painting. Brunelleschi demonstrated the effect by having the viewer stand on the exact spot within the Duomo that he had occupied to make the painting. The image therefore replaced the reality. Ghiberti's solid bas-reliefs became a fiction, a joke. Brunelleschi could have done just as well. At the same time, the complex process Brunelleschi imposed on viewers fixed their eye in line with the vanishing point of the image and forced them into seeing what he wanted them to see. What could have begun as a joke led to what was to become a ubiquitous new way of seeing in the West.

That he sat in the doorway of the Duomo is perhaps a crucial clue to understanding what he was about. It is probable that he imagined that the space of the door was an invisible, transparent sheet upon which the image of the Baptistery and the piazza around it was projected. The space of the doorway was, as it were, the base of a pyramid the apex of which was at the centre of his view of the Baptistery. In his 1435/6 book *Della pictura* another of Brunelleschi's friends, Leon Battista Alberti, explains to the artist how to perform this trick. You need, advises Leon Battista, a *velo*, a veil:

> . . . a thin veil, finely woven . . . This veil I place between the eye and the thing seen, so the visual pyramid penetrates through the thinness of the veil. This veil can be of great use to you . . . you will be easily able to constitute the limits of the outline or the surface [of things] . . . you will be able to put everything in its place.

There are woodcuts by Albrecht Dürer, dating from the 1520s, which show artists using frames with such a transparent *velo* in exactly this way. In one, the veil is divided into a grid of small squares, as is the paper upon which the artist draws. It is an aid to the eye/brain in delineating an 'object which occupies a space' (as Alberti has it) on a flat surface.

There is no evidence that Alberti, Brunelleschi and their circle had direct experience of seeing a projected image and gleaning from that the inspiration for Alberti's 'veil'; but they could have.

> If . . . a small hole is drilled in a wall [of a very dark room] . . . then all objects illuminated by the sun will send their images through this aperture . . . You will then catch these pictures on a piece of white paper which is placed vertically in the room not far from that opening and you will see all the objects on this paper in their natural shapes and colours, but they will appear smaller and upside down, on account of the crossing of the rays in the aperture.

This is Leonardo da Vinci, with a lucidity seldom encountered in the pre-modern scientific writing of his era, describing a *camera obscura*, a dark room, in his secret notebooks half a century after the publication of *Della pictura*. This, however, was no 'invention' of da Vinci's. Knowledge of such dark rooms was widespread and centuries old, even in the West and certainly in the East where the phenomenon had been first noticed, by the Arabs in the ninth century at the latest, as being of use for astronomical observations. It had been recorded in Europe four hundred years later.

The first published notice of the *camera obscura* as an imaging device comes, in the generation after da Vinci, in a far more typically obscurantist account by Giovanni Baptista della Porta. Giovanni's prototypical Renaissance mix of erudition, credulity, self-aggrandisement and naïveté produced many voluminous treatises, including *Magiae naturalis* (1553) in which he gives an account of the *camera obscura*, finally bringing it to the attention of a learned public albeit a small one. The description obscurely begins: 'Now I wish to announce something about which I have kept silent and which I believed I must keep secret' – quite why is hard for the modern mind to grasp. A decade later, in 1568, for the first time in the record, there is mention of a lens in place of the pinhole. The lens massively improved the definition of the image on the wall. In the first decade of the next century, the room was shrunk, as it were, into a tube around this lens. A second lens was fixed in place to close off the other end of the tube to produce a tele-scope. Within six months of the introduction of this device in October 1608, Galileo had heard about it in Venice and, with an improved ver-sion he built himself, soon saw the mountains of the moon and the moons of Jupiter.

There was no reason for the apparatus either to remain room-size or to shrink to a tube – it could be small but retain its shape. Indeed, Alberti had made 'demonstrations' (whatever that may mean) through a tiny opening in a 'little closed box', which could well have been a shrunken *camera obscura*.[1] There is no technical bar to his having done so. Certainly, and without publicity, some time in the first half of the seventeenth century the room shrank with a lens still attached, to become a wooden box, the *camera obscura portabilis*, the direct ances-tor of the modern camera. The lens was fixed on one side of the box and a ground glass was mounted opposite. Like Alberti's earlier veil, this optic box was also of use as an artist's aid. The image it produced can be thought of as being constructed in a variant form of single-van-ishing-point perspective, one that was to be more influential in Northern European, specifically Dutch, art. References to the box were enthusiastic. Constantijn Huygens, who saw one in London in 1622, called the effects of this instrument 'reflection painting': 'It is not pos-sible to describe to you the beauty of it in words: all painting is dead in comparison, for here is life itself.'

It was also discovered that, by putting a source of illumination behind a clear glass, the lens could be made to project any image drawn upon that glass, albeit, if uncorrected, upside down. The earliest refer-ence to the existence of such a projector is in a letter from the scientist Christiaan Huygens, Constantijn's son, in 1656, the year in which he also built the first pendulum clock. Compared with his improved time-keeper, never mind his work on the calculus of probabilities (published when he was 22), Christiaan thought the projector, which he dismissively named the 'Magic Lantern', was a mere 'bagatelle' and he abandoned it, although he did describe it in print in 1659. Two weeks before the Great Fire of London in 1666, Samuel Pepys had noted in his diary: 'Comes by agreement Mr. Reeves bringing an lanthorn with pictures in glasse to make strange things appear on the wall, very pretty.' Reeves had been in the business of marketing magic lanterns at least since 1663. He had in fact built one on Christiaan's instructions.

As Constantijn Huygens's reference to an 'instrument' makes clear, the dark room must have already become a portable box in the first decades of the seventeenth century. The first explicit reference to it as an artist's aid in print, however, dates from 1665. In that year, a *camera obscura portabilis*, complete with moveable lens mounted in its own tube to aid focusing and a mirror arrangement to reverse the inversion of the image, was fully described by Johann Zahn.

These devices emerged from a world of scientific inquiry to which they made little contribution; but, more curiously, there is also a paucity of evidence about their actual use by artists. Despite the recommendations of artists' handbooks as to their utility, no tracing made with the help of a *camera obscura*, *portabilis* or not, has survived – nevertheless, such paper sketches certainly existed. There is, for instance, an engraving of two men inside a full-size *camera obscura* examining a landscape sketch, significantly held upside down, in a medical textbook of 1664. The innovative perspectival systems of the Italians and the Dutch, locking the eye into a fixed position, were of a piece with the new sciences' concentration on observation. The triumph of perspective, albeit at the cost of the previous faith-based medieval system of representation, was an essential precondition for the rise of what has been called a 'lens culture' in the West. Pictorial space was created through the use of a particular code of representation that was both influenced by, and reflected, the lenses of the *camera obscura* and the magic lantern, unaffected by such consideration as the need to, for example, always represent the mature Christ figure as the largest in the image irrespective of where it was placed. Single vanishing viewpoint encouraged the dominance of realism of one sort or another for the better part of the next half-millennium.

Fuelled by the needs of the merchant as much as the imagination of the artist, this illusionism worked, as did printing, as an engine of free expression and a reflection of individuality. The only regular exception to medieval art's limited repertoire of Christian iconography had been pictures of everyday work to be found in miniature in the margins of illuminated manuscripts like the *Très riches heures*. Now, though, pagan gods, contemporary battles and even bowls of fruit and dead game appeared in large-scale works. Yet nowhere had the likeness of the individual established itself as a form. In the post-classical West, only in the funeral effigy could be found any attempt at realistically representing a particular person. The true image of the living individual, the portrait, arrives surreptitiously in European art. At the beginning of the four-teenth century, Giotto inserted likenesses of his friends into large-scale religious paintings as bystanders in a holy scene. More than a century later, just a decade or so before people began to refine moveable type, on 10 October 1432, Jan van Eyck, *valet de chambre* – actually court painter – to Philip the Good, Duke of Burgundy, dated a portrait of a man in his thirties.

Van Eyck is conventionally credited with the 'invention' of oil paint and the picture is in the new medium. The man is plainly but fashion-able dressed in red fur-trimmed coat and green hat. He gazes out of the frame to his right but his head and torso, seen from the waist up, are isolated against a plain dark-hued background. There is not a trace of religious iconography in the image. We do not know for certain who the sitter was but Jan has suggested, in a classical allusion etched into the parapet upon which the figure is supposedly leaning, that the man was either a musician (Gilles Binchois has been proposed) or a sculptor, Gilles de Blanchère. On this same parapet van Eyck has painted, as if engraved in the stone, the legend, LEAL SOVVENIR – 'Loyal Remembrance'. This echoes the effigies of the past but also hints at the verisimilitude of the future. It is van Eyck's guarantee that the picture accurately counterfeits, that is 'imitates', the man. As Gutenberg was dreaming up moneymaking schemes in Strasbourg and as Alberti was publishing in Florence, so van Eyck was adding the portrait of the living individual, *au vif*, to the established genres of painting in Bruges.

Printers soon followed and by the next century images of the famous, such as those published by Jean Thevet in the 1570s, were a commonplace. Some might have been quick to use and reuse the same woodblock or engraving with different captions if they thought it would sell, but authentic portraits were not unknown. A book published in Milan in 1479 featured the author's image and Dürer, master of the *velo*, financed trips amongst the Flemish not only by selling his prints of the Passion at two florins a set but also by executing portrait drawings for a florin. On one trip in the 1520s, he made more than 140 of these and was able to send home assorted luxury items and curiosities including animal horns, a branch of coral and a wooden weapon from India. Lucas Cranach the Elder made three popular likenesses of his friend, Martin Luther, in 1520/1 and Dürer profitably captured Erasmus and Philip Melanchton, also in the 1520s. In the past, only coinage had widely duplicated an individual's image – in the nature of the case, normally the image of the ruler. Now, faces from the ranks of reform and the 'Republic of Letters', as well as the aristocracy, were also to be found in goodly numbers.

In painting, the portrait genre produced variants from full-length figures to head and shoulders, from direct gaze to classical profile, from blank setting to realistic (or fantastical) environment. The rising bourgeoisie in the cities, ever growing in number, wanted to have their image preserved as much as did their betters. On occasion, the desire was prompted by nothing more than the then rather rare acquisition of a new suit of clothes. It became a mark of aristocracy, though, to command large-scale portraits and a protocol developed around what constituted images appropriate for rank. It was usually the case that the more important the person, the more of the body it was suitable to represent. Full-length portraits were normally reserved for royalty. Middling sorts had to make do with nothing bigger than an image from the waist up.

For example, Rembrandt's full-length image of his friend Jan Six, the son of one of Amsterdam's leading merchants, remains an exception that proves the rule. Size conventions were crucial to the decorum of the portrait and were to be long-lived. In general, though, the sense that portraiture was connected to power meant that staking a claim to having one's image produced at any size either as a painting or a print was a facet of the general Western struggle for liberties of all kinds.

Étienne de Silhouette became controller general of France in 1759 and audaciously proposed a land tax on the nobility. He was immediately driven from office but his name became a byword for the basic state to which he wished to reduce the nobles. They were to be, in their view, mere silhouettes of their former grand selves, and this term was popularly used from that time on to describe a basic image – a shadow outline, usually of a profile, infilled with a dark colour. Making these had been a fashionable craze when Silhouette had his moment of power. In the next generation, the same desire for the image of the individual drove the development of the 'physionotrace', which mechanised the process a stage further. All one had to do was follow a person's profile through the cross-hairs of a surveyor's glass and a clever arrangement of pencil and pantograph would reproduce the movement of the glass as a line on a piece of paper.

Silhouettes and physionotraces were indicators that a need for a fully automated mechanically aided system of image making was slowly revealing itself, as the class which developed the taste for such things grew in influence and numbers. The continued popularity of the print, which in a religious form had antedated printing from moveable type, spoke to the same social driver. The range of available images embraced all the subjects of painting, even including pornographic pictures such as those illustrating Piero Aretino's obscene verses, *I Modi* (1525). The first shop dedicated to selling prints had been established in Antwerp in 1550. In 1732 Hogarth had taken 1,240 guineas for his print series 'The Harlot's Progress', about 15 times as much as he made auctioning the six original paintings. It is no wonder that he was eager to protect his prints and in 1735 persuaded Parliament to give copyright protection to

'Designers, Engravers, Etchers etc.' – a piece of legislation known as 'Hogarth's Act'. In 1808, from a modern gas-lit showroom in London, Rudolph Ackermann began offering what would become his first best seller, *Microcosm of London*. The prints were hand-coloured by impecunious refugees from the French Revolution and eventually numbered 107,000. That same year, Alois Senefelder, a failed actor and printer, was bringing to market a chemically based system of print-making from a flat stone, known as lithography. He published a lithograph reproduction of a missal illustrated originally by Dürer, copied by an artist on to the stone.

'La peinture est morte'

In 1816, a wealthy amateur scientist, Joseph Nicéphore Niépce, among whose interests was this new system of lithography, captured images on paper treated with silver nitrate – or so he wrote to his brother. Yet he remained frustrated with his experiments because not only did the images turn black when he attempted to look at them but they also reversed light and dark. Niépce was working in a tradition already nearly a century old. In the 1720s, Professor Doctor Johann Schultze, in addition to his medical practice, had been researching phosphors when he discovered that silver nitrates darkened in light.[2] He had conducted a series of experiments in which he treated a glass pane with a silver nitrate wash or film and by laying objects against these sensitised plates produced a number of what we would today call photograms; but he, like Niépce, had no way of stopping the darkening process and 'fixing' the image. The same problem had frustrated Thomas Wedgwood, a scion of the pottery family and another keen amateur scientist, in the first years of the nineteenth century. His photograms of leaves slowly turned black, even as he inspected them fitfully by candlelight. Wedgwood further thought to place photosensitised material – white leather, for example – against the back-plate of a portable camera but, as he wrote to his contemporary, the scientist Sir Humphrey Davy, 'the images formed . . . have been too faint to produce, in any moderate time, an effect upon the nitrate of silver'.

Niépce was more persistent. To tackle at least one of the problems he faced, he turned from chemicals that darkened in the light to those which light caused to bleach, reasoning that in this way he would be able to capture a positive image rather than a negative one. By 1822, he was using asphaltum and paper first made transparent by oiling. There is some question as to whether or not a *camera obscura portabilis* was involved or whether these were also a species of photogram; but certainly, and in contrast to lithography, no draftsman was needed. By 1826, still in pursuit of what he called 'heliography', writing (or better, etching) by sunlight, he had managed to create a half-toned image by direct contact, in effect a species of what would become known as photogravure. He solved his second problem, fixing, by using a wash of petroleum mixed with oil of lavender. The picture he made was of a copy of a portrait print of a famous man, Cardinal d'Amboise.

That same year, he had the same thought as Wedgwood. He ordered the construction of three *camera obscura*, one as small as a large matchbox. Using a square plate made of pewter and coated with a film of Bitumen of Judea mounted on the back of one of these cameras, after several hours of exposure, he produced a photograph of the view from his window.[3] It seems likely that Niépce was aware of the commercial possibilities of 'heliography' as an alternative system to lithography for reproducing engravings, but that the uses to which images taken directly from nature, like the view from his window, might be put remained somewhat hidden from him. Such was not the case with the artist/showman and proprietor of the Diorama, Louis Jacques Mandé Daguerre, who was to become his partner.

As jobbing artists had done for more than a century at least, Daguerre used a *camera obscura* in the production of his paintings. These huge super-realistic canvases were the heart of his Diorama spectacle, one of the most successful illusionist attractions of the early nineteenth century.[4] He was brought together with the secretive, provincial landowner Niépce by their mutual lens maker. After three years of negotiations amidst much hesitancy, in 1829 they came to a formal agreement to establish a company to exploit heliography. Niépce brought to the table (in the words of this contract) 'the automatic reproduction of the image received by the *camera obscura*', the 'invention'. Daguerre, on the other hand, noting that heliography 'is capable of great perfection, offers to join with M. Niépce to achieve this perfection and to gain all possible advantages from this new industry'. Each provided 50 per cent of the funds needed to set up the firm and each was to receive 50 per cent of the profits.

Daguerre knew little of optics (although he did understand theatrical lighting effects, the other main element of the Diorama) and nothing of chemistry, but he could learn. He returned to experimenting with silver nitrate but it was not until 1837, by which time Niépce had died, that he finally stumbled across the last elements of a complete system. Having left a number of exposed blank iodised copper plates in a cupboard, he discovered, weeks later, that perfect images had formed on them by accident. Among the bric-à-brac stored in the cupboard was an open bowl of metallic mercury, fumes from which had caused the latent images on the iodised silver plates to 'develop'. Daguerre's iodine, mercury and silver nitrate was 60 to 80 times more sensitive than Niépce's bitumen. The heliograph had been 'perfected'. It had become a 'daguerreotype'.

Daguerre, now partnered by Isidore Niépce, Joseph's son, agreed to keep the process secret and reveal it only to adventurous capitalists for not less than 200,000 francs. Although there was increasing scientific interest as Daguerre publicised his breakthrough throughout 1838, capitalists could not see the point and there were simply no takers. Daguerre then turned to François Arago, a prominent member of both the Academy of Sciences and the Chamber of Deputies, to facilitate a deal with the French government. Arago had more success and, for this expression of French genius, it was agreed that the partners were to receive annual pensions of 6,000 francs for Daguerre and 4,000 for Isidore. The government was to retain all rights to the process.

Arago, in selling the idea of the pensions to his fellow politicians, acknowledged that the interests of the 'inventors' could not be 'adequately protected by ordinary patent laws'. It is possible to see why. Daguerre was a painter, a showman and an entrepreneur, not a serious scientist. The fumes of iodine and mercury apart, what else could he be said to have 'invented'? The camera was an object in common manufacture, albeit for specialised artistic uses. The light sensitivity of silver nitrate had been understood since 1727, more than a century earlier. Others, such as Wedgwood, had put camera and silver nitrate together long since. Daguerre, after having used other washes, had by 1839 determined that a hyposulphite would be the best 'fixative'; but the property of such salts to dissolve the silver nitrate effectively had been announced by Sir John Herschel in 1819 (without, admittedly, tying this to the blackening problem). Neither Daguerre nor Niépce could offer any scientific explanation as to why their chemicals behaved in the way that they did. There were, therefore, good reasons for old Niépce's secrecy trait and Daguerre's caution in revealing the process. In his speech to the Chamber, on 3 July 1839, Arago asked, but did not quite answer the question: 'Is the process of M. Daguerre unquestionably an original invention?' In fact, it was no more and no less so than is normally the case with new media.

Arago was on firmer ground when he addressed the usefulness of the process to the sciences (especially archaeology) and the fine arts. He proposed making faultless daguerreotype copies of hieroglyphics *in situ* and recording, on a regular basis, weather conditions, adding images of the sky to thermometer and barometer readings. These, though, were not the applications that, finally, had caused so many elements to fuse together in the 'invention' of photography. Arago's speech made little of the growing pressure in the decades between Wedgwood and Daguerre which caused the breakthrough – the ever-expanding industrialising bourgeoisie's taste for images, including portraits of themselves. Daguerre's publicity in 1838 had stirred up a hornets' nest of opposition among the ranks of jobbing artists who made their living catering to this need, but Arago simply denied that the process 'would be detrimental to our artists and especially our engravers' by hiding behind the painter Paul Delaroche's back. Delaroche's public view was that the daguerreotype could function as a substitute for sketching and save the artist much labour but leave the final business of painting intact; but this was the same Delaroche who had supposedly declared, on leaving Daguerre's studio earlier in 1839, 'La peinture est morte à partie de ce jour', a far more memorable (if probably apocryphal) opinion.

Daguerre got his pension and the French government gave the process to the world (except Great Britain, where it was locally patented by Daguerre's agent). Apart from his official stipend, Daguerre further enhanced his fortune by joining forces with a camera manufacturer. A complete outfit, including chemicals and certified by himself as authentic, cost some 400 francs. Within months the price fell to a quarter of this, but such was the craze for daguerreotyping that Daguerre was soon able to retire to become himself a country landowner.

Daguerre's earliest images, including those he dispatched as part of his publicity campaign, were of views. One sent to the Emperor of Austria was of Notre Dame, framed, as all daguerreotypes had to be because of their fragility, under glass:

> The scale is probably 1/1000 of natural size. It is necessary therefore to use a magnifying glass in order to view the details of the picture. And then the tiny pointed arches of the church windows, the smallest architectural ornament, hardly perceptible to the eye in reality . . . [are] shown in such perfection that any other image is poor in comparison.

Travelling daguerreotypists were on the road before the end of 1839, including some prescient artists such as Horace Vernet. He had specialised in painting battle scenes but now, sensing that a niche market might exist, he took his new camera and chemical apparatus to Malta and Smyrna. The first travel book illustrated with engravings of daguerreotypes, Adolphe Goupil's Excursions daguerriennes, appeared the following year. Soon it was possible to own an album of copies of the paintings in the Louvre; but photography could do more than reproduce. It could offer personalised detailed images, pictures of individuals permitting, for the first time, a true democratisation of the portrait.

It is probable that Daguerre himself did not attempt the making of portraits because of the lengthy exposures required. Yet, given the phenomenon that everything in motion during the long exposures disappears (not being *in situ* long enough to register), a solitary figure does appear in one of his street scenes, the Boulevard du Temple, made before the end of 1839. This anonymous man on the pavement did not disappear because he was trapped into stillness having his shoes polished. He was, unwittingly, the first person to have his photograph taken. Other daguerreotypists would be less deterred and, with the help of devices like neck- and head-rests, pressed ahead with immobilised sitters. Given the old relationship between social status and image, it is perhaps entirely appropriate that the first daguerreotype portrait we know of was taken in that bastion of nineteenth-century democracy, the United States, also in 1839. This picture, made by Professor John Draper of his assistant, required the man to remain still for half an hour.

Like Vernet, but unlike less far-sighted French artists, Professor Samuel Morse, the American portrait painter and Draper's colleague, was much taken with the daguerreotype and saw its potential as a system for producing images of the individual. He had met Daguerre himself in the winter of 1838 when he was in Paris to publicise a technological development of his own, the telegraph. He made his first daguerreotype, the view from his window at what was to become New York University, in September 1839 with a 15-minute exposure. The following year he took the first known group portrait, of his Yale classmates at a reunion in New Haven. The telegraph then took up all his attention but others, tinkering with the chemistry of the process and increasing the aperture of the lens, continued to obtain results with ever-shorter exposure times.

By 1841, exposure times were still forbiddingly long but had fallen considerably; for example, the Viennese firm of Voigtländer, creators of a smaller, metal camera specifically for daguerreotyping, recommended in that year the following procedure 'for the making of portraits':

> The person to be photographed must be seated in the open air. For an exposure by overcast, dark skies in winter 3½ minutes is sufficient; on a sunny day in shade 1½ to 2 minutes are enough, and in direct sunlight it requires no more than 40–45 seconds.

Poor images, using exposures of as little as a second, had already been obtained. By 1842, it was possible to have one's picture taken 'by Daguerre's process in 20–40 seconds, according to the latest and improved method!'

Although daguerreotypes were as varied in subject matter as was painting, the earliest direct commercial exploitation of the process centred on this business of portraits and confirmed this as the fundamental social driver that underlay the technology. The world's first daguerreotype studios were opened in 1840 on a New York University roof and in London on a roof belonging to the Royal Institution,[5] where the world's first course in daguerreotyping was offered in 1841. In the London studio, they were soon taking an astonishing average of £150 a day for portraits made, as the publicity had it, 'by the sacred radiance of the sun'. Open studios rapidly became glasshouses and the superior effect of using blue glass was soon noticed (and patented). Studios proliferated with a rapidity that spoke to the built-up strength of the social need photography was meeting and, unsurprisingly given their original academic locales, daguerreotypists often took to styling themselves as 'professor'. By 1842–3 most major towns and cities in the American West had a studio. The classic phrase, 'Watch the dicky bird' dates from 1843. By 1844 a New York practitioner, Matthew Brady, conceived the idea of a National Historical Portrait Gallery and began daguerreotyping every person of distinction whom he could persuade to sit for him. The first nudes appeared in the late 1840s. By then, New

York City alone boasted 100 (respectable) studios. It is estimated that in 1853, at the height of daguerreotyping's popularity in the United States, some 3,000,000 were made, but it was already an obsolete technique.

François Arago spoke of 'photography' in his July speech, but neither Niépce nor Daguerre had ever used this term. 'Photography' was apparently coined by the astronomer Sir John Herschel in connection with a rival process to Daguerre's even as it was coming to public notice in the early months of 1839. The term was used in a German newspaper article on this other system in February and Sir John employed it himself on 14 March when he spoke before the Royal Academy in London. The system to which he was referring had been developed by Henry Fox Talbot, like Niépce a country gentleman of private means and, like Arago, an MP and a fellow of his country's most prestigious learned society.

Fox Talbot was aware of the Wedgwood experiments but not of the French ones when he began to search for a solution to the problem of fixing the image in 1834. He also knew nothing of Hercules Florence, who had the previous year perfected a system along the same lines. Florence, who had been born in France, had rendered himself *hors de combat* in the 'inventor of photography' stakes by doing his work in Campinas, São Paulo Province, Brazil, where he had taken himself, aged 20, in 1824. As ever, it is less the great man or even the depth of general scientific understanding than the propitious time with its pressing social drivers that really conditions technological developments in the media. All these pioneers, known and unknown, were responding to the same emerging social need for mechanised imaging. By 1835, Fox Talbot had produced his first successful photograph, now lost, of his home at Laycock Abbey. He used silver chloride paper and increased its sensitivity by repeatedly soaking it in a bath of silver nitrate and common salt. At first he also used a solution of salt to fix the image but then Herschel drew his attention to Davy's 1819 'discovery' of hyposulphites. Most importantly, Fox Talbot realised that resolution of the difficulty of the 'negative' image (another term of Sir John's) lay not in the search for more chemicals but in simple repetition of the process. He waxed his paper negative, waxing being an innovation of Niépce's in 1822, and re-exposed it against a second piece of sensitised paper. Upon development with gallic acid, this second sheet became a 'positive' (another of Herschel's neologisms).

In January 1839 Fox Talbot reported to the Royal Society: 'Some Account of Photogenic Drawing; or The Process by Which Natural Objects May be Made to Delineate Themselves without the Aid of an Artist's Pencil'. In March, he communicated his results to the secretary of the French Academy of Science and Herschel formally presented his paper 'On the Art of Photography'. Fox Talbot was obviously spurred to pay greater attention to his photographic researches by Daguerre's prior production of a workable, more light-sensitive system. Yet, if the definition of photography is held to include the easy making of multiple copies as well as 'the automatic reproduction of the image' by the actions of light and chemicals, then clearly the daguerreotype was not quite fully photography, but a wonderfully effective partial prototype. The elaborate process that Daguerre 'perfected' after Niépce's death in 1833 and had completed by 1837 produced a single beautiful image, 'as fragile as a butterfly's' wings'. Fox Talbot's chemically soaked papers, on the other hand, produced an image which, although less finely detailed, could be endlessly duplicated. In February 1841, with no more (and no less) claim to originality than Daguerre, he applied for a patent for this 'Calotype Process'.

Despite the calotypes' soft lines and gentle attractiveness, the point of the new art was its miraculous hard-edged definition and, on this front, not needing the intermediary stages of paper negatives, the daguerreotype had the calotype beat. Calotypes remained in play partly because of the jingoism of the day (it was British, after all!) and, more seriously, because the negative offered real advantages. The first calotype studio opened in London in 1841, but the graininess of the images produced, and the strict control Fox Talbot exercised through his patent in England, limited the popularity of his system. Nevertheless, the archive of the earliest photographic images is much enriched by some calotypes, for example, those of the portrait painter David Octavius Hill. Portrait artists remained among the most avid of early photographers in that they brought to bear coherent aesthetic sensibilities which shaped photography very much in terms of existing artistic practice. Hill, initially drawn to the calotype as an artist's aide, received a commission to paint a commemorative canvas of the convention at which was founded the Scottish Free Church in May 1843. No fewer than 474 clerics were involved in this breakaway and it was suggested to Hill that the calotype might help simplify the logistics of his task.[6] That year, Ann Atkins, a friend of Fox Talbot, published the first photographic book in the UK, *British Algae*, illustrated with 424 calotype prints.

Calotype's disadvantages soon disappeared. Ten years after the patent on negative photography, calotyping acquired the same sparkling detail as daguerreotyping. Lenses had improved and mechanical shutters had been developed, of equal benefit to both systems; but the introduction in 1850/1 of a recently created substance, collodion, to hold the light-sensitive iodised silver-nitrate film in place on a glass plate, was to transform the calotype. The collodion, which was transparent and sticky, could only be handled when wet and the plate had to be inserted into the camera while still damp. Outside the studio, the photographer needed a light-tight tent or a wagon to carry all the tanks and chemicals, including a good supply of water, required to prepare a plate. The paraphernalia and the painstaking manipulations produced, after exposure of only 2 or 3 seconds, a photograph with all the detail of a daguerreotype plus the reproducibility and flexibility of a calotype. The superiority of the negative system had been clearly demonstrated and daguerreotyping slowly but inexorably fell out of use.

The complexity and cumbersomeness of the wet-plate apparatus did not prevent the continuation of that exploration of the world that Vernet had begun with his camera in 1839. The album of views of exotic places became a staple – Latin America, the Middle and Far East, the Alps and the Rockies, Indo-China – all covered before 1870. Nor did inconvenience prevent photographers from developing the techniques of photojournalism. Carl Stelzner's daguerreotype of the aftermath of a great fire in Hamburg in May 1842 is normally considered the earliest news photograph. A decade later Roger Fenton took his horse-drawn camera van to cover the Crimean War. A decade after that, Matthew Brady, with a staff of 19 photographers, went off to cover the American Civil War. The war photograph became a commonplace.

Despite the gestures made in some studios towards the painterly traditions, photography's claim on the real, implicit in Arago's initial rhetoric, clearly meant that it was being situated in society as an irrefutable source of evidence, most popularly but not exclusively as to the look of an individual. A leading mid-nineteenth-century intellectual, Charles Peirce, the pioneer of modern formal logic, considered that photographs were 'physically forced to correspond point by point to nature'. The camera, it was generally agreed, could not lie. Of course, the belief in the photograph's incontrovertibility as evidence was naïve but it is a naïvety that we have yet entirely to shed. Early photographic manuals characterise the entire business from the preparation of the plate on as 'manipulation', but the implications of manipulating exposure of both negative and positive were discounted or simply not understood; nor were even more overt interventions.

Henry Peach Robinson, for example, specialised in combining negatives. His 1858 print, 'Fading Away', is a photographic equivalent of Dickens's description of the death of Little Nell (which Oscar Wilde claimed 'one must have a heart of stone to read ... without laughing'). The pallid 'dying' young woman is attended by sister and mother. The fiancé, hand on brow, gives the viewer his back as he gazes out of the window. Clouds lour in the sky. The final photograph was composed from no less than five negatives. This was a prime example of 'pictorial photography', a most popular 'artistic' genre; but somehow even such highly publicised evidence of the possibilities of photographic manipulation did not impact much on the received view of the camera's inability to lie.

Even easier manipulations of the scene before the camera itself were largely unnoticed. Fenton eschewed disturbing images because he felt they would not sell. His coverage distorts the reality of the Crimea campaign, but none of those who bought his pictures knew that.[7] Or take Andrew Gardner, one of Brady's competitors. He lugged a corpse around the field in the aftermath of the Battle of Gettysburg, recostuming it and re-posing it as he went. The deception remained undetected for more than a century. Photography's reputation as evidence was unaffected by such procedures. After all, the most common photographs were portraits and the accuracy of these could be instantly checked against the reality of the sitter's appearance. The *leal sovvenir* offered by such images was a powerful implicit rebuttal of any taint of subterfuge. Indeed, many considered photography's veracity a weakness in that supposedly it could not, as did the painter, flatter the sitter; but for the multitude there was no choice in the matter.

The search for ever cheaper, less complex systems did not cease, nor did the exploitation of fresh market niches. The first proposal for using photographic portraits in passports was mooted and André Disdéri, the court photographer of Napoleon III, began sticking little photographs on visiting cards in 1853. For cards to be left on ceremonial occasions, the sitter was to be photographed wearing gloves, the head bowed as in greeting, etc., as social etiquette required; when left in inclement weather, the card was to show the sitter with an umbrella under his arm. Disdéri's camera took multiple images along these lines on one negative and the positives cost 20–25 francs a dozen but were, after Louis Napoleon himself had some made in 1859, very popular. 'Cartomania' exploited the allure of the famous. In Britain, John Mayall, a royal photographer, published, with approval, *carte* images of Queen Victoria and her family, encouraging the collection of these into albums. He sold 500,000 a year, but his colleagues and competitors between them probably sold another 300 million or so.

Disdéri's camera was also the most significant step yet towards making photography available to all but the poorest, a by no means uncontroversial outcome. After all, painting which denied the old rules of decorum was still capable of provoking uproar. The nineteenth-century radical artist Gustave Courbet outraged polite society in 1850 by exhibiting what was considered a grossly indecorous work. 'The Burial at Ornans' represented the obsequies of a peasant on a scale – three metres high and six and a half metres long – 'respectable' opinion thought ought to be reserved for paintings of the nobility. No less than 40 'ordinary' people figured in regal full length. In Robert Howlett's famous photograph of Isambard Kingdom Brunel taken in 1857, the engineer stands confidently in front of the launching chains of his ship *The Great Eastern*, hands in pockets, cheroot in mouth, his pose exactly echoing, say, that of the Emperor Charles V in Titian's 1532 painting. The photograph is by virtue of its full length alone an affront to the old aristocratic order. As a photographic journal put it in 1861:

> Photographic portraiture is the best feature of the fine arts for the millions . . . It has in this sense swept away many of the illiberal distinctions of rank and wealth, so that the poor man who possesses but a few shillings can command as perfect a lifelike portrait of his wife or child as Sir Thomas Lawrence painted for the most distinguished sovereigns of Europe.

By this time, there were an estimated 33,000 people involved in the various aspects of the photographic industry in France alone. Over the previous six years the number of studios in London had risen from 66 to more than 200. It was time for the state to deal with the phenomenon of photography. The naïve view of automated picture-making had initially caused the French law to offer no protection to the photographer. The strength of photography's claim to be an image-making system 'without the assistance of a draftsman' worked against the whole French concept of copyright. The Napoleonic code protected intellectual property, but, if there was no draftsman, whose intellect could be involved? The 'professor' with his chemicals and a finger on the shutter? Since too much capital was at stake, the French courts simply rethought the whole thing and declared the photographer to be an artist. Copyright followed but, paradoxically, the transformation of the photographer into an artist did not diminish the automated veracity of the photographic image and its power as evidence. (The English common law did not have this problem since its materialism decreed that the image was owned by whoever bought the plate, irrespective of whose hand clicked the shutter.)

Very occasionally, the deep chasm between the claimed implicit truthfulness of the process and its actual easy manipulation surfaced. For example, in 1877 an irate and naïve English vicar tried to sue Dr Barnardo, who was raising money for his orphanages by selling photographic 'before' and 'after' images of the urchins he was saving from the streets. He sold the images at 6d each or in packs of 20 for 5/-. The vicar was outraged when he discovered the photographs had been taken on the same day, the urchin being swiftly transformed into a clean, well-dressed child. The case collapsed in the face of Dr Barnardo's good intentions (and the vicar's lack of a personal interest the law could acknowledge as giving him a right to bring an action) but it illustrates the depth of public belief in photography's power as evidence 40 years after the introduction of the daguerreotype.

'You press button. We do the rest'

Photography's research tradition was deeply embedded in those pleasures of the eye, what at the end of the nineteenth century Freud was to term *schaulust* – that 'lust for seeing' which had fuelled secularised art practice since the Renaissance. Its earliest practitioners, apart from the savants who pioneered it, were to a large extent artists and soon they were looking to enhance the new medium's capacity for illusion; for instance, with three-dimensionality. The ancients understood the principle of binocular vision, and, in the Renaissance, della Porta made sure his contemporaries knew of their understanding. In the sixteenth century, Jacopo Chimenti had produced drawings to illustrate the stereoscopic effect, but then interest waned until, in the late 1830s, Sir Charles Whetstone repeated Chimenti's experiment. Photography was ideally suited to make good on this insight and it was a simple matter to double the lens of a camera and duplicate the viewpoints of the two eyes in a human head, as Ludwig

Moser demonstrated in 1844. Stereoscopic viewers were a hit at the London Great Exhibition of 1851, especially after Queen Victoria expressed an interest. The production of stereoscopic plates on an industrial scale created a mass mid-Victorian parlour entertainment.

Colour was not so easy. All photographic processes could be, and were, hand-tinted but this was to reintroduce the draftsman. A physical and chemical system not needing artistic input was desired. The concept of primary colours was well understood and, by 1722, it was clear that the superimposition of blue, red and yellow tinted separate copper plates would produce a full colour print. The same principle was applied in lithography. By 1807, Thomas Young had established the wave nature of light and made a creditable if slightly awry set of colour wavelength measurements. He also understood that the cone receptors in the human eye were of three kinds, sensitive to the red, green or blue ranges. In 1861, at the Royal Institution, the great physicist James Clerk Maxwell demonstrated how the three-colour system might work in photography: 'Let a plate of red glass be placed before the camera, and an impression taken. The positive of this will be transparent wherever the red light has been abundant in the landscape, and opaque where it has been wanting.' Repeat this with a green and violet filter, place the plates in three magic lanterns, align them on the screen and a full colour image would result. In 1873, Louis Ducos Du Hauron demonstrated that Maxwell's approach could be translated into a photograph. The next stage would be to discover chemicals which reproduced colours directly in the emulsion, but this was to be the business of the early decades of the next century.

Much more critical to photography was the search for an alternative to the wet plates. Completely dry plates had been developed but they were of reduced sensitivity and therefore required long exposures. Nevertheless entrepreneurs did begin to market them and, by the late 1850s, they were available in all major English cities. At the same time as these 'slow' plates had been introduced, a variant of collodion known as celluloid had been patented as a 'transparent support for sensitive coating' in 1856. John Hyatt, an American printer, produced serviceable celluloid sheets in

1869 but he and his brother were primarily interested in its use (in moulded forms) as a substitute for ivory in billiard balls and piano keys, so the photographic application remained unexplored; anyway, in 1871 gelatine was suggested as another dry alternative instead of collodion.

George Eastman was a keen amateur photographer whose search for an alternative to wet plates was meshed with an entrepreneurial desire to emulate and surpass the success of previous dry-film plate manufacturers. By 1877 he was making his own dry plates at home but a couple of years later he patented machinery for flowing gelatine silver bromides on to glass plates and drying them for sale. Within two years, he was doing $4,000 of business a month. The glass bases of the plates, however, still required careful handling and the alchemical potions and further manipulations needed to develop the latent image, produce and fix a negative, create and fix a print meant that this was still a practice of limited general appeal. Unbreakable bases for the sensitised material were needed, as had been understood as early as 1854 when the idea for a roll of sensitised paper to make calotype negatives had been patented; but this solved only part of the problem.

Thirty years later, in the early 1880s, Eastman returned to the notion of a roll of film, using first sensitised paper and, when that proved too 'grainy', a sensitised paper-backed gelatine layer which could be stripped away to produce the negatives. New chemicals and a new design for the roll-holder allowed him successfully to obtain a patent in 1884. The roll-holder could be used at the back of a camera in place of the plate-holder. Unsurprisingly, Eastman was not without competitors. For example, in 1888 John Carbutt began the large-scale manufacturing of celluloid-based silver-bromide sheets. More seriously, a Reverend Hannibal Goodwin of New Jersey had sought a patent for flexible transparent film in 1887. It took Eastman 27 years of legal wrangling, during which time Goodwin had died, to reach terms on this. In 1914, he had to settle with the film manufacturers to whom the Reverend had assigned his roll-film patent, paying millions in royalties. He could afford to because he had thought of a way to distance himself from straightforward manufacturing by also offering a service. Eastman

173

realised that if the manufacturer of the plate or roll undertook the business of development and printing as well, the photographer could be reduced to being merely the person who exposed the negative.

Eastman sold a box camera loaded with a roll of paper film as a unit to be returned to the factory after the exposures had been made for developing and printing. The camera weighed 1.5 lbs (680 grams) and took 100 circular pictures with a diameter of 2.5″. It was called the 'Kodak No. 1'. A year later, in 1889, a flexible transparent nitro-cellulose base was introduced instead. No draftsman, no artist, no chemist was needed. For the first time, the world could be represented in what was to be called a 'snapshot'. Eastman always claimed that:

> Philologically . . . the word 'kodak' is as meaningless as a child's first 'goo'. Terse, abrupt to the point of rudeness, literally bitten off by firm and unyielding consonants at both ends, it snaps like a camera shutter in your face. What more could one ask?

Eastman's ingenuity allowed him to design manufacturing apparatus capable of producing thinner and therefore more flexible films than his competitors. His managerial skills enabled him to develop quality-control systems to ensure his products' superior consistency. Yet it is the marketing ploy that is the real mark of his genius: 'You press button. We do the rest.' Eastman's reward for making this advertising slogan a reality was that he bought more than a century of world-market dominance for his company.

In 1885, the influential art historian Jakob Burckhardt had already noted the decline of portrait painting. It was, he said, 'certainly not on its deathbed, but . . . far more rarely practised than it used to be'. Painting and all the graphic arts borrowed much from the camera – the distortions of wide-angle lenses, the blurring of moving figures, the odd cropping of subjects in the frame. All pronouncements of the death of traditional artistic modes, however, proved to be premature, though their preeminence as a modes of representation was slowly reduced. The figurative arts did and do survive, not least because the camera's essential obedience to external reality – which could, until the coming of digital imaging, be broken only with effort – released them from their subservience to the production of 'true remembrances' of that same surface world. For the vast mass of people in the West, it was photography which furnished persons with a *leal sovvenir* of their unique, personal appearance. Melding this imaging capacity with other expressions of individuality was to be the central business of the development of modern media.

Sources

Leon Battista Alberti (1435, 1991), *On Painting*, Harmondsworth, Penguin.

Svetlana Alpers (1984), *The Art of Describing: Dutch Art in the Seventeenth Century*, Chicago: University of Chicago Press.

Michael Baxendale (1988), *Painting and Experience in Fifteenth Century Italy: A Primer in the Social History of Pictorial Style*, Oxford: Oxford University Press.

Arthur Booth (1964), *William Harvey Fox Talbot: Father of Photography*, London: Arthur Bake. I am grateful to Peter Twaites for this reference.

Leonardo da Vinci (1970), *The Notebooks*, New York: Dover.

Josef Maria Eder (Edward Epstean (trans.)) (1978), *History of Photography*, New York: Dover.

Colin Ford (1983), *Portraits*, London: Thames & Hudson.

Gisele Freund (1982), *Photography and Society*, Boston: David R. Godine.

Joan Gadol (1969), *Leon Battista Alberti: Universal Man of the Early Renaissance*, Chicago: University of Chicago Press.

P. M. Handover (1960), *Printing in London: from 1446 to Modern Times*, London: George Allen & Unwin.

George Harrison (ed.) (1967), *Elizabethan Journals 1591–1603*, London: Constable.

Arnold Hauser (1951), *The Social History of Art, Volume 4: Naturalism, Impressionism, the Film Age*, London: Routledge & Kegan Paul.

Alpheus Hyatt Mayor (1980), *Prints and People*, Princeton: Princeton University Press.

William Irvins, Jr. (1973), *On the Rationalization of Sight*, New York: Da Capo.

Ross King (2000), *Brunelleschi's Dome*, London: Chatto & Windus.

Aaron Scharf (1964), *Art and Photography*, Harmondsworth: Penguin.

Norbert Schneider (1994), *The Art of the Portrait*, Cologne: Taschen.

4

'WHO KNOWS NOT HER NAME':
THEATRE FROM 1513

'Prose, not verse; modern, not ancient; Italian, not Latin'

In 1513, Bernardo Dovizi's play, *La Calandria*, was premièred at the ducal court at Urbino. Dovizi's plot was drawn from some ancient Latin comedies of Plautus, but his prologue claimed the piece as more original than that: 'Today you'll see a new comedy, *Calandria* – prose, not verse; modern, not ancient; Italian, not Latin . . . If some say the author has blatantly plundered Plautus . . . that big oaf . . ., examine Plautus's comedies yourself. You'll find nothing missing.' The stage set was a realistic representation of Rome. The actors, all scrumptiously costumed men, in the manner of the ancient republican Roman theatre, spoke witty, elegant Italian. The play's theme was, as in Plautus and Terence, the relations between men and women, and its expression overtly sexual. The prologue was somewhat tendentious in downplaying its ancient connections but, derived or not, *Calandria* was a hit and in Rome the following year it was revived before the newly enthroned Pope Leo X, Giovanni de' Medici. That the Pope would allow such a thing is less surprising than it might have been, given that Dovizi was himself a priest – in fact, a prince of the Church, Cardinal Bibbiena.

The Church had long since seen the didactic value of dramas based on biblical, hagiographic and liturgical texts and, indeed, had instituted the Feast of Corpus Christi as a day given over to their performance. From these had grown cycles of religious Mystery Plays, presented by companies of amateurs in urban public spaces, as well as learned *sacra rappresentazione*, saint's plays and other religious performances put on in and around churches themselves. Across the whole of Europe, secular drama too was widespread, in the form of often bawdy folk entertainments, such as one-act Sienese or Neapolitan comedies or English Mummers' Plays. The amateurs presenting these, on occasion, formed themselves into long-lived dramatic societies. The aristocracy also sustained a culture of performance by employing professional jesters and singers in their trains.

The new learning impacted on all these customs, as ancient pagan dramatic models and subjects began overtly to overwhelm sacred dramatic traditions and transmute secular ones. A stage emerged that was centrally focused on the comic or tragic concerns of the individual, delivered to significantly larger audiences on an increasingly regular and, eventually, more or less daily basis by professional actors in a dedicated urban building. The crude impersonation of character (the 'I be St George' of the Mummers) moved through stereotyping of a more complex kind towards the representation of emotionally complicated, unique individuals, just as a demand for verisimilitude came to dominate the image of the individual in the plastic arts.

In the half-century after Gutenberg had begun the work of the books, in addition to the recovery of the classic comedies, hybrid serious dramatic texts had began to appear in Italy – a biblical story in the style of a Roman tragedy or a pagan story written in the religious style. The Latin playwrights, whose works had never entirely disappeared, were once more being performed. In the aristocratic schools maintained by enlightened Renaissance princes, such as Duke Ercole d'Este in Ferrara, boys studied these texts, many recently discovered in old monastic libraries or brought from Byzantium after its final collapse, as part of the curriculum of new learning. The Duke encouraged production of the plays and, thereafter, translations of them and their performance in the vernacular. In 1508 and 1509, the poet Lodovico Ariosto, who had the task of mounting these productions as well as his other political duties at the d'Este court, eruditely wrote two new comedies in the ancient style. Ariosto was Bibbiena's immediate, if unacknowledged, inspiration.

Nicolò Machiavelli was a frequent visitor to the Orti Oricellari, the Rucellai Gardens in Florence, where Cosimo Rucellai presided over regular informal meetings of a society of humanists. Self-consciously in pursuit of antiquity, each 13 November, for example, they observed the traditional date of Plato's death. Although philosophy and politics were discussed, issues such as the viability of Italian as a literary language also occupied their thoughts, as did these new plays, which were read and even performed in the garden. Machiavelli, his political career thwarted, had determined to live by his pen and, among much else, had translated a play by Terence. In 1518, he presented an original work, his own learned comedy, *La Mandragola* (*The Mandrake Root*).

La Mandragola is a perfect *commedia erudita*, replete with the usual characters – old man, young wife, lover – and a plot which turns on the love potion made from the mandrake root which, supposedly, renders any woman who takes it sexually insatiable and any man who takes her, dead. The results are that the virtuous young wife has the child for whom she longed and also discovers the joys of the flesh that her marriage to an old man has kept from her. Her old and foolish husband, who has arranged his own cuckoldom in a positively Machiavellian plot twist, has the heir he desires (albeit not of his begetting) and keeps his young trophy wife. The impoverished, randy young aristocrat, pretending to be a doctor purveying the fake mandrake potion, not only has the virtuous young wife after whom he has lusted but so pleasures her that she takes him as her permanent lover. Since the world of the play is completely amoral, it is tempting to see it as a comic reflection of Machiavelli's understanding of politics. After all, one character, a corrupt priest, justifies fraud and selfishness – adultery even – with the comforting thought that:

> As far as your conscience is concerned, you must follow this general rule: where there is a clear good and an indefinite evil, one must never lose that good for fear of that evil . . . In all things one must look to the result.

Pope Leo not only embraced learned bawdy and new tragedy in the style of the Roman Seneca; he also scandalously relished the coarsest dialect sketches from Siena. In one playlet, for example, by way of denouement, the heroine, having decided to take all her four suitors to bed, invites the audience to join them. Leo was liberal about such explicitness and forgiving of the general licentiousness of his court; although he was himself continent, such tolerance was shocking nonetheless. He stunned a French embassy in 1519 by laughing at the camp jokes in a revival of a play his friend Ariosto had written a decade before. By then the minor disobedience of a German monk, Martin Luther, was mushrooming into a dangerous threat to papal authority. In 1520, the Pope excommunicated the monk. More than a century of upheaval and bloodshed were to follow.

Leo's spendthrift fondness for theatrical entertainment was peripheral to the focus of Luther's attack on what he saw as fraudulent papal revenue raising. Dramatic shows were as nothing compared with, say, the building of St Peter's which Pope Leo had undertaken, being merely an example of the inappropriate papal excess which such ill-gotten funds served to sustain. The *commedia erudita* and Luther's *Ninety-five Theses* could not be further apart, the one being an expression of the new learning that was fanning the wrath expressed in the other. Nevertheless, in another sense, they were different faces of the same coin. Luther's attack on papal authority and spiritual power easily slipped into a revolutionary demand for an individual right of conscience and the freedom to express that right. The learned plays and the other more populist and popular dramatic forms were creating another stage, literal as well as metaphorical, for a different sort of personal expression both by players and playwrights.

The road along which the aristocratic Italian intelligentsia had moved, from sacred plays to the *commedia erudita*, was well signposted with references to what were, supposedly, the dramatic theories of the ancients. The retrieval of Aristotle's *Poetics* was as powerful a model for this self-conscious intellectual work as Terence, Plautus and Seneca were models for the plays themselves.[1] The Italians claimed the rules for drama which they elaborated were ancient but they were not. Horace might have laid down that plays be in five acts but other constraints, supposedly equally ancient, were of more recent coinage – the 'three unities' of time, place and action, for example. These required that a play had to consist of one action without subplots taking place in the course of one day at one place. Although ascribed to Aristotle, the unities were actually articulated as a result of extrapolating from the ancients by Giovanni Giraldi, whose imitation of the *Decameron* was to furnish many plots for Shakespeare and his peers and who published his rules in 1543. Guilio Scaligero's work a generation later continued this tradition. By Scaligero's time, other rules grounded in the misunderstanding of classical authorities were also in place. Playwrights willingly agreed that no character was to appear more than five times; no more than three characters were to be on the stage at one time; no unrealistic soliloquies; no respectable woman was to appear (because the settings were always public places where no such woman would in reality appear).[2]

Slavish duplication, however, did have its limits, beyond the obvious impossibility of replicating ancient barbarity and nudity. For instance, the Italians were not quick to emulate classical theatre building, although they did have an ancient Latin text on the principles involved, Vitruvius's *De Architectura*, which had been rediscovered in the monastery of St Gallen in 1414. Instead the noble hall remained the prime site for drama with a raised stage at one end, a painted scenic illusion behind, and the audience ranged around the other walls. The open space in the middle was occupied by the entertainment's patrons, themselves as much of the spectacle as the actors. It was not until 1584 that the architect Palladio's Vetruvian Teatro Olympico was finished in Vincenza. It opened with Sophocles's *Oedipus*. Its supposed faithfulness to classical practice was not much directly emulated. Instead, the effective model from which the European playhouse descends was built, in 1619, by Gian-Battista Aleotti when he remodelled the great hall of the Palazzo della Pilotta in Parma. The spectators had their view improved by being seated in a horseshoe arrangement of tiered boxes. The space originally occupied by the patron would become the stalls, although it was many decades before the seating there became fixed and the most illustrious members of the audience moved to a box. Most important of all, Aleotti, with no reference to antiquity beyond the use of the name, created a formal divide between this space, the *proskena* in Greek, and the stage – the *skena*. The divide, a proscenium arch, focused the gaze of the audience, enhancing the illusion of the scenery and, curtained, facilitated the creation of scenic effects as well as allowing for the formal marking of starts and stops in the performance.

In some countries the body of rules continued in force for a century or more, before being disregarded everywhere as artificial constraints on artistic expression; but during the time of their dominance, theory was a source of inspiration as well as a brake on imagination. Take the question of music, particularly song. Courtly plays often had elaborate musical interludes, *intermezzi*, between the acts. These involved madrigal-style choral singing and dance, with their own narratives, but there was an argument about the authenticity of this way of accommodating the known ancient Greek practice of using music in dramatic performance. Girolamo Mei, the ranking expert on ancient music, was convinced that the whole approach was wrong. The Greeks, he claimed, sang the whole drama. Not only that: they sang a single melodic line rather than the counterpoint style of Renaissance music. The Florentine composer and mathematician, Vencenzo Galilei, Galileo's father, maintained a correspondence with Mei from the late 1570s on and was to be the channel whereby Mei's theories were tested in practice.

Vencenzo belonged to a conversation circle, the Camarata, dedicated to discussing artistic matters, which met under the patronage of Count Giovanni Bardi. Musicians were prominent in the group and the issue of the use of music in drama much engaged them. It was in the Camarata that, in the name of the recovery of ancient practice, they brainstormed the idea of the *recitativo* to be sung by a solo voice, the words of which would illuminate and advance the action rather than impede it. In 1594, the poet Ottavio Rinuccini and the composers Jacopo Peri and Gulio Caccini, all members of the Camarata, applied the theory to *Dafne*, a tragedy in which all the speeches were entirely sung. In the name of supposedly recovering authentic Greek practice, they had created a new dramatic form – the opera.

'A shew place of all beastly and filthy matters'

In 1600, the word 'celebrity' came into English. Will Kempe was a clown. He had been a member of the Lord Chamberlain's Men, a 'sharer' (that is, one of the original partners who owned the Globe Theatre) and the first 'Dogberry' in *Much Ado About Nothing*. Shakespeare's slap in *Hamlet* at comedians who will not stick to the script – 'Let those that are your clowns speak no more than has been set down for them' – was probably directed at Kempe. An addiction to ad-libbing might well have forced him out since he had just quit the company. Although he was well known in his day as a comic actor, what really distinguishes him is that he is a very early example of a person famous for being famous. This he achieved because of one well-exploited publicity stunt, as we would now call it.

In the February of 1600, on a bet, he danced his way from London to Norwich. He set out on the tenth.

> Will Kempe the clown hath wagered that he will dance from London to Norwich, and this morning before seven of the clock is set forward from the Lord Mayor's to the Mayor of Norwich, accompanied by Thomas Sly his taborer and George Sprat that is appointed his overseer.[3]

He danced out of London for two days, making it to Romford, where he rested for another couple of days. He reached the outskirts of Norwich some three weeks later, delayed by more rests and a blizzard, and because for five days, 'He staid his morris a little before St. Giles gate, procrastinating his dance through the city' so that word of his arrival could spread. The modernity of this stage-managed event, an absurd

parody of a royal progress, is matched by the subsequent exploitation of
the dance by both Kempe and the city: 'The mayor [of Norwich] gave
him £5 in Elizabeth angels, and besides 40s yearly during his life, making
him also a freeman of the merchant venturers.' They then nailed his
buskins to the wall of the Guildhall as a tourist attraction. As for Kempe,
he got the book of the exploit out a mere six weeks later – *Kempe's nine
daies wonder. Performed in a daunce from London to Norwich.* Kempe
was, in the modern sense, the original 'nine-days' wonder'.

As elsewhere, actors in England were merely a class of vagabonds.
The antique legal language of vagabondage – 'common players of
enterludes and minstrels wandring abroad' – persisted well into the
eighteenth century. On the other hand, in 1559, soon after her accession, Queen Elizabeth had licensed the nobility to establish its own
theatrical troupes. The first nobleman to do so, in that same year, was
her favourite, Robert Dudley, Earl of Leicester. The licence made the
situation of English actors distinct. Not only were they not in royal
employ, they were also allowed to take their productions on tour.

In *Sir Thomas More*, a play of the early 1590s, to which Shakespeare
probably contributed, Sir Thomas is seen welcoming the 'Lord
Cardinal's Players' after the fashion of the earlier decades of the century:

More: I prithee tell me, what plays have ye?
Player: Divers, my lord: *The Cradle of Security, Hit Nail
o'th'Head, Impatient Poverty, The Play of the Four P's,
Divers and Lazarus, Lusty Juventus,* and *The Marriage of
Wit and Wisdom.*
More: *The Marriage of Wit and Wisdom?* That, my lads;
I'll have none but that . . . How many are ye?
Player: Four men and a boy, sir.
More: But one boy? Then I see There's but few women in
the play.
Player: Three my Lord: Dame Science, Lady Vanity, And
Wisdom, she herself.
More: And one boy to play them all? By'r Lady, he's loden.

183

By touring, the actors added to the lustre of their lord, but their prize was greater. They achieved a measure of independence few retainers could expect; they found additional and eventually sustaining alternative revenue sources. Even when they gave command performances at court or for their patron, they were paid an honorarium for their services. Soon they were playing to the public too, using the courtyard of a suitably sized inn in which a temporary stage could be erected with an all-important box office controlling entry.[4] In London, seven or eight hostelries regularly hosted these increasingly financially independent troupes, and by the mid-1570s plays could be seen most autumn after-noons somewhere or other in the capital. Eventually, in 1583, the Queen herself appointed a troupe, whose leading player was Will Kempes's great rival, Robert Tarlton; but they were still not quite her 'men', persons so directly in her employ as to require the honour and respect due to royal servants, and to believe that they were was absurd, as the professional writer, Thomas Nashe, makes clear. He tells of a choleric country justice who took his staff to an audience who dared to laugh at Tarlton's clowning, beating them 'unmercifully on the bare pates, in that they, being but farmers and poor country hinds, would presume to laugh at the Queen's men, and make no more account of her cloth'.

In Italy, professional actors, as opposed to those who performed at school, university or court or were members of religious or civic amateur dramatic societies, were also scorned as virtual vagabonds, but, as in England, by the 1570s some had become very well known, an attraction in themselves – Zan Ganassa (the stage name of Alberto Naselli), Giovanni Pellesini, Tristano Martinelli. These players, too, were attached to no court but formed itinerant troupes whose stock-in-trade were cruder, funnier but more accessible improvised versions of the same sort of plots that *commedia erudita* deployed. What they did was known as *La commedia dell'arte*. Significantly, the earliest written use we have of this term, which dates from 1545, was in a contract of employment for a group of eight male players, the Fraternal Company of Ser Maphio, to tour together giving performances in and around Padua. *Arte*, initially in

Italian 'craft', had also come to mean a 'guild' of craftsmen.[5] In 1565, the *capocomico* Ganassa added a woman to his troupe, to great popular acclaim. Soon women – Isabella Andreini, Diana da Ponti – were equalling the men in fame, and sometimes, as in Diana's case, they were also leading companies. The troupes branded themselves – the *Gelosi*, the *Confidenti*, the *Uniti* – the better to market their product and their leading players as they toured the country.

Their main draw was not in the novelty of their plots. On the contrary, these were inevitably a matter of adulterous liaisons, foolish attachments and thwarted romances. The characters were also always the same – frisky young wives and silly ancient husbands, bombastic soldiers and crafty servants, young seducers, wistful suitors and flirtatious maids. What enthralled the public, and continued to do so in parts of Europe for the next century and a half, was the skill these players deployed to revivify the familiar. The troupes were itinerant but stable enough to be secure ad-libbing together, for the *commedia dell'arte* had no scripts. A show, normally three acts, played largely in masks, was a matter of impromptu performance on the basis of an agreed *soggetto* or scenario, more like a jazz improvisation on a 'standard' than a production of a scripted play. The actors might have been masked and playing stereotypes but nevertheless they became well known as individuals valued for their ability to do comic dialects, their general quick wit and their command of the *lazzi* – physical bits of business.

The aristocratic Flavio Scala, who worked in a number of troupes, published a book of scenarios in 1611 outlining their plots ('There was in Rome a Venetian merchant named Pantalone de Bisognosi who had two legitimate children . . .'); listing the casts: ('Pantalone, Orazio – his son, Franceschina – his maidservant . . .') the properties required ('Three women's dresses, Gipsy costume for Pedrolino, many lighted lanterns . . .); and giving detailed instructions for each scene:

Scene: Rome First Act
Enters now the
CAPTAIN who makes his usual boasts. Franceschina tells him

185

of her love. He mocks her. They quarrel. Franceschina
taunts him, saying that she'll make him love her willy-nilly.
They dispute. Enter now
PANTALONE. . .

Commedia dell'arte characters were the direct descendants, in parallel
with the *commedia erudita*, of stock figures who would have been
familiar to a Roman audience 1800 years earlier. Such deep roots in
European culture ensured the *commedia*'s persistent and widespread
popularity. Its very vocabulary has entered more than one European
language. The English word for baggy trousers, for instance, stands for
the whole of Pantalone, the silly old Venetian. 'Zany' is derived from
'Zanni', the *commedia* term for comic servants, itself drawn from
'Johnny' ('Gianni') in Venetian dialect (and the source of 'Zan'
Ganassa). In France, Perdrolino was transformed into Pierrot the clown
in 1665 and survived, for example appearing for many years (in the
person of Paul Legrand) as the star of the *café–spectacle* offered at the
Folies-Bergère which opened in Paris in 1869.[6] The last *commedia*
troop was to be found at the end of the twentieth century playing in the
Tivoli Gardens in Copenhagen. In England, Punchinello also endures
to this day (just) in puppet form as Mr Punch, although his little play
has absorbed as much of the medieval English Mystery and Mumming
traditions as it has preserved its *commedia* origins.

The original Italian troupes were active in spreading their art beyond
Italy. The *Uniti* troupe arrived in London in 1577 but although the
commedia had influence, the English were not predisposed to be
impressed. Thomas Nashe later boasted that:

Our players are not as players beyond the sea, a sort of
squirting bawdy comedians, that have whores and common
courtesans to play women's parts, and forbear no immodest
speech or unchaste action that may procure laughter; but
our scene is more stately furnished . . . not consisting, like
theirs, of a pantallon, a whore, and a zany.

Nor did the English much care for the niceties of the neo-classical rules governing dramatic decorum in more elevated Italian entertainments. They liked clowns to provide relief from the disasters of the main plots of tragedies, and enjoyed historical dramas which ranged far and wide across space and time. (They were also, *pace* Nashe, more than a little partial to bawdy and to plots, comedic and tragic, driven by sexual appetites, misunderstandings and confusions even if no woman appeared on the stage.) English playwrights, including the 'University Wits' who had been educated in the new learning at Oxbridge, were generally unwilling to accept the constraints of neo-classicism when servicing these tastes.

In 1595 Sir Philip Sidney, as vigorous a keeper of Renaissance sensibilities as England produced, published a condemnation (written in 1581) of the barbarous practices of his play-writing contemporaries:

> For where the stage should always represent but one place, and uttermost time presupposed in it should be, both by Aristotle's precept and common sense, but one day, there is both many days and many places inartificially imagined . . . But besides these gross absurdities, how all their plays be neither right tragedies nor right comedies; mingling kings and clowns, not because the matter so carieth it, but thrust in clowns by head and shoulders, to play a part in majestical matters, with neither decency nor discretion.

Sidney's attack fell on deaf ears. Only Ben Jonson, who that year arrived back in London from fighting the Spanish in the Netherlands, took any real notice, but Shakespeare, for example, thought the 'right tragedies'/'right comedies' business was merely good for a joke: 'Tragedy, comedy, history, pastoral, pastoral-comical, historical-pastoral, tragical-historical, tragical-comical-historical-pastoral, scene individible or poem unlimited; Seneca cannot be too heavy; nor Plautus too light'. As for ignoring the unities, he was more measured but just as unrepentant. The audiences must themselves resolve the stresses imposed on their understanding by the use of multiple locations, epic actions and the passage of often indeterminate time; they must, as the Chorus in his *Henry V* insists, work on their 'imaginary forces'; 'grapple' their minds; 'piece out [] imperfections'; 'think'; 'follow, follow'.

English taste was not limited by the constraints of *commedia* stereotyping, even in comedy. With increasing sophistication in the last decades of the sixteenth century, the individual actors were given, by the English playwrights, individuals to play. Take *Love's Labour's Lost*, the nearest thing to a *commedia erudita* that Shakespeare wrote. In it Don Adriano de Armado, 'a fantastical Spaniard', is a type of that ancient military figure of fun, the boastful soldier; the *miles gloriosus* of the Roman stage who had become the *capitano*, Scaramuccia, of the *commedia dell'arte*. Accused of having impregnated a serving wench, Don Armado is the usual absurd braggadocio ('Dost thou infamonize me among potentates? Thou shalt die'). Within lines, though, Shakespeare transforms him into a crestfallen poor old man, withdrawing his challenge, humiliated before the court at being forced to reveal he is too poor to wear a shirt beneath his doublet, as much an object of sympathy as a figure of fun.

Shakespeare's massively popular creation, Sir John Falstaff, is descended from Don Adriano and is even less the Scaramouche. His fall, when he is brutally spurned by his once constant companion, young Prince Hal, now newly crowned as Henry V, is, indeed, most wonderfully neither 'right tragedy' nor 'right comedy':

> *Falstaff.* My king! My Jove! I speak to thee, my heart!
> *King.* I know thee not, old man. Fall to thy prayers.
> How ill white hairs become a fool and jester!

All this is a long way from Flavio Scala's more or less contemporaneous *commedia dell'arte* scenario:

> Enters now the
> CAPTAIN who makes his usual boasts . . .

In 1587, Christopher Marlowe, a newly minted Cambridge MA, sold a 'playbook', the script of *Tamburlaine*, an epic historical drama written in blank verse, to the Lord Admiral's troupe not least because it had a plum name-part for their leading player, Edward Alleyn. From the 1550s on learned playwrights, aping Italian pioneers, essayed such erudite plays largely for educational purposes to be performed, for example, by the popular companies of boy actors. These boys were drawn from the choir schools of the chapels royal and regularly appeared for paying audiences in small specially converted indoor halls. *Tamburlaine* was the first mature expression of what an authentic English version of a Senecan tragedy could be in the hands of a professional adult company. Marlowe provided Alleyn with the challenge of creating a character subject to swiftly changing moods rather than presenting, impersonating, a stereotype. Marlowe followed up the triumph of *Tamburlaine* with a succession of plays all with massive male central roles – *Dr Faustus*, *The Jew of Malta*, *Edward II* – which secured Alleyn's position as the pre-eminent and ultimately the wealthiest English actor of the early 1590s.

By then Shakespeare was performing the same service for Alleyn's great rival, Richard Burbage. Marlowe was dead, knifed in a drunken brawl on 30 May 1593 (or, perhaps, assassinated as a spy in some murky state intrigue) even as Burbage was achieving his first triumph in *Richard III*. By 1596, before Shakespeare had written his greatest plays, the victory of Burbage and the Lord Chamberlain's Men over Alleyn and the Lord Admiral's, was to be seen, for instance, in their monopolising all six command performances at court during the Christmas season. In the first years of the new century, Shakespeare provided Burbage with a series of astounding roles – Hamlet, Othello, Lear, Macbeth. Unlike Marlowe, in whose greatest plays a single voice – Alleyn's – clearly dominated, Shakespeare, perhaps because he was himself an actor, not a 'wit', consistently gave all his company strong parts. He surrounded the great tragic figures with parts which also gave an actor an opportunity to shine. His comedies even more clearly cater for a strong ensemble.

The English troupes, whose names changed at royal whim or as their ostensible lords gained new official titles, had long since acquired, in addition to the inn-yards and halls in which they initially played, custom-built, open-air, public 'stage-houses' in London. The first was erected, in 1576, 'for the acting and shewing of comedies, tragedies and histories' by one of what was then the Earl of Leicester's Men, James Burbage, Richard's father, with capital provided by his wealthy brother-in-law, John Brayne, a grocer. The Corporation of London was especially hostile to this development, ever fearful of 'divers apprentices and other servants' as well as 'masterless men' who were, they claimed, using performances as a cover for planning 'mutinous attempts' or, just as bad apparently, were 'coming together . . . to recreate themselves'. Burbage and Brayne neatly side-stepped this by leasing a site within the liberty of Holywell Priory in Shoreditch. The priory had gone in Henry VIII's dissolution of the monasteries but its ancient ecclesiastical legal entitlements had not and within its grounds the Corporation had no powers. The entrepreneurs named the building 'The Theatre', to the fury of the Puritans: 'a shew place of all beastly and filthy matters . . . a gorgeous playing place erected in the fields . . . as they please to have it called, a Theatre, that is even after the manner of the old heathenish theatre at Rome'. For all the royal and aristocratic support the licensed players had, there was still a real sense that the business was essentially dubious and carrying a nobleman's name did not really alter that; but, fume as the Puritans and the Corporation might, they could do nothing.

Burbage had now only to look out for the intermittently watchful eye of Sir Thomas Cawarden, the royal Master of the Revels, the official responsible for court entertainments and the licensing of all public dramatic performances. His Revels Office functioned for the stage as the Stationer's Company did for the press, and plays could open only 'with the allowance of the Master of the Revells' after vetting.

Plague was a worse threat as all public entertainments were closed, wherever they were sited, as soon as deaths within the city reached 40 a week. This tended to happen in the summer and companies once more took to the road, back to provincial inns and great halls until the pestilence passed. Three summers were lost in the 1570s, five in 1580s (but the theatre did gain Shakespeare almost certainly as a consequence of a metropolitan company playing Stratford-on-Avon). As a result, the theatrical season in London at this time came to stretch from September up to Christmas, despite the worsening weather.

In the stage-houses, people paid 2d for a bench seat under the roof or 1d to stand in the open before the stage in the 'yard'. It was the socially diverse nature of the audience as much as its size, as many as 2,000 a performance, which exercised the authorities. Between 1500 and 1600 the city's population increased between three- and four-fold to 200,000 or more. Since the typical run of a successful play in any one season was six performances, a maximum of 12,000 might see it, six per cent of the population. Today, a similar percentage of Londoners would yield an audience of mass-media dimensions – 450,000, say. The oft-repeated assertion that Shakespeare, were he alive now, would be writing for the television, normally highlights his supposed sensitivity to public taste; but it is also true, in some sense, in terms of audience reach.

Over the last decades of the sixteenth century, as many as 18 public stages – playhouses, inns and indoor theatres – operated in London. Many were concentrated in a liberty south of the river in Southwark on the Bankside, where the Bishop of Winchester's London prison, the Clink, was sited. Long the Tudor city's red-light district, with brothels, gambling dens and animal-baiting pits, it had also always welcomed actors. Philip Henslowe, a dyer who had made good by marrying his late master's widow, built the first stage-house in the liberty, the Rose, in the year of the Armada, 1588. Over the next quarter of a century Bankside also became home to the Globe, the Hope and the Swan.

A troupe now consisted of 12 to 16 actors, only some of whom – half a dozen maybe – were 'sharers', partners with a right to a share of the box-office. The Globe's sharers were James Burbage's sons, Cuthbert and Richard (50 per cent), and Will Kempe, Augustine Philips, John Heminges, Thomas Pope and William Shakespeare (10 per cent each).

Over the years the 'sharers' would change but Shakespeare remained, his 10 per cent becoming the basis of his fortune and his retirement fund. At the Rose, Alleyn, who had married Henslowe's step-daughter and become his partner, was eventually rich enough to found Dulwich College with a £10,000 endowment. The sharers were lucky, for then, as now, only a few made fortunes from the entertainment business while most profited far less from its insecurities and uncertainties.

There were now others employed in the dramatic companies who took wages for which the sharers were responsible. There was a tireman (to look after the costumes); a bookkeeper (to guard the playbooks, texts of a company's plays to which it had exclusive rights); gatherers (to run the box office); musicians; a stagekeeper (to sweep the stage); scribes, and as many as six boy apprentices to play the women. The sharers contracted with the playhouse owner, which in James Burbage's case meant that his company contracted with him. Playbooks were bought outright from the pool of playwrights, dominated by the 'University Wits', and each of the parts was copied out, with cues, for the actor who was to play it. Rehearsals were perfunctory and, although they were familiar with each other, each player operated somewhat independently – a little like a twentieth-century opera singer flown into a production at the last moment to replace an ailing performer. Six performances per play meant that there was a ceaseless demand for new titles. Many scripts were the product of more than one author on a division of labour basis (e.g. *Sir Thomas More*) but that is about as productive as the English ever became. No English playwright, for example, was as prolific as Lope de Vega.

'An object of idolatry on all sides'

A child prodigy and graduate of Alcalá, Lope Felix de Vega Carpio was, like Ariosto, a court functionary. A soldier who had sailed in the Armada, with his womanising he occasioned elopements, abandonments, two marriages and many children, legitimate and illegitimate. In

1614 he took Holy Orders without seemingly giving up his philandering, although he now became known for self-flagellation – which he claimed was good for his soul. Despite having written a continuation of Ariosto's epic poem *Orlando Furioso* and being, by class and education, a potential neo-classicist, Lope was no more impressed by Italian pseudo-antique precepts about the drama than were his English contemporaries. In a poem-come-treatise, *New Art of Writing Plays*, which he published in 1609, he was quite damning about the rules, primarily because they ran against what he knew to be public taste: 'Tragedy mixed with comedy – Terence with Seneca – will cause much delight', he insisted. Causing delight was, as far as Lope was concerned, the point.

Lope drew on exactly the same mix of dramatic traditions as existed in Italy and England but some of the ingredients were for him, and for the Spanish in general, more important than elsewhere. The sacred dramas, for example, remained vibrant while to the north they had become a source of contention between Protestant and Catholic even to the point, as in England, of having long since been banned. In Spain, to the contrary, such *autos sacramentales* were a major agent in professionalising the stage. A number of cities had contracted with a professional to run their traditional amateur religious performances.

In Valladolid, the man chosen for this task was an itinerant actor and playwright, Lope de Rueda. De Rueda had been far from unique in travelling the country with a small professional company of players, including women. They were bound to an *autor* on an annual basis along *commedia dell'arte* lines, but neither de Rueda nor his rivals adopted the particularities of the *commedia* style, although Madrid, like London, was visited by a leading Italian troupe – Zan Ganassi's *Gelosi* – in the 1570s. Instead, the Spaniards played short scripted *pasos* and other secular shows in open squares when they were not involved in *autos sacramentales*. Indeed, it was the popularity of these *pasos* which had suggested to Ganassi that he might do good business in Spain.

In order to liberate themselves from the uncertainties of the collecting tin, the Spanish troupes, like the English, needed an enclosed space accessible only past a box office. Instead of the inns used by English players, they turned to the courtyards of municipal buildings, which in Madrid, for example, were most easily found in the hospitals. As charities, these could always use the hiring fee levied on the players and did so for the first time in 1561. The inconveniences of transforming a courtyard into a roofless performance space led to custom-built courtyard theatres, *corrales*, along the same general lines. A *corral* was a rectangle with a raised stage across one short side facing three sides of audiences in boxes around an open standing space. Women sat separately in the highest galleries, known as *cuezalas* (or 'stewpots'). Public appetite for these entertainments had become insatiable. Apart from Lent, the *corrales* were open all year and, as any new play, just as in London, was seldom seen more than six times (and very rarely that often), new works were always needed. Writing throughout the 1580s, Miguel de Cervantes Saávedra claimed to have created 30 plays, both comedies and tragedies, none of which, of course, has matched the durability of his masterpiece *Don Quixote*; but this was as nothing. It was common for a playwright to knock off a drama in just a few weeks and Lope de Vega claimed to have written around 1,500, a more accurate figure being around 700, of which about half survive. The wonder is that despite this prodigious output, he stands, with some justice, in relation to Spain's theatre exactly where Shakespeare stands in relation to the English stage. In fact, unlike Shakespeare, who was being extensively 'improved' within two generations of his death, Lope remained the living template for all Spanish dramatists for more than a century after his decease.

There is about Lope an entirely modern air of responsibility to his public, a keen sense of what sells being a justification for selling it. He was prepared to defend the popular as being good and worthy exactly because it was popular and it seemed reasonable to him that his audiences' preferences should carry greater weight than did the refined requirements of a humanist elite. Such views chimed well with his ability, which would today be no less admired among professionals than it was in Spain 400 years ago, to churn out material at a pace that would not shame a modern soap-opera scriptwriter.

He dealt with a number of different themes. Some involved contemporary questions of honour, usually in the form of *capa y espada* ('cloak and sword') stories about thwarted couples from the bourgeoisie or the ranks of the lesser nobility. 'Cases of honour', he wrote, 'are best for they powerfully move all people.' He could also turn out *autos sacramentales* – as he did, for example, when the austere Philip II decreed on his deathbed in 1598 that the *corrales* should be closed and, for a time, there was no outlet for secular work. This forbidding monarch had not encouraged his nobles to establish troupes along English lines, nor had he himself done so, but the possibility of using the drama as a tool of royal policy was not unknown in Renaissance Europe and his son, Philip III, took a more sympathetic view of the popular professional stage than had his father. Philip IV in his turn, and his chief minister, the Count-Duke of Olivares, were even more ready to absorb the dramatic energy of the *corrales* into the entertainments of the court. It was in this changed atmosphere that Lope produced the greatest of his historical dramas.

The most famous of these, *Fuente Ovejuna*, was written in 1612 and based on incidents which had occurred in the reign of Ferdinand and Isabella of Aragon over 200 years earlier. The peasant inhabitants of Fuente Ovejuna are driven to murder the Grand Commander of a Christian order of knights because of his rampant oppression, while, in a subplot, another member of this order treasonably resists Isabella by allying against her with the King of Portugal. The main plot is not a radical plea for proletarian solidarity because for Lope, himself of conservative opinion, and his equally conservative audience, the oppression of the peasants parallels the treason of the subplot. The crown and the peasantry are united, both threatened by the knights' failure to fulfil their social bargains and both taking up arms to restore the social order.

This younger Philip had a taste for theatre and commanded professionally acted dramas, known as *particulares*, for his court at a rate of about one a fortnight during the first 15 years of his long reign, easily matching the practice of contemporary rulers anywhere in Europe. The first opera was composed for the court in 1627 (naturally, with Lope as

195

the librettist). A custom-built private royal theatre was opened in 1640. Olivares also was aware of the propaganda potential of the drama and encouraged playmaking on contemporary events, a form of proto-docudrama. For example, the Brazilian town of Bahia, lost to the Dutch in 1624, had been recaptured by the Spanish in the following year. News of this victory was the occasion for Lope's *Brazil Restored*, finished on the 26 October 1625 and presented at court eleven days later. Olivares himself gave another playwright, Pedro Calderón de la Barca, the dispatches from which to fashion a play on the recapture of Breda in the Spanish Netherlands, seized back from the Dutch in June 1625 after a nine-month siege. His *The Siege of Breda* was presented at court the night before Lope's celebration of the restoration of Bahia.

Yet, despite all this activity over 20 years and more, the Spanish king never took it into his head, as the French throne did, to organise the entertainers into official national companies. As the state slipped into decline in the 1640s, losing control of Portugal and suffering a protracted revolt in Catalonia, public *commedias* were banned. The reopened *corrales* never regained their earlier vibrancy and Calderón ceased to write for them after 1651, when he became a priest, confining himself to operatic courtly *zarzuelas*. The Spanish were left with neither a royal national company nor an inventive popular theatre capable of vibrant new work.

The French created both in the course of the seventeenth century, although the effort came to fruition a generation after Vega. The same ingredients – sacred drama, amateur and professional secular theatrical traditions, new learning and royal interest – existed in France as elsewhere, but the last third of the sixteenth century was riven by religious conflict which, among much else, frustrated theatrical developments. By 1600, in contrast to London and Madrid, Paris had but two public theatres and the second had been established only with much difficulty. Humanism, however, had found a warm welcome in France. Early enthusiasts for the new learning argued that new plays in the vernacular on classic secular themes, in the ancient Latin style, were crucial if the French language was to achieve pre-eminence among European literatures.

196

In Paris, staging these works was undertaken by the Confraternity of the Passion, an organisation that had originally had responsibility for the mounting of the Mysteries; but these had been banned in 1548 because they were held to be a source of friction between Catholic and Protestant. Instead there were to be 'honest and decent' secular productions, played by professionals, containing 'no offence or insult'. This change was probably responsible for the banning of women from the stage. That year the Confraternity built Paris's first stage-house, the Hôtel de Bourgogne, for the first time replacing the covered real tennis courts which professional troupes of players had become accustomed to use, much as their English and Spanish peers had erected stages in open courtyards. Although protected from the weather, audiences as many as 1,000 in number stood on the *parterre* before the stage just as they did in the yard of the Globe or the Rose in London. The Confraternity maintained its monopoly strenuously until a second theatre opened, against its wishes, half a century later. Until this point, it had successfully persuaded the authorities to impose a series of inhibiting limitations on the actors who traditionally played at the St Germain fair.[7]

By 1630, Paris had caught up with London, Madrid and the Italian cities. The situation had been transformed and the theatre was, in the view of playwright Pierre Corneille, 'an object of idolatry on all sides nowadays ... It is the talk of Paris and the envy of the provinces, the favourite entertainment of princes of the blood, the pastime of common people and the quality alike.' Catherine de Medici, widow of Henry II and regent of France for decades in the name of her son, Charles IX, was responsible for this change. She had brought all the sophistications of an Italian Renaissance court, including its cooking, north of the Alps. In 1571, Ganassi and his troupe were invited to entertain at her son's wedding, a trip which gave the *commedia* companies in general a taste for travel and which led in the following century to the establishment of a permanent company of Italians in Paris. In 1581, Catherine appointed a corps of dancers, Le Ballet Comique de la Reine, to the court. Before the turn of the seventeenth century, outside the palace, the players at the Hôtel de Bourgogne, now once more including women, were permitted the title, Troupe du Roi.

The ground was prepared, as the first French humanists had argued, for a self-consciously nationalist cultural policy as a tool of statecraft. Corneille himself was one of a group of five playwrights chosen by Louis XIV's powerful chief minister, Cardinal Richelieu, to produce an official drama, a corpus of work to be admired as an expression of French civilisation. Plays were to be another plank in his cultural policy, which was also expressed by his establishment, in 1635, of the Académie Française.

Corneille wrote a smash hit, *Le Cid*, a play so successful that extra seats had to be found on the stage, an extremely profitable innovation from which the French were unable to shake free for nearly two centuries. The piece only just managed to obey the three unities and, even worse from the dramatic theorists' point of view, was a tragi-comedy, 'irregular' in its changes of tone. *Le Cid* became the occasion for a major pamphlet 'war' about dramatic theory, *Le Querelle du Cid*, fuelled by some professional jealousies but also by a real difference of opinion. The upshot of the *querelle* was that the propriety of the play's form and tone was submitted to the decision of the Académie, which pronounced in favour of classical regularity. Corneille fell into line and thereafter wrote tragedies entirely in obedience to Renaissance rules and Richelieu got the stage he wanted for propaganda purposes, a perfect expression of refined, superior French taste.

Inside the box created by these rules, works of major importance to the canon of European drama were nevertheless possible. The generation after Corneille produced, in Jean Racine, a major tragic dramatist whose *Phèdre* (1677) contained an acting challenge for a woman as great as that posed by *Hamlet* for a man. Racine was something of a protégé of Jean-Baptiste Poquelin, whose stage name was Molière. Notoriously ineffective as a tragic actor, Molière had originally ingratiated himself with Louis XIV with a short comic piece improvised in *commedia dell'arte* fashion. Installed in the Palais-Royal, a theatre Richelieu had built in 1660, he staged Racine's first play, *La Thébaïde*, but it was the comedies he mounted there and at court which ensured Molière's place among the canonised giants of European drama.

In part, his reputation rested on his collaboration with the court composer Giovanni Battista Lulli. Lulli had arrived from Italy in Paris as a boy of 14, and it was his dancing that had first brought him to the attention of the young king. Despite *Le Ballet Comique de la Reine*, the line between dancing for pleasure and appearing in a dance for the entertainment of others remained unclear. Louis himself played the Sun God in a work called *Le Ballet de la nuit* in 1653. In 1661, the King established the Académie Royale de Danse for the training of dancing masters and then, nine years later, he opted for professional dance as a distinct form. He decreed that dancing as performance was not the business of the aristocracy. The first prima ballerina, Mlle La Fontaine, debuted in 1681 in *Le Triomphe de l'amour*. Lulli had been deputed to run the Dance Academy and, working with Molière, developed the *comédie-ballet*, which integrated dance and comedy at a new level. In *Le Bourgeois gentilhomme*, for example, M. Jourdain, the bourgeois of the title, has a daughter whose lover poses as a Turk in the fourth act, so that the dance which concludes it quite naturally, as it were, takes a fashionable oriental theme.

French drama was admired as the acme of modern classicism but the Italians, in developing the lyric stage, were once again being seen as more up-to-the-minute. Claudio Monteverdi had been transforming the experiments of the Camarata into a more finished artistic form. For example, in 1642, in old age, he composed *The Coronation of Poppea*, charting Poppea's progress from harlot to the imperial throne as Emperor Nero's consort. Monteverdi had been liberated from the need to be polite about courtly behaviour because he was composing for a public opera house in a republic, Venice, whose citizenry exhibited a truly insatiable passion for the new form. Tourists were impressed:

> We went to the opera, [wrote John Evelyn in his diary in 1645] where comedies and other plays are represented in recitative music, by the most excellent musicians, vocal and

instrumental, with variety of scenes ... and machines for flying in the air, and other wonderful notions; taken together it is one of the most magnificent and expensive diversions the wit of man can invent.

It was this popularity that Lulli encouraged his paymasters to pursue after he parted with Molière and in 1672 he took over the Académie Royale de Musique, transforming it, in effect, into the Paris Opera.

Molière was playing Argan the hypochondriac in *Le Malade Imaginaire* on 17 February 1673 when he suffered a haemorrhage during the play's fourth performance. He was taken home and died four hours later, aged 51. Louis's last gesture of support for him was to overrule clerical objection to burying an actor in hallowed ground – but even the King's order could do no more than force a consecrated interment under cover of darkness. Molière's death provoked a crisis in the organisation of the theatre companies in Paris from which emerged *La Comédie-française*. Royal decree had, at last, created a proper French reply to the *Comédie-italienne* – the permanent *comedia dell'arte* company which, after repeated visits, had eventually settled in the Boulevard des Italiens. The price for status and permanency was close royal control. Regulations were drawn up by Madame la Dauphine. Oversight was given to the four First Gentlemen of the Bedchamber who in turn charged the *Intendant des Menus Plaisirs*, the official responsible for court entertainments, with the daily management of the companies. It was the job of a *premier gentilhomme* to vet all candidates for membership and the terms of their engagements. The heavy hand of this aristocratic bureaucracy soon brought the golden age of French Renaissance spoken drama to an end.

'Public stage plays shall cease'

Across the Channel, the Stuarts had been quick to assert Bourbonesque control over the vibrant London stages. A mere eight weeks after becoming King, with the theatres closed for the first time in nearly a decade because of plague, James VI & I found time to license his own group of players, including Shakespeare and Burbage, 'freely to use and exercise the art of faculty of playing comedies, tragedies, histories', ordering all 'justices, mayors, sheriffs, constables, headboroughs and other our officers to suffer them . . . without any of your lets and hindrances or molestations'. The Lord Chamberlain's Men were now the King's Men and the other companies were distributed to other members of the new royal family. It is no wonder that Thomas Dekker called his pamphlet on the events of 1603, plague and Elizabeth's death notwithstanding, 'The Wonderfull Yeare': 'The worst players' boy stood upon his good parts, swearing tragicall and busking oaths . . . he would be half a sharer (at least)'.

Soon enough, however, such close royal patronage revealed its downside. Plays offensive to the court occasioned arrests, fines and closure, despite all having been individually licensed by the Revels Office and performed by companies licensed by the King himself. There was always a serious threat that pressure from any courtly or ambassadorial quarter would force James swiftly to impose his own arbitrary 'lets and hinderances or molestations' on the actors and playwrights. In 1604, for example, Ben Jonson and George Chapman were imprisoned for having upset the King's Scottish favourites in *Eastward Ho!* Their partner, John Marston, was not arrested, although the offending lines were probably his. The experience was not new to Jonson, who had spent two months in jail under Elizabeth in 1597 for a controversial piece, *The Isle of Dogs*, written with Nashe (and now lost).[8] In 1608, the French ambassador managed to close Chapman's *Brion*, a play about recent events in France, dangerously closer to journalism than to history. The offence which had particularly incensed the ambassador, as he reported back to Paris, was that the living French queen was shown beating up one of her ladies. Three of the actors, but not Chapman, were imprisoned.

In that year also the boy companies were deemed to be too outspoken, the mask of their supposed innocence no longer a protection. The

Children of the Chapel Royal were effectively closed, denied a renewal of their lease on the Blackfriars Theatre. This had been held by Cuthbert Burbage, who now used the theatre as winter quarters for the King's Men. The company also kept the Globe, the indoor theatre being perhaps one tenth of its size, but the indoor performance space was the shape of things to come.

Ben Jonson, reasonably enough, sought refuge in the escapism of masque writing. Although they were to be seen in other great houses, under the Stuarts masques became the court entertainment par excellence. Jonson wrote 20 of the 37 mounted during the reign of James I. On one occasion he received the princely fee of £40. The entire production had cost an enormous £2,000, over half of which had been spent on costumes. Inigo Jones, the architect, with whom Jonson constantly feuded, used these ruinous sums of money to advance the nascent art of scenic design in England, substantially increasing the range of effects that the indoor theatre could accomplish. Acted by the court and the royal family, the themes were invariably antique and allegorical – a princess representing the Thames, for example, with 12 other English and Welsh rivers personified by the ladies of the bedchamber. Women might have been banned from the public stage but at court it was a different matter. There Lope de Vega's opinion, that *sin ellas todo es nada* – 'without women all is nothing' – was shared. This did not meet with general approval:

> At night we had the Queen's Maske in the Banquetting House . . . At the further end was a great Skallop, where were four seats; on the lowest sat the Queen with my Lady Bedford; on the rest were placed the Ladies Suffolk, Darby, Rich, Effingham, Ann Herbert, Susan Herbert, Elizabeth Howard, Walsingham and Bevil. Their apparel was rich, but too light and Curtizan-like for such great ones.

The Puritans were, of course, even more outraged by the court's dramatics than by the public stage. William Prynne lost his ears, was fined

£5,000 and sentenced to 'perpetuall imprisonment in the Towre of London', for his 1632 tract *Histriomastix*. His reference to 'women actors, notorious whores' was read as clearly meaning Queen Henrietta Maria, Charles I's consort and often the leading masquerader. It was to describe her that the very word 'actress' had first appeared in English in 1626.

Those involved with the professional public theatre found it ever harder to avoid political difficulties. One option was to leave the country: Dekker's demanding boy actor threatened that, if he were not made 'half a sharer', he would 'else strowle (that is to say travell) with some notorious wicked company abroad'. Such was the reputation of English players that they could, emulating the Italians of the previous century, now export their art. Companies of English actors were becoming something of a commonplace across northern Europe. By the 1620s, English companies were established at the courts of Hesse and Brunswick and had been seen as far east as Poland. Such was their popularity that two hundred years later, long after their day, shows were still being sold as the work of *Engliche Komödianten*.

For the majority who stayed, still enjoying massive public support, the consuming debate about the central problem of state power, against the backdrop of religious strife, was unavoidable. Within years, the issue would be brought to the decision of the battlefields of a civil war. The stage could not but reflect the intellectual currents that were fuelling this deepening crisis. For Shakespeare, in *The Tempest* (1611), utopian social arrangements, notwithstanding the sombre reflections of Sir Thomas More (the real one) in his essay *Utopia* a century earlier, were still a matter for jocularity, echoes of the medieval Land of Cockaigne:

> *Gonzalo*: I' the commonwealth I would by contraries
> Execute all things . . .
> No occupation, all men idle, all;
> No sovereignty.
> *Sebastian*: Yet he would be king on't.

Antonio: The latter end of his commonwealth forgets the
   beginning.

Just over a decade later, political arrangements are a matter for tragedy.
In *The Bondman*, Massinger chose a slave revolt in ancient Greece as a
vehicle for this agenda. The slaves' leader Marullo justifies revolt:

>   Your tyranny
> Drew us from our obedience. Happy those times
> When lords were styled fathers of families,
> And not imperious masters.

But this is no *Fuente Ovejuna* looking for the re-establishment of the
old order of beneficent masters and overlords. The slaves demand:

>   Liberty
> To all such as desire to make return
> Into their countries; and, to those that stay,
> A competence of land freely allotted
> To each man's proper use, no lord acknowledged.

The joking was over.
   Early in September 1642, less than two weeks after Charles I had
declared war on the Parliament in London, the politicians acted to
close all the theatres:

> Whereas, the distracted Estate of England, threatened with
> a cloud of blood by a civil war, calls for all pallible means to
> assuage and avert the wrath of God . . . it is therefore
> thought fit and ordained by the Lords and Commons in
> the Parliament assembled, that . . . public stage plays shall
> cease and be foreborn.

The character Jonson had once called Zeal-of-the-Land Busy had finally won the argument. The most misnamed play in the annals of the English stage, the innocent *A Jovial Crew*, with the most maladroit line in English drama – 'Away with all grief and give us more sack' – was the last play to be seen before the ordinance took effect.

The ranks of the *Engliche Komödianten* on the continent swelled as many players fled, but Zeal-of-the-Land Busy was not quite busy enough to stop all performances in England and Wales during the next 18 years. Mounting a production was a dangerous business but in noble houses, among the students of the Inns of Court and even, on occasion, surreptitiously within the closed theatres, it was done. Eventually, Cromwell weakened the Puritans' resolve by permitting the pageantry of London's annual Lord Mayor's parade once more and in 1656 the royalist, Sir William D'Avenant, was allowed to mount *The Siege of Rhodes*. D'Avenant, who claimed without much evidence to be Shakespeare's bastard son, divided the piece (after the fashion of a masque) into entries, rather than acts, and mounted it, not in one of the old theatres, but in Rutland House. Safest of all, it was that new Italian thing – an opera. He was allowed to transfer the production to his old theatre where *The Spaniards in Peru* followed in 1658. A year later, in the midst of what John Evelyn called the 'anarchy and confusion' following Oliver Cromwell's death, *Sir Francis Drake* was staged.

D'Avenant was therefore already in place when Charles II entered London in triumph on 29 May 1660 to restore the throne. It took the King a little longer than it had either his grandfather James or the vengeful Puritan Parliament to get round to the stage, but, less than three months after the Stuarts returned, he allowed two patented theatres to reopen. These prospered and, despite the efforts of the authorities, other stages, eschewing – or pretending to eschew – spoken drama opened as well.

D'Avenant, one of the victorious patentees, leased an old real tennis court in Lincoln's Inn Fields and converted it into the most up-to-date playhouse, the Duke of York's. It had a proscenium arch, the country's first, an apron stage and a capacity for creating scenic 'clap-traps' – whereby a breathtaking scenic effect (or an audacious actor) seduced the audience into applauding. Among Sir William's bright ideas was the selling of coin-like tokens, the ancestor of the ticket, in advance of a performance. (Before this innovation, shows would start when enough money had been collected as the house filled up.) His rival at the other patented company, Thomas Killegrew, went further and erected, from scratch, a custom-built theatre in Drury Lane which opened in 1663.

The abandonment of the open-air playhouses meant that the old Elizabethan 'stack 'em high' logic of the large diverse audiences paying comparatively little was cast aside in favour of smaller audiences who, because a run was still only half a dozen performances or so, had to pay a lot more to see a play – a shilling for the cheapest seats. Instead of the 2,000+ held by a Globe, a big indoor theatre, Killegrew's new Theatre Royal for example, could only manage a maximum of 700. Even when, in the next century, the indoor theatres grew – for instance the house in Covent Garden that opened in 1737 sat nearly 3,000 – despite the raucousness of the gallery which had replaced the noisy yard of the old open theatres, the old diversity was never quite restored.

A changed dramatic diet served this changed audience. D'Avenant routinely updated the works of his putative 'father' to conform with both these new acting conditions and the supposedly more refined taste of the new age. This was to be the fashion for the next century, the treatment of Shakespeare being very different from that accorded to Lope de Vega in Spain. The biggest development, however, was the arrival of the professional actress. Sir William, who had been in the court entertainment business all his life, knew the truth of Lope's opinion about women on the stage: *todo es nada* without them. Even before the Restoration, he had risked having a Mrs Edward Coleman sing in the *Siege of Rhodes*, albeit with her husband, who was also in the cast, as some sort of earnest of her respectability. In 1660, for the first time in more than a century, an English woman – we do not know her name – appeared in public, in a play, almost certainly as Desdemona in Shakespeare's *Othello*. This did not mean that D'Avenant had given up entirely on boy actors: he cast Ned Kynaston (who was to be a leading adult male Restoration player) as Olympia in Beaumont and Fletcher's

The Loyal Subject. Young Ned 'made the loveliest lady that I ever saw in my life', thought Samuel Pepys, Secretary of the Navy and an obsessive theatregoer.[9] The new opinion was that women posed a lesser moral danger than did sexually ambiguous young men in drag. Killigrew, obviously believing that there cannot be too much of a good thing, revived his own pre-Civil War 'loose and obscene' play, *The Parson's Wedding*, with an entirely female cast. That novelty did not catch on, but the 1662 patents, by insisting on women because 'some had taken offence' against the boys, soon enough killed off the female impersonators.

On the afternoon of 5 October 1667, there was not even standing room at the Duke of York's playhouse in London for Sir Thomas Saint Serfe's new play, *The Coffee House*. Pepys, thwarted at the Duke of York's, instead betook himself to the rival house, the King's Theatre in Drury Lane.

> And there, going in, met with Knepp[10] and she took us up into the tiring rooms and to the woman's shift where Nell was dressing herself and was all unready and is very pretty, prettier than I thought. . . But, Lord! To see how they both were painted would make a man mad and did make me loath them.

But not really.

Nell (or Ellen) Gwynn (or Guyn) had made her debut in John Dryden's *The Indian Empress*. She was, perhaps, 15 but she was already in the bed of a leading actor, the handsome Charles Hart. She was always more to be valued for her loveliness, vivacity and charm than for her dramatic talent. It is no wonder that she was thought good at impersonating men in 'breeches parts', once a neat way for helping boys who had to play women, but now an excuse for actresses to display their legs in form-hugging menswear. In *Secret Love*, Dryden wrote an exchange about a sort of seventeenth-century pre-nuptial agreement, a 'proviso scene', an innovation that was to be often repeated in

207

Restoration drama. The lovers wittily outlining the rules they required their partner to obey after marriage were played by Gwynn and Hart, giving their original audience, who well knew they were an 'item', an entirely modern frisson:

> *Celandon, a courtier* (Mr Hart): As for the first year, according to the laudable custome of new married people, we shall follow one another up into Chambers, and down into Gardens, and think, we shall never have enough of one another. —— So far, this 'tis pleasant enough I hope.
>
> *Florimell, a maid of honour* (Mrs[11] Ellen Guyn): But after that, when we begin to live like Husband and Wife, and never come near one another —— what then, Sir?
>
> *Celandon*: Why then our onely happiness must be to have one mind, and one will, Florimell.
>
> *Florimell*: One mind if thou wilt, but prithee let us have two wills; for I find one will be little enough for me alone.

Pepys went on four occasions to see the original production and twice to both revivals in the following two years:

> So great a performance of a comical part was never, I believe, in the world before as Nell do this, both as a mad girle, then most and best of all when she comes in like a young gallant; and hath the motions and carriage of a spark the most that ever I saw any man have. It makes me, I confess, admire her.

He was not alone. King Charles went twice and had the piece given at court a month after its run. In 1669, he was again smitten, this time by Gwynn's delivery of an epilogue. Epilogues were not quite 'clap-trap' but were nevertheless designed as crowd-pleasing speeches, often given to the star actress to display her wit. A year later, Gwynn's last role as royal mistress removed her from the stage. In Lely's portrait of her in the character of Venus, a prototype pin-up image probably painted for Charles's eyes only, she lies nude on pillows and a sheet, a somewhat conventional beauty of the time – oval face, straight nose, Cupid's bow-lips, hooded eyes and a slight, almost boyish, figure – 'a killing dame', the poet, wit and rake John Wilmot, Earl of Rochester called her.[12] Other Restoration actresses, Anne Bracegirdle (whose 'unique selling point' was a strident insistence on private respectability) or Wilmot's mistress, Elizabeth Barry, say, were far more well-regarded; but Nell's celebrity has ensured that it is she rather than they who is best remembered.

Celebrity is often claimed as a modern obsession, the engine driving what are now economically significant industries, but it emerges in exactly this contemporary form in the seventeenth century, an enduring by-product of European individualism. Our current obsession with the stars of stage (and now screen) demonstrates that, in 350 years, however much the world has changed, the glamour of the stage and the fame it bestows on individual players has not. It was not only in prints of the famous that the modern European individual, by virtue of skill and talent rather than birth or status, stood forth. She also emerged under the soft glow of a hundred flickering candles, most brilliantly, for good or ill. Of Nell Gwynn, whose trustee and advisor he was in the 1670s, Rochester wrote: 'Who knows not her name?'

Sources

John Allen (1983), *A History of the Theatre in Europe*, London: Heinemann.

James Bowen (1975), *A History of Western Education (Vol. Two)*, London: Methuen.

Julian Bowsher (1998), *The Rose Theatre*, London: Museum of London.

Oscar Brockett and Franklin Hildy (2003), *History of the Theatre*, Boston: Allyn & Bacon.

John Russell Brown (ed.) (1995), *The Oxford Illustrated History of the Theatre*, Oxford: Oxford University Press.

John Dryden (1966), *The Works of John Dryden, Volume IX*, Berkeley: University of California Press.

Deborah Payne Fisk (ed.) (2000), *The Cambridge Companion to the English Restoration Theatre*, Cambridge: Cambridge University Press.

Anthony Masters (1992), *The Play of Personality in the Restoration Theatre*, Woodbridge, Suffolk: Boydell.

Leslie Orrey (1972), *A Concise History of Opera*, London: Thames & Hudson.

Samuel Pepys (1953), *The Diary*, London: Dent.

Sandra Richard (1993), *The Rise of the English Actress*, New York: St Martin's.

Alexander Schouvaloff (1987), *The Theatre Museum*, London: Scala Books.

Michael Sidnell *et al.* (eds) (1991), *Sources of Dramatic Theory: 1 Plato to Congreve*, Cambridge: Cambridge University Press.

Claire Tomalin (2002), *Samuel Pepys: The Unequalled Self*, London: Viking.

David Vieth (ed.) (1962), *The Complete Poems of John Wilmot Earl of Rochester*, New Haven: Yale University Press.

Stanley Wells (ed.) (1986), *The Cambridge Companion to Shakespeare Studies*, Cambridge: Cambridge University Press.

Glynne Wickham (1985), *A History of Theatre*, Oxford: Phaidon.

John Dover Wilson (1911, 1944), *Life in Shakespeare's England*, Harmondsworth: Penguin.

5

'SO MUCH FOR STAGE FEELING': STAGE AND SCREEN FROM 1737

'The gaiety of nations'

On 2 March 1737, two very different young men set out together from Lichfield in Staffordshire to travel the 116 miles to London seeking their fortunes. They had one horse between them, on which they rode turn and turn about. One was a heavy, ungainly and scrofulous 28-year-old, son of a poor bookseller who had managed to afford but four terms at Oxford. The other, eight years younger, was of small stature, handsome and lithe. He was the child of an army officer (originally of asylum-seeking French Protestant descent) with wine-importing connections but too poor to go to university at all. The elder of the pair, having failed to establish a grammar school, now had a plan to make his mark on the stage and carried with him his five-act tragedy, *Irene*, already written and ready to sell. The younger, a former pupil at the school, was on his way to continue his education in the cheapest fashion possible at another school in Rochester, Kent. Ultimately, he was bound for the law.

Decades later, the elder, Samuel Johnson, recalled 1737: 'That was the year I came to London with two pence half penny in my pocket.' David Garrick, the man who travelled with him, 'overhearing him, exclaimed, "Eh? What do you say, With two pence half-penny in your pocket?" Johnson: "Why yes; when I came with two pence half-penny in *my* pocket, and thou, Davy, with three half-pence in thine".' Johnson never fulfilled his theatrical ambitions although 'Little Davy' did loyally produce *Irene*, with no success, in 1749. (The failure caused a rift

211

between them.) Garrick was equally unsuccessful in that he never got to the Inns of Court; nor did he prosper at a wine-importing business set up in partnership with his elder brother. As an actor, on the other hand, he triumphed. His contemporaries thought him 'a bright luminary in the theatrical hemisphere . . . a star of the first magnitude' – indeed, he was the first player to be called such a thing – a 'star' – in English, in print.

He began acting in London in amateur performances staged in the somewhat lavish home of the proprietor and editor of the *Gentleman's Magazine*, Edward Cave, an early employer of Johnson's journalistic talents.[1] Garrick was still a wine-merchant when he began infiltrating the green rooms of the theatres, much to the detriment of his business and the annoyance of his brother. In 1740, he wrote a play, an 'after-piece' to be performed after the main five-act play. Afterpieces were short comical, often farcical, one-acters. Curtain up was now at 6.00 p.m. but half-price tickets were sold for the last two acts and the afterpiece was offered to make buying late tickets worthwhile. For Garrick, there was no social problem involved since playwriting was a perfectly respectable activity for a gentleman, or indeed an aristocrat, to undertake.

Garrick had become close to Henry Giffard, who ran Goodman's Fields, a popular but unpatented theatre, ostensibly given over to musical shows but actually illegally offering pure dramatic entertainment. His afterpiece was produced there as part of a benefit performance for Giffard. Benefits, which were special productions, with ticket prices doubled and the profits going to a named actor, were a common occurrence at this time. In the spring of 1741, Giffard gave Garrick his first opportunity to act professionally in London masked as Harlequin. Giffard was engaged to bring a company to Ipswich that summer and he took Garrick. When they got back to Goodman's, Garrick decided that for his London debut he would play Richard III, in a suitably genteel version of Shakespeare's play concocted by the actor-manager and writer, Colly Cibber. The playbill proclaimed: 'N.B. The part of King Richard by a Gentleman (who never appeared on any stage).' This was not true, quite, but nor was it an inducement. New actors often debuted using this format and Londoners knew better than to spend money on seeing them. The house was half empty, as might have been expected, but Garrick's performance set the audience 'on a roar'. The *Daily Post*'s anonymous critic wrote that his reception was 'the most extraordinary and great that was ever known on such an occasion; and we hear he obliges the town this evening with the same performance'. As acting, unlike playwriting, was no job for a gentleman, Garrick soon had to come clean to his family, which he did by explaining: 'as I shall make very near £300 per annum by it, and as it is really what I dote on, I am resolved to pursue it'. And pursue it he did – for the next 35 years, totally dominating the English stage.

He played Richard III 15 times in that first season as well as giving 151 other performances in 17 different roles. He had a prodigious memory and he was willing to take on parts which, in the fashion of the time, 'belonged' to other, older actors. Cibber, for example, so much deemed the comic role of Bayes, in the Restoration satire, *The Rehearsal*, to be his that he handed it on to his son. Garrick nevertheless seized it and swiftly made it his own. Drury Lane immediately snapped him up for the 1742–3 season, for £500 per annum plus a percentage of the box office. He took Giffard and also Mrs Giffard, a talented actress, with him. Five years later, having suffered from incompetent managers, he raised £8,000 to buy himself 50 per cent of the patent and, with it, the post of sole artistic director. He took one break between 1763 and 1765 to tour the Continent in a private capacity, until, after a triumphant performance in the summer of 1776 in *The Wonder, a Woman Keeps a Secret*, a then old (1714) and now forgotten comedy by Susannah Centlivre,[2] he retired. He died three years later and was buried in Westminster Abbey. Samuel Johnson wrote that little Davy's death 'eclipsed the gaiety of nations'. Garrick was not the first theatrical to be buried in the Abbey (Ben Jonson preceded him); nor was he knighted for services to the stage (nobody was until 1895); but he was the first actor to enter the elevated social milieu of London's *bon ton* as something other than a servant, mistress or toy-boy. The benefits of his celebrity considerably enhanced the status of the actor, although his colleagues were still, for the most part, a déclassé crew.

As a manager he followed and expanded on Giffard's practices. He too insisted on proper rehearsals and a drum was beaten to alert actors in the coffee-houses around the Covent Garden piazza when they were beginning. He was interested in improving stage techniques and introduced hidden lighting, although the auditorium still remained lit throughout a performance. It was also still the habit to allow the quality to sit on the stage, but now only at benefits. In 1755, Garrick arranged a benefit performance of *Hamlet*, with Charles Holland, whom he had trained, playing the title role. Tate Wilkinson, a Westminster School pupil at the time, recalled that when Holland's hat fell off during his initial encounter with the Ghost, a traditional bit of business that audiences expected:

> An inoffensive woman in a red cloak (a friend of Holland's), hearing Hamlet complain that the air bit shrewdly and was very cold, with infinite composure crossed the stage, took up the hat and with the greatest care placed it fast on Hamlet's head.

Garrick banned seats on the stage, although this had a potentially adverse effect on the size of the benefit. He avoided trouble with his company by squeezing more seats into the house so that another £135 a night could be taken and their share maintained.

Running a company was stressful. All managers excited animosities which piled up over the years, and Garrick, although continually praised for his performances, was no exception. Sometimes squabbles would occur when plays were turned down or actors turned away. Even when, as with Johnson, a piece failed, Garrick would be blamed. These private spats had a habit of becoming public rows, fought through the medium of the pamphlet. The audience could also be problematic. It might have become less diverse than the Elizabethan groundlings, but it was somewhat readier to turn into a mob. Apprentices and other rowdies yet flooded the gallery and could easily be infuriated by a manager who misjudged the attractions of an offering. Garrick was more usually right than wrong, but he made a major mistake when he decided, in 1755, to import a French ballet company led by Jean-Georges Noverre.

In France, the ballet had continued to develop since the days of Lulli. Masks and wigs had been abandoned and Rameau, Lulli's successor, had encouraged the adoption of new steps such as the jump. In 1734, a leading ballerina, Marie Camago, gave up heels and shortened her skirts. Her rival, Marie Salle, threw off her corsets and danced in a Greek tunic. Garrick, in serious need of new afterpieces and conscious that Covent Garden had the edge when it came to spectacles, imported Noverre, ballet's leading choreographer and theoretician, and 60 dancers for the season at an unheard-of cost of £2,000. He and the Frenchman were both blithely naïve about the political situation.

In 1755, because England and France were facing up for their third armed confrontation of the century, hostility to all things French was running high. Garrick thought to avoid trouble by giving his Richard III and inviting King George II, who had never seen it. The ploy did not work. The King slept through the performance, although afterwards he did say he liked the Lord Mayor (who has all of 11 lines in Act III, Scene 5). Anyway the crowd was so raucous that the King withdrew – happy when he was told the noise was expressing anti-French sentiment. Within days the uproar had grown so great that the dancers could not perform, and Garrick had to buy the French out of their contract. (A decade later, Noverre, now working for the court in Stuttgart, created the modern story-telling ballet by introducing the *pas d'action* which enabled a narrative to be told entirely in dance.[3])

Garrick was also less than successful when he tried to stop issuing late half-price tickets. In 1763, working in concert with the management of Covent Garden, both houses abolished half-price admittance. A well-organised mob tore up the benches (which had only comparatively recently become fixed to the floor) in the two theatres. This would never have happened in less liberal European lands where the threat of unruliness had led to armed guards becoming a feature of the auditoria.[4] The London 'Old Price' riots forced both managements to capitulate.

'On the stage he was natural'

Garrick was honoured at home and abroad not simply because he was a great actor, but rather because he was a great actor in a revolutionary new style, which his contemporaries called 'natural' – although this term must be understood in the context of highly formal eighteenth-century society. We share an understanding of how behaviour should be represented to us in performance, 'natural' or realistically represented behaviour always being the distilled essence of actual observed or potentially observable demeanour. As modes of behaviour change, so the code to reflect them also changes; which is why, ever since Garrick, despite the dominance of the 'natural' over the declamatory on the English stage, one generation's acting style can look quite arch, if not stilted, to the next.

By the 1740s, the old declamatory style, already in Shakespeare's time prone to 'tear a passion to tatters', had become stultified. Tragic actors were primarily valued for their stentorian voices. Of one, the novelist Tobias Smollet said: 'His utterance is a continual singsong . . . his action resembles that of heaving ballast into the hold of a ship.' Delivery had become mannered to the point of travesty, gestures to express emotion codified and mechanistic. Books were available to explain how to do it.

John Rich, Garrick's rival at the Garden, was a very effective manager. In 1728, he had staged a musical play, *The Beggar's Opera* by John Gay, an enormous hit which brought to London a French innovation, a *pièce-en-vaudevilles*.[5] *The Beggar's Opera* had made, the wits said, 'Rich gay and Gay rich'. So wealthy did it make Rich that he had built the theatre in Covent Garden on the proceeds. As an actor, though, Rich was very much of the old school. During one performance, he left the stage to box the ears of the prompter for feeding him a line unnecessarily, thereby interrupting, as he explained to the audience on his return, his 'grand pause'. It is easy to see why Garrick's great friend, the actor Charles Macklin, thought that the dominant manner on the stage was 'hoity-toity'.

Macklin was an Irishman, 20 years Garrick's elder, who had joined the Drury Lane company in 1733.[6] In February 1741, just as Garrick was making his anonymous debut, Macklin determined to give *The Merchant of Venice*, which had not been seen since 1701 when a hit adaptation, *The Jew of Venice*, replaced it in the repertoire. Not only did Macklin insist on the original, he also researched the part, spending time observing London's Jews, discovering that in Venice they wore red hats, reading Josephus's history of the Jews. In his diary, he noted: 'Jews, their history . . . Go through the history of it – act the great characters.' Before the curtain went up on the evening of 14 February, there was a row. Under the old-style rehearsal where everybody did their thing, still in vogue at Drury Lane at this time, Macklin's colleagues were unaware that he was plotting a revolution – a realistically villainous Shylock, rather than a stereotypical comic one. The other actors were convinced that disaster was staring them in the face and it certainly must have been an odd evening. Portia flirted with the crowd as usual and Antonio was booming away while, instead of the comic turn the audience were expecting, they got Macklin's carefully observed, sinister Jew. By the end, though, Macklin had won. He noted that, 'The whole house was in an uproar of applause'.[7]

The following October, the 'Gentleman (who never appeared on any stage)' opted for Macklin's approach. Garrick's Richard III was far more physical than the audience was used to, full of movement, changes of expression and variations in the voice. He listened to what the other actors were saying and he never slipped out of character at the end of a speech; nor did he assume a character after he came on the stage, having entered as himself, expecting applause. Old-school actors decided Garrick and Macklin's new method of acting was a nine-days' wonder but they could not have been more wrong. The new-school actors were completing a development long in the making from the original process of acting as impersonation to acting as the emotionally rounded delineation of an individual character. In doing this, they raised two basic questions.

The first was a paradox – that psychological truth is reached through dissembling. As Shakespeare had put it:

> Is it not monstrous that this player here,
> But in a fiction, in a dream of passion,
> Could force his soul so to his own conceit
> That from her working all his visage waned,
> Tears in his eyes, distraction in his aspect,
> A broken voice, and his whole function suiting
> With forms to his conceit?

Which raises the second issue. Does the actor perform this lying truth intuitively or consciously? This was the basis of an eighteenth-century theoretical 'war' between 'sentiment' and 'calculation'. Dr Johnson once asked the actor John Kemble, very much Garrick's successor as an effective manager,[8]

> Are you, Sir, one of those enthusiasts who believe yourself transformed into the very character you represent?
> *Kemble*: No.
> *Dr Johnson*: If Garrick really believed himself to be that monster, Richard the Third, he deserved to be hanged every time he performed it.

Garrick did not so believe. Once, during *King Lear*, having as usual brought the house to tears, he said (turning upstage, *sotto voce* and ironically) to the actor with whom he was performing, 'Damme, Tom, it'll do! So much for stage feeling.' Garrick's art depended on an ability to recollect emotion in tranquillity and reproduce it; hence the importance of observation and research, the need for careful rehearsal, to create a character who was not himself – night after night and, in the case of his most popular roles, year after year. In all this, he was seeking psychologically valid justifications for every word and movement. As was noticed at the time, 'Garrick was, so to speak, searching after nature'; or rather, searching after an expressive code which struck his audiences as 'natural'. Oliver Goldsmith, the witty playwright, said of him, 'On the stage he was natural, simple, affecting', but added: 'T'was only that when he was off, he was acting.'

The European stage was becoming everywhere, as in London, rather the property of the players than of the playwrights who had sustained the rebirth and flowering of the drama (*commedia dell'arte* apart) over the previous two centuries. Now it was the theory of acting rather than the elaboration of supposedly ancient rules governing dramatic conventions that conditioned intellectual debates about the drama. The new theoretical focus produced no conspicuous flow of new plays and Macklin's and Garrick's innovative acting style was deployed in old pieces; no new Shakespeare, Racine or de Vega emerged. Creativity was far from dead but a golden age of dramatic writing had passed.

'The liberty of the stage'

In Great Britain, as elsewhere, censorship of the stage remained a given, despite contemporary British moves towards press freedom. An anonymous piece in 1737, *The Golden Rump*, concentrated on the King's bowel functions and finally gave Sir Robert Walpole, the long-serving leader of the Whig government, the excuse he needed to replace the creaking Master of the Revels system of stage censorship. It might well have been that he encouraged the production exactly to engineer such a pretext – after all, he controlled the press by recycling the newspaper taxes to toady editors in the form of bribes, so such a stratagem would not be beyond him. For Walpole, trying to protect the King was a necessary ploy. It would silence those who would attack him if he tried to stifle a play that merely mocked him – for example, he had been widely seen as the model for the master-criminal Peachum in *The Beggar's Opera*. Walpole rushed through Parliament a new theatrical Licensing Act giving the Lord Chamberlain the censor's role with increased powers. Prior constraint on the liberty of the stage was strengthened, even as such censorship was being declared generally illegal under the common law. Lord Chesterfield, then an ally of Walpole and the most admired speaker in the House of Lords, complained that the measure 'seems designed not only as a restraint on the licentiousness of the stage; but it will prove a most arbitrary restraint on the liberty of the stage'.[9] During the era of direct censorship which followed, and for the 231 years it lasted, few new plays prior to the late nineteenth century were admitted to the canon. By then, some – George Bernard Shaw, for example – were convinced that this dearth was entirely the fault of the Lord Chamberlain. His Examiner of Plays did prove to be just the restraint Lord Chesterfield feared – surviving the abolition of the leaky patented theatre duopoly by a new Theatre Regulation Act in 1843, the rise of the musical hall thereafter and the coming of the movies, radio and television. The Act of 1737 made the concept of free expression, in one of the few societies that legally acknowledged its existence as a principle in the first place, media specific; that is, it was limited to the press and not automatically assumed to be available for other forms of expression.

The eighteenth-century European spoken stage was in general better at creating new comedy than at producing enduring tragedies: in Britain, for instance, there are the late Restoration-style comedies, Goldsmith's *She Stoops to Conquer* (1773) and Sheridan's *School for Scandal* (1777). In Italy, a stage-obsessed young lawyer, Carlo Goldoni, determined to transform the ad-libbed tradition of the *commedia dell'arte*. In 1738, he added one fully written part to the indications given in the *soggetto* for a *commedia*, *Man of the World*. Five years later, he produced a complete script, written in the style of *commedia* ad-libbing, *The Servant of Two Masters*, one of 150 plays he was to write. Unlike Shakespeare and Kemp, Goldoni gave in to his top clown, Antonio Sacchi, still allowing him to improvise; but when the text was published all the clown's speeches were printed – probably created as much by Sacchi as by Goldoni.

Otherwise, Italian spoken tragedy was completely eclipsed by the lyric stage. The courtly *opera seria* continued to flourish, expanding its musical resources by adding horns and trombones and finally clarinets to the original strings, woodwind and trumpets. In Naples, Alessandro Scarlatti developed a tripartite overture form which was to give rise to the symphony; but the Italian opera, as the palace entertainment par excellence, found its most welcoming home in the Hapsburg court in Vienna. Conversely, in London, when Handel attempted to operate in an open entertainment market, he found building a ticket-buying audience for opera more difficult. In France, to escape from Lulli's strictures, a public *opéra-comique* was instituted in 1715 at the Theatre de la Foire, home of the *pièces-en-vaudevilles* which Gay had aped. The *opéra-comique* also produced parodies of the *opera seria*, which were to metamorphose into the operetta in the following century and, especially across the Atlantic, into the musical a century after that.

The French spoken stage still held itself bound by the strictures of neo-classical composition, reinforced by the increasingly atrophied acting style of the *Comédie-française*, and by various levels of direct state control – including official ticket inspectors to monitor tax and calculate royalty payments – and a claque in the audience to condition a play's reception. French admiration for the English stage, at least among the enlightened, seldom translated into fresh works. Voltaire, besides everything else, was a most prolific dramatist. Despite his early fondness for Shakespeare, the most daring break with the neo-classical in the 53 plays he wrote was the introduction of occasional spectacular effects. Denis Diderot, whose theoretical musings on the nature of acting were much inspired by Garrick's innovative acting style, reduced the players of the *Comédie* to a complete funk in 1758 by having them speak, at least in part, in prose instead of verse. The play, *Le Père de famille*, came some 30 years after its model, George Lillo's *The London Merchant* – a bourgeois (or 'lachrymose') tragedy which attempted 'to show, in artless strains . . . a Tale of private Woe' – opened at Drury

Lane. The English had long had a taste for non-aristocratic milieux, going back to the Elizabethan *Arden of Faversham*, but it had been catered for by very few plays. *The London Merchant*, although often revived into the nineteenth century, like its predecessors fostered little emulation.

Paris failed to appreciate Diderot's effort and other continental European audiences did not take the *drame bourgeois* to their hearts either. Gotthold Lessing's *Miss Sara Sampson* (1755) – in which the eponymous heroine is murdered by her lover's mistress, causing the lover to commit suicide – was, like *The London Merchant*, a runaway hit in the German-speaking lands, but it did not mark the start of a tradition of middle-class dramas in German. The German lands had proved unresponsive to Renaissance neo-classical theatre although, on a more popular front, Hans Sachs, an early supporter of Luther in Nuremberg, had been allowed to mount new productions for amateur performers in the city's Marthakircher. These combined the old sacred plays with new short, satirical *Fashnachtsspiel*, an equivalent of the English Mummers.[10] *Miss Sara Sampson* marked a turn from 'a period of boring French taste' (as Johann Goethe put it) which had replaced Sachs's pioneering effort to English models. The domestic did not take, but Shakespeare, finally, did. *Shakespearomanie* fuelled the 'storm and stress' of German romantic drama in the decades that followed, eventually producing masterworks – Goethe's *Egmont*, for example, or Schiller's *Maria Stuart*, both set in Shakespeare's century and influenced by his way with history.[11]

In Spain, the eighteenth-century Bourbon court was indifferent to the theatre and the public stages came, as in London, to rely on the repertoire. Lope de Vega was never revised to suit contemporary sensibilities as Shakespeare was and he, Calderón and their less well-remembered contemporaries continued to be performed but under the beady eye of the authorities. The government even banned ad-libbing. On the other hand, in Russia, the Romanovs were theatrical enthusiasts. The Empress Elizabeth was so fond of drama that she compelled her court to attend performances by the company she had created; and Catherine the Great was a prolific playwright. But in Russia too, by 1800, the stage was firmly controlled by the secret police.

Few canonical works were produced under the eye of the court in France either, although some comedies have endured. In 1784 Pierre-Augustin Charon de Beaumarchais followed up his 1775 success, *Le Barbier de Seville*, with one of the century's greatest hits, *Le Mariage de Figaro ou la Folle Journée*. It played an unprecedented 80 perform-ances and immediately crossed the Channel as *The Follies of a Day*, but it had been licensed in Paris only with difficulty. Marie Antoinette had persuaded Louis XVI to hear the playwright read the script. Louis, offering a running commentary in the accepted aristocratic style, was eventually apparently moved to comment that the play would 'never be performed: for this play not to be a danger, the Bastille would have to be torn down first'. Nevertheless, Beaumarchais – so effective an oper-ator that he was among the first to collect royalties on performances of his plays – had a more positive reception from court officials. They were persuaded by his charm and the wit of the piece to allow a pro-duction. Louis also agreed, hoping the play would fail; but he had been right the first time. On the opening night, prolonged applause greeted Figaro's great speech: 'No, Monsieur le Comte, you shall not have her . . . Because you are a great lord you imagine you are a great genius! Nobility, wealth, titles and appointments, they all make you so proud.'

'Pictures in glasse to make strange things appear'

Voltaire might have been loath to kick against the constraints of the classical rules in his playwriting but he was not unwilling to embrace an entirely new medium, to wit: the magic lantern. His slide-shows, com-plete with comic commentary delivered in a funny Savoyard accent (because itinerant lanternists in France stereotypically came from the poor province of Savoy), would, said Madame de Graffiny, who was present at one in 1738, 'make you die laughing . . . No! there was never anything so funny!'

The magic lantern had been known for more than a century, since the days of Christiaan Huygens. By 1664 a Thomas Walgensten was giving professional magic-lantern shows as entertainment but, in a pattern that has been endlessly repeated with each successive communication technology down to the present, some were quick to trumpet the device's radical educational potential. In 1702, Johann Creiling, in the course of a lecture at Tübingen University, suggested that the magic lantern would revolutionise face-to-face teaching. In the event, the lantern was to find real popularity in the fairground tent and the salons of the aristocracy, creating more opportunities to misbehave than to learn anything:

> La Fare [that is, le marquis Charles Auguste de La Fare] offered to show us a magic lantern which he had made. The room was prepared, and he passed in front of us a series of the engravings of l'Arétin [almost certainly images of copulation inspired by Aretino] ... During the darkness, everyone grabbed hold of a woman ...

including, it must be assumed, the guest of honour at this early eighteenth-century soirée, Philippe d'Orléans, Regent of France from 1715 to 1723 and a noted rake.

Magic-lantern shows were like musical performances in that they were given in the home and people sat or stood around haphazardly in order to enjoy them. In the theatres of the day, especially in mainland Europe, similar moveable seating was to be found in the welter of boxes tiered around the walls in a U-shape, in chairs on the stage itself or in the benches that had filled up the standing space of the pit. Unordered, moveable seating was also reflected in audience behaviour at home and in public. It was by no means the case at either theatrical or musical public entertainments that people were silent during the performance. In fact, aristocrats seemed to regard quiet attentiveness as an unforgivably bourgeois trait. Performances were social gatherings and the done thing was to circulate – exactly as is still done at modern parties even on those rare occasions when live rather than recorded music is provided.

Fixed benches and then stalls, rows of fixed individual seats, only slowly replaced the moveable benches. The word 'auditorium' with its connotation of fixed seating is not even found in English before 1727. Lantern shows shared the informality of the private musical soirée until, at end of the eighteenth century, like public musical performances, they were being offered as ticketed entertainment and domestic casualness gave way to orderliness. The lantern shows became, through this process of seating the audience, much more theatrical both in the complexity of the illusions presented and, all importantly, in the narratives attempted. The possibility of slides being arranged in sequence, a narrative, had been noted very early. The first recorded slide show is of a screening of a set illustrating a journey – which easily fell into a basic narrative form – to China by Jesuit missionaries before 1671.[12] The possibility of other sorts of story took longer to develop:

> Sounds of a belfry, view of a cemetery illuminated by the moon. Young carrying the inanimate body of his daughter. He enters an underground passage where we discover a series of rich tombs. Young strikes on the first; a skeleton appears, he flees. He returns, works with a pickaxe; a second apparition and renewed terror. He beats on a third tomb; a ghost rises and asks him: What do you want of me? A tomb for my daughter, replies Young.

This unexceptional, unsophisticated little horror-film scenario was the script of an animated slide show, presented with sound effects, voices and music. It is dated 11 May 1802, and was written by Étienne-Gaspard Robert.

Robert adopted the name 'Robertson' apparently to give himself a more scientific, British air, the better to sell his *Fantasmagorie*, a smash hit, bells-and-whistles (literally) entertainment, which was the main attraction in Napoleon's Paris at the turn of the nineteenth century. He did not devise the Phantasmagoria, this sort of lantern show had been in business from the 1780s. It involved back projection, which not only heightened the illusion by hiding the apparatus but also allowed images to be enlarged and diminished by the moving of a large variable-focus lantern on rails behind the screen. Sound was also used – effects, speech and music, some from the eerie glass harmonica. The audience sat in fixed pew-like rows.

> The total darkness of the place, the choice of images, the astonishing magic of their truly terrifying growth, the conjuring which accompanies them, everything that combines to strike your imagination . . . Reason has told you these are mere phantoms, tricks done by mirrors . . . your weakened brain can only believe what it is made to see, and we believe ourselves to be transported into another world and into other centuries.

Such was Robertson's success that the room he was using, which held 60, proved too small for the crowds and he moved to the abandoned Convent of the Capucines, the nuns having been driven off during the Revolution.

Robertson's *Fantasmagorie* performance mixed the thrilling single image or effect (e.g. Robespierre rising from his tomb) and stories (e.g. *Young Burying His Daughter*). This oscillation between narrative and non-narrative spectacle was to characterise all such shows until the early cinema, in its dominant commercial manifestation, unambivalently embraced the story in the middle of the first decade of the twentieth century.

'A child could take his parents'

Like Robertson, Guilbert de Pixérécourt responded to leisure predilections engendered by political upheaval and the Terror by popularising, essentially, horror. He offered the Parisian public an alternative down-market theatrical genre of tragedy, with a happy ending, expressly, he claimed, 'for those who could not read'. He called it *mélodrame*. In 1812, Napoleon, who thought *The Marriage of Figaro* was 'revolution in action', had attempted to limit the number of Paris stages to eight, although in a more sympathetic mode he had returned the venerable national companies to the actors involved as partnerships, granting them shares and a job for life. Following Napoleon and the overthrow of the restored Bourbons in 1830, attempts at limiting the number of stages ceased. Where once in the Boulevard du Temple theatrical licences had forbidden speech and even limited a house to entertainments as specific as 'rope dancing', now melodrama became a staple and the street was soon nicknamed the *'Boulevard du Crime'*. In its theatres were born those stock nineteenth-century characters, the damnable villain, the unsullied virgin heroine and the innocent but manly hero.

As nineteenth-century urbanisation progressed, in contrast to the comparative stagnation of the older more 'legitimate' forms, such unregarded but vibrant popular entertainments flourished. In London in the 1770s, animal shows with juggling and tumbling had been transformed by Philip Astley, an ex-sergeant-major of the Dragoons and an expert horseman, into the modern circus. This progressed from the original bill of horse dressage and jugglers to 'equestrian dramas', a re-enactment of the Battle of Waterloo, for example, which packed them in well into the 1820s. By the 1850s, Astley's Amphitheatre, the fourth structure to be raised on the site of his original equestrian ring at Westminster Bridge and bigger than Covent Garden, had a full-scale proscenium arch and stage but also housed a 42ft-diameter ring in the pit. Equestrian versions of Shakespeare's histories were not unknown; nor were 'dog dramas' (which were to be reborn in the cinema a century later) or 'aquatic dramas'. At Sadler's Wells, naval battles were staged in a tank, with children playing the sailors on the reduced-size ships to help maintain the illusion. So extreme was the taste for spectacle that audiences could be found for all sorts of 'attractions', a word which acquired this meaning by the 1860s, including, for example, going 'up West' in London to watch chickens hatch in an incubator.

No wonder then that such *Schaulust* embraced shows which presented nothing but scenery. A rival attraction to the *Fantasmagorie*, the *Panorama*, was housed in a specially constructed cylindrical building, eventually some 40 metres wide, whose wall was covered with a single, realistic painting. Daguerre's *Diorama* involved complex scene changes effected by the gas lighting introduced in the 1820s, and augmented its painted backdrops with models of, for example, chalets and fir-trees to enliven the representation of Mont Blanc. The appeal of such spectacles without actors to the shows' proprietors is easier to understand than the audiences' taste for them. Not only were they cheaper than conventional popular theatre or music hall to mount, they attracted less attention from the authorities since the heavily licensed and censored stage was defined by speech in many countries' legislation. For the audience, though, these attractions did meet that fundamental Western taste for verisimilitude, which had been manifesting itself from the fifteenth century on. The Diorama was nothing but Masaccio's 'imitation of the truth' or van Eyck's 'loyal memorial' writ large.

In the 1830s, the popularity in Britain of French and German melodramas, which had been quickly translated and copied, was melded with 'free and easy' singsongs at the pub. By the 1840s, enterprising publicans were setting aside rooms, some equipped with a simple stage but still with chairs and tables rather than rows of seating, for singers and speciality acts. In 1852, Charles Morton went further by building a large hall adjacent to his tavern for these various types of act. Substituting theatrical seating for the tables was all that was now needed to transform a music hall into a palace of varieties.

In mid-century America, a rather risqué form of popular theatre designed for male audiences, burlesque, developed which sandwiched an 'olio' (or variety) of specialities between two sets of 'bits' – sketches, monologues. Smut was left for a 'blue' afterpiece:

> We came to a potato patch, she wouldn't go across,
> The potatoes had eyes and she didn't wear drawers
> sang one Johnny Forbes in an early hit.

228

In 1869, a more time-honoured form of burlesque arrived and caused a sensation. An English dancer, Lydia Thompson, toured a troupe of 'British Blondes' (many of whom were neither) in a tradition satirising classic drama dating back to the Duke of Buckingham's *The Rehearsal*, which had mocked Dryden's heroic tragic style in 1671 (and afforded Garrick a hit part). By the early nineteenth century, songs had been added and burlesque had become, with comic opera, the perfectly respectable forerunner of operetta and musical comedy. Thompson was less interested in satire than in titillation. The big attraction of her *Ixion* (in which she acted the title part, an ex-king of ancient Thessaly) was that the all-female cast played men in tights and very short tunics – in the mode of 'breeches parts' – while the women characters were also in tights with short slit skirts. In Thompson's hands, the word 'burlesque' itself began to acquire its twentieth-century connotation, feeding a taste for erotic display first catered for in the disreputable contemporary English *poses plastiques* and the 'blue' afterpiece. It was on the road to its twentieth-century manifestations in strippers, stand-up 'patter men' and the smutty sketch.[13]

Burlesque also absorbed elements of the minstrel show, a black-face entertainment. This persisted on British television nearly into the 1980s, in defiance of rising racial sensitivities, more than 130 years after Tom Rice, a black-face impersonator, had first created the character 'Jim Crow' as the basis of his hit song-and-dance act. African-Americans had been forming dramatic companies since the 1820s and one, Ira Aldridge, although blocked on the American stage, did enjoy considerable success in Europe, as many entertainers were to do after him; but white Americans preferred their African-Americans to be fakes in the Tom Rice mode. Rice never joined a troupe, although his success led to their proliferation on both sides of the Atlantic. The formula was a semi-circle of seated blacked-up players (and later African-Americans) singing songs and rising to perform soft-shoe dances, monologues or sketches interspersed with backchat between the two 'end-men', 'Bones' and 'Interlocutor'. In America, 'Jim Crow' was long remembered in the dismissive name given to subservient blacks and to the humiliating post-Civil War segregation laws of the Deep South.

As ever, the pleasures of the poor aroused the anxieties of the authorities and in Britain, where Morton's innovation had spawned a host of variety venues all over the country, a Suitability Act was passed in 1878. This was, ostensibly, a safety measure; there had been a disastrous fire at the Royal Palace of Varieties the previous year. Ensuring that the halls presented a reduced fire risk (by requiring an expensive iron safety curtain and the mechanism to raise and lower it) had the not unwelcome effect, as far as the government was concerned, of closing some 200 popular theatres.

The greater economic sense of seeking 'double audiences', that is women as well as men, eventually produced a more seemly form and the old French term *vaudeville* was imported into America to describe what the British were by then calling variety. Vaudeville became so respectable that, as a wit remarked, 'a child could take his parents'. On 6 July 1885, two ex-circus entrepreneurs, Benjamin Keith and Edward Albee, opened a continuous show at the Bijou Theatre in Boston, Massachusetts which ran from ten in the morning to eleven at night. Instead of a $1.50 theatrical ticket, admission was 10c (plus 5c more if you wanted to sit down). The bill included a singer, an illusionist, a man who played the bones and a short lecture on the Arctic moon. Backstage, a notice to the artists stated: 'If you are guilty of uttering anything sacrilegious or even suggestive you will be immediately closed and will never again be allowed in a theatre where Mr. Keith is in authority' – which by the time he died in 1914 meant a sizeable percentage of the theatres where vaudeville played.

Keith's chain was modelled on the contemporary organisation of the 'legitimate' theatre. By the later eighteenth century, individual actor-managers, such as Tate Wilkinson in Yorkshire, had toured an established circuit of provincial theatres on a regular schedule with a fairly stable company of players. Wilkinson had done much to create the 'tour' by building theatres himself and also by encouraging municipalities to follow suit. He had given up acting but still managed the company, in effect becoming a producer. Other entrepreneurs opened theatres as speculative ventures and had no part in creating the shows that appeared on their boards. Business logic moved some of them to accumulate more than one house, creating a chain. One show in many theatres, instead of each theatre producing its own shows, started to make economic sense. This was especially true if the company, as tended to happen increasingly in the United States from the 1840s on, just presented this one stock production instead of offering a repertoire as acting troupes had been doing for the previous three hundred years.

Single productions meant a fresh cast as the play demanded and although the company system persisted, English and American actors increasingly began to swap its comforts for the uncertainties of constantly finding new productions, hoping for a long run or new touring opportunities. This was not so much a problem for leading players; indeed, the first to abandon the companies were those who ran them, like Thomas Cooper, the star and manager of the Park Theatre in New York, who went on the road as a leading player as early as 1815. Transatlantic tours by individual stars – Edmund Kean and Fanny Kemble westwards, Edwin Forrest and Charlotte Cushman eastwards, for example – began even sooner, in 1810, and continued thereafter until the present.

The decline of permanent companies in the English-speaking world allowed managers greater flexibility in casting, encouraging the idea of fitting parts to players according to type, rather than players to parts as the troupes had required. A more specialised, typecastable actor emerged and the offences against realism sometimes produced by the old system slowly disappeared. As repertory decayed, actor-managers increasingly maximised their successes. Charles Kean, a major innovator who was one of the first to establish the primacy of the director, abandoned rep in the 1850s, playing *A Midsummer Night's Dream*, for instance, for 150 consecutive performances in 1856. Henry Irving – who was to achieve ultimate respectability by accepting the first theatrical knighthood – gave his Hamlet on 200 consecutive play-nights in 1874. Freelancing players now had agents who represented their interests with managements. Selling theatrical experience in Britain and the

United States came to turn more and more on advertising the celebrity of the actors. Stardom became too essential to be left to playbills, notices in the papers and the chance of word of mouth; an assiduous cultivation of the press became an essential part of theatrical enterprise and a new role, that of the publicist, emerged to perform it.

In 1830, Victor Hugo brought English theatrical disorder (as it might be) to that bastion of dramatic neo-classicism, the *Comédie-française*. *Hernani ou l'Honneur Castillan* echoed Corneille's *Le Cid* of 1637. It too broke the rules and provoked a row – in this case *La battaile d'Hernani* as opposed to *Le querelle du Cid*; but the nineteenth-century dispute was conducted by repeated rioting in the theatre, not by pamphlets. *Hernani* is also distinguished from *Le Cid*, despite both plays sharing a Spanish setting, because, while Corneille's is a masterwork written in a golden age, Hugo's is unconvincing farrago about a Robin Hood-like bandit (who is actually a noble) taking poison at his wedding because of some daft oath. Leading English romantic writers, including Byron, Coleridge and Shelley, also essayed verse tragedies, uniformly antiquated and artificial, all almost never now performed. Equally ignored are works by less elevated figures, although Dion (or Dionysius) Boucicault's *London Assurance* (1841), staged by the period's most far-sighted theatrical producer, the actress Lucia Elizabetta (Eliza) Vestris, did enjoy an unexpectedly successful revival in the 1970s. Most of the supposedly serious drama written for the 'legitimate stage' between the Napoleonic era and the rush of European imperialism in the last decades of the nineteenth century has been largely forgotten.[14]

In 1817, gas lighting had been introduced at Drury Lane and the Lyceum. For the first time the audience sat in the dark, their vision concentrated on the bright illumination of the scene. Their taste for spectacle was fed as lighting became ever brighter in the course of the century, with limelight in the 1820s and finally electric bulbs in the late 1870s. Meticulous scene painting had long been a given, including back-cloths with angled perspective. In 1804, in Manheim, the traditional wings, borders and backcloth were replaced by a box-set, with flats making a more realistic room setting. Mme Vestris introduced this innovation to London, with a cloth ceiling, for *The Conquering Game* (another forgotten play) at the Olympic in November 1832. She also used real furniture, props and carpets for the first time. Soon, doors were equipped with real doorknobs and by the 1870s the proscenium arch had become, on occasion, a sort of transparent 'fourth wall' looking over a domestic space, although sometimes the stage housed interiors and their exteriors simultaneously. Theatres became ever more grandiose to accommodate epic realistic effects. In the German lands, where in the eighteenth-century theatres and opera houses had been trophy structures for the dukes and princelings, state and municipal theatres continued to be built and run as public amenities, expressions of civic pride as well as a middle-class entitlement. They tripled in number between 1870 and 1896 and were expected to astound their publics. Wagner's demands that the new Bayreuth Festspielhaus stage in 1876 should accommodate the Rhine bursting its banks, the Valkyries' flying steeds and a collapsing Palace of Valhalla were not completely out of line. A decade later, Irving had established the convention that scenes would be reset behind the dropped curtain.

The convention governing the historical accuracy of costume was almost the last of current Western theatrical practices to slip into place. In 1761, Marie-Justine-Benoiste Chantilly, a stalwart of the *Comédie-italienne*, imported an authentic Turkish dress to play a Turkish princess, despite the fact that informed opinion of the day held such authenticity to be a distraction. She also wore peasant clothes when appearing as a peasant. In 1773, Macklin astonished audiences by appearing as a kilted Macbeth.[15] The following year, Goethe's early attempt at a Shakespearean play, *Götz von Berlichingen*, was performed in medieval costume. François-Joseph Talma took to playing Roman parts at the *Comédie-française* in a toga, both encouraging and echoing the fashion for Roman republican styles and the imperial pretensions of Napoleon, whose favourite actor he was. The matter was still in dispute until the 1830s, but thereafter authentic costuming matched realistic settings and within decades Charles Kean was seeking the help of an Oxford scholar to ensure the accuracy of his Shakespearean productions.[16]

As the public stage had moved indoors, so the heterogeneity of Shakespeare's and de Vega's audiences had become increasingly threatened. Overall, theatre certainly did not escape that general intellectual turn of the late eighteenth and early nineteenth centuries which saw the European taste-making elite determine that some activities – those they enjoyed, essentially – were 'art' whilst others – essentially those which gave pleasure to the lower orders – were not. The concept of 'high' (that is bourgeois) culture replaced aristocratic taste, quickly creating, by contrast, 'folk' culture (even as the 'folk' who had created it disappeared into the urban maw). Then, by a process of supposed dumbing-down which has gone on for rising two centuries, 'folk' (good) culture was distinguished from 'popular' (bad) and, eventually, 'mass' (worse). Early on in this process, Goethe, in charge of the courtly theatre at Weimar, was so appalled when his ducal master requested a production of Pixérécourt's 1814 hit, *Le Chien de Montargis*, actually starring a real dog (the prototype Rin-Tin-Tin), that he, supposedly, handed in his notice. Theatres could be found everywhere even in 'the lowest neighbourhoods'. In London, just south of Waterloo Bridge, for instance, was the Royal Victoria (now the Old Vic) with an audience, according to William Hazlitt, 'of the lowest kind – Jew-boys, pickpockets, prostitutes and mountebanks'.

The potency of the popular, nevertheless, could not be denied. Eliza Vestris (who had first made her name singing in a traditional respectable burlesque of Mozart's *Don Giovanni* in 1817), had a big hit song 'Cherry Ripe', Charles Horn's 1825 setting of a seventeenth-century poem by Robert Herrick, which became so popular that it was still being taught to English school-children decades after the Second World War – long, long after she had been forgotten. She had on occasion been prepared to appear outside the West End, for example in 1846 at the Surrey Theatre, which was normally marketed as 'THE FIRST NAUTICAL THEATRE IN EUROPE', but sold tickets for its boxes in the West End. So was William Macready, very much the Garrick of his day and a patentee. The Surrey was just round the corner from the Old Vic and, when it was not devoting around a month a year to such 'legitimate' productions, offered much the same popular fare. At the Alhambra Music Hall in 1861, the sensation was Jules Léotard and his tumbling innovation, the trapeze, the rage of Paris. After a number of visits in the 1860s, he left behind his name (for the one piece garment he designed to wear on stage) and another enduring popular song, 'That Daring Young Man on the Flying Trapeze'.[17] Theoreticians of the day were busy elaborating an elitist notion of bourgeois art and culture ('the best that has been thought and said in the world' as leading pontificator Matthew Arnold famously put it), but the public adored pop songs and trapeze artists and the like.

Despite the persistence of the popular, the occasional slumming (as it were) of 'legitimate' players and the shared taste for spectacle, the nineteenth century produced self-consciously class-bound performance environments. Confusingly, the bourgeois legitimate theatre and lyric stage on the one hand and melodrama, vaudeville or variety (as well as even more déclassé variants) on the other were housed in similar buildings, especially, in Britain, after the Suitability Act took effect. Like cinemas built in the twentieth century, nineteenth-century popular theatres were opulent and huge, some seating as many as 3,700, a thousand more than the contemporary Covent Garden. The provision of theatrical experience for both the bourgeoisie and the masses had become industrialised. By the 1890s, around one million theatre tickets a week were being sold in America.

As in other industries, both management and workers tended to group together to advance their interests. Every large American city had at least one vaudeville but there were only five chains. The American Theatrical Trust, established in 1895 and soon known as the Syndicate, gave the agents, managers and owners a stranglehold on the entire American legitimate theatre while a parallel Association of Vaudeville Managers was formed in 1900 to achieve the same level of control over the popular stage. The Keith–Albee–Orpheum chain controlled over 100 vaudeville theatres and ran the United Booking Office, an operation constricting enough to be sued under the anti-trust laws.

In response, American theatrical workers moved beyond the benev-
olent societies they had been establishing since the 1880s to a full-scale
Actors' Society which became Actors Equity in 1912/1913. In Britain,
musicians revived a moribund guild – the Worshipful Company of
Musicians – while the musical hall operatives and variety acts formed the
Variety Artists Association. And there were strikes. In 1901, in the
USA, the White Rats, who were the equivalent of the British Variety
Artists Association, struck the Association of Vaudeville Managers. The
stage had been transformed from what was in the 1860s just a 'show' (a
new term) – into what was by the 1890s – 'show business' (a new
phrase).

'Living Moving Pictures'

The Eidoloscope made its debut on 20 May 1895 at 156 Broadway,
New York, promising 'Living Moving Pictures': 'You'll sit comfortably
and see fighters hammering each other, circuses, suicides, hangings,
electrocutions, shipwrecks . . . just as if you were on the spot during the
actual events.' The spectacle attracted the cinema's first paying audience, but was far from being a runaway success. Compared with the
contemporary sophistications of the lantern show – needle-sharp, brilliantly coloured, often animated in a simple way but with complex
techniques of fades and dissolves – the black-and-white and rather shaky
Eidoloscope image seemed less of a wonder than it might. It also failed
to match the current versions of the indoor spectacle, actorless shows of
scenery with complex effects which had been a feature of nineteenth-
century urban attractions since the time of Robertson. By the 1890s
these included Hales Tours, where patrons sat in a full-scale replica of a
railway carriage with mechanically jolted seats while a painted scene was
rolled past the windows.

Amidst the Victorian addiction to spectacle, all sorts of visual toys
had also flourished in the Victorian parlour. In 1832, the first animated
figure of a 'little man in silk stockings, knee breeches and puffed sleeves'

danced into the history of the moving image endlessly pirouetting in one of these, the Phenakistoscope. The affinity of these animation gadgets to the magic lantern was instantly recognised. The lantern itself had become more powerful after the introduction of limelight in 1822 and audience numbers at slide shows increased as more powerful projectors permitted enlarged screens. Phenakistoscope animation projectors were a commonplace from the 1840s on, so images on the screen, even if drawn, had been moving for 50 and more years before the coming of the cinema.

In 1864, Louis Ducos du Hauron, who is also credited with the perfection of the first effective photographic colour system, patented a device using up to 580 lenses: 'By means of my device, I make myself able particularly to reproduce the passing of a procession, a military review . . . the grimaces of the human face . . . This will be in some fashion a living representation.' It seems probable that he never quite managed to do this, but the idea was not exactly remote given the ubiquity of Phenakistoscopes and the like and advances in projection.

It is no real surprise that, one Saturday in February 1870, 1,600 Philadelphians bought tickets for a show that included Henry Hyle's Phasmatrope. Hyle had devised a projector with a complex wheel of slide-holders. As these passed through the projector a shutter opened and closed. When the wheel was rotated quickly enough, the audience's eyes would see only the photographic image and not the blackness. Although Hyle had only a few slides of an acrobat and a couple waltzing, by endlessly recycling them he created the illusion of movement, reinforced with the help of live musical accompaniment.

On Saturday 25 February 1888 Edwearde Muybridge, who had made his reputation by capturing the motion of a galloping horse in still photographs, played the music hall in Orange, New Jersey. Illustrated lectures were a high-toned night out and commercial lanternists had moved on from limelight and were employing powerful calcium light projectors which allowed them to perform for large audiences in theatrical venues. Muybridge, who made a living in part with a travelling lecture-cum-show of his work, projected both his stop-motion photographs and brief moving sequences of drawings (not photographs) in his Zoopraxiscope. On the following Monday, he visited Orange's most famous citizen, Thomas Edison, to propose, not the photographic moving image, but that the Edison phonograph should be used in synch with the animations in the Zoopraxiscope.

Edison's lab at Menlo Park was organised for the structured investigation of technology on a number of fronts simultaneously in a way that was to become the norm in the next century. In the late 1870s, the 'Wizard' had been caught up in what became a race to develop a 'speaking telegraph', the telephone. While he was tinkering with this in 1877, Charles Batchelor, one of his staff of engineers, discovered him with:

> a telephone diaphragm mounted in a mouth-piece of rubber in his hand, and he was sounding notes in front of it and feeling the vibration of the centre of the diaphragm with his finger . . . [He said:] 'Batch, if we had some point on this, we could make a record on some material which we would afterwards pull under the point and it would give us the speech back.'

By 6 December of that year Edison and a mechanic, John Kruesi, had built the first tin-foil phonograph. If a crank was turned as one spoke into the ear-trumpet attached to the device, the stylus was pulled along the foil drum, inscribing the pattern of the sound, which was 'given back' when the stylus was pulled across previously recorded foil. High fidelity it most assuredly was not but it worked, although for what purpose Edison was not quite clear. Recorded music stretched the capacity of this simple, non-electric device and perhaps because its sound quality was so limited, he did not see any particular role for the phonograph as an automatic music-making machine. That was just another possibility in his list of applications: books for the blind; the preservation of spoken language and pronunciation for various purposes; a sort of audio-camera for making family records; an alternative to the telegram, deliverable from a central office to people who had no telephones; a substitute for visiting cards (via a recorder fitted at the front door). Although pre-recorded material could be produced for the phonograph, its descendants were primarily to be office recording and dictation machines, as Edison himself was beginning to suggest in 1878 when he added a vision of the phonograph as a substitute for a stenographer to his initial list of potential uses.[18] He never took up Muybridge's suggestion about mechanical sound for lantern shows, but he did become interested in the problem of reproducing motion.

Motion pictures were not a high priority at the lab. After some false starts, Edison and his research team had determined to use a strip of George Eastman's wonderfully thin and miraculously consistent celluloid, and to ensure the correct positioning of the strip with toothed wheels and corresponding sprockets in the film. The idea of sprockets would seem, judging from a sketch in his own hand, to be easily Edison's most significant personal contribution to the technology of the cinema. Edison had no more inkling that the team's work implied projected images for audiences arranged in darkened auditoria than that recorded music was the point of the phonograph. Instead, he came up with the peep-show, the Kinetoscope, which offered a small image to be seen by one person at a time. It is possible he was influenced by Louis Glass of San Francisco, one of his agents, who in 1889 attached coin-operated listening tubes to a phonograph, thereby 'inventing' the jukebox and, incidentally, finally demonstrating that music was the point of the thing.

The Kinetoscope was not rolled out until 1894 but it became immediately popular. Beyond the fairground, where they had a natural home, the machines also became a permanent fixture in cities. They were to be found in specialised store-front parlours where the customer could view a single-shot film, initially from the series of 75 photographed by Laurie Dickson, mainstay of the development team. They were mostly photographed at a specially built studio, nicknamed the Black Maria, in the garden of the labs – Fred Ott, an Edison employee, sneezing; a couple waltzing; the reconstruction of a prize fight; or more saucy stuff like a belly dancer or the actors, John Rice and May Irwin, kissing each other as they had done in the popular Broadway play *The Widow Jone*.[19] This was tame as compared with, say, Aretino's seventeenth-century 'Postures', but excitable legions of those who had made a tradition of what Milton had long before called the 'crowding of free consciences' swooped. The self-defined 'decent' were on to the cinema as soon as its images moved, although film censorship, as opposed to illiberal ranting, was not to be put in place until the next century.

Just as it took Glass to show Edison the way with the phonograph, it was the brothers Otway and Gray Latham, Kinetoscope parlour proprietors, who correctly identified the most effective application of the Kinetoscope's technology – projection. They secured the services of Dickson, who was not happy at the way the 'Wizard' took (or was given by the newspapers) all credit for moving pictures and had quit. Working in secret with another disaffected ex-Edison employee, Eugène Lauste, Dickson had built for the Lathams the Eidoloscope, in effect a 'projecting kinescope'. Its film, wider than the Kinetoscope's, had no sprocket holes because these were quite clearly an idea of Edison's, and he was ever quick to move against any actual or potential infringement of his patents, as his ex-employees well understood; but the lack of sprockets led to extremely unsteady images and contributed to the Eidoloscope's uncertain debut.

Edison was less than excited about this development and promptly sued for patent infringement anyway; nor was he pleased by 'THE MARVELLOUS ELECTRIC PHANTOSCOPE' unveiled in September 1895 at the Cotton States Exhibition in Atlanta by Thomas Armat and Charles Jenkins. The Phantoscope had an effective intermittent mechanism to hold each frame in the shutter aperture for a fraction of a second, producing a far steadier picture than that of the original Kinetoscope, never mind the Eidoloscope. Armat and Jenkins did not seek any protection for their device and they also used Edison's films – dubious dancing, a cockfight and two acts of another 1895 hit Broadway hit, *Trilby*.[20] The Phantoscope was not a success, most probably because its illumination source was inadequate; but Edison ('inventor' of, among much else, the electric light) moved to acquire Armat's patents, obviously seeing the writing on the wall, as it were, for the Kinetoscope.

The Phantoscope, re-christened by Edison the Vitascope, was relaunched on 23 April 1896 in Kost and Bial's Music Hall, one of the large vaudeville houses at Herald Square in Manhattan. It was billed as 'Thomas A. Edison's Latest Marvel' and it promised 'selections from the following: "Sea Waves," "Umbrella Dance," . . . "Venice, showing Gondolas," "Kaiser Wilhelm reviewing his troops"'. The attraction was eighth on the bill, just before the intermission. Until about 1905, most American viewers saw moving pictures either in these circumstances or in local opera houses, church halls and public lecture theatres as well as at travelling shows. The movies were by no means an exclusively fairground attraction.

Meanwhile, in Europe, others had been as content to follow Edison's lead as had Armat and Jenkins, especially since Edison had not bothered to patent his device abroad. Auguste and Louis Lumière, major photographic equipment manufacturers based in Lyons, knew about the Kinetoscope film strip in 1894 and saw the failure to patent as an opportunity. They took the precaution of opting for projection rather than peep-show and used a different-shaped single-sprocket hole, round not square, on each side of the frame as opposed to two square ones as in the Kinetoscope system; and they used a narrower gauge, 35mm wide. (The actual width of the image between the sprockets was equally acceptable to the Anglo-Saxons at one inch, or as near as dammit.) Louis also designed an effective intermittent mechanism, almost certainly without reference to the Americans.

The Lumières originally thought to call their combined camera/projector 'Domitor' simply to indicate that it was superior to all others. At the first demonstrations in spring 1895, the device had become a 'Projection Kinetoscope'. Their first film, some 800 frames lasting barely a minute, was of their workers leaving the factory in Lyons. On 28 December of that year, they unveiled their system to a paying audience at the Grand Café, 14 Boulevard des Capucines, round the corner from where Robertson held his shows at the beginning of the nineteenth century. There were ten films, including that of the workers. Thirty-three customers, at one franc each, were greeted by a still image

241

of some factory gates. One was heard to mutter, 'The magic lantern again'; but then the operator, Lumière engineer Charles Moisson, turned the handle of the projector/camera and, on the screen, the gates swung open. The Lumières' workforce hurried past the lens to their dinners, pushing bikes, smiling, a dog gambolling among them. 'It was life itself, it was movement captured in real life.'

The only major technological advance between the animated toys of the 1830s, the dreams of moving photographic slides of the early 1860s and the various 'inventions' of the mid-1890s was the admittedly crucial introduction of celluloid; but the date 1895 was not determined by any new knowledge of that substance. Celluloid was being investigated from the late 1840s on. It was there, had any sought it or seen a need for this application. The real difference between these decades was not in essence technological at all, but business. The cinema was, as it were, the 'invention' of its audience – the people buying a million theatre tickets a week in the USA alone – rather than of any of the 'great men' normally credited with this achievement.

Although France was the dominant European cultural arbiter and was also at this time a technological powerhouse,[21] it is nevertheless curious that the 28 December Paris show is inscribed on popular consciousness as the date of the birth of the cinema. The Lumières had not even themselves come up with the name that stuck – the flexible and easily translated *cinématographe-cinéma*, cinema, *ciné*, *Kino*, cinematography. They had certainly rechristened their Domitor/Projection Kinetoscope the *Cinématographe* for the December screening but the term was not theirs. *Cinématographe* had first appeared in an 1892 patent by Léon-Guillaume Bouly, another of those proposing movie systems along du Hauron lines. Bouly had allowed his patent to lapse the following year and with it all claims to his coining. Received history has nevertheless accorded to the Lumières the privilege of Adam – they had demonstrated and, supposedly, *named* the cinema and they are therefore remembered popularly as the 'inventors'.

Their business was immediately threatened. Robert Paul, for instance, was Edison's London Kinetoscope agent whose first public screening was on 9 March 1896 in the Empire Music Hall, Leicester Square. With a partner, Birt Acres, Paul went into production himself and was soon selling titles back to Edison in the United States. One of Paul's French clients was George Méliès, owner and chief performer at the Theâtre Robert Houdin, which specialised in magic and shadow shows. Méliès's first film in 1896, *The Game of Cards*, was a trick, unlike the realistic, documentary single shots of everyday doings and everyday sights which constituted the Lumières' catalogue; although it must be said that trick possibilities had occurred to the Lumières. One of their original films, observing a wall being demolished, cuts to the shot reversed so the wall magically reassembles itself. But it was Méliès who more systematically exploited the camera's ability to create either non-realistic or fake realistic effects by halting filming in mid-shot. This allowed him to alter the scene and then continue without the audience being able to witness his actual manipulation. He also soon learned how to superimpose images, a well-established still-photographic technique. The Lumières decided, despite their takings – 600 francs a day in January, 4,000 francs a day by April – to limit themselves to making film equipment rather than producing the films themselves. Their *laissez-faire* approach allowed Méliès and many talents from the French theatrical and photographic worlds fully to exploit the new medium as well as giving scope to the entrepreneurial genius of others, notably Charles Pathé, who had made a success of marketing Edison's phonograph in France.

The hyperbole surrounding all new media suggests that older forms are always quickly obliterated, but, as in the case of the cinema, this is never true. Long periods of changeover and adjustment are the norm before the older form even becomes peripheral, let alone disappears. With the coming of the cinema, Victorian Panorama-like spectacles lost their popularity but they took a long time to shrink to the size of dioramas in museum display cases.[22] Lantern shows too were absorbed. Indeed, in the very first distribution catalogues, films were listed as 'cinematographic slides' and these could be as pictorial, and as saleable, as any glass slide. Animation had, as it were, merely come of age. In the first Lumière reel – a single-shot film, *Baby Having Breakfast* at a table in the garden – it was the animated movement of the rustling leaves of the tree behind the baby that most fascinated the first audiences. That was what was new, not the hands moving to feed the child. Audiences were not, however, so overwhelmed by movement as to leap out of the way of the train arriving at La Ciotat station, another single-shot film on the same reel. The train obliquely crosses the screen rather than heading towards the lens, and there is no contemporary evidence that anybody was confused.

The myth that they were is significant. We are so in thrall to the idea of progress that we seem to need to rewrite history constantly to bolster the supposed impact of the new. The tale of the naïve viewer is a very good example. It ignores the fact that people had been watching screens for a couple of centuries and that the images on the screen had been capable of movement, if not of such complexity, for 50 years or so. The tendency to falsify the historical reality of cinema's reception by the public is typical of the way in which every advance we make is seen as a revolution. Such 'revolutions' rely on our collective amnesia.

Popular theatre also influenced the content of the earliest films, for among the first to troop over the river from Manhattan to Edison's Black Maria in New Jersey in 1894/5 were a whole succession of vaudeville acts – animal trainers, contortionists, the strong man Eugene Sandow. Showcasing moving pictures as a variety act, and conceiving of them as moving lantern slides, worked together to stress the attractiveness of the moving image as spectacle rather than as a potential story medium; and there was certainly a possibility that the cinema might emulate the variety acts it was recording and with whom it was sharing the bill by eschewing narrative.

For example, the voyeuristic movies that were to turn the Kinetoscope into 'what-the-butler-saw' machines relied on attractions which had little to do with story. When Charles Pathé was looking for material to put in the peep-show machines he had imported to Paris, he had his associate Henri Joli shoot *la Bain d'une Mondaine* (*The Society Lady's Bath*). In *The Bride Retires*, a bride undresses with winks and nods towards the audience. There is here the possibility of a simple tale whose attractive frisson might turn, at least in part, on the narrative trajectory from dress to undies, but it clearly had far more to do with that non-narrative pleasure, Freud's *Schaulust*.

The drive to organise images according to narrative logic seen in the development of the lantern show now repeated itself with the movies and, over the first decade or so of the cinema, narrative came to dominate the mainstream film. At first, though, this outcome was not so obviously likely. In June 1894 two boxers, Michael Leonard and Jack Cushing, were filmed by Dickson at the Black Maria studio reconstructing a recent fight. By more than doubling the length of the film strip to 150 feet and slowing the running speed from 40 to 30 frames a second, about one minute of coverage per round was obtained. The six-round bout was presented on six separate machines in a Kinetoscope parlour in lower Manhattan. It would stretch the normal notion of narrative to describe a prize fight as a story but it does have a clearly defined beginning, middle and end and the events at any one point do condition what follows, which is what narratives do. Patrons unwilling to invest in six viewing experiences went to the machine showing the last round because, as with 'once-upon-a-time' narratives and all stories, closure – knowing how it all turned out – is crucial to enjoyment.

Putting the rounds in separate machines, however much this was conditioned by technical limitations and entrepreneurial savvy, avoided the issue of transition between shots. It was by no means clear that the well-established 'vocabulary' of the slide show would transfer to 'cinematographic slides'. There were some worries about jerks or 'shocks to the eye' and suggestions that blank screens be inserted between every shot. On the other hand, exhibitors were quick to experiment with projected images, putting together complex mixtures of slides and single-shot films. In 1897, an event such as the Spanish American War was featured in a display using 20 films and slides. Before 1900 a 20-shot film had been made by Méliès – *Cinderella*. In Australia in 1900, 13 short films and 200 slides were constituted into a show which lasted for more than two hours.

Elements of narrative obviously existed within the single-shot films. It was already present in the Kinetoscope movies – *The Execution of Mary Queen of Scots*, for example. There is not much of a narrative but the film does progress from a living to a dead queen – an effect achieved in two shots, from exactly the same position, because the camera is stopped to allow a manikin to be substituted so that the actress can keep her head. (This was one of the basic tricks that attracted the magician Méliès to the cinema.) Our propensity to find narrative everywhere cannot be ignored, even in such simple material as *Workers Leaving the Factory*. The factory gates open, a dog suddenly emerges – itself a somewhat curious mini-event and one created when, for a second take, canine interest was introduced to pep up the shot – and the people move away and the gates close. *Fin*.

Achieving a sense of closure even at this level was not inevitable and not all the first single-shot films managed it. For example, in that first Lumières reel a troop of the 7th Cuirassiers charges towards the camera and, when it gets there, mills around in an aimless fashion clearly wondering what to do next. Such mere fragments of action were not going to hold the audience's attention for long. The future of the cinema is much more clearly delineated in the reel's most obvious fiction, *L'Arroseur arrosé* (*Watering the Gardener*). Within the single shot and static frame of the film, a gardener is discovered with a hose in hand, watering the garden. Behind his back a boy steps on the hose, halting its flow. The gardener inspects the suddenly inoperable hose; the boy removes his foot; the gardener is soaked; the boy, laughing, runs off, is caught and has his ears boxed. Set-up, punch-line, *Fin*!

'Yesterday,' wrote the Russian writer Maxim Gorky in July 1896,

> I was in the kingdom of the shadows. If only you knew how strange it is to be there. There are no sounds, no colours. There, everything – the earth, the trees, the people, the water, the air – is tinted in a grey montone . . . This is not life but the shadow of life . . . I must explain . . . I was at Aumont's café and I was watching Lumières' cinematograph.

'Merde!'

Five months later at Théâtre de L'œuvre in Paris, there was yet another of those audience commotions which punctuate Western theatre's history, caused, as usual, by the new generation's forceful rejection of the old ways.[23] Alfred Jarry's *Ubu Roi* opened on 9 December and closed on 10 December. The first word of the play – 'Merde!' – provoked a 15-minute uproar and nothing that followed calmed the tumult. W. B. Yeats, who was present on this opening (and penultimate) night, wrote: 'After our own verse, after all our subtle colour and nervous rhythm . . . what more is possible? After us the Savage God.' No savage god had been invoked in the *battaille d'Hernani*, which merely, if passionately, pitched new romanticism against old Renaissance classicism. The *querelle du Cid* was even more polite in questioning but then accepting those same neo-classical rules. The theatrical uproars of the last third of the nineteenth century tended to be provoked by a play's subject matter rather than by its style. That thrust to realism which sought to make the proscenium arch a fourth wall voyeuristically revealing, not spectacle, but the dramatic tensions of domestic life, had produced dramas about subjects hitherto unknown to the stage. Major playwrights emerged in a number of societies that had come late to the Renaissance theatre – Henrik Ibsen in Norway, August Strindberg in Sweden and Anton Chekhov (with equally dark but far funnier situations) in Russia. The oppression of women, the legitimacy of privilege, the legacy of syphilis, the inevitable corruption of local politics – all became the uncomfortable subjects of plays. Playwrights now regularly exceeded the tolerance of their bourgeois publics in their remorselessly accurate portrayal of the mores of the day. They also took an opposite but equally challenging tack by moving towards symbolism – dramas set in no place at no time, characters assuming allegorical roles in the name of exploring the inner mind. Again, this was difficult stuff for the increasingly predominantly middle-class audience which the 'legitimate' stage attracted with its canon of classic texts and 'well-made', uncontentious plays of contemporary middle-class life.

Ubu Roi was more radical than either of these strands and the scope of the row it provoked in 1896 was far wider than mere matters of taste and form. The new offensive taste-makers were *fin de siècle* bohemians who saw the bourgeois society in its entirety as a 'vicious villain'. They were giving the 'Savage God' of modernism a voice:

> I [Jarry wrote] wanted the stage to stand, as soon as the curtain went up, before the public like one of those mirrors in the fairy tales . . . where the vicious villain sees himself with bull's horns and a dragon body, the exaggerations of his own vicious nature.

Jarry was 23 when the play appeared, but *Ubu Roi*'s earliest manifestation was a schoolboy's sketch for puppet theatre he had written eight years earlier, destroying, at least to his own satisfaction, M. Hébert, a hated and absurd schoolmaster at the lycée Jarry was attending in Rennes. 'Père Ubu' is a pure untrammelled expression of personal will, a dark conclusion to the logic of the West's insistence, after the Enlightenment, on the value of every last individual. A self-obsessed prefiguring of the 'me generation', he is unreflective, lacking doubts, ideals or real objectives beyond the gratification of his own desires. A latter-day Macbeth, he seizes the throne of Poland by murdering the king, one of whose officers he is. Bombastic and stupid, he is driven out, making a last, opaque yet authoritative (and incontrovertible) observation as he is exiled to France: 'If there were no Poland, there would be no Poles.'[24]

The unveiling of photography had suggested to some observers that painting, realistic painting, was henceforth dead, rendered redundant. The cinema, silent and monochromous, uncertain of its possibilities as a narrative form, did not immediately provoke parallel pronouncements as to its impact on the theatre. In the event, of course, photography did not 'kill' painting, nor did cinema close the theatres. In fact, despite film, live popular theatre did even better than other nineteenth-century spectacles and remained a major force, culturally and economically viable, for another half-century at least. The legitimate stage persists still, once more perhaps with an audience overly skewed to the privileged; so do its overtly sexual manifestations in the form of strip-clubs and the like. But photography did impact on painting and so did the cinema on the theatre.

That drive towards naturalism which had played a part in the development of both photography and cinema had also been expressed in ever more realistic stage presentations and attractions throughout the century; but now the cinema unquestionably delivered such realism more efficiently. The overlap was to become clear although it was there from the outset. Ibsen, for example, wanted his theatrical audience to feel that it was 'sitting and watching something taking place in real life' – exactly the same sensation as the Latham brothers promised viewers of their Eidoloscope: that they would be 'on the spot during actual events'.

With hindsight, *Ubu Roi* is a declaration that the two media could have different objectives. Like the ever less figurative modes of painting from Impressionism on, *Ubu Roi* signals (however much *en passant*) a response to the new medium. In effect, it vacates the field of realism, leaving it to the cinema (while kicking the pretensions of symbolism into touch at the same time). The rules of the game by which the theatre, with its celebration of increasingly complex individuals, had been playing for three centuries in representing the real were rewritten. So much, then, for stage feeling. As 'Père Ubu' once cried, 'Merde!'

Sources

John Allen (1983), *A History of the Theatre in Europe,* London: Heinemann.
Robert Allen (1977), *Vaudeville and Film,* (Dissertation: University of Iowa).
Kathleen Barker (1976), *Bristol at Play,* Bradford-on-Avon, Wilts: Moonraker.
Jean Benedetti (2001), *David Garrick and the Birth of Modern Theatre,* London: Methuen.
Oscar Brockett and Franklin Hildy (2003), *History of the Theatre,* Boston: Allyn & Bacon.
John Russell Brown (ed.) (1995), *The Oxford Illustrated History of the Theatre,* Oxford: Oxford University Press.
Michael Chanan (1980), *The Dream That Kicks: The Prehistory and Early Years of the Cinema in Britain,* London: Routledge & Kegan Paul.

Seymour Chatman (1990), *Coming to Terms: The Rhetoric of Narrative in Fiction and Film*, Ithaca, NY: Cornell University Press.

Jim Davies and Victor Emeljanow (2001), *Reflecting the Audience: London Theatre Going 1840–1880*, Hatfield: University of Hertfordshire Press.

Thomas Elsaesser (ed.) (1990), *Early Cinema: Space, Frame, Narrative*, London: British Film Institute.

Martin Esslin (1969), *The Theatre of the Absurd*, Garden City, NY: Anchor Books.

John Fell (1974), *Film and the Narrative Tradition*, Berkeley: University of California Press.

Robert Friedel and Paul Israel with Bernard Finn (1986), *Edison's Electric Light: Biography of an Invention*, New Brunswick, NJ: Rutgers University Press.

Douglas Gilbert (1940, 1963), *American Vaudeville: Its Life and Times*, New York: Dover.

Bernard Hewitt (1970), *History of the Theatre from 1800 to the Present*, New York: Random House.

Eric Hobsbawm (1995), *The Age of Empire*, London: Weidenfeld & Nicolson.

Teresa de Laurentis and Stephen Heath (eds) (1980), *The Cinematic Apparatus*, New York: St Martin's Press.

Laurent Mannoni (2000), *The Great Art of Light and Shadow*, Exeter: University of Exeter Press.

David Mayer and Kenneth Richards (eds) (1980), *Western Popular Theatre*, London: Methuen

Brooks McNamara (1974), 'Scenography of Popular Entertainment', *Drama Review* 18–1.

Charles Musser (1990), *The Emergence of Cinema*, New York: Charles Scribner's Sons.

Geoffrey Nowell-Smith (ed.) (1996), *The Oxford Book of World Cinema*, Oxford: Oxford University Press.

Leslie Orrey (1972), *A Concise History of Opera*, London: Thames & Hudson.

Samuel Pepys (1953), *The Diary*, London: Dent.

Alexander Schouvaloff (1987), *The Theatre Museum*, London: Scala Books.

Michael Sidnell *et al.* (eds) (1991), *Sources of Dramatic Theory: 1 Plato to Congreve*, Cambridge: Cambridge University Press.

Claire Tomalin (1995), *Mrs. Jordan's Profession: The Story of a Great Actress and a Future King*, Harmondsworth: Penguin.

Kenneth Tynan (1967), *Tynan Right and Left: Plays, Films, People, Places and Events*, London: Longmans.

Glynne Wickham (1985), *A History of Theatre*, Oxford: Phaidon.

Raymond Williams (1968), *Drama in Performance*, Harmondsworth: Penguin.

Brian Winston (1996), *Technologies of Seeing*, London: Routledge.

6

'GIVE THE PUBLIC WHAT WE THINK THEY NEED': RADIO FROM 1906

'Peace to men of good will'

On Christmas Eve 1906, aboard the ships plying the North Atlantic routes, radio operators, the newest class of crew-member, were on watch by their Marconi morse receivers. Suddenly, instead of the usual clicks, Handel's Largo was heard, after which a violin played 'Oh Holy Night' with a man's voice singing the last verse and reading from the Gospels: 'Glory to God in the highest and on earth peace to men of good will'. Christmas wishes were given and a promise to return on New Year's Eve. Then, just as suddenly, it was gone. The listening ships were not entirely shocked by all this, but only because a morse message had warned them to expect their machines to start talking and making unexpected noises.

It had been just over a decade since Guglielmo Marconi and Valdimir Popov had demonstrated the viability of shipboard wireless telegraphic signalling during the 1895 summer manoeuvres of the British and Tsarist imperial fleets. Thereafter, the technology of wireless telegraphy spread rapidly from the ironclad navies into the merchant marine, destroying the isolation of deep-sea voyages forever. But, with foreign governments fearful of radio's military importance and therefore hostile both to the British Marconi Company's monopoly and each other's imperial ambitions, the protocols for its use were still being forged.

The voice heard that Christmas Eve belonged to Reginald Fessenden, a former professor of electrical engineering now conducting commercial wireless experiments at Brand Rock on Blackman's Point in

Massachusetts. Like the pioneers of printing, photography and the cinema, he was not an inventor, in the sense of discovering new science or even building, from scratch, an original device. The technology he was manipulating had its beginnings in theoretical physics, in the idea propounded by James Clerk Maxwell in 1865 that all electromagnetic phenomena took the form of waves and in the machines, coherers, that were built to demonstrate his theory. In 1880 David Hughes – who had previously knocked up a loose contact microphone essentially out of nails, a block of wood and a battery – transmitted a signal 500 yards along Great Portland Street in London. But the mucky-mucks of the Royal Society called in to observe this demonstration of Maxwellian wave radiation insisted it was induction. Hughes gave up.

There were to be 15 years of growing imperial naval rivalries and ever-bigger ironclad battleships before Marconi and Popov came up with an application. Radio was essential to the communication needs of dreadnaughts. These huge ships steamed into battle so far apart that the van was out of sight of rearmost vessels in the fleet, creating an insoluble, but crucial, communications problem. So pressing was it that the British Admiralty, in contrast to its usual behaviour,[1] was eager to embrace the advance. Hence the pioneering demonstration of wireless telegraphy using the phenomenon of radio was at sea in 1895.

For all its effectiveness on the ocean, wireless for general communications remained another matter. Across the landmass and under the oceans ran the telegraph; on land there was also the telephone. Why duplicate their facilities? As a general substitute for the telegraph and the telephone, wireless telegraphy had one overwhelming disadvantage: anybody could intercept the message. It was worth risking this with morse messages to ships at sea only because nothing else would do, but not otherwise. Anyway, the landline telephone had conspicuously failed to make a mark as anything other than a one-to-one communications system. In the late 1870s loudspeakers were attached to phones to enable more than one person to listen. A live performance of Donizetti's *Don Pasquale* was transmitted in this manner in Switzerland in 1879, and a church service brought to an invalid. In 1884, a London firm offered a programme of live relays from theatres, concert and lecture halls and churches. For £10 per annum your phone-line would be adapted to take four headsets. The service, which lasted for twenty years, was duplicated in Chicago. Of even greater duration were 24-hour services offered in Paris and Budapest. Telefon Hirmundó (Town Crier Telephone), created by Tivadar Puskás, who had worked at Menlo Park with Edison before returning to Budapest, was in business from 1893 until 1917. The service started with news on the hour, read aloud like the contents of a *gazzetta* and followed by a lot of silence. By 1896, Puskás had expanded his programming. There was a constant stream of general news, specialised stock-market reports and cultural reviews as well as musical concerts most evenings, children's programming and famous authors reading their works in instalments. The system employed 150 people. Nowhere else was telephony's potential as a mass medium seriously explored. Even in Hungary, Hirmondó had only 6,000 subscribers (although this was ten times more than the London system ever achieved).

Radio's appearance as a medium of expression was delayed because people persisted in thinking telephone when they should have been thinking phonograph (or gramophone). Unlike an expanded telephone service on the Budapest model, by 1906 recorded music was popular enough to have become big business. Of course, not least because Edison was involved, there had been a patent battle. A decade after the introduction of the Edison phonograph, Emile Berliner patented an alternative system for audio recording which etched the sound pattern on a zinc platter by pouring acid on it as the stylus cut the groove.[2] It was first sold in Germany in 1887 as a nursery toy, with a library of seven-inch discs, but obviously, given the acid, the point of the gramophone was in the listening not in the recording. It was being marketed for adults with pre-recorded music discs by 1894. Two years later, Eldridge Johnston produced a spring-driven player and in 1901 he and Berliner founded the Victor Company. Edison, by now preoccupied with Kinetoscope and the Vitagraph, reached a compromise in 1902 and a patent pool was established. Over the next 15 years the Victor

Company's value went from $2.72 million to $17 million, and in the UK and the US alone there were nearly 300 firms issuing records. The soprano Alma Gluck's recording of 'Carry Me Back to Old Virginny' was the first million-selling record. By the time he died in 1921, Enrico Caruso, who made his first recording in 1904, had earned some $2 million from his discs and that same year 100 million records were made in America alone. Mechanised home entertainment had arrived.

The thought that radiotelephone technology could be used to reach on a mass basis people you did not know never occurred to Fessenden but it was not rocket science. Apart from general SOS calls at sea, people eventually began to explore this application by land, using morse. In 1914 and 1915, the *New York Herald* telegraphed shipping in the city's harbour with news and weather reports as a public-relations 'stunt'. More unexpectedly, at the same time, universities in North Dakota, Nebraska and Wisconsin did the same to land-based morse hobbyists, adding crop reports to the New York agenda. The Germans sent demoralising propaganda messages in morse across the Allied lines during the First World War. The most radical example of these telegraphic attempts to be widely heard was the proclamation of the Irish Republic from the roof of the Dublin Post Office during the Easter Rising of 1916 against the British.

Adding a voice for a land-based mass audience, wireless telephony rather than telegraphy was also demonstrated prior to the First World War. In 1908 Lee de Forest, one of those who had developed the amplifying valve (or tube) upon which Fessenden had relied, transmitted an operatic concert, on records, from an aerial installed in the Eiffel Tower. To take another example, in 1912, Charles Herrold, proprietor of a training school for electricians in San Francisco, advertised his school over the air. Privacy, it turned out, was not everything after all but there was a problem: all receivers were also transmitters. How could that work on a mass basis? A receive-only radio and a central transmission mast designed primarily to send signals did not exist. The obscured vision of receive-only radio was a reflection of another confusion. Charles Herrold not only used wireless telephony to advertise his business, a time-honoured process for all the newness of the medium, he also transmitted his newborn baby's first cries to anybody who was listening. Radio's comparatively slow development to the early 1920s was due to these cultural uncertainties more than to any technological advance; in fact there were no advances of a fundamental nature after the introduction of the triode valve in 1906. As for other distractions, even the First World War lasted only four of these years.

With the peace, though, came a flurry of activity. The staff of the Marconi wireless telegraphy station in Montreal began voice transmissions on an experimental basis and were given a licence to do so by the Canadian Government as XWA/CFCF. Licensing was, of course, a natural corollary of radio's importance to the shipping industry and there was also a need to regulate signal characteristics to prevent interference. The British General Post Office, which had stunted the growth of telephony to protect its own telegram business, had been quick to get its hands on wireless telegraphy in the aftermath of the first international conference on the matter in 1903. A UK Wireless Telegraphy Act was passed in 1904 to ratify the agreements reached at such meetings. As far as the British Postmaster General of the day was concerned, its purpose was also 'to provide against the growth of monopoly in the hands of any one Company' – which could mean only Marconi's. Given the international nature of Marconi's business, takeover was resisted but strict licensing was not. In Germany, the first broadcast was transmitted in December 1920, totally arranged by the Post Office, which had acquired the army's wartime wireless telegraphy station. There was no question but that in Britain too radio would need GPO sanction. A reluctant Post Office gave Marconi's a licence similar to that which the company had obtained in Canada and for 10 months in 1920 it transmitted from its Chelmsford wireless telegraphy station. In that summer, the *Daily Mail* sponsored Dame Nellie Melba to sing into the microphone as a publicity stunt. (As with the gramophone and phonograph, strong operatic voices worked best with the new technology.) She finished her recital with a rendition of 'God Save the King'. Yet even a live operatic recital by the greatest diva of the day did not alter the official

British view that the entire business was essentially frivolous – which, compared with nautical communications, military and civil, it undoubtedly was. The licence was withdrawn.

In the United States, radio was for hobbyists, a mode that was to persist as 'ham radio'. After the wartime restrictions were lifted, the Navigation Section of the Department of Commerce granted hundreds of licences. The airwaves were flooded with talk, a species of wireless chat-room exactly prefiguring internet public exchanges 80 years later. There were even worries about lady ham operators becoming involved with unsuitable men as a result of having made contact through the 'ether'. Some of the amateurs had grander ambitions and tried to entertain their listeners, mainly by playing records; but one station was operated by a laundry promoting its services and from another, on a farm in Ohio, came advice on hog, cattle and chicken feeding as well as uplifting talks 'on art, education and religion' as a way of advertising its products. Leagues of operators and radio clubs sprang up all over America, and by the early 1920s these organisations constituted a most significant Washington lobby.

Dr Frank Conrad was not untypical of these American 'hams'. What distinguished him was that he was also a professional electrical engineer who had supervised the Westinghouse production line making the US army's transceivers during the war. Now, in the peace, he was in charge of manufacturing electric switches. In 1919, in a purely private, amateur capacity, he began transmitting music from records as a hobby, just as so many others were doing, using Westinghouse apparatus installed in his Pittsburgh garage. When he started to repeat himself, a local suburban music store supplied him with new discs in return for a mention as suppliers. Among those of the '100,000' core ex-military signalmen and the radio hams who happened to be living in greater Pittsburgh, Conrad's transmissions on Wednesday and Saturday night on 8XK were a great hit. A downtown department store saw a way to sell records by listing Conrad's concerts as part of its own press advertising. The store's ads caught the eye of Conrad's boss, Westinghouse vice-president H. P. Davis, and in September 1920, the company took a decision to build a transmission mast to which the Navigation Section assigned the call letters 8ZZ. Fourteen months later Westinghouse received the eighth of the new 'Class B' radio licences to be issued and the station became KDKA.

These Class B licences marked the line that the Commerce Department was now trying to draw between amateur and professional. Class B licencees were forbidden to use recorded music, equating professional programming with liveness, while Class A were not licensed to carry 'weather reports, market reports, music, concerts, speeches, news, or similar information or entertainment'. By regulation, the amateurs were now confined to a chat-room of the air and nothing else. It was a very crowded and noisy space. Although the B-licence professional commercial stations were quite capable of ignoring the bandwidth and power restrictions placed on them by Commerce, it was the A-class cacophony of amateur transmissions that was a primary source of the widespread perception that American radio was in chaos. The Secretary of Commerce himself, Herbert Hoover, spoke of radio being as if '10,000 telephone subscribers were crying through the air for their mates'. The numbers contributing to the noise, however, were no longer growing exponentially because possessing a set no longer necessarily meant being able to transmit as well as to receive. The receive-only radio had at last become obvious to many – David Sarnoff, for example.

Sarnoff's was the classic New York immigrant story. He had made it from Russia to Manhattan, and, when there, from Yiddish newspaper street-seller to telegraph operator.[3] He was to claim that he conceived of radio as a mass medium as early as 1915, for which there is no evidence at all. After nationalising Marconi's during the war (as the US navy demanded), the United States government spun it off in 1919 as a private, wholly American, company, the Radio Corporation of America – RCA. RCA had been created specifically to be bought by General Electric, which was soon joined by Westinghouse and AT&T as principal shareholders. Sarnoff found himself working for the new firm. In 1920 he conceived of the one-way home receiver with a loudspeaker rather than a headphone. With a colleague, he had visited an independent engineer who had perfected a single control knob to tune, or 'rectify' to use the term of the day, a wireless receiver. Sarnoff's colleague was dismissive, claiming that half the fun of radio was finding the signal and listening through the headphones. Sarnoff disagreed: 'This is the radio music box of which I've dreamed.' He then wrote a famous memorandum to his line manager suggesting that one million radio music boxes at the handsome cost of $75 each could be expected to sell within three years of the start of manufacture. In short order Sarnoff was RCA's 'Broadcasting Manager'. Whether he really had this insight prior to the award of the Class B licences remains in question but it is clear that by the early 1920s, he and many others saw that a 'radio music box', with a loudspeaker and easy controls, fitted into the culture. It was an obvious alternative to the Victorian parlour piano and all the other totally mechanised sources of home music making – the paper-driven automatic player-piano, the phonograph and the gramophone. The new thing for bright young things was very soon to be the 'radio dance' party at home.

With such radios to sell and the Class A licences now limited to amateurs, the electrical manufacturing industry and the retailers who marketed their goods sought Class B licences as being essential to their prosperity. Dr Conrad's little hobby had been transformed. Twenty-five of these new licences were issued in 1921 and over 600 in 1922. Westinghouse took the lead, erecting masts in Newark, Chicago and Springfield, Massachusetts, where a production line was also established to make receive-only sets. After the electrical industry, the largest group of Class B operators was drawn from the newspaper press and other publishers. Educational establishments and department stores constituted the next largest major groups of owners. There was now a new question: 'Could you make any money out of radio programming?'

For all the commercial interests involved, the first idea was that the programmes would have to be given away free, as it were, to get people both to buy the sets and thereafter, in a general way, to bear in mind the name of the station owner. For example, the *Detroit Daily News*, operators of WWJ, which was awarded its B-class licence three months before KDKA, claimed to have created the first regularly transmitted schedule: religious programmes, university extension courses, time signals, news and a bedtime story for the children. The cost of providing this service was in the same category as the cost of buying billboard advertising space for the paper. WWJ's general manager said, 'Good will is about the only return we expect from our station'. Earning revenues from radio operations, even if the owner was in a profit-making business, was by no means a given.

The sponsorship/advertising-driven business model was just one of many ideas being canvassed throughout the 1920s. Some were still suggesting subscriptions and the amateurs continued to be a powerful voice. Sarnoff himself had first thought that the taxpayer should fund the content. After all, municipalities paid for bands to entertain the populace in parks, why shouldn't they run radio stations? On this basis, a large number of municipal and educational stations, including eventually more than 200 universities, were granted licences. The issue was becoming more pressing. From 1923, the American Society of Composers, Authors and Publishers, which had been founded in 1914 to collect royalties from record companies, began to flex its not inconsiderable muscle about royalty payments for live radio transmissions. Operating a 'B' licence was becoming more costly.

'Say "goodnight" Gracie'

By privatising Morse's telegraph in 1845 and allowing private telephone companies in the 1880s, the American Congress had long since got out of the communications business – except for its eighteenth-century constitutional responsibility for the mails. Even if First Amendment issues were set aside, Congress was not going to obstruct commercial interests. Europe was different and in the UK, inevitably, the General Post Office was at the heart of the debate about radio. Marconi's 1920 experimental programming attracted an unexpected amount of attention, convincing potential British set manufacturers that there would be a market for domestic receivers if there were something to listen to. Over 100 companies applied for licences over the next two years but the GPO did nothing – apart, of course, from closing the Marconi station down. This position could not be maintained and when potential set-manufacturers formed a cartel with the wireless telegraph companies for programme provision, the GPO was forced to come to terms. The cartel established, as an agent of the GPO, a British Broadcasting Company, elegantly using 'broadcasting', an eighteenth-century agricultural term for sowing seeds. In the background the press barons were eager to ensure that, whatever else, the outcome was not a commercial service. BBCo was to be financed by fees raised from extending the licensing system to cover individual receivers (as opposed to fees for transmitters or transceivers) and a tariff on the sale of radios (or 'wirelesses') themselves. The licence, otherwise an hypothecated tax of the sort to which the British treasury has always been (and remains) implacably hostile, solved the problem of how to pay for programming. BBCo, which had already begun transmissions from London, Manchester, Birmingham and Newcastle in late 1922, received its own licence on 18 January 1923. The arrangement, which was to run for two years, was confirmed as a more permanent solution by a committee of inquiry, led by Sir Frederick Sykes.

The close control of the GPO, including its seat on the BBCo's board, raised real questions about how legal, in a fundamental sense, this solution could be in a country with, supposedly at least, a 'free' press. The initial agreement, which among other things required BBCo to avoid contentious material of any kind, did not augur well for the new medium's claim on the right of free expression. Broadcasting was beginning in the UK far closer to the censored theatre than to the liberated press of the newspaper barons. In fact, as a result of their hostility, the agreement prevented the BBCo from carrying news, including coverage of sporting events. Even in musical matters, it was also being treated very differently from the unfettered world of recording.

Over the two years of BBCo's licence, John Reith, the company's first general manager, steered a brilliant course between the Scylla of such political control and the Charybdis, equally worrying to him, of private commercial ownership. Not least by pursuing an elitist programming policy, which found space for a succession of 'talks' by the great and the good, he had earned the golden opinions of a number of key players. In 1925, a second inquiry led by Lord Crawford supported Reith's vision of a third way. Crawford's opinion was much influenced by a trip his committee had made to America, where the uncertainties of federal policy and the cacophony of the amateurs appalled the British visitors. Using as a model the official boards set up in the First World War to control various aspects of British life – everything from forestry to water and electricity – and the medieval legal mechanism of a royal corporation, the BBCo was transformed into the British Broadcasting Corporation.

In 1926, there was a general strike in the UK and the real editorial independence of the BBC, even before the royal charter was actually signed, was immediately put to the test. A dispute in the coal industry had spread to other sections of the trade-union movement. The country was shut down. In a West paralysed by fear of the communists then ruling in Moscow, the British ruling class treated this event as a revolutionary precursor. Members of the Cabinet, Churchill prominent among them, thought the newborn BBC ought to be taken over directly; but Churchill's own government newspaper, specially produced during the strike, was widely derided as a propaganda sheet and the radio take over option was not exercised. Instead, a civil servant was inserted into the Corporation to ensure its good behaviour. The bureaucrat expressed satisfaction at the end of the nine-day crisis, when the TUC collapsed the strike, that he had had nothing to do. Self-censorship preserved the Corporation's third way even as it was being born.

Reith famously wrote to his managers explaining that the BBC, in the best traditions of the press, was independent: 'but, on the other hand, since the BBC was a national institution, and since the Government in this crisis were acting for the people, the BBC was for the Government in the crisis too'. In the light of this, it is easy to dismiss claims of independence on the part of the BBC as cognitive dissonance or false consciousness of a particularly debilitating kind. The real brilliance of the arrangement was to convince the British public that there was any independence at all. Among the 15 chairmen[4] of the board of governors in the first 75 years of the corporation were numbered one earl, one viscount, four lords, four baronets and a right honourable. Of the four commoners, one, George Howard, owned one of the largest houses in England – where the television version of *Brideshead Revisited* was shot in 1981. Of course, there was always a trade unionist, usually of safe conservative bent, and female representation was not unknown even in the early years, normally, and unsurprisingly, titled. Successive Post Masters General denied, whenever controversies about programmes were brought to the floor of the House of Commons, that they had any responsibility for the content of the Corporation's output and there was, despite these connections to the Establishment as well as the secret service official who for years would vet all supposedly sensitive BBC appointments, a daily truth in these protestations. Journalists and other programme makers were in reality left alone almost all the time. Nevertheless, the government-appointed BBC governors were charged with content control. Self-censorship was normally the key to promotion. Square pegs, however brilliant, bumped against glass ceilings for decades. The price of the BBC's independence, which was perceived as being real within the Corporation and by its listeners, was a profound self-censorship to which reference was never made.

In America, as early as 1922, 'driblets of advertising', as one astute observer noticed, 'are floating through the ether every day . . . once the avalanche gets a good start nothing short of an Act of Congress . . . will stop it'. In 1923, one of the stations licensed to AT&T, WEAF in New York, accepted commercial sponsorship, that is product plugs and programming packaged together, which other leading stations were allowing on their air for nothing. WEAF's different approach was largely because AT&T had been founded and had prospered as a rental business, selling time on its telephone wires to its subscribers. Why not sell time to firms to broadcast commercial messages from its radio studio? Here was the elusive, effective business model, the key to unlocking the riches of radio, but even so the commercial interests did not automatically prevail.

The Commerce Department had been regulating the airwaves on its own initiative but when in 1926 its right to do this was challenged in court, its regulatory behaviour was found to be illegal. An Act of Congress the following year created the Federal Radio Commission but this did nothing to halt the flow of advertising driblets. In fact, under the FRC, the driblets did indeed become an avalanche, although in the public debate about broadcasting the Commission was repeatedly urged to protect non-commercial broadcasters such as the universities. It did the opposite and by 1934, when the FRC was transformed into the Federal Communication Commission (FCC) with responsibility for all modes of electronic communication, the dominant commercial nature of American broadcasting had been set.

Commercialism did not buy the freedoms enjoyed by the press, such as they were, any more than non-commercial arrangements did, either in the US or elsewhere. In 1923 the senior AT&T vice-president responsible for radio had written:

> We have been very careful . . . not to state . . . that the Bell system desires to monopolise broadcasting, but the fact remains that it is a telephone job, that we are telephone people, that we can do it better than anybody else.

No, it wasn't and they couldn't. WEAF's management proved to be particularly insensitive to the idea of creative freedom. For example, it determined that its first star, Roxy (Samuel A. Rothafel), who in 1914, as an entrepreneur, had built the Strand, the first 3000-seat US picture palace, was too slangy and populist a figure, as a performer, to be associated with the phone company. Roxy's show was a test bed for outside broadcast (OB or 'remote') transmissions. A vaudeville mixture of sketches, music and monologues, it came live from the stage of the Capitol Theatre in New York. In 1925, after two successful years, the telephone men started to edit Roxy's scripts, or 'continuities' as they were then called, which Roxy quickly turned into a public-relations disaster for the phone company. Given that AT&T was also engaged in renegotiating its relationship with other radio licence holders and anyway being more aware than were its partners in RCA of the threat implied in charges of monopolistic practice, it gave up on programming. It passed its broadcast licences over to RCA, which used them and those it held itself to form the National Broadcasting Company.

NBC, under Sarnoff, created two networks, the 'Red' and the 'Blue', which both began transmission in November 1926. Municipal or other non-commercial broadcasting was no longer an objective for him. Such alternative funding notions were now quite clearly a menace to what had already become a most lucrative business. Networks were both a major consequence of, and a further driver for, the emerging dominance of the commercial radio. If the purpose of the system was to deliver audiences to advertisers with programming between sponsorship messages as bait (as it were), then the larger the audience delivered, the more the sponsor could be charged. This was an especially sweet possibility because such increases in the size of the audience required no increase in production costs.

AT&T's contribution to this development was the provision of the high-quality cables the new networks needed, a much more familiar business for the telephone company than the hazardous creation of programming. The infrastructure was therefore privately owned but licensed, on a local basis, by the federal state. Networks were not formally acknowledged by the regulators in the FRC. In 1928, NBC Blue and Red acquired a rival, the Columbia Broadcasting System. A fourth network did not follow although it was attempted, but the logic of the radio market prevented any other players from developing into chains.[5]

The three dominant networks were built on the massive success of radio's earliest years. The new medium absorbed the star system of vaudeville, creating a new generation of attractions like Wendell Hall.

Hall had played the circuits as 'The Singing Xylophonist' but, with his ukulele and a signature tune ('It Ain't Gonna Rain No More'), he was a far bigger hit than he had ever been on the stage. Hall, born in Kansas but raised in Chicago, presented a somewhat racially ambiguous figure over the air. The microphone, like the internet computer decades later, was a very effective veil. Equally well disguised were the Caucasian features of Freeman Gosden and Charles Correll, who created the most popular, and one of the most long-lived, of all American broadcast series, *Amos 'n' Andy*.

Gosden and Correll were travelling producers helping amateurs to mount community shows. These usually involved blackface. The act the pair offered to the radio station of the 'World's Greatest Newspaper', the *Chicago Tribune*'s WGN, meshed piano and ukulele music with a lot of traditional 'dialect' banter. What the *Tribune* wanted to add to its programming was an equivalent of its comic strips. With Gosden and Correll, the idea was to transfer a comic strip's dialogue balloons to the air, thereby expanding the vaudeville sketch or dialogue. After an unsuccessful stab at this with white characters, the duo suggested the impersonation of blacks. The show, *Sam 'n' Henry*, debuted on WGN in January 1926 and was unlike anything else on the air. It ran every day except Sunday at 10.00 p.m. for ten minutes and it carried its story lines forward from day to day. The duo became so popular that within a year a massive schedule of personal appearances, *Sam 'n' Henry* merchandising and a new syndicated newspaper comic strip propelled Gosden and Correll into national stardom. They proposed pioneering a technique of recording their routines on to disk for a new sort of syndication to other radio stations but, despite the paper's long experience of selling material to other titles, the idea was rejected. Gosden and Correll jumped, with the format, to WGN's rival, the *Chicago Daily News*'s WMAQ. There the programme director, Judith Waller (one of a number of women to hold key positions in the earliest phase of American broadcasting), gave them the syndication rights they sought. Since 'Sam' and 'Henry' had to be left behind at WGN, they tried various names until 'Amos' and 'Andy' were unveiled on 19 March 1928.

By the following year, they were on the NBC network.

They played stereotypical minstrel types, one biddable and the other 'uppity':

> *Andy*: Listen, Coolidge is a Republican an' fo' de' las' fo' years or so he's done had Hoover locked up waitin' to put him in office.
> *Amos*: What you mean he done had Hoover locked up?
> *Andy*: Well, I was readin' on de paper right after Hoover was nominated dat Coolidge was getting' ready to take Hoover out of de cabinet.

The shows were recorded six weeks in advance for syndication but transmitted live, on WMAQ, in a slot starting at 7.11 p.m., the very time echoing significant dice throws in craps, a gambling game to which African-Americans were supposedly addicted. The stereotyping of the minstrelsy extended even into their sponsorship with Pepsodent, white teeth, like craps, being icons of caricatured blackness. Until its popularity peaked in 1935, *Amos 'n' Andy* commanded an audience in the region of 40 million people a night, a third of the entire population. It is no wonder that George Bernard Shaw, on a visit to the USA, ranked *Amos 'n' Andy* with the Niagara Falls and the Rocky Mountains.

As it declined, the show's time slot expanded first to 15 minutes then, in 1943, to a full half-hour. The original two voices had become a full-scale company of characters and 'Amos' slowly gave way to 'Kingfish', 'Sapphire' and other habitués at the social club which was the show's primary setting. *Amos 'n' Andy* spoke both to the traditional function of the minstrel show, a vehicle for safely defusing the threatening otherness of the black presence, but also to radio's ability to create a new national community of listeners. It did nothing, of course, to salve the wound of America's racism. Happy as Pepsodent were to have their product's name brought into millions of American homes by the show, their bigotry suggested that the product should nevertheless be insulated from the programme. For one thing, the product name did not figure in the programme's title, contrary to the usual practice of the time, nor were references to it made in the course of the show in the usual sponsorship manner. Instead, discreet advertisements were inserted. The broadcasting spot commercial was therefore created as a consequence of America's racism.

Nor did *Amos 'n' Andy* open the door to a fuller and more meaningful media representation of the American black experience. On the contrary, as with the minstrel show itself, it laid down the lines which such representations must not cross. Take, for example, the behaviour of J. Walter Thompson. Although the advertising industry had revenues of more than $100 million a year by the turn of the twentieth century, the full-service agencies that had emerged in the last decades of the previous century, J. Walter Thompson prominent among them, exercised little overt control over newspaper and magazine content. Radio offered another chance and JWT was the first firm to grasp this. It became a major producer of sponsored shows throughout the era of radio dominance. It and the other agencies were not about to resist racist stereotyping. In 1937, JWT hired Louis Armstrong to do a programme for Fleishmann's Yeast but insisted that he spoke, like Amos or Andy, in the style of the minstrelsy. His refusal to do so killed the programme in six weeks. The networks were no better. When Arturo Toscanini was tempted out of retirement to conduct a new house symphony orchestra for NBC in 1936 as part of its response to the revised regulatory regime following the creation of the FCC, no black musicians were allowed. The radio did not follow the record companies in ghettoising black music – jazz (especially the blues) – as 'race records', yet, given such pervasive racism, it is no surprise that, although 'crossover' records were not unknown, the first massively popular mainstream jazz band of the 'jazz age' was an outfit as lily-white as the NBC Symphony Orchestra led by the appositely named Paul Whiteman. (Nevertheless, he and the other white jazz players caught the fall out from an ongoing moral panic about jazz.)

Amos 'n' Andy buried this reality. The show was, in that sense, powerful propaganda for a vision of an implicitly harmonious America, one in which, because of the ambiguities of the microphone, they could even be heard to interact with possibly white characters without tension. Eventually, though, in the general post-Second World War collapse of this myth, *Amos 'n' Andy* became the site of the first major battle over such misrepresentation. The show transferred to television in 1951 with an African-American cast but the increasing protests of the black community against its stereotyping forced its withdrawal two years later. The next television prime-time series with a black setting did not happen for nearly two decades.

In its radio incarnation, *Amos 'n' Andy* was of a piece with a dominant strand of early programming which reflected the immigrant experience, albeit the internal post-First World War immigration from the rural south to the northern cities. Other shows gave voice, equally stereotypical it must be said, to communities whose members had travelled further to find 'the Golden Land'. Gertrude Berg began her radio career by broadcasting, on behalf of the Consolidated Edison electric utility company, a recipe for Christmas cookies – in Yiddish. She sold NBC the idea of a family-based situation comedy in 1929. This became *The Rise of the Goldbergs*, a series she was to write and star in, on both radio and television, for the next 30 years. She played 'Molly Goldberg', who, like the other older characters on the show, yielded nothing as stereotypes to Amos, Andy and their friends in the 'Mystic Knight of the Sea' social club:

> *Molly:* Vat's de matter so late, Sammy? Let me look at your hends. Playing marbles, ha? For vat is your fadder slaving for vat I'm esking you? A marble shooter you'll gonna be? A beautiful business for a Jewish boy!

Subsequent worthier documentary attempts to introduce the ethnic communities to each other (such as those aired in the Second World War) failed; typically each group listened only to the show about itself. It was left to long-running series like *The Rise of the Goldbergs* to suggest a common Americanness to the entire audience. Sammy Goldberg, unlike his parents, had no ethnic accent and unlike the contented blacks in the 'Mystic Knights of the Sea' club (who remained, as it were, in 'the cabinet') the Goldbergs were, as the title of their show loudly proclaimed, on the rise.

Against the urban theme of learning to be an American, radio also pitched the popular concept of a lost rural America in hillbilly hits such as *Lum and Abner*. Set in a fictional Pine Ridge, Arkansas, this pioneering show was so successful that it quickly moved from the local Arkansas station where it began to WMAQ and soon the entire nation was speaking hillbilly – 'Well, wouldn't that just paint yer purple'. One Arkansas village went so far as to change its name officially to Pine Ridge.

With more than 10,000 acts from which to choose, radio found a rich source of talent in the world of vaudeville. The transfer was easy for singers like Bing Crosby or Al Jolson who shared, turn-and-turn about, the starring spot in *The Kraft Music Hall*. Music apart, the microphone obviously favoured the sketch over the speciality act; so, as was not unknown in the musical show or film, radio shows were given a theatrical or club setting. For *The Fleischmann's Yeast Hour*, JWT gave its original star, Rudy Vallee, the band-leader, a night club and a role of emcee to showcase his guests. In 1932, Jack Benny, who had once promised vaudeville audiences 'Fiddle Funology', was among the first to appear on the *Ed Sullivan Show*, a format emceed by Sullivan, a show-business journalist, to showcase new talent. A few years later, with his own programme, Benny played himself, a character named 'Jack Benny', who was in the radio business. He was surrounded by an assortment of other characters, including, from 1937 on, Eddie Anderson as Rochester van Jones, his African-American manservant.

When one double act that Vallee had showcased, Burns and Allen, was given a programme, the sketch came to dominate almost the entire proceedings. George Burns was an unsuccessful vaudeville act until he met Gracie Allen in 1922. On radio and then on television their immaculate timing ensured decades of popularity but their vaudeville routine gave way to extended comedy narratives in a domestic setting. Only a closing duologue, with Gracie explaining to a bemused George the curious idiosyncrasies of her relatives, remembered their roots. For 40 years these duologues always finished the same way:

> *George*: Say 'goodnight' Gracie.
> *Gracie*: Goodnight Gracie.

Gracie finally said goodnight in 1964 while George died in 1996, aged 100, the last great vaudevillian.

Drama was slower than comedy to secure a prominent place but by the mid-1930s over half the networks' daytime schedules were taken up with professionally acted melodramatic serials specially directed at 'housewives'. The popularity of the fragmented story, normally in the thriller genre, had been demonstrated throughout the 1920s by the cinema serial. Now some companies, neither broadcasters nor advertising agencies (for example, Proctor and Gamble), established departments to make multi-part melodramatic radio plays in house; as a result, the serials were known dismissively as 'soap operas', although their sponsors included many firms other than household cleaning-product manufacturers. With open-ended story lines they ran for years; *The Guiding Light* started in 1937 and finished in 1956.[6]

Over ten per cent of the day was given to programming for children and this too took populist dramatic form. Series – where in each episode characters reappeared but story lines were concluded – dominated and, as with the soaps, some ran for years and even survived transfer to television. *The Lone Ranger*, for example, began as a local radio programme in 1933 and became an early network hit TV series in 1949. The medium's educational potential was as marginalised as the magic lantern's had been; children were not well served by commercial radio. In 1932 CBS had created an Education Department but this turned out to be more a publicity stunt than a programming reform. Its head, Alice Keith, resigned when she realised she could not access airtime for programming.

Influenced by both the old silent film serial and the popularity of magazines such as *True Story*, the networks inserted an ever-increasing number of thrillers into the prime-time schedule through the 1930s. In 1937, the heavily distorted voice of Orson Welles, already the boy wonder of the Broadway stage, was heard to cackle: 'Who knows what eeevil luuuurks in the heart of men? "The Shadow" knows!!! Hhehhehhehehhhe.' There followed half an hour of hokum with Welles as Lamont Cranston, the crime-fighting 'Shadow' whose powers of hypnosis were so great he could make himself invisible. He needed this ability, or something like, because most weeks his girlfriend Margo Lane, played by fellow Mercury Theater actor Agnes Moorhead, managed – literally – to fall into the hands of the villain.

The following year, the Mercury Theater company transferred wholesale to CBS, initially as a sponsorless summer replacement, to perform literary adaptations under the banner *Mercury Theater of the Air*. *Dracula* was the first, not untypically chosen by Welles a week before air instead of *Treasure Island* on which John Houseman, dragooned into being a radio script writer, had been working. Although they rehearsed the seventeenth script of the series, written by Howard Koch and Ann Froelich and based on H. G. Wells's *War of the Worlds*, on Thursday 28 October 1938, because of rewrites Welles encountered the full text for the first time after finishing his theatre rehearsal on the following Saturday just hours before the live broadcast.

The opening half of the show was constructed as a series of fake breaking-news interruptions to music programmes supposedly coming live from two ballroom locations around New York. Such interruptions had indeed become a rare but real radio characteristic as the international crisis of the 1930s had worsened. Nevertheless it is hard to know why so many listeners were fooled into believing that they were hearing genuine eyewitness reports of an actual Martian invasion, if indeed they actually were so fooled. Only the middle of the programme comes anywhere close to echoing the feel of on-the-spot news reporting and even that was broken up by unlikely eyewitness speeches, a full network ident and a genuine spot commercial. Moreover, compared, say, with the run-of-the-mill *The Shadow*, *The War of the Worlds*

271

showed its 'just-in-time' nature and is a very thin auditory experience, lacking convincing sound effects and with much dead air. At the end, Welles, whose voice is heard both as himself and as the play's leading character, reinforces the fiction, explaining the show as: 'The Mercury Theater's own radio version of dressing up in a sheet and jumping out of a bush and saying "boo". . . You'll be relieved I hope to learn that we didn't mean it. . . . That was no Martian – it's Halloween'. As indeed it was.

Although positioned, with the NBC Symphony, as part of radio's serious contribution to American culture, the taint of commercialism was of course never far away from these drama series. The uproar after *The War of the Worlds* not only got Welles to Hollywood and *Citizen Kane*; it brought him a naming sponsor, Campbell Soup. Welles closed each *Campbell Playhouse* with an interview segment. After *Rebecca*, for example, he spoke to both its original author, Daphne du Maurier, and Margaret Sullivan who had played the title role in the dramatisation. Sullivan said: 'You know, two things I like very much are good stories and good soup. And when I tell you my idea of a good soup – that's Campbell's chicken soup – that, Mr Welles, is no story.'

The War of the Worlds confirmed radio's power, if by 1938 any such confirmation were needed. When the network ran a 'Why I hate Jack Benny' contest as a publicity stunt they got 217,000 replies. A product-showcase daytime series received 250,000 requests for a brochure about the show. Yet, curiously, the medium's power was shared. The residual telephone time-leasing idea led to a system where the advertiser, or more often the advertiser's advertising agency, created the sponsored programme as a species of telephone message which they paid the broadcaster, an equivalent of the telephone company, to carry. This meant that much programming, the most popular in fact, was in the hands of the advertising agencies, not the radio networks or the stations that subscribed to them.

The networks sought such a division of labour because it was profitable, allowed them to claim they were offering a 'general public service' as the law required and stilled any suspicions the Justice

Department might harbour about monopoly. In the wake of the establishment of the FCC, the networks created internal censorship operations in the form of 'Continuity Acceptance Departments', just as Hollywood was tightening its industrial prior-approval system with ever stricter enforcement of its production code. As with censors at all times everywhere, the actions of Continuity Acceptance, later called Network Standards, were, when they were not reinforcing bigotry, largely asinine. The censors were endlessly confused by the innuendo that was stock in trade of the vaudeville stage whence came so many of radio's stars. For example: 'Oi! Am I sick. I was in bed all day with three doctors and two nurses' struck them as having a 'possible double meaning'. Miss Fanny Brice, whose gag this was, cannot have been too shocked to have this drawn to her attention. The NBC's chief censor after 1936 was Janet MacRorie. She eyed the soap scripts with hawk-like attention. No 'dope fiends'; no 'confinement cases'; no 'neglect of wife for other woman'.

As for popular drama, its reliance on the detective story had made it in MacRorie's view far too prone to violence. *Dick Tracy*, for example, glorified 'the colourful deeds and skill of miscreants' and there were excessive gunshots and screams. MacRorie's colleagues were not above resisting her arguments, largely on the grounds that the overall popularity of radio was paying her wages. Such realists also had a transatlantic example to throw in Network Standards' face. Just as the British used US amateur radio cacophony in 1920s as a species of awful warning, so in the 1930s the American radio professionals cautioned against the po-faced solemnity of the BBC. One asked MacRorie, 'Are we to give the radio audience what they apparently like to listen to or what we think they ought to have? The advertisers pursued the former course; the British Broadcasting Company[7] the latter.'

'Heard echoing in the loneliest cottage in the land'

There was much truth in the charge. Reith had adopted a morally and culturally improving agenda for the BBC. In 1924 while it was still

BBCo, he had written: 'It is occasionally indicated to us that we are apparently setting out to give the public what we think they need – and not what they want – but few know what they want and very few what they need.' In part this elitism may have arisen from his own rigorous class-conscious Presbyterianism, but it also made sense in the face of Post Office hostility and the perception that populist American radio was in chaos. Anyway, clothed as 'public service broadcasting' it secured the BBC a monopoly of the airwaves for 30 years and ensured its continued vibrancy for at least another half-century after that. In effect Reith hijacked the term 'public service' to mean only that broadcasters should make no profit, not that they should serve the public by meeting popular needs. Their purpose was a tripartite one: to educate, to inform and to entertain, which in a class-stratified Britain meant meeting middle-class cultural standards. There was an important ideological consequence to this.

The issue of national identity and radio's role in reinforcing it was a central, if implicit, agenda item for the BBC. The current political entity that is the United Kingdom of Great Britain and Northern Ireland is, following the establishment of the Irish Free State, just two years older than the BBC itself. The United Kingdom can be thought of as an artificial construct and the BBC as a major instrument of its continued viability. Certainly the BBC was, almost from the beginning, and in defiance of the limitations of the technology, a network dedicated to distributing the same programme over the entire country rather than a collection of semi-autonomous broadcasting stations. In 1924, Reith wrote that the BBCo would allow the chimes of Big Ben, that potent aural symbol of national unity and imperial power, to be 'heard echoing in the loneliest cottage in the land'. The technology was bent to this purpose.

At a 1926 conference, the Corporation yielded half its internationally assigned wavelengths to the ever-expanding number of stations in the rest of Europe and after 1928 set about building one single national service via nine main and ten 'relay' stations linked by high-quality GPO landlines. Peter Eckersley, the engineering genius who fashioned this system, created the possibility of a dual service since the transmitters were built to handle two signals, the national (relayed by landline from London) and, in the main stations, a locally produced regional service. A lively tradition of local programme origination emerged with, for instance, 2ZY Manchester becoming, because of the Hallé orchestra and other regional professional musicians, a centre for classical music. Nevertheless, from the outset London ruled. The relay stations, sometimes against a background of vociferous local objections, were simply not equipped to originate material.

What was at work here was the dominant myth of 'one nation', a most necessary propaganda thrust for the ruling establishment given that events such as the birth of the Irish Free State, the General Strike and the exacerbated economic disparities of the Great Depression clearly revealed a nation very far from being at one with itself. This overt need for nation building was then refracted by the 'one nation' nature of much of the programming. For example, British radio's first huge outside broadcast (OB) audience, estimated at ten million listeners, heard King George V open the Empire Exhibition at Wembley in 1924. After a decade of cajoling, Reith then persuaded Buckingham Palace to allow a royal Christmas broadcast in 1932. Its informality was sensational: 'I wish you all, dear friends,' said the King, 'a Happy Christmas'. These transmissions, which continue on television in the twenty-first century, became as much part of the British Christmas Day as fir trees, holly, turkey and presents. In the early decades, the transmission of the National Anthem at the end of the broadcast day as well as during the outside broadcast of ceremonials raised the vexed question of whether or not it was proper to rise and stand by one's loudspeaker.

The official voice of the BBC – BBC English as it soon became – was the accent of the ruling class, Southern Received Pronunciation. Regional voices, even educated ones, were, outside of entertainment, more or less excluded from the national output. Much, for example, was made of the use of Wilfred Pickles, a Yorkshireman with an educated regional accent, as the only non-SRP national newsreader in the 1930s. Through the faithful echoing of this vision of unified national life in the impeccable accents of the ruling class, the BBC fulfilled Reith's vision – in contrast to America, where such an identity-creating objective was a by-product of popular ethnic programming produced in the relentless search for mass audiences. Needless to say, unexamined institutional racism kept any ethnic programming along American lines well away from the BBC's microphones.

In Britain, the rich variety of Britain's voices, drained of any foreign overtones, merely signified comedy and only slowly was comedy allowed to achieve its potential. Public service broadcasting most assuredly did not mean prioritising populist fare. On the contrary, Reith's vision injected a measure of pomposity into the BBC which turned it into an object of fun, even to its own entertainers. The first of these to achieve any public acceptance, Helena Millais, played a cockney lady called 'Our Lizzie': ' 'Ullo, me old ducks! 'Ere I am again with me old string bag.' Lizzie, though, was not ecstatic about the company she was keeping on the airwaves:

> Mind you, I don't always 'old with the programmes. They're too 'ighbrow; I like the comics and the Saverloy Band,[8] and some of the Hentertainers ain't bad; but them simfunny concerts and them virtuoso stunts! Of course, I'm glad them singers is virtuous, but I'd like 'em to be a bit brighter about it.

The BBC was easy to mock. Reith, his controller of programmes, Cecil Graves, and the head of the Music Department, Adrian Boult, were all to be knighted – Reith indeed eventually becoming a peer. Announcers were given a dress allowance in 1925 so they could wear black tie to the microphone in the evening. The Corporation was never a hotbed of low show-biz types.

In the UK, as elsewhere, all who thought themselves rivalled by the radio had been initially hostile – the church, the Football League, the press barons. The Corporation's 'stuffed-shirt' antipathy to the 'low brow' specifically soured relations with the vaudeville industry. Despite public enthusiasm for radio comedy, the new medium was made a trifle hazardous for practitioners of the old. For example, the following joke got the comedians who made it banned from the studios for five months in 1935:

> — What is the difference between a champagne cork and a baby's bottom?
> — A champagne cork has the maker's name on its bottom.

London ticked off BBC Midland Region for playing the supposedly risqué number 'The Window Cleaner' by George Formby and was undeterred to be told that the song figured in a U-certificate (general audience) film and the star himself had been singing it without objections in a local pantomime. 'The people who complain of vulgarity in broadcasting may be those who think it immoral to go to a pantomime or even to a film' came back the snooty metropolitan admonition.

As late as the eve of the Second World War, John Watt, then head of Variety, asserted, somewhat wearily one cannot help feeling: 'It has been said there are only six jokes in the world, and I assure you that we cannot broadcast three of them.' Nevertheless, variety programming was increasingly popular with the audience, if not with the BBC's hierarchy; in fact it was more popular than straight dance-music shows. A Radio Variety Department was created under Eric Maschwitz in 1933 and its output grew rapidly from three hours a week to 15 hours three years later. Among its innovations was the concept of the fixed time slot – 6.30 p.m. every Saturday for *In Town Tonight*, for example – instead of the previous day-to-day unpredictability. Out of this, the idea of a complete schedule with regular slots for established programmes slowly grew; and the popular finally secured a pre-eminent place.

Comedians Ted Ray and Tommy Trinder adapted to British taste the American stand-up one-liner routine. Others moved towards the extended sketch: in 1937, for instance, Rob Wilton created 'Mr Muddlecombe J.P.', the judge of the 'Court of Not-So-Common-Please!' in the town of 'Nether Backwash'. Soon he was the mayor:

Muddlecombe: But we must keep up with the time, be up to date. Bless my life, every decent town these days has its by-pass.

Buttersbun: My argument is that we don't have enough passers-by to want a by-pass.

Muddlecombe: No, but the passers-by who do pass by, if they had a by-pass to pass by, would be able to pass by the by-pass.[9]

Variety Department's biggest pre-war hit, *Band Waggon*, appeared the following year. Faced with cancellation after the first six editions, the BBC's original 'resident comedian', Arthur Askey, and his upper-class sidekick, Richard Murdoch, invented for themselves a location and a style which turned this disaster around. Their success was rewarded with one of the still rare regular time slots. Askey and 'Stinker' Murdoch moved themselves into a fictitious flat on top of Broadcasting House populated by two pigeons, a goat, Mrs Bagwash, the cleaner, and her daughter Nausea, neither of whom was ever heard to utter. The show was punctuated by the pioneering use in Britain of comic sound effects and endless catchphrases – 'Hello, playmates!'; 'Aythangyow'; 'Don't be filthy!' – as well as Arthur's comic songs which had been the mark of his stage act.

Music was everywhere but, again, the BBC had a problem with the popular. In its internal organisational terminology, 'Music', as an unadorned epithet, meant the classical tradition. In 1926, in an inspired early decision, Reith had agreed to sponsor the Promenade Concerts, a fixture in the musical life of the capital since 1895. The BBC made the Proms into another regular national annual radio event. Eventually, the Corporation also supported Covent Garden, Sadler's Wells and a touring opera company. At his death, the country's most prominent classical composer, Sir Edward Elgar, was working on a BBC commission. The BBC had 266 musicians on its books, 119 in its own symphony orchestra (under Adrian Boult) and the rest in five regional orchestras as well as the Theatre, Variety and Empire Orchestras and the Military Band.

By 1934, 65 per cent of its output was coming from this one department.

Three-quarters of this programming was distinguished from classical music as 'light' or 'dance' music. This did not mean jazz or anything close to it. As a distinct area of programming, jazz remained unthinkable. Even 'crooning', that quiet, intimate American 'mezzo-voice' singing style which had made stars of people like Bing Crosby, was beneath the BBC's notice before the mid-1930s, although Rudy Vallee had been softly wooing his listeners through a megaphone a decade earlier and the microphone was the mezzo-voice's natural ally. The Controller of Programmes, Cecil Graves, thought it 'a particularly odious form of singing' and demanded that it be banned from the air. Swing, it was decided, was a minority taste to be catered for in the odd 'concert'. A full six years after Duke Ellington had asserted in America that 'It don't mean a thing if you ain't got that swing', in March 1937 the BBC nerved itself to broadcast its first such 'concert'. Announced as a 'jam session', it threw Graves into his best 'Lady Bracknell' mode: 'A jam session?' he memoed, 'What on earth that means I don't know. . . . Is it a new Americanism? . . . We must introduce some sort of supervision to prevent this sort of thing.'

On the other hand, the audience was equally hostile to the modern classical avant-garde – characterised by one irate listener as 'Bartok-Stravinsky type of organised musical noise' – to which the BBC was committed, but the Corporation was no more to be swung by public hostility to the high brow than it was by public appetite for the low. Reith, secure in the ivory tower of public service, did not care to acknowledge public opinion much at all. He resisted any measurement of the audience. Ever swift to possess the moral high ground, he called upon the authority of Chronicles 1:21, wherein the impulse to make a census is ascribed to Satan; but knowledge of the audience's size posed problems for him greater than mere biblical transgression.

'A conspiracy of silence'

The International Broadcasting Company, in offices cheekily round the corner from the BBC's Broadcasting House in London, had made arrangements with a number of the French commercial stations, one of which in Normandy was directed at south-east England, to broadcast in English. The company sold sponsorships in the contemporary American style and recorded programmes, mainly dance-music records linked by disc jockeys, to carry these commercial messages in London, first scratchily on 16-inch discs and then, more cleanly, on optical film via a sound camera. These were then transported physically to the continent for transmission. The IBC's potential to threaten the BBC came after 1933 when it began to programme a private radio station licensed by the government of Luxembourg.

As elsewhere, radio began in the Grand Duchy as an amateur affair, in this case in 1924. The operation was transformed into a local commercial company in 1928 and chartered by the government two years later at 100 kilowatts, far more power than was needed to cover Luxembourg's 1,000 square miles. For example, the BBC's Daventry transmitter, 5XX, on 1600 metres longwave, which had been licensed by the usual international agreement to solve the BBC's domestic reception problems in 1925 but which could be heard all over Europe, transmitted at 30 kilowatts.

Luxembourg was unique in its wholehearted adoption of American-style commercialism. Elsewhere on the continent, despite the long tradition of state ownership of the communications infrastructure, the emerging system often embraced at least elements of the American commercial model. The reason was quite clear. Radio telephony interests, Marconi and Western Electric for example, already had a presence in many countries. From 1924, before the fascists came to power in Italy, these two firms dominated the slow growth of a commercial network via the Unione Radiofonica Italiana, licensed by the state to provide a service, and Italian Society for Radio Advertising, SIRPA. Take-up was very slow, a mere 50,000 receivers in 1928, a year when in (admittedly more populous) Britain over two million sets were in use. (This number was not reached in Italy until 1942.) The Italian company only opened its first national transmitter in 1930, and later that decade the fascist state did operate a rural service as well as shortwave transmissions to the diaspora community in the United States, or in Arabic to areas where Mussolini had political ambitions.

Before the war, France failed to make a choice between public and private. Fourteen commercial stations faced twelve state-operated stations, both serving the more than five million receivers the country had in use by 1939. In Germany, on the other hand, the post office had remained in greater control than even the GPO in Britain, beginning a service in 1923 and opening a shortwave transmitter in 1929. As in the UK, by the end of the 1920s over two million sets were in use but the Nazis saw radio as a prime communications tool and, with the provision of cheap Volksempfänger receivers, ensured its pervasiveness. The RRG (Reichs Radio Gesellschaft) authority became a centre for technological development – audiotape, for example. Plastic-based tape, to replace a flexible steel system, had been patented in the late 1920s but it was at the RRG labs, just in time for the Nazi leadership's wartime speeches to be perfectly recorded, that a crucial noise suppression system was developed, making a tape-recorder truly viable for all recording purposes.

The BBC was not happy with Luxembourg but, despite the lack of international sanction for its slot on the dial and the power it was using, Radio Luxembourg remained defiant. By 1935 established British variety artists were recording for it. By 1938, the British branch of J. Walter Thompson, which had built a London studio in Bush House (which, ironically, the BBC's world radio service was eventually to make its home), was providing 44 sponsored programmes a week. Sponsors also filled the Scala Theatre in London for popular music concerts. Reith fumed about 'this monstrous stuff from Luxembourg' and the BBC mounted endless counter-attacks. It complained in international fora. It attempted to ban artistes who broadcast for Radio Luxembourg from BBC studios. It successfully persuaded newspapers not to carry commercial radio listings and the GPO not to provide the IBC with a high-quality landline to the continent. (The BBC had one as it was part of the internationally agreed European broadcasting system.)

Nevertheless, particularly on Sunday, gathering an audience was not hard for the IBC. Supported by religious opinion and by his own convictions, Reith (who had fired the crucially important Eckersley just because the man had been cited as a co-respondent in a divorce case) had cast the BBC's Sabbath in an authentic austere mode. Nothing before 9.30 a.m. when there were 15 minutes of prayer. Nothing after that until a suitably sombre diet of classical music and talks began at 12.30. These concluded with a full-scale classical music concert and an epilogue at 11.00 p.m. Radio Luxembourg, which only transmitted in English on weeknights, spoke English all day on Sunday when spinning its usual diet of popular records. It is entirely plausible that, as commercial audience research claimed, 60 per cent of the BBC's audience also listened at one time or another to Luxembourg or one of the other commercial stations broadcasting in English.

The BBC survived the threat. It needed to because its finance depended on the hypothecated tax that was the licence fee, and the political will to increase it, as was from time to time necessary, or even to leave it in place would quickly wither if the audience were seriously eroded. The BBC did therefore come to terms with the variety artists and, in the last years of the 1930s, offered increasingly accessible fare. It was also the case that as the Listener Research Unit (when it was eventually established) unexpectedly demonstrated, Radio Luxembourg's speciality, dance music – especially recorded dance music – was not as popular as the live variety.

Radio Luxembourg never really developed a full range of popular genres beyond the spinning discs. The BBC did, although drama both 'serious' and 'light' – at 3.5 per cent of output in the early 1930s – was no more prominent in the schedule than were religion, schools and children's programmes. Again, as with music, 'serious' at first outweighed 'light'. Avant-garde dramatic features, 'Posters in Sound' as they were sometimes called, and classic dramas were heard before 1930 whereas the first equivalent to the popular American thrillers, *Paul Temple*, did not appear until 1939.

After music, the biggest genre of programming was talk. Nearly a fifth of BBC airtime was taken up with 'talks' and news. The reason for the distinction lay in the hostility of the press. New technologies, however attractive and however pervasive they eventually become, always occasion suppressive hostility (as well as technological hyperbole, confusion of purpose and misplaced applications) and this inevitably blunts their potential for radical change. Radio was no exception and its history features all of these factors. Among those overtly hostile, no group's enmity was more powerful or more sustained than that of the British newspaper owners, however formally uninvolved they were. Even in America, where the proprietors owned a significant percentage of all radio stations and the stunted nature of non-commercial public service broadcasting was no threat, the broadcasting of news bulletins remained problematic. Early experiments in reading the news on air, which dated back to 1909, merely confirmed radio as a potential threat. Broadcasting election returns in 1916 and 1920 ensured that when the push to full-scale professional broadcasting began, newspapers would do their best to deny material to the new medium. Although there was a measure of local news, as the press collectively owned the wire services, it was a simple matter to refuse to let the radio networks have national and international reports.

The 1932 election which put Franklin Delano Roosevelt into the White House, and print-media hysteria over the Lindberg kidnapping, forced the issue. The networks established news departments. In response, the American Newspaper Publishers' Association ordered its members not to carry station listings. To resolve this standoff, in December 1933, the two parties signed an agreement at the Biltmore Hotel in New York. In return for restored listings, the broadcasters agreed once again to limit the news. Crucially, the agreement did allow the radio to cover exceptional stories and wars in Spain, Manchuria and Abyssinia, Hitler's aggressions and the tension of the Depression occasioned enough of those so that, by 1938, the flash news report was sufficiently a feature of the radio to enable Welles, faking the technique, supposedly to create a panic about a Martian invasion. By this time, the proprietors of the press, who were increasingly at odds with themselves because some but not all were cross-media owners, had seen that the radio did not stop people buying newspapers after all. Full access to news sources was now as available to broadcasters as to the press.

In Britain the parties were less intertwined since the press had no part in BBCo nor, of course, in the public corporation that succeeded it. The original BBCo licence prohibited the controversial in general and it was agreed in particular that there would be no news bulletins prior to 7.00 p.m., the time of the last edition of the evening papers. The very success of the radio as a news source during the newspaperless days of the General Strike confirmed the hostility of the press. When the papers once more hit the streets, the restrictions were reimposed. Not only was the time of bulletins laid down but the contents were delivered from one of four approved news agencies, which were, as in America, obviously the creatures of the print medium. The result was often absurd; for example, the 1926 Derby was covered but the result could not be reported on air. By 1927, the time restriction had moved forward to 6.30 p.m. and the following year to 6.15 p.m. Soon there were more than 400 eye-witness accounts of events a year being read to the studio microphone. No editorial viewpoint was allowed, although how its inevitability might be avoided in the selection and presentation of even the flattest of reports was never addressed. By 1932 the BBC had its own news operation and, as the pressure of major stories meshed with the same growing realisation as the Americans' that newspaper sales were not affected by broadcast news, the bulletins became a crucial part of the BBC's schedule.

Despite the early restrictions during the late 1920s on straightforward news bulletins, the BBC had sought to produce informative spoken material in the form of 'talks'. Ignoring the PMG's uneasiness about 'controversy', even before the Corporation was formed, in 1923,

BBCo broadcast a 'debate', 'Does communism have a future?', complete with a real live communist. Such programming, as well as the continuation of Reith's use of the famous as broadcasters in the run-up to the acquisition of the Charter, led in 1928 to the establishment of a Talks Department under Hilda Matheson. This imposed distinction between news and current affairs was reflected in the BBC's organisation of its factual programming well into the age of television.

Not only did the parade of famous Britons continue in the 1930s, squeaky-voiced H. G. Wells to the fore, but the distinction in some way licensed Talks, relieved of the burden of direct news reporting, to adopt a more investigative and editorially challenging role. In the early 1930s under Matheson the studio-based radio documentary developed and, in contrast to the far better-known but far less committed documentary films being made at the same time on the same topics by the Grierson group at the GPO Film Unit, these transmissions were amazingly outspoken for their time and source. *SOS on Unemployment* was a 1932 series of eleven programmes about the Depression:

> Here is an S.O.S. message, probably the most urgent you will ever hear and it vitally concerns you. You are called upon to create a entirely new social order. . . There is plenty for you to do and you must do it at once if you care about your fellow countrymen.

Two years later, Talks producers began to bring working-class voices to the studio microphone to give their views of unemployment and poverty. This was so powerful that ministers felt the need to attack the veracity of their witness in the House of Commons. Faced with the first licence renewal in 1935, the BBC backed away from such controversial programming. The entire liberal/radical Talks Department team was dispersed – to start radio services in Palestine and India or to training. One, Felix Greene, the radical producer who had caused the most trouble, was sent to the non-job of being the BBC's 'Representative' in the USA.[10] In London, a far safer pair of hands was put in charge, ex-diplomat Sir Richard Maconachie. The Corporation's licence was renewed. For all the occasional rows, the organisation survived by repeatedly censuring itself – as, indeed, it had first done during the General Strike.

If the Head of Light Entertainment could complain that half the jokes in the world could not be broadcast, a senior BBC journalist, John Coates, writing in late 1938 could say much the same about fascist Europe:

> I say, with a full sense of responsibility and, since I was for over three years Chief News editor, with a certain authority, that in the past we have not played the part which our duty to the people of this country called upon us to play. We have, in fact, taken part in a conspiracy of silence.

The BBC had been a reluctant participant in the radio propaganda war which began to develop in the 1930s. Certainly, deliberately targeting overseas populations by broadcasting in other languages than English had been rendered politically suspect. But the BBC was, after all, secure in the sense that its signal, in English only of course, could be heard over all of Europe. It resisted broadcasting in foreign languages as Moscow, Rome, Berlin and the Vatican were doing. It was only when the Italians began their Arabic transmissions that the BBC felt the need to respond to political pressure and followed suit. The BBC's shortwave Empire Service was financed not by the licence fee but by a direct grant from the Treasury.

The Empire Service was also responsible for overcoming the disinclination to record and thereby produce 'bottled' radio. Much had been made of liveness not least because of Radio Luxembourg's canned output, and the BBC acquired steel-tape audio recorders[11] for the shortwave Empire Service only. The BBC, unlike the Nazi RRG, therefore played little role in the development of recording technologies during the 1930s. The RRG's *Echo Des Tages* used radio cars effectively but the BBC's version, a 27ft long van weighing seven tons and recording to disc, proved too unwieldy for the news and was banished to the regions. Live remote broadcasting was, of course, a different matter. Richard Dimbleby, scion of a local newspaper-owning family, began to build the reputation which would over the next three decades make him the county's most respected broadcaster, with a live report of the Crystal Palace fire from an adjacent phone box. Although no reporters had been sent to Spain, much less Manchuria, the BBC's 'silence' on the international situation was broken as the European crisis deepened in the last years of the 1930s, so much so that listeners started complaining that the news was unsettling them, making them ever 'more certain that war must come'.

Having cleared their own domestic problems, the American networks also took the international crises of the 1930s seriously. CBS in particular used shortwave pick-ups from European studios, no fewer than 151 during the Nazi invasion of Czechoslovakia in 1938, to demonstrate vividly radio's immediacy. William Shirer, based in Berlin, provided the network with unrivalled coverage of Hitler's regime. After hostilities broke out, Edward R. Murrow, the CBS man in London – in his publicity photographs slouch-hatted, raincoat-belted and Bogart-handsome – proved even more important, insisting on British resilience during the Blitz. Christmas Eve 1940:

> This is not a merry Christmas in London. I heard that phrase only twice in the last three days . . . It can't be a merry Christmas, for those people who spend tonight and tomorrow by their firesides in their own homes realise that they have bought this Christmas with their nerves, their bodies and their old buildings . . . I should like to add my small voice to give my own Christmas greetings to friends and colleagues at home. Merry Christmas is somehow ill-timed and out of place, so I shall just use the current London phrase – so long and good luck.

It had been exactly 33 years since Reginald Fessenden first used the airwaves to wish peace on earth to all men of good will.

Sources

Asa Briggs (1995), *The History of Broadcasting in the United Kingdom*, Oxford: Oxford University Press.

John Cain (1992), *The BBC: 70 Years of Broadcasting*, London: BBC.

Michael Chanan (1995), *Repeated Takes: A Short History of Recording and its Effects on Music*, London: Verso.

Jonathan Dimbleby (1975), *Richard Dimbleby: A Biography*, London: Hodder & Stoughton.

Patrice Flichy (1991), *Une histoire de la communication modern: Espace publique et vie privée*, Paris: La Découverte.

Andy Foster and Steve Furst (n/d), *Radio Comedy 1938–1968*, London: Virgin.

Geoffrey Hare (1992), 'The Law of the Jingle, or a Decade of Change in French Radio', in R. Chapman and N. Hewitt (eds) *Popular Culture and Mass Communication in Twentieth–Century France*, Lampeter: Edwin Mellen.

Geoffrey Hare (1997), 'The Broadcasting Media' in J. Flower (ed.), *France Today*, London: Hodder & Stoughton.

Michelle Hilmes (1997), *Radio Voices: American Broadcasting 1922–1952*, Twin Cities: University of Minnesota Press.

Timothy Hollins (1984), *Beyond Broadcasting: Into the Cable Age*, London: British Film Institute.

David Morton (2000), *Off the Record: The Technology and Culture of Sound Recording in America*, New Brunswick, NJ: Rutgers University Press.

Graham Murdock (1992), 'Citizens, Consumers, and Public Culture' in Michael Skovmand and Kim Christian Schröder (eds), *Media Cultures: Reappraising Transnational Media*, London: Routledge.

Ed Murrow (1941), *This is London*, New York: Simon Schuster.

Richard Nichols (1983), *Radio Luxembourg: The Station of the Stars*, London: Comet.

Paddy Scannell and David Cardiff (1991), *A Social History of British Broadcasting Volume* 1, Oxford: Basil Blackwell.

John Snagge and Michael Barsley (1972), *Those Vintage Years of Radio*, London: Pitman.

7

'AMERICAN SHOTS': CINEMA FROM 1925

'The same scene shot three times'

The opening shot is masked in black, the image – of a spiral staircase – confined to the middle third of the screen. Down the steep stairs, in their brief dancing costumes, run chorus girls (cut to high angle, full screen) out on to a theatrical stage. With these two assured shots, and a perfectly fluid sequence of seductive dancers and their audience of mainly elderly leering men, both *The Pleasure Garden* and the career of Alfred Hitchcock as a film director began. The year was 1925. *The Pleasure Garden* was a British film, produced by Michael Balcon at Gainsborough Pictures, but it had American stars, Virginia Valli and Carmelita Geraghty, and was shot by an Italian, Baron Giovanni Ventimiglia, with an otherwise British crew in the Emelka studios in Berlin and on location in Italy and Germany, those countries standing in for the Orient and England.

Michael Balcon was a figure new to the nascent British film industry, a producer as opposed to the more usual producer/director, such as Herbert Wilcox. Balcon had been a rather unsuccessful distributor who had exploited his network of exhibition and distribution entrepreneurs to fund his first movie in 1922. Both of these Englishmen had made deals with a Berlin producer, Erich Pommer, whose career had also progressed, like Balcon's, from salesman (of French movies in Germany) to producer.

By the time of these Anglo-German arrangements, Pommer had to his credit, for example, the 1919 expressionist horror movie, *Das*

Kabinett des Dr Caligari. Its acting style was unchanged from what had become the histrionics of the nineteenth-century stage but the settings – jagged, hysterically angled, obviously false – revealed the cinema's anti-realistic, modernist potential. *Caligari*, although it had few imitators, marks the beginning of what is inscribed as a golden era of filmmaking in Germany where such *Autorenfilmen* took a proper place alongside other high-culture avant-garde artistic expressions. (More popular fare, *Sensationsfilmen*, also contributed to Germany's success but are not to be found in the canon.)

In 1923, Pommer was made the head of Universum Film AG (Ufa), a post-war integrated company created by the merger of a number of older production firms. Ufa was specifically designed to put German films on the national screens and on the map internationally. Its specially built Berlin studios at Neubabelsberg offered facilities unmatched anywhere in the world, even in Hollywood. Striving for his trademark Film Europe productions to rival American movies, Pommer, apart from his relationships with the British, also worked closely with the Danes, which, among other things, brought the great director Carl-Theodor Dreyer to Ufa. To a certain extent this business plan paid off and for a time the Germans did rival the Americans in some European markets, but the films were shot using different national stars for simultaneous versions, even though, as there was no speech, there was no linguistic reason for doing this. As Balcon recalled, the project was fundamentally doomed: 'The difficulties of working in this way are infinite, impossible to exaggerate. And the boredom! The same scene shot three times, with however many "takes" required on each.'

Hitchcock had first arrived in Berlin in 1924 as an assistant director and editor, not for one of Pommer's early 'Euro-pie' efforts but as part of the Balcon's Ufa deal which allowed British productions to use the Neubabelsburg facilities. One of Pommer's most important *Autorenfilme* directors, Friedrich Murnau, was shooting *The Last Laugh*, a film that would turn out to be another of the canonical masterworks of the silent cinema, although in a very different style from *Caligari*. It reflected the 'New Realism' that was coming to dominate

Weimarian production and, despite a bathetic ending, is inscribed in the canon of the silent cinema as a masterly study of the assumed effects of camera angles. The elderly Emil Jannings, the greatest German stage actor of his generation, plays a pompous and overbearing head porter at a grand-lux hotel. He is constantly shot from a slight low angle so we are forced, as audience, to look up to him. But he is getting old and heaving the travelling trunks of the rich is getting too much for him. He is called into the manager's office and given a letter. The camera looks over his shoulder as he reads it. Suddenly, we are looking down at him, just as he is being told that he has been demoted to lavatory attendant. It is easy to move the camera for no reason to achieve such an effect; but to do so because the narrative motivates the change of angle is perhaps a crucial mark of the film director's talent. Such finesse represents how quickly in the 1920s the dominant cinematic language was refining and complicating the cinema as a means of expression. In 1924, Hitchcock spent all his spare time observing Murnau at work and picking his brain. In later years, Hitchcock was to claim that he was 'American trained' because his first job in the movies had been to design intertitles for the London studio in Islington of the major Hollywood film company Famous Players-Laskey, but, arguably, it is Murnau's influence which lies behind the fluidity of *The Pleasure Garden*'s opening.

Four years after *The Last Laugh*, Murnau was in Hollywood. By then Pommer himself had made two trips to Los Angeles. A decade after that, Hitchcock was summoned to the West Coast by producer David Selznick. Not least because of the rise of the fascist dictators, this had become a one-way traffic westward; but it had not always been so. Hitchcock was far from alone in the 1920s in using American stars. Dorothy Gish, for example, was in London in 1926 at Herbert Wilcox's invitation to make *Nell Gwynn*. Many found themselves on the transatlantic liners going to Europe yet still working for Hollywood. Gloria Swanson's French hit of 1925, *Madame Sens-Gêne*, was made in a Paris studio run by the American firm Paramount (as Famous Players-Lasky had become). As well as Paramount, Fox had arrived and the other

American majors followed. All such interchanges, a commonplace of cinema's history in the first decades of the twentieth century, spoke to the fact that film was fundamentally an international art form and an international business.

Of course, there had been national preferences and local developments of considerable significance – the initial Russian fondness for more or less static tableaux, the Italian taste for ancient epics, the French fashion for stage stars and high-toned history; but language was no barrier and intertitles could easily be translated. As a means of communication – with a 'language' of its own for representing time and space – cinema was international from the beginning. Its mainstream conventions of shots and editing, its basic modes of operation – even its marketing ploys – had been developed, in effect, as a multi-national project.

Multi-shot films, such as the four-shot reconstruction of the execution of President McKinley's assassin – two exteriors of the prison, the prisoner in his cell and the execution – had begun to appear at the turn of the century. By 1907, a film was no longer coterminous with a shot. Films had many shots and the sequence of shots told a story. Initially there were worries about the audience's ability to understand a straight cut between moving images although the first single-shot films had been joined together by exhibitors to make up reels. With the help of full-screen intertitles, the audience clearly understood the transition from one shot to another. It was probably projectionists who learned from experience that audiences could cope with cuts within a film, because they repaired the inevitable breaks in the celluloid that occurred during projection with the same special cement they used to make up reels and the audience did not rebel. Straight cuts with continuous action are found as early as 1901, for example, in films made in Brighton by James Williamson; but most producers took no chances. Méliès in *A Trip in the Moon* (1902) had a model rocket hit the moon, which has a man's face, in the eye and the face grimaces. In the next shot, the 'rocket' again lands on the surface, a studio set of fantastic rocks. The double action is an aide to audience comprehension, not, as it would be today, an offence against logic. In the Edison 1902 film, *Life of an American Fireman*, now credited to his employee Edwin Porter, an entire rescue is repeated in interior and exterior shots of the same action, but soon the straight cut became a norm, denoting continuous time. Alternatives – fades and dissolves – came to indicate the passage of time.

Much of *The Great Train Robbery*, a film made by Porter at Edison's in 1903, duplicates the straight-on tableaux-like shot of all early movies, the action happening as on a stage with the camera firmly fixed in the stalls, far enough away to capture the entire scene. Nine feet between the camera and the action, which, with a standard lens, produced the image of the whole figure to fill the screen from top to bottom, had become another norm. During the chase sequence at the film's climax, the camera, although still at a distance and with somewhat confused coverage, was set-up at an angle and the film cross-cuts in an entirely modern way between the robbers and the pursuing posse in an early example of parallel action. It is no accident that Porter began his movie career as a projectionist.

It was some years before the camera moved relative to fictional action. Changing the spectators' angle of view within a shot was obviously something that had never happened in photography or in the theatre, although it had been possible with magic lantern shows of the Phantasmagoria type. Early films were taken with a moving camera if the platform on which it was mounted itself moved – the view from the elevator in the Eiffel Tower, or from a boat floating down the Ganges or, most commonly, from the front of a train. These last 'phantom rides' became a particularly popular way of transferring the attractions of the Panorama's cityscapes and dramatic landscapes to the screen in a dynamic way.

Obviously, the technology of mobile platforms presented no obstacle. To move the photographic tripod only needed wheels and stability, which could be provided by laying lightweight tracks. Porter was soon using a dolly to track in for closer views, but again, audiences were deemed to need help if the angle of view changed as the action of a scene continued, as when the cut was from a long-shot to a close-up. In *As Seen through a Telescope*, made in 1900 by G. A. Smith, another of the so-called 'Brighton School', a voyeur in the foreground spies on a couple in the distance, using a telescope. The young woman is being shown how to ride a bicycle and the second shot reveals in close-up a man's hands around a trim female ankle as her floor-length skirt is raised and her foot is placed on the pedal. The audience is helped to relate the two shots because the close-up is masked to reveal only a circle of action, as if being seen through the telescope.

The most important developments were to use the potential fluidity of the sequence in such a way as to not confuse the audience. As the camera began to move its position from shot to shot maintaining the direction of action, and later, when the close-up became common, the eye-line of a character required considerable control. If, for example, the camera moved from one side of a line of action (or a look) in a shot to the other side of the same action (or look) for a subsequent shot, the direction would be reversed, 'crossing the line' of action.

Cecil Hepworth quite understood these 'grammatical' or encoding rules of spatial and temporal representation by 1905. In *Rescued by Rover*, he transferred a time-worn racist tale of a Romany woman stealing a baby into a fluid sequence which avoided the confusions of earlier multi-shot films, such as *The Great Train Robbery*. It takes three shots for the young nanny to upset a Romany woman; to let the woman kidnap the baby while nanny is distracted chatting up a boyfriend; and for the nanny to run home to alert the family, including the dog Rover, to the crime. There then follow 16 shots in which the dog jumps out of a window, runs down a street and round a corner, swims across a stream, finds the slum house and enters the room where the baby is – all the time maintaining direction and continuity. This order of shots is then repeated in reverse – Rover exits the house, swims back cross the river, runs back to the window, rouses the father. Then for a third time the sequence is repeated but with the father following (and using a conveniently tethered rowing boat to cross the water). The kidnapper is gone but the baby has been abandoned and is rescued.

294

Hepworth spares us a fourth repetition of the sequence linking house and hovel by using a shot of the kidnapper's return to her room, followed by a contrasting shot of the father, mother, baby and Rover rejoicing in their home. Perhaps the film's most remarkable testament to the growing understanding of these early filmmakers about how stories could be told in the new medium is in these last two shots. Hepworth assumed that the audience did not need to see father, baby and dog return to the house but would guess this was happening while looking at the kidnapper re-entering her hovel. The duration of this last shot is not, realistically, related to the time it would have taken dad, baby and Rover to get home but it does not offend against the audience's sense of the logical representation of time on the screen.

Transitions from shot to shot allowed for a considerable degree of manipulation. Some produced tricks as in Méliès's works but the vast majority were hidden, in the sense that they were simply absorbed by the audience, who remained unconscious of what went on between any two camera set-ups. Continuity between shots, to prevent the audience becoming distracted by jumps, became crucial as this breaking down of the action within the old tableaux into discrete shots increased. Such grammar was primarily deployed in the service of narrative, privileging the Lumières' tendency to realism over Méliès-style fantasy. Possible manipulations of time and space were constrained in the name of this realism. Filmmakers came to deliver seamless streams of images which accorded with their audiences' actual experience of how the world did, or might, work. Spectacle as spectacle, which had so entertained nineteenth-century audiences, no longer stood alone, paradoxically given the capacity of the new medium to deliver it. Without stories, it has been claimed, the audiences soon grew bored with non-narrative 'cinematographic slides' and it was this that forced showmen into perfecting cinema's story-telling capacity in the first couple of years of the twentieth century. It has even been suggested that the short reels of plotless single-shot movies, the norm of the late 1890s, had become so boring to theatre audiences that, within the first half-decade of the twentieth century, such reels were being used in vaudeville houses with continuous shows to 'chase' the audience out. If this was so, it was but a misfire in the cinema's relentless early drive to mass popularity. The victory of story, aping theatrical norms, over plotless spectacle, grounded in the lantern show, was secured in mainstream movies.

'Out of the cradle endlessly rocking'

The French had been first to exploit the possibilities of full-scale integrated industrial production, distribution and exhibition. By 1905, Charles Pathé's firm, Pathé-Frères, was combining specialised cinematographic equipment manufacture, constructing 250 cameras, projectors and ancillary devices a month, with a massive programme of film production. It was shooting and processing six or more titles a week – an hour to 90 minutes worth of finished, edited screen-time. When the first custom-built film theatres, cinemas, began to appear on both sides of the Atlantic around 1906, Pathé undertook a massive building programme. By 1909, the firm owned and operated 200 screens across France and Belgium. The distribution division, servicing independent exhibitors, ran six wholly owned regional agencies, renting rather than selling Pathé titles. They were the core of a rapidly developing worldwide marketing network.

In contrast, the Americans at first failed to realise the implicit internationalism of the new medium, and even the logic of integration along Pathé-style lines escaped them. This was largely because of the litigious Edison, using his patents (as usual) to assert his position. By 1901, Edison had no less than 23 infringement suits pending. Dickson and Lauste had progressed from the projecting Kinetoscope to found a rival firm to Edison's Vitagraph, Bioscope, which used its own 70mm film, producing superior image quality. This had rapidly established itself as the preferred format in first-class vaudeville theatres, charging a premium because of its superiority to Edison's 35mm. A number of others also sought to undercut Edison. On the basis of his British legal position,

William Friese-Green, for example, one of the many who had been working on motion picture devices in the late nineteenth century, had been able to obtain a US legal declaration that his was the master patent for the whole technology. Despite these hitches and confusions, enterprising independent American exhibitors were able to create a mass cinema-going public, gleaning its huge numbers from among those who constituted vaudeville's vast audience, and seating them as cheaply as possible.

A seat at the movies, in the basic converted store-front spaces which began proliferating after 1905, cost only 5c (a nickel) as compared to the cheapest vaudeville seat – then 25c – never mind a Broadway show or a serious illustrated lecture where a ticket could cost as much as $2. These 'Nickelodeons' escaped Edison's complete control not only because of other American producers but also because of Pathé. Up to a half of all the films screened in nickelodeons came from this one French company, which was flooding the American market with 200 copies of each film it made. Pathé's success concentrated the American mind. Edison and Biograph resolved their patent stand-off with a cross-licensing agreement. In 1908, this became the basis of the Motion Picture Patents Company, the MPPC or the 'Trust', which consolidated its position by signing an exclusive deal with Eastman Kodak for celluloid. It also created a subsidiary to organise a nationwide distribution system for finished films. The Trust, which included some foreign-owned production companies, was a success as a protectionist manœuvre and Pathé was soon being cut down to size. By 1911 they were commanding only 10 per cent of American exhibition.

It is not true that only unlicensed, non-MPPC filmmakers, led by Universal's Carl Laemmle, fled to the sunshine of a Los Angeles suburb called Hollywood to escape the Trust's reach, because of course the Trust knew they were there. Indeed, some Trust members themselves were attracted away from New Jersey to work in California. In 1912, Edison's movie patents were declared void and in 1915 the Trust itself was found to be an illegal cartel. It was wound up by 1917, by which time war had intervened and Hollywood was already emerging as the site of a concentration of major studios. Anyway, many of the MPPC's positions were (or would have been, had it been more efficient) a brake on film's potential.

Film was also no more successful than theatre at acquiring for itself the same rights of free expression enjoyed by the press. All over the world police forces and other local authorities took it upon themselves to censor the new medium. In England the ancient Watch Committees of the municipalities were empowered to regulate cinemas by the Cinematographic Act of 1909 on a safety basis but quickly began to censor contents until, in 1912, the industry successfully petitioned for its own licensing board to prevent the confusions which arose more than once because one committee censored a title another committee allowed. A similar National Board of Film Censors had been established in the United States in 1909. In France a national commission within the Interior Ministry censored all films from 1916 on. Film, in fact, confirmed what the theatre had already demonstrated, that freedom of expression was media specific and the specific medium to which it applied was the press. The US Supreme Court in 1915 declared that as cinema was a business 'pure and simple' it could enjoy no rights 'as part of the press of the country or as organs of opinion'. First Amendment protection did not apply.

Despite the MPPC and the censors, film nevertheless advanced. The received history of the cinema credits much of the elaboration of its mainstream 'language' to the Americans, *pace* the Trust's posturings, naming Biograph's leading director, an ex-actor, David Wark Griffith, as the person most responsible. Although Griffith's camera remained more or less at a standard height and moved little unless mounted on a travelling platform to film chariot, car or train, shots were varied. The wide establishing shot was explored in subsequent shots of details within the scene. The impact of a performance could be exponentially increased by cutting from the establishing shot, to a mid-shot of the figure, to a close-up of the face. Ensuring that any movements were matched shot to shot – which required a careful monitoring of the action to ensure gestures, body positions, details down to the length of burning cigarettes were accurately repeated – turned into a serious job on the set. In the cutting room, overlapping action allowed for minute differences of pacing as cutting-point choices were made between multiple possibilities. This breaking down of the scene and its fluid reconstruction on the editing bench became the essential mark of the American style. The psychological refinements of the 1920s – Murnau's in *The Last Laugh*, for example – would have been impossible without these advances.

A problem for Griffith with the Trust was the issue of length. Film reels lasted 15 minutes maximum, as long as the average variety act.[1] This length, somewhat paradoxically, was the norm in the Nickelodeon and when, after 1912/13, custom-built cinemas became common, films became more usually multi-reeled, although the terminology of 'reels' persisted. A half-reel of five to seven minutes became the dominant mode in some forms of mainly comic filmmaking, enduring as the standard length of cartoons for decades. The 1913 Italian epic *Quo Vadis* lasted a couple of hours but was a big hit internationally, including in America. The Trust sought to preserve the single-reel film. Biograph, already scared by the expense of the fourth reel of *Judith of Bethulia*, which Griffith had insisted on adding in emulation of the Italians, forced him into the arms of Mutual, who proved to be no happier with his grandiose ideas. With Mack Sennett and Thomas Ince, Griffith then set up an independent production company for which, in 1915, he made *Birth of a Nation*. It runs for twelve reels, more than three hours. Despite being awash with sentimentality, it is a bloodstained racist tract, faithfully reflecting its sources, two novels by Thomas Dixon, in making heroes of the Klu Klux Klan and stereotyping African-Americans as subhuman. The Klan welcomed it with a massive march in Atlanta but the then recently formed National Association of Coloured People boosted its own standing by organising a nationwide boycott. This did not prevent the film from being a massive hit but even Griffith, although a loyal son of the South, knew that hostility and controversy were not good for business in the long term and could not be justified by the fact that his father, a Confederate officer, had died of his war wounds when David was ten. Griffith therefore spent the next three years coming up with *Intolerance* as a four-fold corrective and, in the process, enabling these two films to establish the American blockbuster.

Although Griffith's great epics remained somewhat static in terms of any one shot, the exuberance of the editing created a cinematic vibrancy. He was particularly flamboyant in exploiting the possibilities of parallel action. At the end of *Intolerance*, the four stories which had been intertwined throughout the film are all cut together in a fast-moving montage. Since three of the stories involve rescues, Griffith juggles no less than ten different elements. In the contemporary story, they are preparing to execute the hero ('Boy'), while his would-be rescuers, in a racing-car, chase a train on which sits the governor who can stay the hanging. To these three elements are added a further three from the story of the fall of ancient Babylon. 'The Mountain Girl', driving a chariot, races ahead of Cyrus's army to warn Belshazzar in Babylon that his city is about to be attacked. (Belshazzar is having a party, as usual, surrounded by lady extras lightly draped in transparent gauze, which is more clothing than their Italian predecessors wore in *Quo Vadis*.) In Paris, it is St Bartholomew's day, the Protestants are being massacred and one races to save his beloved from the hands of a mustachioed mercenary. The ninth element concludes the most familiar of these four stories, that of Jesus, with two interspersed long shots of the Hill of Golgotha and the crucifixion. Finally, through all the 197 minutes of the film, a shot of a shadowed woman rocking a wooden cradle and the title 'Out of the Cradle Endlessly Rocking' are used to mark transitions from one of these stories to another. They appear again, more than once, at the climax.

The only clues that Griffith might have anticipated his audience finding all this a bit hard to follow lie in the overt guidance given in a couple of early intertitles: 'Therefore, you will find our play turning from one of these four stories to another'; or, 'And now our fourth story'. Otherwise, there is no evidence that the original viewers found the film any more difficult to follow than we do, except that unlike *Birth of a Nation* it was a box-office bust that destroyed the production company.

Ensuring audience engagement acted as a brake on creative flamboyance. It limited cinematic 'language' and also encouraged generic productions so that brands of stories – genres – could guide individuals to the sort of film they preferred. By 1911 Vitagraph were producing a domestic drama, a drama with a military setting, a comedy, a Western and a costumed piece a week. The range of genres, like the basics of editing or the expected length of a feature film, had been determined internationally. Of the Vitagraph list, only the Western can claim a more or less pure North American lineage. *The Great Train Robbery* had transferred the substance of the popular Western novel to the screen, creating the story-type. In the 1920s, when made by major studios, Westerns often had a historical epic feel, as in Cecil B. De Mille's series of panoramic dramas with a Western setting from *The Covered Wagon* (1923) to *Cimarron* (1930). Otherwise, it was left to the 'B' picture end of the business to exploit the low-budget 'oater'. It was not until the end of the 1930s, after the success of *The Plainsman*, that the majors made the Western their own, but even then creating them was no guarantee of glory. John Ford, for example, worked within the genre from 1917 (*The Tornado*) until 1964 (his elegiac *Cheyenne Autumn*) and over half of the more than 100 films he directed were 'oaters'. He won six Oscars, but not one of them was for a Western.

Vitagraph's other film types all had foreign inspiration. For example, it was Pathé in America who produced the exemplary melodramatic serials featuring Pearl White[2] and from France itself came the first hit thriller series, *Fantômas*, directed by Louis Feuillade. Animation too begins in Europe. Within the box of cinematic tricks that characterised the Méliès approach, the possibilities of animated drawings, on a blackboard for instance, altering them frame by frame, was well established by 1906. In that year Émile Cohl began providing animations for Gaumont in Paris. He was copied in America in 1911 by a famous newspaper cartoonist, Winsor McCay, but the real advances came when other Americans, John Bray and Earl Hurd, introduced the celluloid overlay sheet so backgrounds did not have to be endlessly redrawn. Dave Fleischer (who with his brother was to give the world Betty Boop and Popeye the Sailor) developed the 'rotoscope', which allowed single frames of live action to be redrawn as cartoon. Although until the 1950s cartoons were designed for all ages, their potential for adult expression became even more a matter for experimental filmmaking, especially in Europe.

Nothing was more exportable than American slapstick but this, too, was initially an imported form. The cinema's first star clown, André Deed, had worked for Méliès. Deed's successor, Max Linder, who achieved an international following, was also French. The necessarily physical comedy of the silent screen meshed with the older foreign tradition of the slapstick.[3] This shared European convention lies at the heart of America's universally adored screen comedy. The players who made the world laugh were children, sometimes quite literally, of the slapstick stage. Charles Chaplin had a clog-dancing act in the London music halls by 1899. He was ten. A year later, in America, Joseph Keaton, aged five, was a major success as a comic acrobat. By 1914 Chaplin was working for Mack Sennett in Hollywood. Keaton, 'Joe' having become 'Buster', was in Hollywood by 1917. The mastery of the physical world for comic effect was the essence of the joke: impossible numbers of Sennett's Keystone Cops falling out of the police van; the starving Chaplin and Mac Swain tucking into a boiled boot; Harold Lloyd endlessly hanging from the hands of some huge clock-face and, above all, the eternally po-faced Keaton, as the entire facade of a house neatly falls about him, leaving him unharmed in its open doorway.

The Americans did not invent the idea of the movie star either. Again, it was the Trust which inhibited development, leery that if any employees who appeared before the camera became famous their wage-bargaining power would be enhanced. The star of the cinema was, as it were, the phenomenon of motion itself, and the brand attracting the audiences was the producing company. Edwin Porter, after all, was merely an Edison employee, as anonymous as those he filmed. *The Life of an American Fireman* and *The Great Train Robbery* were marketed as Vitagraph pictures.

The presence of contemporary stage acting was always noticeable. In

The Great Train Robbery, the robbers, the posse and the telegraph operator go through the motions – working in the movies was considered 'slumming' by most thespians – but the little girl who finds the tied-up telegraph operator and raises the alarm is another matter. She has at her command the entire histrionic vocabulary of what we now see as the exaggerated, codified gestures of the late Victorian theatre. Outside the gloom of the gas-lit stage (which anyway was a thing of the past in the age of electric-lamp theatrical lighting), she does not of course need them, but she still uses them – hand on heart in sorrow, arms flung wide in shock. It took some decades to meld the less stylised playing with such antiquated stage-based methods of performance to produce for the camera the 'true-to-life' realism that came to mark screen acting.

Professionals, of course, were not anonymous. They were essential to the cinema's early attempts in a number of countries to find respectability by using literary and dramatic titles. In France, in part to produce films which would, because of their artistic legitimacy, find a ready market in the USA, the Film d'Art company produced the cinema's first self-conscious attempt at high bourgeois seriousness. Its 1908 hit, *The Assassination of the Duke of Guise*, had a scenario by a member of the Académie Française, players from the Comédie Française and incidental music by Saint-Saëns.[4] In 1912 Sarah Bernhardt reprised a famous performance in *La Dame aux camélias* for Film d'Art. The same year, her film *Queen Elizabeth* was successfully presented in the United States as if it were a live theatrical event – 'road-showed'. At first, the art film was far too bound to its theatrical antecedents to do anything for the emerging art of the cinema, although it did preserve the work of a number of late nineteenth-century stage giants such as Bernhardt in unprecedented, if still incomplete, detail.[5] Film d'Art worked well however, even without the synchronous sound of speech. In America its success suggested to an entrepreneur, Adolph Zukor, that there was appetite for 'famous players in famous plays' and the studio he created under this banner, Famous Players, became, as Paramount, one of the most enduring in Hollywood history.

As far as we can tell from surviving films, from 1907 on, the camera discovered the close-up on a regular basis, virtually forcing the industry over the following years to acknowledge the movie star. In 1908, the studios established more permanent stock companies and in 1909 began to advertise some of the players as an attraction using their real or stage names. Laemmle promoted Florence Lawrence as another company, Kalem, introduced cards of its players to be displayed in the lobbies of the nickelodeons. In 1910, the stage actress Asta Neilsen's erotic dance in a Danish film made in Germany, *The Abyss*, delivered an international reputation.

An alternative to the named player, used by some American companies, was the use of generic names in the style of the *commedia dell'arte*. According to her autobiography, when in 1912 the young actress Lillian Gish visited a friend from the theatrical circuit, Gladys Smith, who was working between seasons at the New York 14th Street brownstone studio of Biograph, the doorman denied that the girl had a job there. 'But we saw her in one of your pictures, *Lena and the Geese*,' Lillian's sister Dorothy protested. 'Oh, you mean "Little Mary"? Wait a minute!' The 'Mary' stuck and 'Smith' had already been changed for stage appearances by the theatrical producer David Belasco to 'Pickford'. As the Gish sisters waited for her, they were spotted by Mr Griffith: 'They were blondish and were sitting affectionately close together. I am certain that I have never seen a prettier picture.' They started work the same day as extras, but only after they had obtained Mr Griffith's assurance they would have time to visit the agents to find a legitimate play for the next season. The screen was always able to find a space for amateurs which the theatre tended to deny them, but professional stage actors made cinema their own, even though working for the one required significantly different techniques from working for the other.

Consider the dancer Louise Brooks. Brooks was not the first young Hollywood leading lady to bob her hair. Colleen Moore cut her tresses in 1923 for *Flaming Youth*, the original flapper picture, directed by John Dillon; but despite the pancaked white make-up, to hide her Kansas freckles, no other actress of the decade had quite the Brooks look. 'I wanted a different type of girl,' recalled director Howard Hawks, who had first featured her in 1928 in *A Girl in Every Port*, 'a new type'. She was indeed so 'new' that, at the time of her rediscovery in the 1960s, she seemed to be an almost entirely contemporary figure. Recovered for insertion into the roll of memorable silent films were, not her American pictures, but the two she made in Berlin in 1929 for the German director George Pabst, *Pandora's Box* and *Diary of a Lost Girl*.

In *Pandora's Box*, Pabst cast Brooks to play the film's liberated and destructive sexual force, 'Lulu'. Opposite her he cast Fritz Kortner, the Emil Jannings of his generation, a major theatrical figure of the German speaking stage. In Berlin, Kortner, the leading exponent of the contemporary German style of expressionist acting, was outraged by Brooks. It was not her sexuality, although Pabst did his best to ensure she was unnecessarily provocative by, for instance, having her wear nothing under her peignoir in one crucial scene. Rather it was her acting, or, as Kortner and informed German opinion saw it, her non-acting; but, as a fully trained dancer, much influenced by the young Martha Graham, with Broadway and a number of films behind her, Brooks knew exactly what she was about.[6] She used her considerable acting ability to project herself through the lens on to the screen, without the artifices of previous generations of players. One of those who rediscovered her, the film archivist Henri Langlois, wrote: 'The camera seems to have caught her by surprise, almost without her knowing it.' In one sense, this is new; but in another, it is the old business, discovered by Garrick and Macklin, of producing a code of performance which looks natural, realistic, to a new generation.

After the war, the cinema's transborder fluidity resumed. The international nature of cinema's 'language' remained an established fact underpinning the exchange of movies, but the early sense of a balanced trade in people and ideas shifted in favour of the Americans. The American presence in Europe began to feel more like colonisation as Hollywood studios overwhelmingly embraced European partners – Metro with Aumount, for instance, and Goldwyn with Gaumont in 1922 – and nowhere did the Americans dominate more than in Britain.

The British film industry's infrastructure had been largely the creation of foreign interests. Unlike continental Europe, in Britain the creative community did not take to film, maintaining a snobbish attitude towards it well into the post-Second World War era. It is certainly possible that the strength of the British theatre drained creative effort from the movies but, for whatever reason, Britain produced neither *Autorenfilme* nor Hollywood populism and British films did not dominate local screens nor have much international status. Cultural hostility was one of the reasons why Hitchcock was moved to cross the Atlantic in the 1930s. The British had even been colonised by the French. Lime Grove Studios in Shepherd's Bush were built by Leon Gaumont, two years after Zukor had established Islington. Local interests took stakes in both studios after the war but, despite the efforts of Balcon and some others, British production, even with foreign backing, could account for only five per cent of screen time in the early 1920s and the industry was soon screaming for government protection in the form of import restrictions. Four of every five films exhibited in Britain were American-made.

In France, the pattern of post-war exhibition was prefigured by Cecil B. De Mille's *The Cheat*, which played in Paris for six months in 1915. A decade later, nearly two-thirds of all films on French screens were American-made and only a dozen French productions a year were being exported to America. In 1927, only 13 per cent of domestic releases were French-made and overall there were more German titles released than French, never mind American productions. Despite the collapse in production, among the reduced numbers of films being made were many that vividly advanced the art of film. The Société Générale des Films, backed by the Russian émigré fortune of Jacques Grinieff, provided Abel Gance in 1927 with the funds to finish his enormous epic, *Napoléon*, with its specially designed, triple-screen, panoramic climax. Of equal importance, the SGF funded Carl Dreyer's *La Passion de Jeanne d'Arc*, more modest in scale but more ambitious in technique. Dreyer's film is nothing less than a descant on the established rules of Hollywood grammar, every one of which he breaks without losing his audience. Its idiosyncratic way with matched cuts and eye-lines is, paradoxically, a testimony to how deeply embedded these norms had become by 1928.

The Italians were soon in trouble, but this was not immediately apparent. A trust brought the dispersed production companies, scattered throughout the major cities, together under one umbrella and in 1920, 400 titles were produced. The Italian public maintained its pre-war taste for magnificent leading ladies, 'divas', generally swamping, by their 'bigness', the 'smallness' of the melodramas in which they were seen. This taste influenced Hollywood's ideas about how its stars might develop: Theda Bara, for instance, was a totally ersatz 'diva', transforming Theodosia Goodman (b. 1890, Cincinnati, Ohio) into a figure of mysterious allure and commoditised sexuality. The male hero of Italian cinema's hit, *Cabiria* (1914), a slave character called 'Maciste' played by Bartolemeo Pagano, became the prototype for a series of films with the same characters and many emulators. It was, of course, a time for big men in Italy; Mussolini came to power in 1922, but, despite the divas and 'Maciste' and his emulators, the trust had begun to collapse and production levels shrank.

Unlike the Nazis a decade later, the Fascists were not overly active in the face of this decline. In 1926 they had taken over the Union of Cinema and Education (LUCE) which had been created two years earlier to produce short subjects and in 1929, faced with sound films, they banned all non-Italian soundtracks. Dubbing became the norm and even Italian-language pictures tended to be shot silent for later post-production synching. The first Italian sound picture, *La canzone dell'amore*, was simultaneously shot, Film Europe-style, in French and German as well as Italian but did no overseas business. The touch that had so successfully brought the Italian epic to foreign screens 20 years earlier had long gone. The Fascists simply left the industry floundering in the face of popular American – dubbed – imports.

The Germans did not manage to resist American dominance either; although, after the war, as Pommer's ambition indicated, they initially made a better fist of it. Pre-1914, two-thirds of the German industry had been foreign owned. Following the wartime seizure of foreign-owned facilities, in the peace, over 90 per cent of the industry belonged to German firms but Ufa, under Pommer's Film Europe banner, never produced more than a fifth of the movies made in the Weimar Republic, despite its ambitions. The flood of American product threatened even this, and overwhelmed its German rivals so much that in 1925 a quota law was passed to protect the domestic industry. By 1926, Ufa was drifting towards financial disaster, not least because Pommer was betting the studio on Fritz Lang's great sci-fi vision of a dystopian totalitarian future, *Metropolis*, which was way over budget and shooting schedule.[7] The quota system, more typically, encouraged far less ambitious 'quota quickies', one of a number of ways in which US firms circumvented the German law. Many of these were never even released. By 1928, the law was abandoned as unworkable. Over the decade the number of German films fell by two-thirds to some 200 titles a year.

Undeterred by the German example, the British industry had achieved its own quota act from Parliament in 1927 but this did local filmmakers as little good. Production remained mired at 40 titles a year and audiences' preference for the American product persisted unabated. When sound film arrived, the British industry, in contrast to the rest of Europe, was particularly vulnerable because of the shared language. The audience had no reason to give up their taste for American films.

The international language of the cinema, a product of Western sensibilities, technology and performance traditions, had become a matter of 'American shots' and 'Hollywood grammar', yet American films owed their transborder appeal exactly to a common system of representing space and time, the result of supranational creativity and the heterogeneity of the filmmakers who settled in Los Angeles. The American film industry can be seen as the most spectacular twentieth-century American immigrant enterprise of all, itself an expression of the whole of Western culture. So American films conquered the world but in a real sense they were the cultural property of the world rather than only of the United States. It is not for nothing that the industry has always been organised around 'territories' and 'markets', not 'nations'. Film 'nations' are the concern of criticism, history and cultural politics. In the aftermath of the war, the French critic Louis Delluc was already fretting about the future of the French cinema and Alfred Hitchcock was claiming to be 'American-trained'. But, in the sense of film as an international mode of expression, as opposed to a multi-national capitalist enterprise, the remarks are meaningless – like novelists worrying that they are in thrall to the Spanish because the first modern novels appeared four centuries ago in that language, and reflected that culture not theirs.

'Of all the arts for us the most important is cinema'

There have been two sustained attempts to develop alternative film 'languages' to that which had evolved in the interdependent commercial cinemas of the West. The first formal effort to break the mould was made in post-war revolutionary Russia; the second was a project of the artistic avant-garde in the West.

As everywhere in Europe, the arrival of the Cinématograph in Russian had taken only a matter of months. The first St Petersburg screening, during the interval of an operetta, took place in May 1896 and, as elsewhere, Gorky's 'kingdom of shadows' soon became a staple of the popular theatre and the fairground, and Russia merely another territory dominated by Pathé-Frères. Local production was delayed and it was not until 1908 that the first film was made in a *kinofabrika* (film factory) in the tableaux, Film d'Art style which was to dominate the next few years; but this was swept away, with the rest of Tsarist culture, in the revolution of 1918.

There was a quite consciously formal attempt to produce a new sort of cinema that reflected communist ideology not just in its stories and acting but in its very essence. In Marxist hands, film editing especially acquired a theory. The cinema was deemed to reflect the truth of the Marxist law, derived from the nineteenth-century philosopher Hegel, that all 'theses' produce 'antitheses' which, in turn, create 'syntheses'. In just this way, a shot in a film can be thought of as a thesis, a subsequent shot an antithesis and the two together produce a synthesis of meaning in the audiences' minds. The 20-year-old director, Lev Kuleshov, conducted a famous experiment in 1919 in which he juxtaposed the still face of a stage star, Ivan Mozzhukhin, with shots of a plate of soup, a corpse and a happy child in order to show how differently an audience would interpret the actor's unchanging look in each case. Kuleshov understood that these were technically known as 'American shots' edited together in the process of 'montage'; but for him the experiment demonstrated a Marxist truth.

In the hands of the Soviet master filmmakers – Sergei Eisenstein, Vsevolod Pudovkin, Alexander Dovzhenko – the principles of montage were taken to their limits to produce a number of films which have never been removed from the cinema's canon of great works. For example, in Eisenstein's *The Battleship Potemkin*, made to celebrate the twentieth anniversary of the abortive 1905 revolt against the Tsar, mutineer sailors nervously steam towards the shadowy outlines of the rest of the fleet while the signalman taps out the message 'Don't Shoot, Brothers'. The threatening fleet was merely old newsreel footage of the pre-war German navy (although some in Western intelligence agencies read the images as evidence of Soviet naval power). The battleship used in the film was of the Potemkin class but, reduced to being a munitions store, it was anchored. The illusion of its movement was created by swinging a camera into a close-up of the bows. And the meaning of these shots – the distant fleet, the close-ups of the tense sailors, the cross-cut tapping morse key – was secured by the intertitles: 'Don't Shoot, Brothers'. 'Don't.' 'Shoot'. 'Brothers'. 'DON'T'. 'SHOOT'. 'BROTHERS'. Western bourgeois censors were right (by their own lights) to be alarmed at the power of such sequences.

When the symbolic or metaphoric intention of the filmmaker was of a piece with the realism of the sequence, the effect is still vivid. In Dovzhenko's *Arsenal* (1930), on war and revolution in the Ukraine, the ineffectual Tsarist war effort becomes a runaway troop train. The exuberant editing is abruptly curtailed as the train crashes and a central character, a munitions factory worker drafted into the army, walks away washing his hands of the whole business – Tsarist Russia, effectively, as wrecked as the train. But, as proof that the norms of cinema language were not so malleable as the theorists supposed, these highly sophisticated filmmakers quickly overreached themselves with their primary public, the audience of workers, peasants and soldiers. In Eisenstein's tenth anniversary film of the revolution, *October*, the arguments of the Mensheviks in the Petrograd Soviet are cross-cut with harpists. For the audience such cutting did not suggest that the harpists were a symbolic comment on politicians, as Eisenstein intended; rather it meant that they were playing somewhere else, their presence in the narrative obscure. It was clear from the audience surveys conducted at the time that such conceits could not be 'read'. Russian audiences knew how the cinema 'worked': American shots, Hollywood grammar.

The Commissar for Education, Anatoli Lunacharsky, who had command of the film industry, remembered Lenin telling him 'that the production of new films imbued with Communist ideas and reflecting Soviet reality should begin with the newsreel. . . . Then, smiling, Vladimir Ilych added . . . "You must remember that of all the arts for us the most important is cinema".' These fascinating films startled the West, where intellectuals endlessly held them up as alternatives to the increasing post-war domination of populist genre movies from the big American studios. Nevertheless, back in the USSR, however imbued the filmmakers were with Marxist ideology, politically the films themselves were seen as a sterile indulgence, as was the ferment of sophisticated arguments about the very nature of cinema that swirled around them – the most sophisticated and vibrant that had yet been aired anywhere in the world. Soon, dangerous questions were being raised. Of these masterpieces, a rival director could write in 1929:

> We have nothing to offer our own dear worker and peasant. Name something we can offer them. It is not with *October*s . . . that we must begin to build Soviet cinema. Does Soviet cinema need [such films]? Let them be. We need them like Soviet diplomacy needs tail-coats.

The All Russian Association of Proletarian Writers pushed the Revolutionary Cinematography Workers Association, which had grown from an organisation originally founded by Eisenstein and Kuleshov, into an equally critical position:

> There can be no doubting the fact that some of these films are either almost inaccessible to the mass audiences, or include particular sequences which contain, at the expense of social content, experiments of a formal kind that are contrary to the films' fundamental purpose.

In the atmosphere of repression that was to characterise Stalin's dictatorship, the word 'formal', a synonym for any kind of experimentation, became a deadly term of abuse. The search for an authentic alternative cinematic language faltered in the face of audience disapprobation and Stalinism.

The second sustained attempt to escape from the mainstream prison-house of naturalistic drama took place in the West itself. Its concerns were far from those of the Soviet experimentalists but the outcome, as far as audience was concerned, was much the same. It too failed to reach a mass; in fact, such an objective was not even part of its agenda.

An intertitle: 'Once upon a time'. A man gazes at the moon as he sharpens a razor. A cloud crosses the moon. In big close-up, the razor slashes a young woman's eye. A second intertitle: 'Eight years later' but what follows bears no relationship to the opening horror. We are in the world of dream, of nightmare. Ants crawl out of hands, blood dribbles from mouths, books become guns, pursuing characters left in one room are found waiting in the next. A woman's dress vanishes as her lover caresses her breasts. There are more meaningless titles: 'Around three in the morning'; 'Sixteen years before'; 'In the spring'.

Artists, especially the non-English-speaking avant-garde, were excited by film, especially if they could liberate it from any trace of story. One escape route from narrative was to treat film as the stuff of dreams. The man with the razor at the start of *Un chien andalou* (An

Andulusian Dog, 1928) was Luis Buñuel, the film's director. The film was made in France in collaboration with the surrealist painter Salvador Dali and it marked Buñuel's debut as a director. Two years later, another collaborative surreal experiment, *L'Âge d'or* (1930), provoked the far right into rioting and the French authorities into a ban.

Buñuel and Dali were not alone in sensing the similarities between film-watching and dreaming, as Freud's innovative psychology was explaining it, and in being moved to explore the extraordinary capacity of film to reproduce the dream state. In 1943, in Hollywood, Maya Deren, sometime journalist and poet (and, like Brooks, a startlingly contemporary-looking beauty), and her husband, filmmaker Alexander Hammid, shot another dream, *Meshes of the Afternoon*, on amateur 16mm stock in and around their home over a couple of weeks. They used themselves as the figures in the film. Echoing an ancient trope from Celtic myth, she runs after but cannot catch the slowly walking figure in front of her. Where there should be a face, there is a mirror. Keys emerge from mouths, turning into knives. The figure of the woman confronts and threatens her own sleeping self. 'The film', Deren wrote, 'is concerned with the interior experiences of an individual.'

This thin stream of work on the possibilities of using film to illustrate the subconscious and the surreal constitutes one aspect of the avant-garde's search for alternatives to mainstream narrative. The other experimental approach is to treat film as a surface, like a canvas. This second avant-garde itself contains a continuum of approaches. Before the First World War some artists were experimenting by painting directly on to the celluloid, a mode of expression that was to be picked up again in the 1930s. Others turned away from the infantilised mainstream animation to use its techniques in pursuit of abstraction. In *Rythmus*, the series made by Hans Richter between 1921 and 1924, the abstraction was pure, total; but non-narrative montages of representational images were also possible, as in painter Fernand Léger's *Ballet mécanique* (1924). In Richter, the image is drained of all representational meaning – two white squares on a black ground, for example. In the Léger, an elderly washerwoman laboriously and repeatedly, as in a

loop, climbs the steep stairs of a Montmartre lane; a man, curiously formally dressed, slides on a helter-skelter in a curve across the screen, a
movement echoed by the revolving wheel with which it is cross-cut.
Such associative editing substitutes for narrative causality; but the ticket-
buying masses of the West were no more interested in these
flamboyances than were 'our dear workers and peasants' of Soviet
Russia taken with their film avant-gardists.

The final proof of the mainstream's tyranny lies with another genus
of production – the documentary. Some in the avant-garde applied
non-narrative logics to filming *sur la vif*, from life. Jean Vigo, for example, produced in *À propos de Nice* (1930) a short visual diatribe against
bourgeois affluence and excess on the French Riviera. Footage, shot
often out of kilter, of the town, its cemetery and the carnival is unexpectedly cross-cut with surrealist images: an inserted table-top shot of a
toy train and model tourists; or an elegant woman sitting at a terrace
table who magically undresses – they were fond of this transgressive
effect – without moving. Buñuel himself turned to filming seemingly
unrehearsed images, as opposed to highly structured dream-states, as
part of a row with surrealism's founder, André Breton. In *Land Without
Bread* (*Las Hurdas*)(1932), he melded a devastating critique of poverty
in a remote rural area of Spain with an equally pungent attack on the
whole idea of realistic representation. A goat is seen climbing a rock and
then is obviously shot while the commentary announces, shamelessly,
that goats often loose their footing.[8]

Despite these connections with the avant-garde, the documentary
orthodoxy that emerged from the late 1920s and after did not challenge
the essence of Hollywood's representational conventions. The roots of
the tradition are to be found, first, in single-shot news movies, such as
The Derby (1896) or the *Funeral of President McKinley* (1901), which
had early demonstrated film's capacity to document events. By 1917,
the term 'newsreels' had been introduced to describe these efforts, by
then issued weekly and containing several items. There was also the tradition of the lantern show. Lanternists with series of travel plates had
been part of screen culture from the very beginning in the seventeenth

century. The journey with its logical narrative progressions and transitions was the template by which 'cinematographic slides' might be assembled into narratives. The first movie 'travelogues' to do this effectively appeared in 1908. Another basic narrative structure – the events of a day – provided a second obvious organising format for non-news actuality material.

In 1914 the photographer Edwin Curtis, having completed his 20 volumes of sepia stills, *The North American Indian*, made a movie among the Kwakiutl of the American Northwest, *In the Land of the Headhunters*. In line with a contemporary vogue for *documentaires romancés*, this was a piece of Western melodramatic hokum in an exotic setting involving a plot line that had nothing to do with Kwakiutl culture. The details of the costumes, the sets and the ceremonies, though, were as accurate as Curtis could make them – though reflecting the tribe's life as lived a generation or more earlier. The film was to be the first of a series, to parallel the photographic books, which Curtis promised his potential backers would be 'one of the most valuable documentary works which can be taken up at this time'.

Curtis made no other films but a year later he discussed his plans with a young prospector, explorer and stills photographer, Robert Flaherty, who had been shooting movie footage of the Inuit on Baffin Island. It was not until some years after the First World War that Flaherty, backed by a fur company, completed Nanook of the North (1922) in another part of the Canadian sub-Arctic, establishing a form that was to combine the travelogue, news actuality authenticity and melodrama. Flaherty's genius was in realising that the details of Inuit everyday life (despite this being, like his mentor's picture of the Kwakiutl, a generation or more out of date) could be edited into a dramatically satisfying structure, utilising, for the most part, the established representational norms of the fictional cinema. To match this obedience to Hollywood, instead of fantastic magic and witchdoctors, Flaherty presents, realistically, hunger and hunting, kayak-making and igloo-building, blizzard and threatened death by exposure. When coupled with observational Western city documentaries – which had attracted the talents of many of the avant-garde – a new form was established and enjoyed some commercial success in the 1920s. Nanook, for example, opened in two Paris theatres simultaneously in 1922 and was still being exhibited twelve years later.

In general documentary, as an alternative film genus, was no more successful than revolutionary montage or either of the two avant-gardes at supplanting Hollywood-style fictional feature movies in the affections of the public. The public turned away and so did filmmakers. For instance, Ernest Schoedsack, sometime camera operator on Keystone Cops films, made his reputation, with partner Merian Cooper, making documentaries about tribal peoples before turning to fiction: Schoedsack and Cooper are not remembered for, say, *Grass* (1926), a film about Iranian nomads. *King Kong*, made in Hollywood seven years later, is their memorial.

'You ain't heard nothin' yet'

From the first, movies had inherited that long tradition of sound – commentary, music and effects – which had been part of lantern slide shows and nineteenth-century scenic spectacles. Although live music in the cinema rapidly became the industry norm, on occasion there could also be lecturers explaining the film or even actors reading a script behind the screen. As Muybridge had suggested to Edison even before the cinema was 'invented', phonograph and projector begged to be linked in some way, which is exactly what Edison's assistant Dickson achieved using the Kinetoscope. Laemmle equipped 45 of his cinemas with a synchronised disc system in 1908; Gaumont and Edison himself repeated the experiment in 1913; but none made lasting headway, not against the ease and cheapness of the solo nickelodeon piano-player, nor versus the full-scale orchestra employed by fancier cinemas.

It was therefore a mere repetition of a previous failed marketing ploy when in August 1926 *Don Juan* was premièred by Warner Brothers, a smaller Hollywood studio backed with capital provided by Goldman Sacks, using the 'Vitaphone' disc system developed by

316

AT&T's subsidiary manufacturing arm, Western Electric. *The Jazz Singer* with its snatches of dialogue – including Al Jolson's famous 'You ain't heard nothin' yet' – followed in October 1927.

In the later 1920s, things were different. A series of technological changes eased synch sound shooting. Hissing arc lights, a presence since studios went 'dark' (i.e. were windowless and entirely artificially lit) in 1903, had finally given way to silent incandescent tungsten bulbs, long common in the theatre. Panchromatic film was replacing slower, cheaper orthochromatic film stocks because, needing fewer lights, it was realised to be nevertheless more economic. Most importantly, Hollywood, which had early adopted an astonishing technological conservatism as a major barrier to new entrants, was prepared in 1926–7 to contemplate change because it was suffering its first major decline in box-office receipts.[9] Hence, finally and without any major technological advance, the sound film arrived – but it was not on disc.

The phone company, using an idea Bell himself had toyed with in the nineteenth century, had another method to hand. Sound could be converted into light and, in the form of a narrow optical track, recorded on to the same celluloid base as the picture. Lauste had patented this idea in 1907 and is believed by 1910 to have made it work, using a system of rocking mirrors and a light bulb flickering in response to the modulated wave coming from the microphone. In the next decade, Theodore Case, a partner of Lee de Forest, took such a system, christened 'Movietone', to another of the smaller Hollywood studios, Fox. Such an obvious application of existing technology was bound to be widely investigated and the Germans and the Danes were on to it at the same time. The usual patent battles ensued but were brief.

This was because the success of Warner's vaudeville shorts and Fox's *Movietone News* thrust the big five studios – Paramount-Famous Players-Lasky, Metro-Goldwyn-Mayer, United Artists, Universal and First National – into AT&T's (and de Forest's) embrace. Electrical Research Products Inc (ERPI), the AT&T subsidiary which owned the de Forest patents, rapidly became the dominant player in Hollywood. As one of its executives noted in a memo to AT&T's main board in

1934: 'It is true today, as it has been for three or four years, that the Telephone Company can control the motion picture industry.' The phone company, already locked in battle with the federal government over monopolistic practices, behaved with restraint and was even pleased to welcome a rival optical sound-recording process created by GE and Westinghouse and marketed by RCA as the 'Photophone'.

Conversion to sound was to cost the American industry between $23m and $50m but industrialised Hollywood, once pushed into change, did not mind pricey solutions which, after all, were barriers to potential rivals. In the case of sound, the cheaper, ignored, alternative was audiotape. Wire recording had been introduced in 1898 and it had also been linked to a projector by Lee de Forest in 1913. It was eventually being demonstrated as an alternative to Vitaphone in 1928. In 1929 Tobis, a German sound film company, established that the quality of sound recorded on a flexible steel tape was superior to that of any of the optical systems then available. BASF produced a lighter, more flexible plastic tape in 1934.[10] The film industry disregarded these developments and certainly did nothing, in the form of research and development, to speed them. Hollywood first used audiotape as the primary sound-recording medium on the set of *Son of Cochise* in 1962, long after its widespread use in radio and in the home.

The same tendency to pursue the most expensive solution can be seen with colour, a technology being introduced at the same time as sound. Just as ERPI was given considerable control over one aspect of their product, the studios were in the process of handing monopolistic control over another to Technicolor, the most expensive, complex and indeed old-fashioned colour film system available. Before the turn of the twentieth century, films were being hand-tinted, frame by frame, and it was also common for whole sequences to be printed on differently tinted stocks to reflect content and mood – dark blue for night-time, vivid red for wicked drinking dens and so on. True still colour photography, using multiple negatives – one in each of the three primary colours – dated from 1873, but it was difficult to keep different-coloured film strips together for cinematography. Beginning in 1928,

Herbert Kalmus slowly perfected a system involving two negatives (red-blue/green) exposed via a beam-splitter located behind the lens in a specially developed camera. If studios wanted to use the system, patented as Technicolor, they needed to hire his cameras as well as his operators and agree that a 'Technicolor Consultant' had veto power over sets and costumes. Kalmus's wife Natalie, the senior 'consultant', became the veritable 'tsar' of American colour movies. The studios saved Technicolor for the fantasies of cartoons and musicals and the colourfulness of history, as in *Becky Sharp* (1935) or *Gone with the Wind* (1939). But, again, there was a cheaper way.

Kodachrome, Kodak's single negative 'monopak' stock, developed a few years after Technicolor, required no special apparatus. Its German rival, Agfacolour, did not even need to be processed by the manufacturer. Although these films would have allowed the studios to escape from the expensive Technicolor enchanter which added 30 per cent to production costs, they did not offer a unique product. It was not until 1942 that the first Hollywood feature, *Thunderhead*, was shot on Kodachrome. After the war, as all movies came to be made in colour, pressure on the Technicolor labs, where Kalmus used 'imbibing', a largely abandoned complex nineteenth-century process which had been developed for photogravure printing, grew almost to breaking-point. The cross-patent agreements followed and Technicolor was slowly reduced to being, though still significant, an international chain of laboratories using Kodak film.

All the cinema's technological developments had equally long lineages and were usually introduced, as sound had been, by second-rank, smaller studios. The 3-D fad of the early 1950s, for example, was pushed by Columbia, Universal and a by then shrunken Paramount in the face of an audience dispersed to the home comforts of the suburbs and seduced by both radio and television. Two photographs of the same scene taken from slightly different angles viewed in a special viewer had amused Queen Victoria in 1851. Spectacle frames with one red and one green lens, to look at superimposed red and green projected still images taken from slightly different angles, date from 1858. Friese-Greene had patented a separate dual-image system for a 3-D movie peep-show in 1900 and the first audience to don the glasses for a movie did so in 1909. Entrepreneurs tried to break 2-D's stranglehold on the cinema with the glasses in 1922, in 1936, and, with a sophisticated Polaroid superimposition system which allowed for colour images, in 1939. In the USSR, a totally different system using a special, glass-beaded 'integral' screen enjoyed some success and a version of *Robinson Crusoe* played in five cinemas for a decade after the war. The 1952/4 American 3-D fad produced movies, *Kiss Me Kate* for example, where a lot of things get thrown towards the lens, but it had no lasting impact on the cinema. The glasses reappeared, yet again, with the giant Imax system in the 1990s.

Imax also stands in a line of repeated attempts to increase the size of the screen. At the climax of Abel Gance's epic, called with Napoleonic hubris *Napoléon vu par Abel Gance* (1928), the young General Bonaparte arrives in the Alps to take command of the bedraggled French forces in Italy. The screen suddenly trebles in width to show the full extent of the army's camp. Gance's system, Polyvision, used three linked cameras and projectors which allowed for different, as well as melded, images – Napoleon in heroic close-up on the centre screen, long lines of marching men on both flanks, for example. It was not copied until three-camera/projector Cinerama was marketed with considerable hoopla in 1952 by one of radio's most famous newsmen, Lowell Thomas. *This is Cinerama*, the first feature, was the last film directed by Schoedsack and produced by Cooper. Although Cinerama remained marginalised, like the Imax today, it did prompt a more permanent use of wider, bigger cinema screens.

The story is that both 20th Century Fox and Warner Brothers were so impressed by the thought of a big-screen response to television that they literally rushed out of the Cinerama opening to race each other to France where lived, in retirement, Henri Chrétien. Chrétien had been long ignored by Hollywood despite his having developed, by 1927, 'Anamorphoscope', a single-camera wide-screen process, producing, with a special lens, a 2.35:1 image on ordinary 35mm stock.[11] Spyros Skouras, the boss of 20th Century Fox, got to Chrétien first and his studios presented the first anamorphoscopic movie, *The Robe*, to the public in 1953. By then, at a cost of $50,000, Skouras had bought a new name for the process – Cinemascope.

Such technological pace-setting by the largest studios was exceptional. Their technological conservatism was persistent and comprehensive. On their sets, for example, zoom lenses never replaced primes even when their quality would have allowed them to.[12] The studios did not even take to 'safety' film. Less dangerous than unstable and highly inflammable nitrate, it had been patented as early as 1902 but was ignored by the industry until after the Second World War. Nitrate rendered cinemas even less safe than theatres and underpinned the stringent regulations which everywhere in the West governed public projection (and which also, of course, had the attendant advantage of facilitating any system of censorship). In the United States, limiting screenings to licensed cinemas, which they then largely owned, was just fine with the studios and worth the odd disastrous conflagration. Nitrate was another effective barrier to entry.

None of these advances, not even the upheaval induced by sound in the late 1920s, occasioned anything like a fundamental rethink of the grammar of film. The mainstream silent cinema had, in essence, offered two versions of 'American shots'. One relied on a quick montage of elements within the master shot establishing the scene. (This approach was what the Soviets had seized on and converted to their own purposes.) The other varied the original approach to fictional filmmaking – longer takes replicating the experience of the theatre, played across the depth of the scene with close-ups inserted to focus audience attention and response. André Bazin, the most influential post-Second World War film critic, argued that sound ensured the comparative mainstream triumph of the latter approach over the former and claimed for it a greater capacity to represent reality. Nevertheless, realism was not all. For example, essentially unrealistic continuous music in the new synch sound films still set the mood behind dialogue and effects.

This is not to say that the introduction of synch sound was not disruptive to film at every level. All American cinemas were re-equipped by

1930. In Europe it took a bit longer but by 1935 the conversion was complete. Some British audiences might have found the unfamiliar American-accented English from the loudspeakers behind the screen amusing, but to non-English-speakers the talk was simply incomprehensible. Moreover, in some countries – Fascist Italy, for instance – incomprehension was reinforced by a politically motivated legal prohibition against synch sound films which were not made in the native language. For whatever reason, synch encouraged a revival of production in a number of countries where the public had come to prefer the internationalised American product – with intertitles in the local language – over the silent output of their own studios; for example, in France the number of features rose from a low in 1929 of 52 silents to three times that number of talkies three years later.

Once again multiple versions of the same film were shot concurrently with different stars – even, on occasion, in Hollywood itself. Better, because cheaper, dubbing (for larger linguistic territories) and subtitling (for smaller) were soon proved to be acceptable. Audiences became used to one or other method but exhibited a reluctance – which persists – to cope with the one to which they were not accustomed. Anglophones, of course, resisted both but the acceptance of these methods by non-English-speaking audiences allowed the Americans to re-establish their dominance. Musicals became a new genre for Hollywood since singing and dancing transcended linguistic barriers and, after all, the American musical stage was, like the cinema itself, an outcrop of older European traditions.

Local revival was something of a chimera. The increased cost of sound film production was proving too much for smaller linguistic communities, especially during the Depression. Even in America, audiences and the number of screens both shrank by a third, although this had less effect on the flow of production than it did elsewhere. Hollywood was also unaffected by the pressures of dictatorship or other political uncertainties and by the middle of the Thirties, the status quo ante-synch sound had been more or less restored. By the decade's end, 65 per cent of the world's movie business was American. One-third of

322

Hollywood's revenues came from abroad, half of that from the UK alone; Hollywood remained home to the world.

The set is of 'The American Bar' in Casablanca, 1942. The suave croupier is asked by the owner Rick, 'How's takings?' Having just obeyed Rick's orders to fix the wheel so a young Bulgarian refugee can win enough money to buy exit visas from the town's corrupt Chief of Police, he says: 'A few thousand less than I was expecting.' The film is, of course, *Casablanca* and 'Rick', Humphrey Bogart. The bit player is Marcel Dalio, himself a European refugee, a once and future star of the French cinema.

In the 1930s, Dalio played the lead in two of Jean Renoir's (and the cinema's) most highly regarded films, *La Règle du jeu* and *La Grande Illusion*. In the first he is cast against type, not his usual sophisticated villain, but an aristocrat and a Jew (which takes some explaining). With Renoir, Bazin's cinema of depth implies more than long takes and complex multiple planes of action. It also means, as in the case of characters like Dalio's Marquis de la Chesnaye, the depth and complexities of rooted humanity. The Marquis seldom does what is expected of him. As his game-shooting is being plagued by rabbits, he orders his head warden not only to release a poacher who has been catching them with greater efficiency than the warden himself, but also instantly to employ the villain. De la Chesnaye has, as one character says of him, '*la classe*', unsurprising in le Marquis perhaps but, in the view of 1930s anti-Semitism, remarkable in a Jew.

In *La Grande Illusion*, Renoir's sympathy embraces the prison-camp commandant, played by Austrian-born Hollywood émigré director Erich von Stroheim, as well as the French prisoners of war. When the French aristocrat, played by Pierre Fresnay, sacrifices himself to cover the escape of the working-class flight lieutenant Jean Gabin (and the wealthy scion of a Jewish department-store family – Dalio, again) Fresnay tells von Stroheim he is doing it because, '*le devoir, c'est le devoir*': 'duty is duty'. When, towards the film's end, a young German soldier asks the war-widow who is hiding the runaways Gabin and Dalio how far he has to march to his destination, he sighs, on being told it is

16 kilometres: '*Dienst ist dienst*'. *Dienst, devoir*, duty – these are all words for the great illusion that would, shortly, transform millions of young men into soldiers once more as the world plunged into a second war. It would also bring Dalio to Hollywood until the conflict was over.

In 1952, *La Règle du jeu* figured, just, in a list of the cinema's ten greatest films which the British Film Institute's magazine *Sight & Sound* compiled by polling leading critics from around the world. Every decade since then the magazine has repeated this exercise. Some rather curious titles have inevitably appeared and disappeared. In that first list, for example, was Flaherty's picturesque paean of praise to the beneficence of oil exploration, *Louisiana Story* (1948), and David Lean's *Brief Encounter*, but a core has remained more constant, thereby creating some sense of a slowly changing canon. Hollywood figured in this first list, of course, but apart from the Flaherty only Orson Welles's maverick 1941 masterpiece *Citizen Kane*, which was placed first, dated from the sound era. Hollywood's major contribution was deemed to be less the genre pictures of the 1930s and 1940s than silent features – two from Chaplin and one from Griffith as well as von Stroheim's *Greed* which, when released in 1925, was still, at ten reels, a mere fraction of the ten-hour length Stroheim had planned.

Even *Citizen Kane* is scarcely a monument to Hollywood's studio system. The 24-year-old Welles had come to Hollywood trailing Broadway glory and the scandal of the *War of the Worlds* radio broadcast. There he fell in with Herman Mankiewicz, whose massive talent as a script doctor had protected him from the consequences of his fondness for the bottle. Mankiewicz could tell studio honchos, 'Idiocy is all right in its own way, but you can't make it the foundation of a career', and get away with it. Between them – with help from John Housman, Welles's theatrical collaborator; Oscar-winning cinematographer Greg Toland, who would provide shots with unprecedented depth of focus (often using manipulations in the camera, Méliès-style); Perry Ferguson, whose sets were designed with ceilings; Bernard Hermann's music and a talented cast, largely members of the Mercury Theater stock-company – they created a film of startling originality. *Kane* is a broken narrative told from multiple viewpoints with, on occasion, repeated shots. It is replete with extreme camera-angles and voices that talk, as in life, over one another (and were recorded by Bailey Fesler and dubbed by James G. Stewart). But above all it is *about* something: the corrupting power of the mogul, not a subject much treated of in the bastion of American capitalism Hollywood had become. *Kane*, in five decades of *Sight & Sound* polling, has never been dislodged from its top position. Critical opinion still deems it the greatest film ever made.

Otherwise the polls have favoured post-Second World War European art-movie directors (Ingmar Bergman, Renoir, Fellini, *et al.*) and their Eastern peers (Ozu, Mizoguchi, Kurosaka and Ray). Their works mesh seamlessly with the standards of expression which normally inform the canons of the other arts; but Hollywood's scintillating exploitation of the popular does not sit so easily with such essentially class-bound, nineteenth-century ideas of 'art'. It is seductive to seek to correct this by establishing connections between the cycles of genre production and the world beyond the film studios. For example, it has been suggested that melodramatic 'women's pictures' of the late 1940s, where social independence always brought heroines low, had the obvious ideological purpose of getting women out of the workforce, where they had replaced their drafted menfolk, and back into the home. The viability of such connections is hard to sustain and, anyway, is no earnest of 'art'. It was not until 1982, after French cinéastes of uncompromising intellectual profundity had invented a theory of 'auteurism' – which transformed workaday Hollywood directors into artists like any others – and this had been translated and absorbed by Anglophone critics, that the first American genre titles entered the *Sight & Sound* canon. In that year, Stanley Donen's *Singin' in the Rain* (1952) and Alfred Hitchcock's *Vertigo* (1958) were admitted to the *Sight & Sound* list; but by then the studio system in which such 'auteurs' had laboured was long gone. Indeed, it was on its last legs in the 1950s when these films were made.

There had always been a tension between the creative talent and the money. At Universal and then again at MGM, von Stroheim, for example, argued with producer Irving Thalberg, then a boy-wonder in his mid-twenties who had curtailed *Greed*. The Hollywood production system owes much to Thalberg's concept of an interventionist executive being in charge of a studio's entire output and exercising control both through script approval and in the cutting room. Thalberg was less the 'Last Tycoon', which character Scott Fitzgerald modelled on him, than the first such; neither purely money nor, clearly, an artist, but a crucial link between the two.[13] The system Thalberg pioneered nurtured the seeds of its own destruction. Industrial logic led to degrees of genre specialisation and within the studios production units, each under an executive specialising in a certain type of picture, emerged to replace his centralised production operation. At Warner's, the 'B' pictures were all handled by the Foy unit, led by Bryan Foy, whose career had begun as one of the 'Seven Little Foys', one of American vaudeville's most famous acts. Many units were yet more specialised. Because George Arliss had picked up one of Warner's rare Oscars in 1929/30 for his performance in *The Life of Louis Pasteur*, biopics had become synonymous in the company mind with quality and prestige and so a unit was created to make them. Its 'production supervisor' Henry Blanke came up with a new job title – 'Associate Producer'. Units attached to stars associated with specific genres became common. The Durbin Unit, for instance, produced musicals for Deanna Durbin.

Soon some creative figures were breaking out of the studio and coming back in only on their own terms. Director Howard Hawks, for example, was being hired in specific one- or two-picture deals at a time, and by 1936 he was getting the credit 'A Howard Hawks Production'. (A level of critical acclaim to match the reality of his professional clout had to wait until it was bestowed on him by the French auteurist theoreticians of the *Cahiers du cinéma* magazine in the 1960s.) Actors were also seeking independence. James Cagney won a legal battle with Warner's because he successfully claimed they were not offering him reasonable projects within the terms of his contract. By the start of the Second World War (for America late in 1941), Bette Davis was selling her services to Warner's through her own company. All this had been eating away at the studio's hegemony so that when, after the war, they were compelled by the Justice Department to sell off their cinemas (and forced by technology to face the challenges of broadcasting), they were ready to fall.

The irony is that the canonical worth of the popular was only acknowledged after the system that produced its masterworks was long gone. *Singin' in the Rain* is a product of one of the most coherent and prolific of all the units, that producing musicals, run by Arthur Freed for two decades at MGM. *Vertigo*, on the other hand, is one of five pictures (the others are *Rear Window*, *The Trouble with Harry*, *The Man Who Knew Too Much* and *Psycho*) made for Paramount but eventually wholly owned by Alfred J. Hitchcock Productions Inc. And just as he had moonlighted in Germany a quarter of a century earlier to learn his craft, so, while Hitch was waiting to begin work on *Vertigo*, he occupied himself with other projects. He knocked off a couple of short thrillers for the TV networks. One, *The Perfect Crime*, with Vincent Price, was the eighty-first episode of the hit CBS television series, *Alfred Hitchcock Presents*, then in its third season with a title sequence entirely focused on the director's unmistakable, individual portly silhouette.

Sources

Michael Balcon (1969), *Michael Balcon Presents . . . A Lifetime of Films*, London: Hutchinson.

Charles Barr (2002), *Vertigo*, London: British Film Institute.

André Bazin (1967), *What is the Cinema? Volume One*, Berkeley: University of California Press.

André Bazin (1971, 1986), *Jean Renoir*, New York: Simon Schuster.

David Bordwell (1981), *The Films of Carl-Theodor Dreyer*, Berkeley: University of California Press.

David Bordwell, Janet Staiger and Kirstin Thompson (1985), *The Classsic Hollywood Cinema: Film Style and Mode of Production to 1960*, London: Routledge.

Stephen Bottomore (1990), 'Shots in the Dark: The Real Origins of Film Editing', in Thomas Elsaesser, *Early Cinema: Space, Frame, Narrative*, London: British Film Institute.

Louise Brooks (2000), *Lulu in Hollywood*, Twin Cities: University of Minnesota Press.

Simon Callow (1995), *Orson Welles: The Road to Xanadu*, London: Jonathan Cape.

Michael Chanan (1980), *The Dream That Kicks: The Prehistory and Early Years of the Cinema in Britain*, London: Routledge & Kegan Paul.

Seymour Chatman (1990), *Coming to Terms: The Rhetoric of Narrative in Fiction and Film*, Ithaca, NY: Cornell University Press.

Thomas Elsaesser (ed.) (1990), *Early Cinema: Space, Frame, Narrative*, London: British Film Institute.

John Fell (1974), *Film and the Narrative Tradition*, Berkeley: University of California Press.

Hugh Fordin (1975), *The World of Entertainment: The Freed Unit at MGM*, New York: Doubleday.

Robert Friedel and Paul Israel with Bernard Finn (1986), *Edison's Electric Light: Biography of an Invention*, New Brunswick: Rutgers University Press.

Lillian Gish (1969), *The Movies, Mr Griffith and Me*, New York: Prentice Hall.

Douglas Gomery (1992), *Shared Pleasures: A History of Movie Presentation in the United States*, Madison: University of Wisconsin Press.

Tom Gunning (1990), 'The Cinema of Attractions: Early Film, Its Spectator and the Avant-Garde' in Thomas Elsaesser, *Early Cinema: Space, Frame, Narrative*, London: British Film Institute.

Teresa de Laurentis and Stephen Heath (eds) (1980), *The Cinematic Apparatus* New York: St Martin's Press.

Jay Leyda and Zina Voynow (1982), *Eisenstein at Work*, New York: Pantheon.

James Limbacher (1968), *Four Aspects of the Film*, New York: Brussel & Brussel.

Leonard Matlin (1980), *Of Mice and Magic: A History of American Animated Cartoons*, New York: McGraw Hill.

Laura Mulvey (1972), *Citizen Kane*, London: British Film Institute.

Charles Musser (1990), *The Emergence of Cinema*, New York: Charles Scribner's Sons.

Geoffrey Nowell-Smith (ed.) (1996), *The Oxford Book of World Cinema*, Oxford: Oxford University Press.

Kevin O'Brien (1984), *Kino-Eye: The Writings of Dziga Vertov*, Berkeley: University of California Press.

Roberta Pearson and Philip Simpson (eds) (2000), *The Critical Dictionary of Film and Television Theory*, London: Routledge.

Hans Richter (1986) (trans. Ben Brewster), *The Struggle for Film*, Aldershot: Gower Publishing.

Thomas Schatz (1981), *Hollywood Genres: Formulas, Filmmaking and the Studio System*, New York: Random House.

Thomas Schatz (1998), *The Genius of the System*, New York: Pantheon.

P. Adams Sitney (1974), *Visionary Film: The American Avant Garde 1943–1978*, New York: Oxford University Press.

Donald Spoto (1983), *The Dark Side of Genius: The Life of Alfred Hitchcock*, London: Plexus.

Janet Staiger, 'Combination and Litigation: Structures of US Film Distribution 1896 -1917' in Thomas Elsaesser, *Early Cinema: Space, Frame, Narrative* London: British Film Institute.

David Thomson (2002), *The New Biographic Dictionary of Film*, New York: Knopf.

William Uricchio and Roberta Pearson (1993), *Reframing Culture*, Princeton: Princeton University Press.

Brian Winston (1996), *Technologies of Seeing*, London: Routledge.

Peter Wollen (1975), 'The Two Avant-Gardes' in *Studio International* 190 (Nov.Dec.).

Peter Wollen (1992), *Singin' in the Rain*, London: British Film Institute.

8

'SEE IT NOW': TELEVISION FROM 1954

'The fault, dear Brutus, is not in our stars'

At 10.30 p.m. on Tuesday 9 March 1954, the American ABC television network presented an asinine quiz show in which a celebrity panel was invited to guess the name of the contestants. The people were chosen because they shared cognomens with famous persons or objects – a Mr Napoleon Bonaparte or an A. Garter, for instance. Although the series lasted for four years, *The Name's the Same* cannot be counted amongst the greatest hits produced by Mark Goodson and Bill Todman – their masterwork being *The Price is Right*. Against *The Name's the Same*, the struggling DuMont network scheduled no programme but left its few affiliate stations to their own devices. For the first half of the slot, NBC, one of the two main networks, ran a news bulletin and current-affairs interview show, *On the Line with Considine*, conducted by veteran jour-nalist Bob Considine. CBS, the other leading network, also had a news programme fronted by a veteran, Ed Murrow, but its *See It Now* lasted the full half-hour.

On this particular evening, Murrow began: 'Tonight *See It Now* devotes its entire half-hour to a report on Senator Joseph R. McCarthy, told mainly in his own words and pictures.' There followed a trawl through the news-film archive. The demagogic Wisconsin senator was seen questioning a witness: 'You know the Civil Liberties Union [ACLU] has been listed as a front for . . . the Communist Party?' Murrow rebutted by telling the audience: 'The Attorney General's List does not and never has listed the ACLU as subversive. Nor does the

330

FBI or any other federal government agency.' And so on and so on. After footage of McCarthy mocking the Secretary of the Army on the witness stand with a Shakespeare quote, 'Upon what meat does this our Caesar feed?', Murrow asked, 'Upon what meat does Senator McCarthy feed?'

Although the American media, much of which was anyway in thrall to the senator's red-baiting, had been quelled into silence by his threats, Murrow's attack was not unique. Radio in particular had been increasingly running unsupportive stories and, on television, *See It Now* itself had first mounted a short item in December 1951 along the 'investigatory' lines now deployed, as well as dissecting the plight of one of the senator's innocent victims in October 1953. Murrow had done enough for McCarthy to have him marked down as 'soft on Communism', complete with a file on his involvement, when president of a national student organisation 20 years earlier, with a summer school in Moscow. It was show-down time. Murrow began his final 'continuity': 'Had he [McCarthy] looked three lines earlier in Shakespeare's *Caesar*, he would have found this line which is not altogether inappropriate: "The fault, dear Brutus, is not in our stars, but in ourselves".' He concluded, directly addressing the lens:

> We will not walk in fear, one of the other. We will not be driven by fear into an age of unreason. . . . The actions of the Junior Senator from Wisconsin have caused alarm and dismay amongst our allies abroad and given considerable comfort to our enemies. And whose fault is that? Not really his. He didn't create this situation of fear, he merely exploited it; and rather successfully.
>
> Cassius was right. 'The fault, dear Brutus, is not in our stars, but in ourselves'.
>
> Good night and good luck.

American broadcast news, partly because of establishment worries as to its power and partly as a result of the deals it had needed to do with the newspaper industry in the 1930s, had been prohibited by regulation from editorialising. In the late 1940s, as more people applied for radio licences than could be accommodated, the FCC in Washington rethought this prohibition and suggested that stations, as 'public trustees', had an obligation to air all the different points of view in their communities, including their own, on controversial issues. This soon became a sort of right-of-reply requirement, known as the Fairness Doctrine. Joe McCarthy had been using it successfully to demand air-time from anybody who dared to cover his activities, and this had been a factor in silencing the broadcasters. Murrow had begun his attack, that March evening, by promising that the senator could take the *See It Now* slot to reply (which he did in a slick filmed rebuttal, counter-productively ranting about the Moscow summer school and much else, three weeks later). The following December, the Senate voted 67–20 to censure McCarthy and his hold was broken. Murrow was always to claim, with much justice, that he was not solely responsible for McCarthy's fall; insults to fellow senators and threats to the army contributed much more than television. Nevertheless, this *See It Now* played a significant role. After all, 15 months earlier, a young Californian politician, Richard Nixon, had used the NBC TV studio in Los Angeles to talk his way, triumphantly, out of a corruption charge with a tearful tale of the gift of a little dog, Checkers. *See It Now* confirmed what Nixon had already demonstrated; television had inherited all the supposed power and influence, which had long been validated by commercial advertising and Hitler, of radio.

'The ideal way of sending messages'

The year 1954 was the seventieth anniversary of the earliest television patent. In 1884, Paul Nipkow, inspired by the recent introduction of the telephone, patented the use of a selenium block as the heart of what he called an 'electric telescope'. Nipkow suggested that a spinning disc punched with a spiral of holes mounted between a lens and a block of selenium, a metal whose resistance to an electrical current varied when exposed to light, would convert light-waves into a modulated electrical signal – just as sound-wave pressure on carbon varied its resistance to electricity and was therefore at the heart of the recently introduced telephone. Ideas were soon being floated for a videophone, some mocking. *Punch*, for instance, ran a cartoon of a 'telephonoscope', a contraption with a screen as long as a mantelpiece. Less whimsically, others thought it could perhaps be of more service as an alternative to 'copying-telegraphs', facsimile machines which had existed from the time of Morse for the transmission of handwriting. A device for doing this, using selenium and a sheet of paper soaked with potassium iodide to interact with the incoming electrical signal, had been demonstrated in 1881. At a scientific conference held during the Paris Exhibition of 1900, Constantin Perskyi introduced a neologism for this experimental field – not the *Elektrisches Teleskop* Nipkow had patented, but 'television'. He had no clearer idea about applications for the technology than anybody else. Television was either another sort of facsimile machine (probably flawed in that it produced no copies); an add-on visual facility to the telephone which (as the next hundred years were to demonstrate) no one really wanted; or the reinvention of the telescope which nobody, despite a certain obsession with surveillance that some have seen as a central characteristic of nineteenth-century Western civilisation, had need of either.

In 1908 a senior electrical engineer, Alan Campbell Swinton, outlined in theory the essentials of the system that was eventually to be brought to market in the mid-twentieth century. He suggested that an effective television system should be entirely electronic using 'two beams of kathode [sic] rays (one at the transmitting and one at the receiving station) synchronously deflected by the varying fields of two electromagnets'. Cathode ray tubes (CRTs) had been around for about a decade when Campbell Swinton published this concept. Boris Rozing, a scientist in the St Petersburg Institute of Technology, tentatively demonstrated its viability in 1911, when he transmitted black and white bars to a screen, using a CRT as the 'pick-up' in the camera as well as the receiver. Nevertheless, more than a decade after that, Campbell Swinton could still complain:

> If we could only get one of the big research laboratories, like that of the G.E.C. or of the Western Electric Company – one of those people who have large skilled staffs and any amount of money to engage on the business – I believe they would solve a thing like this in six months and make a reasonable job of it.

For the rest of the 1920s and into the following decade, firms with 'large skilled staffs' did explore, with no great urgency, both Nipkow-style spinning discs and Campbell Swinton's CRT-based cameras. In 1927, a team at Bell Labs introduced a mechanically scanned videophone with a minuscule screen a couple of inches square. Rivals at General Electric that same year made the crucial connection to show business, unveiling a screen seven feet square in a cinema as well as obtaining an experimental licence to broadcast pictures from its Schenectady radio station. Among the transmissions was a popular melodrama, *The Queen's Messenger*, the medium's first theatrical effort. It had a small cast and, apparently, concentrated on the hands and feet of the actors. In the year following, 21 other stations were also licensed to experiment with television. For the most part, their systems did not work very well: MIT students, monitoring reception of signals transmitted from W1XAV in Boston, invented a game guessing which members of their team were on camera in the studio, so poor was the resolution. This did not deter the independent British entrepreneur John Logie Baird, whose mechanical system was then producing only 30 or so horizontal lines of resolution, from trying, with little success, to sell 'televisors' to the public. In the next decade, the Germans opened a mechanically scanned videophone wired link with 180-line signal between Berlin and Nuremberg but it thrived no better than the Bell Labs one had. By the mid-1930s, the German company Fernseh had refined mechanical scanning, with a spinning disc encased in a vacuum revolving at 6,000 r.p.m., to produce what were then considered high-definition images of 440 horizontal lines – more or less the electronic equivalent of 16mm film at that time.

It took the all-electric systems a little longer to achieve as much but by 1932, a team lead by Rozing's pupil, Vladymir Zworykin, working for RCA, had created the 'Iconoscope' camera capable of 240 lines resolution. Increasing the lines and, equally importantly, cleansing its signals of unwanted 'noise' – 'artifacts' as engineers curiously name them – took a sister team at EMI in Britain (led by Isadore Schoenberg, another of Rozing's pupils) and the independent American researcher Philo T. Farnsworth until 1936. In that year, Baird, whose showmanship was always more impressive than his engineering, was given a chance publicly to test his by now poorer-quality system against EMI's essentially American one. The BBC, which had been entrusted with the run-off, soon abandoned mechanical scanning but Baird's spurious British reputation as the father of television somehow persisted. In Germany, a similar run-off was occasioned by Nazi pride in Nipkow and Fernseh and the two systems ran parallel until the Second World War.[1] The German television network grew to embrace five cities and after the invasion of France, the Eiffel Tower was pressed into service as a transmission tower; but programmes, even coverage of the Berlin Olympics, had produced little public enthusiasm. There were only around 200 domestic *Volksfernsehempfänger* because Nazi authorities hesitated about placing them in homes lest Hitler be mocked in private, and no more than 1,000 other sets were installed, almost all in halls seating between 40 and 400. Even in democratic Britain, the 1936 Coronation, like the Olympics, had failed as a draw and only 20,000 home receivers were sold prior to the outbreak of the Second World War. One reason was that a decade of Baird-inspired hype about barely discernible pictures on minuscule screens had deterred potential buyers – offering what was to be a seldom-heeded warning about the dangers to the market of hyping a technology too early.

In America, the situation was more complex. Sarnoff at RCA supported television research because the technology would allow him to

compete, not with his own radio networks, but with AT&T's phones –
or so he claimed. 'The ideal way of sending messages', he announced,
'is to hold up a printed sheet that will be immediately reproduced at the
other end.' The FCC did not believe this ploy and from 1936 on
refused to license a regular TV service because it would have enshrined
an RCA broadcasting monopoly. The Americans persisted in treating
television as 'experimental' when, as the two European services showed,
it was quite obviously no longer any such thing. It took until 1941 to
break the deadlock but a National Television Standards Committee
(NTSC), designed to contain RCA, finally agreed a standard for television which almost exactly matched the one proposed by Sarnoff's
engineers at the outset. The NTSC deal was, in reality, a pact to access
the technology while avoiding creating a monopoly but within months
of this settlement, the United States entered the war and the introduction of the new medium faltered. The BBC had also given up, although
the Nazis continued despite hostilities.

With the peace in 1945, official American opinion immediately positioned the stalled medium as a vital engine for post-war recovery both
as a consumer item and as a channel for advertising other consumer
items. Americans had a long tradition of associating consumption of
locally produced goods with patriotism, and of seeing advertising as the
clue to encouraging this. After all, George Washington had insisted on
an all-American suit of clothes for his inauguration, and had found the
'superfine American Broad Cloths' from which to have it tailored in an
advertisement in the New York *Daily Advertiser*. From the 1830s on,
newspapers had maintained their independence of politicians in large
part because of advertising revenues. A hundred years later, 'driblets of
advertising' had come to swamp American radio. It is not too surprising that James Fly, the war-time chair of the FCC, could write of TV: 'I
think it quite likely that during the post-war period television will be
one of the first industries arising to serve as a cushion against unemployment and depression.' The medium, in short, would prevent a
repetition of the economic disaster of 1930s.

In 1946 there were 5,000 televisions in the USA but by 1948, an initial post-war licensing flurry had created 52 TV stations, affiliated to four networks serving nearly a million sets in 29 cities. Originally, the Commission had determined that broadcasters using the same VHF channel should be 200 miles apart, giving a city a maximum of five channels. Since the driver of the new medium was to be advertising, the industry protested, wanting more. The FCC reduced the distance to as little as 150 miles in the crowded north-eastern region, allowing New York, for example, seven stations instead of the four originally allocated. This was against the advice of its engineers and they were in the right. The new signals interfered with each other and the Commission therefore abruptly stopped all licensing in 1948. Although the number of sets continued to increase exponentially, so that by 1950 there were just under ten million of them, a further 292 applications for station licences were held up. The growth of the number of televisions alone meant that the easiest solution, moving all stations up to the UHF band, was resisted. Instead, the Commission determined that the demands of the broadcasting market for multiple VHF channels be met by reducing power, even at the cost of condemning viewers to watching shadowed, fuzzy images, especially for those living amidst mid-town skyscrapers.

Reception problems were exacerbated by the other major area of technical debate: colour. Sarnoff's technicians had refined a colour system, patented in Germany in 1938, using three colour-sensitive pick-up tubes in the camera transmitting to a specially treated CRT tube. The FCC replayed the business of containing RCA by, at first, supporting an alternative system which had been developed by CBS; but then, when the manufacturers refused to make CBS-compatible receivers, it was forced back to RCA and cross-licensing agreements. Colour languished.

The Freeze, as it was known, had the more immediate effect of encouraging entrepreneurs to import signals from the few existing broadcasting stations. In 1948, with no new stations coming on stream, four electrical appliance dealers in Panther Valley, Pennsylvania had the bright idea of rebroadcasting signals from Philadelphia, 70 miles to the south. They captured them with an 85ft-high antenna on a hill-top and using broadband co-axial cable, which AT&T, with its usual astuteness, had developed before the war to enable the radio networks to build their television connections, to carry the signals to subscribers' homes. The dealers were able to sell sets, their primary business, and also make some money from offering the service, for a $100 installation fee and $3 a month thereafter. They paid nothing to the broadcasters.

In using wires, the Panther Valley Television Company was following in a radio tradition, though not one much seen in the US. In Europe, radio by 'relay' had been a reality since the mid-1920s with millions paying a subscription to receive broadcast stations through a wire rather than the air. This was either because of reception problems or to obtain signals, often from across a border, which could not otherwise be heard. In the Netherlands, by 1939, 50 per cent of households were wired for radio. Even in Britain, where the ideology of radio as a national cultural resource had constrained network opt-outs and dictated the engineering of a single universal system, three per cent of households subscribed to cable and the BBC had to lobby, successfully as it happened, for restrictions to be placed on its growth.

Neither cable, nor colour, nor even signal interference can account for the 43-month duration of the Freeze. The ostensible problem, interference, could have been solved, more or less, by any competent team of engineers with contour maps more quickly than this. What took the time was finding a balance between the radio industry and Hollywood, just as in the previous decade, a modus vivendi was needed for RCA and its rivals within radio. Hollywood had pressing reasons for reaching an accommodation with television. A connection to radio had been made in the 1920s, essentially to advertise the movies, but it proved crucial to the introduction of sound film. It also alerted the studios to television research so that, for instance, the contractual arrangements made with the sound-recording people that most of Hollywood preferred using, AT&T's subsidiary ERPI, dealt with television rights long before a viable TV system existed. Hollywood's first post-war thought was to use the technology in direct competition with radio by transmitting materials to the cinemas for large-screen display. The technology to do this, big-screen 'Eidophors',[2] had been developed in Switzerland in 1939. By 1948, Paramount's own system was installed in their Times Square showcase and live transmission of major boxing events was established as a popular draw. Four years later, as the Freeze ended, more than 100 cinemas were equipped with electronic systems. On another front, however, Hollywood was in deep trouble with the Justice Department over its monopolistic integration of production, distribution and exhibition. By a consent decree of 1948, it had been forced to spin off its cinemas into independent chains. The times were not propitious for the film industry and the broadcasters were able to insist with the Commission that the cinemas not be strengthened as a rival to television. The FCC refused to extend the use of the spectrum to cinemas.

Hollywood refocused. Instead of seeking to rival radio's new business, the film industry would instead service it. Making movies for television, which RKO was already thinking about when it set up a subsidiary for this purpose in 1944, soon became a major activity. By 1955, raw film-stock consumption for television was ten times greater than that of the feature side of the industry. Of course, many new production entities emerged but the studios also remained deeply involved. After an initial refusal to deal, they also realised that their archives were of immense value to the new medium and old feature films were licensed for transmission. The consequences of these moves would take most of the rest of the 1950s to play out; but the result was already clear when the FCC lifted the Freeze with its *Sixth Report and Order* in April 1952. Whereas in 1948, the nascent television schedules were dominated by live variety shows from New York, in 1952, *I Love Lucy*, shot on film in Hollywood, was TV's biggest hit. The accommodation between the east and west coasts not only facilitated this process, it also provided America with cans of readily exportable filmed material for the rest of the world. By now, the world was waiting.

The Germans' last TV transmission in Paris had occurred as the Allies approached the city; then there was silence. Despite austerity and post-war reconstruction priorities, the BBC recommenced its television transmissions in 1946. By the end of 1952, there were still fewer than two million receivers in the UK but 78 per cent of the population was within range of the TV signal. Two years after that, against considerable political and cultural opposition, a heavily regionalised competitive commercial service was licensed, setting in place a duopoly that was to survive, augmented by a second BBC channel in 1964, into the 1980s. This was to be something of a pattern for Europe. Television began almost everywhere in the West as a state monopoly, only slowly to add commercial elements. In West Germany, the occupying powers installed a public regionally based broadcasting system, ARD, which carefully balanced, in the management teams, Christian Democrat and Socialist interests. In Italy, the dominance of the Christian Democrats led to the perception that the state broadcaster, RAI, was their creature. The French state broadcaster, Radio-Télévision de France, was made over more than once as one post-war republic succeeded another. RTF insisted on a unique 819-line standard, ignoring both the American 525 lines and the German and (eventually) British 625 lines. In the Netherlands, the most responsive of radio systems had existed, with stations licensed to the radio clubs established by 'pillars' of Dutch society – for instance, religious (Protestant or Catholic) or political (socialist or liberal). These now got slices of the television schedule according to the size of their membership, which continued to fund production through the sale of programme guides with inflated prices. In Sweden, the 'pillars' of society included newspapers and other commercial interests which were represented in the management of the state broadcaster.

Although only in Luxembourg was the American advertising-funded, privately owned model whole-heartedly accepted, most countries soon found ways of accommodating commercials: Francoist Spain established a completely commercially funded state-run service; West Germany allowed an isolated band of mid-evening ads; and, in the UK, Australia and Canada, entirely separate commercial channels coexisted with the state broadcaster.

The Germans also managed to revive their pre-war tradition of technological innovation. Their audiotape recording lead had been lost to the Americans, who seized their patents after the war and by 1956 developed an effective system for video recording. Nevertheless, the southern German network in Stuttgart contributed in the early 1950s to the development of 16mm magnetic sound-recording techniques which were important both for television news production and for general use in documentary filming. German engineers also created a trichromatic colour-tube system, PAL (phase alternating line), as an alternative to the RCA (NTSC) method on which they had been working before the war. Not least because PAL was adopted by the British, who began using it to transmit colour in 1967, it became a worldwide rival standard to NTSC colour. The French ignored both, opting instead for a Soviet system.

Behind the Iron Curtain, television, like all media, was overtly part of the states' ideological apparatus. Having confiscated all but a few of the paltry million radio sets that were individually owned at the outset of the war, the Soviet Union, constrained in any case by severe economic hardships, did little about television in the 1950s, though Kremlin propaganda vigorously claimed to have patented the entire technology in the late nineteenth and early twentieth centuries. These were not entirely without foundation given the historical importance of the Tsarist Institute of Technology in St Petersburg. The push for television occurred in the 1960s and by 1967 colour was being transmitted using a third system, one that was to be adopted by the entire Second World, Cuba and, alone among non-Communist states, France. By 1970, thanks to the dedicated Molinya (Lightening) satellite systems, two channels were available all over the Soviet Union and many big cities had a further two. Molinya encouraged control and centralisation, as only the ground stations in Moscow and Vladivostock could both transmit and receive – the rest were receive-only.

341

'A vast wasteland'

Television was a remarkably derivative medium, its content largely dictated by radio, but its mode of visual representation was essentially
cinematic, using the 'Hollywood grammar' that audiences expected.
The perceived need to emulate the norms of cinema had entirely, and
expensively, determined the design of the TV studio, setting challenges
in the engineering of mixing panels, to allow discontinuous shooting by
a single camera recorded on film to be replaced by continuous shooting
on multiple cameras transmitting live. Figures unknown to radio –
camera operators, make-up artists, set-designers – appeared; but, despite
these technical and personnel differences, in essence, television simply
took over the forms of radio, not only institutionally but also program-
matically. No entirely new popular genres emerged although, obviously,
television favoured some types of programming over others.

Talk, as a radio staple, was not easily transferred – although many
societies were to be more tolerant of 'talking head' discussion programmes on TV than were the Anglophones. In English-speaking
lands, television conversation became a species of variety, the 'talk
show', with, usually, celebrity guests, music and, often, stand-up
comedy and sketches interspersing the talking.[3] The new medium was
also unsympathetic to musical performance of limited visual interest
whether by the symphony orchestra or its emulator, the seated popular
or swing band. Like talk, they had had a significant presence on radio
but during the 1950s, as even the most popular of these forms was
being overtaken by the informalities of emergent rock and roll, they
played a far less prominent role on television. Comedy, drama and
news, on the other hand, flourished.

Milton Berle was the new medium's first American star, created by a
classic variety show in 1948, the *Texaco Star Theater*. He had never
been a headliner, although he had begun his career long before as a
child actor in Biograph pictures during the First World War. Now he
was 'Mr Television', wowing the audience with a new informality, often
injecting himself into the acts he was introducing. Berle was a song-and-

dance man; obviously, vaudeville on television could be more generous than radio had been towards the visual element in such acts and, of course, comfortably accommodated specialty acts that radio had perforce ignored – jugglers, say, or magicians.[4]

Sid Caesar, for instance, was the sort of physical comedian who could never make radio his own, but he too flourished in the new medium. He had played in New York revues and nightclubs and in tough summer seasons in the 'Borscht Belt', as the Jewish hotels of the Catskills, with their unforgiving audiences, were known. His exploration of TV's potential went further than Berle's. In *Your Show of Shows*, a weekly 90-minute theatrical revue transferred to the small screen, he offered the audience material somewhat closer to the sophistication of contemporary Broadway. Among others, Mel Brooks, Neil Simon and Larry Gelbart (who were to have stellar careers respectively as a Hollywood director and star, a Broadway playwright and the driving force behind arguably American network television's greatest situation comedy thus far, *M.A.S.H.*)[5] provided sketches:

> *Caesar* (as 'The Professor'): After many years, I haff found
>   the secret of Titten-Totten's Tomb.
> *Interviewer*: What is it, Professor?
> *Caesar*: I should tell you?

Parodies could embrace Italian cinema's neo-realism as well as *From Here to Obscurity* or *Aggravation Boulevard*.

Audiences fundamentally favoured more realistic comedic situations with plot lines more extended than were possible in brief sketches. By the end of the Freeze, Berle was in trouble and had to recast his formula in a more situation-comedy mode. In 1952, *The Buick/Berle Show* found 'Uncle Milty' each week backstage rehearsing his TV programme. There was still song and dance, but guests were fewer and there was a rudimentary back-stage plot. *Your Show of Shows* did not last either and was over in 1954. Unlike Berle and other even more clownlike entertainers such as Red Skelton, Caesar was to become a totem of

343

American television's lost potential for any other than the most populist programming.

Radio had long favoured show-biz settings for its situation comedies and many of these transferred with little change; for example, George Burns and Gracie Allen, whose show-business milieu had become more or less domesticated, moved from radio to television in 1950, live from New York. Burns added asides to the camera. He claimed, 'That was an original idea of mine; I know it was because I originally stole it from Thornton Wilder's play *Our Town*.'

Lucille Ball was indebted to nobody. She had cut her teeth, as a performer, in Broadway reviews in the late 1920s. She was soon in Hollywood, a Goldwyn girl in 1933 and first on the radio, although not a dominant presence, in *My Favorite Husband* between 1948 and 1951. She transferred to television that year in *I Love Lucy*, but Ball, who produced through her own company, insisted that the programme be filmed in Hollywood, not performed live from New York as CBS had wanted. Her clout was such that she further demanded that the programme be shot on linked film cameras as if live. It allowed for a slickness in editing which no show filmed discontinuously with a single camera could match. She also, in perhaps an even more significant victory, co-starred her real-life husband, Desi Arnaz, a Cuban, in defiance of broadcasting's persistent racial bigotries.

Ball played a ditzy, but glamorous, blonde housewife in approved 1950s fashion but she uniquely combined this with the slapstick tradition which Caesar and Skelton had brought to the small screen. It was not for nothing that she had once shared an office on the MGM lot with Buster Keaton. In one sense this was just another situation comedy in a show-biz milieu – Desi was supposed to be the star of a TV band programme – and it differed little from the programmes older and better-established radio stars than her were bringing over to the television schedules. In another sense, though, she was a veritable 'Ms Television'. Her public persona, as the owner of Desilu Productions and one of the shrewdest players in Hollywood, was set against the stereotypical brainlessness (and unexpected comic physicality) of her character in the show, thereby undercutting most of the notions then current about women on the screen, big or little. The public instantly loved her. By spring 1952 *I Love Lucy* was the top-rated show, capturing two-thirds of the available audience, and over the five years of its run it managed to average a 53 per cent rating; only in 1955 was Ball beaten to the top spot, by a quiz show – *The $64,000 Question*. It was Ball's insistence, at the outset, on Los Angeles and film which confirmed the arrangements reached between the radio and film industries during the Freeze. As this ended, *Burns and Allen* also moved to the West Coast and film. Live vaudeville transmissions still came from New York but, as these gradually lost out to filmed situation comedies, Hollywood came to be the prime light-entertainment production site.

The same thing happened with drama. Popular dramatic radio genres – thrillers, soap operas, Westerns and police series – transferred wholesale. Cycles in their proliferation were to become a feature of the TV schedules. Despite the popularity of soaps,[6] it was an industrial given that the prime-time audience preferred self-contained episodes, series rather than serials. Outside series, individual programmes – 'plays' as the British called them – were 'anthologised' under an umbrella title such as NBC's *Goodyear TV Playhouse*. Again live from New York, such showcases were considered, like *Your Show of Shows*, to have delivered the new medium's first masterworks; but, as in light entertainment, these were squeezed off the screen by the early 1960s, replaced with filmed formulaic product from Hollywood. What was lost was original teleplays such as Paddy Chayevsky's *Marty*, directed by Delbert Mann and transmitted under the *Goodyear* banner in May 1953 with Rod Steiger in the title role. These productions were constrained by the limitations of live transmission and developed a very particular sort of realism. Scripts with multiple settings required that each location be shrunk to a minimum in order to get it on to the studio floor, and time and cost dictated that set dressing also had to be pared down. Marty's butcher's shop, for instance, was merely a counter and a flat with hanging joints of real meat.[7] These transmissions spoke to the same range of concerns as did the legitimate theatre, which was hardly surprising since that was where most of the talent came from, with many making live television drama a way-station on their journey to the Hollywood feature film studios. On CBS's *Studio One* and *Playhouse 90*, for example, a group of directors including John Frankenheimer, George Roy Hill, Frank Schaffner and Sidney Lumet made shows – *The Miracle Worker*, *Days of Wine and Roses*, *Judgement at Nuremberg*, *Twelve Angry Men* – all of which had a Hollywood afterlife, as did their directors. Nevertheless, *succès d'estime*, replete with regular acknowledgement in the Emmy awards, was not enough. *Kraft Television Theatre*, the first anthology series, was removed in 1958. By then, *Goodyear Playhouse*, which had in only one year garnered sufficiently large audiences to figure in the top 15 rated shows, had been reduced to a half-hour and was shot on film. New York was left with the live daytime soaps, sustained by Broadway's pool of thespian talent.

In 1959, Rod Serling, a comparatively minor Broadway playwright, moved from writing single live dramas such as *Playhouse 90*'s first major hit, *Requiem for a Heavyweight* (with Jack Palance, directed by Ralph Nelson), to create the early Hollywood cult series, *The Twilight Zone*, shot, of course, on film. 'There is a fifth dimension beyond that which is known to man', each episode began. 'It is a dimension as vast as space and as timeless as infinity.' The then head of the FFC, Newton Minnow, also had limitless expanses on his mind when in 1961 he famously described American television as 'a vast wasteland' created as a result of the industry's 'squandering of the airwaves'. What he so sloganised was exactly the formulaic Hollywood product – *The Twilight Zone*, say – which had killed off shows exemplifying what was already being thought of as a 'Golden Age' – *Playhouse 90*, for example.

Not least because of First Amendment inhibitions, Minnow's FCC, despite its regulatory powers, could not intervene to bring back programming of a sort the public had began to spurn. The audience wanted formulas and that is what the industry was supplying. This product-line approach to programming had first become glaringly obvious in 1957. In that season, ten new prime-time cowboy series began – including *Wagon Train*, *Have Gun, Will Travel* and *Maverick*. These joined the returning posse of, among others, 'Wyatt Earp', 'Jim Bowie', *Gunsmoke*'s 'Marshall Dillon' and cavalry private 'Rin Tin Tin', a dog. Oaters, such as *The Cisco Kid*, also dominated the syndicated programme business – shows sold to independent stations or to affiliates to be used in their own local early prime-time slots, allocated to them as a result of FFC regulation. As ever, the truth of economist Harold Hotelling's 1927 theory about competition was proving evident. Just as rival ice-cream sellers on a beach tend to cluster together to maximise sales, so the networks bunched their Westerns and, when taste moved on, bunched another genre to replace them.

The first of these replacements was concerned with crime, one way or another. In the year of Minnow's speech, *Perry Mason* was already in the fourth season of its nine-year run and prime-time detectives could be found in twelve other series. Prime-time drama, dominated by private investigators and Westerns, was a highly masculine world. In 1969, to correct this, shows featuring doctors and hospitals, a presence in the daytime world of the soap opera, began to appear, following on from the pioneering prime-time success of *Dr. Kildare* between 1961 and 1965. Good-looking male medics were served up for the delight of the crucial 18–34 female demographic.

Not for nothing was the Nielsen ratings report book, which contained demographic breakdowns, known as 'The Bible' but, just as with Holy Writ, belief in its veracity required a certain faith. No doubts about the principles and outcomes of such audience 'research' were (and are) allowed, even though occasional changes of methodology have revealed the artificiality of these data.[8] Academic research into television, which has been extensive, has all too often been little better. Take scholarly inquiry into the effects of children's TV. The American TV industry had begun to replace programmes such as *The Howdy-Doody Show* and *Captain Kangaroo* – host and puppet pap, in many people's opinion – with animated series. A panic about violence was added to the previous complaints about mindlessness. At the heart of the disquiet stood a weighted, inflatable doll marketed as 'Bobo':

347

> In one corner, the child found a set of play materials; in another corner he [sic] saw an adult . . . with a set of tinker toys, a large inflated plastic Bobo doll and a mallet . . . the adult sat on the doll and punched it repeatedly in the nose, pummeled its head with a mallet, tossed it up in the air aggressively and kicked it around the room.

Unsurprisingly, except perhaps to the psychologists at Stanford University who designed this 'experiment' in 1958, the children witnessing such violence were more violent in their play than those in the control group who saw the adult 'playing' quietly. The essential problem of extrapolating conclusions about the 'real world' obviously had little impact on the thinking of these academics; nor have any reservations about the exercise's inherent artificiality ever seriously undercut the common assumption, which the 'Bobo doll' report is deemed to 'prove', that violence on television *causes* violent behaviour. 'Bobo doll'-style research was still being funded, executed and quoted with approval in the twenty-first century. It is part of received wisdom as to television's general influence, which has never been much questioned in public debate.

The industry has, of course, remained unrepentant about the quality of its children's programmes and about violence in general. After all, however much observers might fret, violence sells. As Quinn Martin, the producer of *The Untouchables*, the first drama made by Lucille Ball's production company and a rare major hit for ABC, the then trailing third network, memoed one of the show's writers in the early 1960s: 'I like the idea of sadism'. Only external events, such as the assassination of Robert Kennedy, could on occasion give the industry pause; but basically mayhem remained essential to popular drama. A decade after *The Untouchables*, for instance, producers of *Charlie's Angels* (a show which many observers considered was really about hair, bikinis and glamorous evening wear) altered the writers' brief: instead of each of the three heroines being put into violent jeopardy three times an episode, one jeopardy each would, they thoughtfully determined, do.

Not all the emerging sociology about television was as flawed as the 'Bobo doll' caper. In the UK, for example, a 1950s study of children revealed that they were more frightened of everyday violence – verbal abuse between adults in a realistic drama, say – than they were of greater brutality in a fantastic setting – a Western gun-fight, for example. Of course, given that most of us do not imitate the media representation of transgressive behaviour in our 'real' lives, any connection between actual violence and such representations might be merely a symptom of socio- or psycho-pathology in the persons so behaving. To claim that their violence was 'caused' by the media could be like insisting that it was the shaking of leaves in the trees which 'caused' the wind; but this has never established itself as a viable alternative hypothesis in the public mind where television's 'power' remains a given. Billions were being spent (and are still) exactly to affect consumption of everything from beer to politicians and, surely, all that money could not be wrong? Had not Ed Murrow destroyed Joe McCarthy?

In the first decade of its real diffusion as a mass medium, American television did, though, manage to reveal itself as corrupt. After an FCC ban on give-away prizes on television was declared unconstitutional by the Supreme Court in 1954, CBS transferred its successful radio quiz, *The $64,000 Question*, as a late replacement to its schedule in June 1955. Adding the image of a contestant sweating out the answers in a closed 'isolation booth' and increasing the prize money a thousand-fold created a show so popular that, in the following season, *The $64,000 Question* beat the seemingly unassailable *I Love Lucy*. Its success spawned a host of other shows but the money involved – *The $64,000 Question* alone gave away $1 million and ten free Cadillacs in prizes that first year while earning millions more in advertising revenue – was clearly too important to be left to chance.

Quiz shows were the first to deliver that most desired of all outcomes for the industry, really cheap programming which attracted massive audiences. This chimera was still being actively pursued with the 'real-ity television' fad half a century later; but, brought up on film, where lavish production values and the most expensive technology had always

349

been used as a barrier to entry, audiences usually rejected anything but high-priced, professional product. By the 1980s such expectations cost, for prime-time drama, $1 million an hour. Spending less, in essence, does not look quite like 'television' to the audience, for all that they might not be able to put their finger on exactly why. Other genres were cheaper than drama – old-style filmed social problem or political documentaries, for example, cost a third as much; costumed dramas obviously cost even more – but very little truly popular programming costs more or less nothing. The quiz shows of the 1950s, despite the size of the prizes, were the first to come close.

In May 1958 Edward Hilgemeier Jr., a 24-year-old part-time butler and bit player, failed to make it on to the screen as a contestant in *Dotto*; but, while waiting for his try, he found written evidence left lying around that another contestant had been given the answers. Dissatisfied with the hush-money he was paid by Colgate, *Dotto*'s sponsors, he blew the whistle and protested to the New York State Attorney General. One Howard Stemple then came forward with another story. Some 18 months earlier, he had been the losing contestant on another show, *Twenty–One*. With even more prize-money at stake than on *The $64,000 Question*, the programme was an extraordinarily elaborate concoction which required considerable coaching; but that is what Stemple and his opponent, Charles Van Doren, were given. The adlibs they came up with, though, were their own. Van Doren made himself a star with these apparent insights into his mental processes: 'I've seen the ad for those books a thousand times'; 'She's that lovely frail girl???'; and, crucially, 'Oh! I know!!' Van Doren won and became an instant celebrity with a spot on NBC's pioneering morning lightweight newsmagazine, *Today*.

In November 1958 the New York Grand Jury convened and more than 100 witnesses – broadcasters, sponsors and contestants – swore up and down that the shows were honest. The state prosecutor complained that 'nothing in my experience prepared me for the mass perjury that took place'; but when the judge sealed the proceeding's outcome, Congress, ever ready to pursue a high-profile issue, began its own investigation. A year later, in Washington, finally, Van Doren sang: 'I was involved, deeply involved, in a deception.' His career as a television personality was at an end – as were, for the moment, the game shows. There was, however, no crime as the fraud was, in fact, victimless. The concept of a 'contract' not to deceive the viewer, which was to become, for instance, a cornerstone of British content regulation, was as yet undreamed of. Television's integrity was, of course, damaged but not to the point where the rest of the output – news and documentaries, for example – was questioned.

Minnow's 'vast wasteland' speech was less of a slur and more a reasonable description, yet there is a question about the assumptions behind his attack and, indeed, the general disdain in which by then many held (and still hold) television's output. Serling, for example, can be seen as a minor Broadway playwright who, with these others, had distorted the power the new medium had to bring meaningful entertainment and information into the mass of homes by rendering it less accessible than it might have been. It was, by this reading, *The Twilight Zone* rather than *Requiem for a Heavyweight* which was the more significant work. Critics, ensnared by an essentially class-based vision of culture, might sneer but successive generations of audience have marked their mental maps with the programming they have experienced, both as children and as adults. They have, as with the popular cinema and radio before it, constantly accorded television an importance in their lives as great as any claimed by the apostles of culture for the canons of high art in theirs; and to entertain and satisfy millions, surely, is no small thing?

'Television has come to stay'

'Television has come to stay', opined paragraph 78 of the 1943 British official inquiry, chaired by Lord Hankey, into the medium's post-war future. The report further recommended that the BBC should provide it. The BBC was having a 'good war'. The call sign, '*Ici Londres . . .*',

351

symbolised its significant role in supporting European underground resistance to the Nazis and its home provision, especially the popular Forces Network introduced in 1940, was widely acknowledged as a crucial morale booster. Television transmissions had been closed down on 1 September 1939 at noon, with a Mickey Mouse cartoon. Hankey's conclusion that television belonged to the BBC was of course satisfactory to the Corporation and on 7 June 1946 they restarted the service, continuing where they had left off in 1939, with the same cartoon. It was transmitted, it is safe to say, to a minuscule audience. By 1948 there were still only some 45,000 TV licences and sets cost £50, about two months' average industrial take-home pay. In fact, for many in the BBC, Hankey's belief that television's future was theirs was somewhat less than welcome. Massive costs were being incurred in advance of the revenue gained from new TV licences and there was, to all intents and purposes, no audience.

A somewhat paradoxical consequence of this lukewarm response of the radio professionals was that the enthusiasts within the BBC who did commit to television were less bound than were their peers in America by the modes of radio production. Although, in broad-brush terms, British television's output echoed the genres of radio programming just as it did across the Atlantic, there were far fewer direct transfers and there was no distorting pull from the weak British film industry, as there was with Hollywood. In Britain, television was neither film nor was it, quite, radio with pictures. Novel mongrel techniques, many of which did not survive beyond the mid-1950s, were essayed; for example, there were periods of dead air, minutes long, filled with repetitive images – a spinning potter's wheel was particularly remembered – between programmes, functioning as 'intervals', just as were found in the theatre.

Most original was the use of film and live material in the same programme turn-and-turn-about. In part, economic necessity underpinned this procedure since film was an expensive consumable (because of raw stock, processing and editing costs) whereas live television, its capital costs already accounted for, was not. The British public continued to accept the filmed insert even after the later 1950s when the flow of transatlantic series shot completely on celluloid began to have a serious impact. They were still tolerant of it in the era of videotape (which the Americans had developed from the German audiotape technology they had seized after the war) and 'as-if-live' studio recording.[9] Television had inherited the British distrust of audio recording – 'bottled radio' as they had called it in the 1930s – which had now expanded to embrace programming recorded on film. 'We have never cheated you with film and we never will', promised Derek Burrell-Davies, a senior BBC OB producer in 1957. The general assumption in the 1950s was, in the words of Philip Dorté, then head of BBC Film Operations, that 'Television should have as little film as possible'. Between the theatrical Scylla of Shaftsbury Avenue and the filmic Charybdis of the studios in Pinewood, Denham and Ealing, BBC-TV was pioneering, as it were, a third way.

In 1949, Michael Mills, BBC-TV's first specialist Light Entertainment 'producer' (as the Corporation insisted on calling its directors) took a couple of shots on film at Paddington Station to use under an opening title. 'It may not sound much now,' he recalled some 40 years later, 'but at the time it was a sensation.' The collective skills needed to cue film sequences or even single shots into the body of a live transmission were no easy matter given that the telecine machines which were used to play film on television required at least seven seconds before they were up to speed. In the 1950s, Mills's pioneering effort was most extensively developed by the BBC's first major television drama director, Rudolph Cartier.

Cartier specialised in big-event studio-based classics, either adaptations from great literature (upon which rock was to rest an entire tradition of British 'heritage' television) or plays from the theatrical canon. Film not only permitted the introduction of 'real' exterior locations, it also allowed him, with the use of single brief shots, to expand the space of interior action. 'Rudi', as he was universally known inside BBC-TV, was also, stereotypically, the German high-art director, always pushing for the biggest sets he could accommodate on the BBC's stages. This was not particularly surprising for, beyond simply wanting to deliver the most spectacular results he could, he had learned his craft in the early 1930s at the Ufa film studios in Berlin, which had become known for, among much else, the elaborate realism of their sets.[10] He also rejected the constraints of that limited realism which characterised contemporary New York live TV drama. Take an instance from the 1954 dramatisation of George Orwell's *Nineteen Eighty-Four*, starring Peter Cushing and Yvonne Mitchell and adapted by Nigel Kneale, a drama which can lay claim to being British television's first canonical production.

For the climactic torture scene in Room 101, his floor manager Paddy Russell recalled:

> Rudi insisted that we had genuine dyed-in-the-wool sewer rats. But we had to use such a hell of a lot of lighting in those days . . . that when we got those rats into the studio they all passed out from the heat. White rats had to be procured from a local pet shop instead.

They had, indeed, to be 'dyed', using Leichner No. 3 make-up, but they were nevertheless realistic enough for an outcry, demonstrating that the new medium was as tricky as the old when it came to public relations. There were now over two million sets, a quarter of which had been purchased, it was believed, as a consequence of the coronation of Queen Elizabeth II, which had been covered in a live seven-hour OB transmission the previous year. This was in contrast to 1937, when coverage of the procession for the Queen's father's coronation had done little for the new medium. Rudi's rats provoked the usual infinitesimal number of complaints (infinitesimal, that is, as a percentage of the whole television audience) and a predictably outraged press. The customary BBC response – a high-level inquiry – ensued. This was made more meaningful because, again echoing the stage, such television plays were scheduled for more than one transmission. These were re-done live, although they could at this time have been recorded on film with, admittedly, a certain loss of image quality. After the Sunday transmission and the row on the Monday, the question was asked at the BBC Programme Board as to whether it might not be too close to Christmas to put *Nineteen Eighty-Four* out again on the Thursday, a mere nine days before the holiday. The Board decided that television could well, on occasion, offend some sensibilities and it was retransmitted.

Nowhere in pre-war British television had the essentially middle-class nature of its minuscule audience been more clearly acknowledged than in the taste which informed the drama output. The first British TV drama in 1930 was a production, in Baird's Long Acre studio, of Luigi Pirandello's avant-garde *The Man with a Flower in his Mouth* (rather than a popular work of the sort the Americans had used in 1927 for their first effort). It was towards the London theatre rather than the British film industry that the BBC-TV pioneers turned in the later 1930s. After all, the head of television drama until 1952 (who had been the director of *The Man with a Flower in his Mouth* and was the senior pre-war radio drama producer) was a person from the heart of English theatre, Val Gielgud, John Gielgud's brother. He was an unrepentant elitist, complaining, for instance, that a popular, and very long-lived, post-war radio serial, the soap opera *Mrs Dale's Diary*, was: 'socially corrupting by its monstrous flattery of the ego of the "common man" and soul-destroying to the actors, authors and producers concerned'. 'Mrs Dale' was the wife of 'Doctor James Dale', and the soap's setting could not have been more genteel – initially a 16-room detached house in South London. Accents were cut-glass. The serial was on the air from 1948 to 1969 and a spoof catchphrase attributed to Mrs Dale, 'I'm awfully worried about Jim' (or some such), was a sure-fire gag for comedians of the day. It became more a joke about the BBC's irredeemably bourgeois programming than about middle England's supposed phlegm.

The BBC had implicitly acknowledged a class-based differentiation of taste by dividing its radio output into three. A Light Programme service had replaced the Forces Network in July 1945 and three and a half months after television restarted, the national Home Service was relieved of its high-culture remit, most of which – but not Shakespeare, for example – moved over to a Third Programme. If television were ever to reach out beyond the limitations of its audience demographic, it would have to find ways of shutting up the Val Gielguds and privileging Light Programme-style material, but instincts remained tilted towards output that was not 'socially corrupting', that is popular, even as elements of all three radio services were being decanted, as it were, on to one television channel. Cartier was one of those who in effect demonstrated how the cultural division of the radio output could be transferred to television. In the summer of Coronation year, he and Kneale came up with a popular science-fiction serial, *The Quatermass Experiment*. It was British TV's first massive hit and Cartier was always to alternate the production of such 'lighter' series with his 'Third Programme'-style canonical plays.

In 1951, Beveridge became the fourth peer to chair a committee of inquiry, this time into the case for the BBC's charter renewal.[11] Beveridge determined not only that the charter should continue but that the BBC should also maintain its monopoly. The leading Tory politician on the committee, Selwyn Lloyd, took a different view of this last matter, however, and submitted a minority report arguing the case for a competing commercial television service, which his party then introduced when next in power. Dire warnings of what today would be called 'dumbing-down' along what were perceived as the lines of the US output were heard from the Labour opposition and much of the cultural establishment.

ITV began transmitting on 22 September 1955 and the predicted flow of American material (*I Love Lucy* and *Dragnet*, for example) or American formats (British versions of *The $64,000 Question*) led the schedule. The new service seized the heartland of English variety with *Sunday Night at the London Palladium*, an OB series which was to last over a decade. The regulations about advertising were exploited to produce daytime consumer shows of risible quality using vaguely dramatic conventions. Soap operas appeared, although the most successful of them, *Coronation Street*, did not start until 1960. (Chat-show host

Russell Harty, a star of the 1970s, once said: 'There was life before *Coronation Street*. But it didn't add up to much.')

The BBC ignored (as it had to) the advertising magazines. It also eschewed the give-away quiz shows to stick with its early hit, the cerebral *Animal, Vegetable or Mineral*, in which three stereotypical elderly dons – one with a white beard, another called 'Sir Mortimer' – guessed the nature of museum objects presented by a chap in a bow tie. Otherwise, it was prepared systematically to offer a more popular mix than before. It licensed a popular American formula, *This is Your Life*, which lasted until 1964 and then, after a five-year break, achieved an even longer run on ITV.[12] Many of the BBC's worries proved to be unfounded. The serious weekly current-affairs magazine *Panorama* or *Zoo Quest*, David Attenborough's first natural history series, were thought, despite their success, to be unlikely to meet the challenge of the flood of give-away game shows and formulaic Hollywood film-series on ITV – yet they survived. *Panorama* was still being transmitted 50 years later, as were Attenborough's animal documentary series.

In 1955, radio, where BBC's monopoly was as yet untouched, was far from dead. The country's most innovative and popular comedy programme was still on the old medium:

> *Grytpype-Thynne* [Peter Sellars]: Now Neddy, the prisoners are growing restless.
>
> *Seagoon* [Harry Secombe]: What, what, what, what, what? . . .
>
> *G-T:* . . . What the lads really need is a holiday.
>
> *S:* Holiday? Where?
>
> *G-T:* Well, I've spoken to the lads and they've all got their heart set on the South of France.
>
> *S:* But I can't let them out of prison.
>
> *G-T:* Of course not, Neddy. We'll take the prison with us.
>
> *S:* You can't move the prison. People will talk.
>
> *G-T:* Neddy, we're going to leave a cardboard replica.

The *Goon Show*'s sixth series began two days before ITV went on air.

Radio's popularity was not all of such surreal quality as to be difficult to translate to the screen. Another big star, Tony Hancock, was ideally suited to front the BBC response to ITV. Hancock had first appeared on stage in 1938 at the age of 16, and he was not alone in refining his craft as a comic at London's most famous burlesque house, The Windmill Theatre, after his war-service. He was on the radio by 1950 but in 1954, on the Light Programme, he starred in a situation comedy series, *Hancock's Half-Hour*, written by Ray Galton and Alan Simpson, which rapidly turned him into a national institution. Self-centred, delusional and opinionated, gullible, pompous and snobbish ('Anthony Aloysius St John Hancock' was the character's pretentious full name), Hancock inhabited a recognisable world – a Britain, like him, much put upon and increasingly uncertain of its place. The show was to last until 1960 but in 1956, concurrently, Hancock started to appear on television using the same title, the same writers and the same formula. The 57 episodes transmitted over the next five years laid down a marker for British television situation comedy that is still in place. Galton and Simpson had discovered that all the small screen needed was, essentially, duologues with strong writing and consummate playing, the one provided by them and the other by Hancock and his co-star, Sid James. Hancock, in reality a driven perfectionist, was never satisfied and, increasingly troubled by (among other things) James's ever-growing stature, he forced the show to finish its run in 1960.

It took a couple of years to find a classic variety programme but in 1956 the BBC poached a cockney band-leader, Billy Cotton, who had done a few shows at the end of the previous year on ITV. He was given a showcase, at first entitled *Wakey, Wakey*, which kept him on the screen and in the forefront of popularity for the next twelve years. On the dramatic front, the most immediately successful counter-programme was *Dixon of Dock Green*, a popular police series based on a 1949 feature film, which was to last for 21 years.

Of course, none of this assuaged the left and the intellectual elite, although the cries of woe were, absent the sin of popularity, almost entirely ill-founded. In fact, for the BBC the arrival of a challenger forced a better solution to the issue of programming balance on a single TV channel than the Corporation had been able to discover in the first half of the 1950s. But competition also sharpened an implicit problem which continues to haunt the BBC into the new millennium: if a BBC programme or genre of programming is popular, why is it not provided commercially? If it is not popular, why is it being paid for by all licence holders? The BBC successfully fended off the answer to this conundrum for the better part of half a century, although whenever its audience share fell significantly behind ITV's the issue loomed larger and was deemed by the BBC's highest management to require response. For the rest of the time, when it achieved a measure of parity with the commercial service, it could defend itself in part because its popular material was of a quality which silenced its critics (e.g. *Hancock's Half-Hour* or even, in its early years, *Dixon of Dock Green*). Moreover, the BBC was long able to trade on goodwill accumulated during the war, to the point where its timidity and failings were (and are) forgiven, even as ITV's serious contributions to widening the range of mainstream television expression are, equally, forgotten.

ITV was also challenged in return by the BBC. It might have brought Lucy and quiz prize-money to Britain but, unnoticed by its critics, it tended to match the BBC's programming mix rather than copy an American network's. It was bound by the terms of the Television Act which established it – requiring, for example, 'due impartiality' in its coverage, forbidding religious and political advertisements; but it was even more constrained by previously established audience tastes, which had been conditioned by the BBC. Funding method, it turned out, was not the sole determinant of a TV channel's output range or its quality. ITV not only produced specific replies to the BBC – *This Week* v. *Panorama*, or *Survival* instead of Attenborough's series – it, rather than the BBC, was also responsible for a number of breakthroughs, especially in drama and news.

The BBC did have a somewhat attenuated tradition of new 'serious' drama on both media. In 1954 Dylan Thomas had provided the Third

Programme with radio's only canonical play, *Under Milk Wood*. The live New York TV dramas were not unknown either. For example, a young Canadian director, Alvin Rakoff, persuaded the BBC to let him mount a British production of *Requiem for a Heavyweight* in 1957.[13] In 1958, another Canadian, Sidney Newman, was poached from CBC in Toronto to take over as producer of *Armchair Theatre*, an anthology drama series, for ABC Television, which held the weekend licence for London and the Midlands. The series, which had started in 1956, was already a success, but Newman thought to hold the audience he inherited from *Sunday Night at the London Palladium* with a new approach: 'I said we should have an original play policy with plays that were going to be *about* the very people who owned TV sets – which is really a working-class audience.' This shameless massaging of 'the monstrous "ego" of the common man' immediately produced British television's first original masterwork from an original script – Alun Owen's *No Trams to Lime Street* with Billy Whitelaw and Jack Hedley. Even the accuracy of the Liverpool accents was fresh; Newman was instructed by the head of ABC TV's parent company, 'You tell those darn actors next time to speak fucking English'.[14] But the audience understood well enough and Newman and commercial television brought the revolt against the drawing-room gentilities of the live stage, where rebellion had been heralded by John Osborne's 1956 stage-play *Look Back in Anger*, to the small screen.

Given his ideological position, Newman was, of course, more than willing to mount unashamedly popular drama. He was the executive under whom *The Avengers*, a fantastical witty espionage series, was commissioned. It started in 1961, but the 50 episodes made with Patrick Macnee and Diana Rigg from 1965 were among the very few contemporary (i.e. non-'heritage') British shows to have any impact in North America, as well as being a hit at home. In the 1960s, the sense of oscillation between discrete 'levels' of culture, as these had been enshrined in the BBC's radio output, was being eroded. Casting Rigg, a star of the Royal Shakespeare Company, as sexy, leather-clad 'Avenger' Emma Peel raised no eyebrows and certainly had no negative impact on her career. After *The Avengers* she returned, in the 1970s, to the National Theatre.

ITV also forced the BBC to rethink its news coverage. News had been a problem for television from the outset – unlike, say, sport, which obviously worked very well on the small screen. The Germans had covered the Olympics in Berlin in 1936 and the BBC OB unit was at Wimbledon in 1937 and a year later televised its first soccer international (England v. Scotland) and its first cup final (Huddersfield Town v. Preston North End). In the US, boxing – a dramatic, contained, live evening affair – dominated the nascent post-war schedule throughout the late 1940s, to be joined by wrestling and other indoor events, including rodeo or horse-trotting races.

News was another matter. The issue was straight forward: how to meld the unvisual yet, especially after the war, journalistically authoritative radio bulletins, with the visual, but widely despised, cinema newsreels (which were characterised at the time, with some justice, by the musician and wit Oscar Levant as 'six catastrophes concluded by a fashion show').

The earliest news preserved in the CBS archive is a tele-recording of Douglas Edwards presenting the main evening bulletin on 7 April 1949.[15] The programme oscillated between what was essentially the radio bulletin with Edwards talking to camera as the main image, and two film reels, one international – replete with continuous orchestral music in true newsreel style – and the other domestic, both being voiced-over, live, by Edwards. Some attempts at illustrating the 'radio' sections, holding up pictures, in this case of the baby Prince Charles, to the camera, were to be soon abandoned; others were the shape of things to come. The first item was a complex story about the introduction of the farm subsidy system. Edwards's piece to camera was illustrated by three shots from the film archive of combine-harvesters at work plus an animated caption-card (actually mounted on a stand in the studio and manually manipulated), to explain, using reveals, how the new system was to work. Such integration of various inputs was to solve the problem and, by the mid-1950s, the form of American television news was set.

Although by 1948 the BBC had a news-film exchange programme with NBC, it did not develop such a flexible, integrated, illustrated style. Instead it used its American film and, more, its own to produce a *BBC Television Newsreel* several times a week, its only gesture to the new medium being the opening title, which featured a television transmission mast. As for a news bulletin proper, there was a fear that any journalist in vision would, by their expression, betray bias. Instead, from July 1954, an uneasy mixture of newsreel intertitles, as headlines, and single pictures ('seen here in the wire photograph') was deployed for five minutes or so as 'an illustrated summary of the news' prior to the newsreel.

This was the hesitancy that the threat of ITV killed off. The companies who had been successful in their bids for TV licences established a wholly owned but distinctly managed news subsidiary, ITN, which began broadcasting using an American-style in-vision news*caster* and no newsreel. ITN also deliberately adopted a less deferential approach to interviewing. Robin Day, a barrister by training, deployed a briskness with powerful interviewees that was as revolutionary in its way as anything the 'Angry Young Men' were putting on stage.[16]

ITV continued in other ways to make the running, for example, challenging the reporting restrictions on elections enshrined in the Representation of the People's Act. In the *Morecambe and Wise Show*, the network managed to transfer the traditions of the variety stage to the television studio more successfully than any had done before or since. Eric Morecambe and Ernie Wise even worked their tab act in front of curtains, which were hung, of course, from the studio lighting grid. By the early 1960s, the BBC had acquired the sobriquet 'Auntie' and in the 75 per cent of British homes capable of receiving both services, it was being beaten by ITV 2:1. Nevertheless, in 1962 the next government inquiry into broadcasting, chaired by Sir Harry Pilkington, roundly (and more than a little unfairly) condemned ITV for fulfilling all the negative outcomes predicted for it by the Beveridge Report eleven years earlier.

Thus protected, Director-General Hugh Carlton Greene, who had master-minded the BBC German Service during the war and had played a central role in the rebuilding of broadcasting in the Western zone of occupation after it, took BBC-TV into its most effective era. An anthology launch pad for situation comedies, *Comedy Playhouse*, began in the Light Entertainment department and produced hit after hit, among these *Steptoe and Son*, essentially another brilliant set of duologues by Simpson and Galton. This time they used actors Wilfred Bramwell and Harry H. Corbett to play the central roles, father and son rag-and-bone men.

In the Drama department, the logs moved with the departure of Gielgud's successor, the equally elitist Michael Barry, and Newman transferred from ITV. All drama had been divided into three: plays, now occasionally with new writing; serials; and, at the bottom in the Light Programme position (as it were), series. In 1962, script-writer Troy Kennedy Martin and director John McGrath had already decided to ape, very self-consciously, the American cops series, notably the syndicated *Highway Patrol*, starring Broderick Crawford. The result was *Z–Cars*, studio-based with filmed inserts but done at an American pace, very much a northern reply to what was by then being seen as *Dixon of Dock Green*'s southern softness. To this new openness, Newman added a most significant anthology series, *The Wednesday Play*, which became the hothouse of British television's own 'Golden Age' of drama, a new testament to complement *Armchair Theatre*'s old.

The focus on realistic themes and settings and what one of the Newman's team, producer Tony Garnett, has called 'self-righteous idealism' engendered drama with consistently disturbing authenticity, shot on 16mm, using the recently introduced news and documentary film equipment with aesthetically appropriate gritty results. BBC Film Department objected but Newman insisted. 16mm's cheapness also allowed Garnett and the director with whom he came to be most closely associated, Ken Loach, entirely to dispense with the studio element, recorded on tape 'as if live'. Loach had begun as a director on *Z–Cars* but with film he developed a particular improvisational style, giving actors, for instance, different cue lines before each take to maintain freshness. In this way, the lessons of contemporary French Nouvelle

Vague features, especially the early titles by Jean-Luc Godard (although these were actually shot on 35mm) and the even older Italian tradition of Neo-realism came to Britain. On the big screen the sclerotic, nepotistic local film industry was also having its own *Look Back in Anger* moment, in a few films such as Karel Reisz's *Saturday Night and Sunday Morning* (1960). A more vibrant British cinema, it can be argued, was being watched on television, in the work of Garnett and Loach and their colleagues. *Cathy Come Home* (1966), with adlibbed dialogue and handheld camera, deployed for fiction a look indistinguishable from a documentary on homelessness and caused an immense stir. Another of the group around Newman, Dennis Potter, was to spend three decades into the 1990s exploring the medium with increasingly non-naturalistic experimental 'plays'.

Apart from nurturing such talents, at the BBC Newman was also still capable of dreaming up the unashamedly popular – a little children's sci-fi series featuring a 720-year-old time-travelling doctor, for instance. His one instruction, 'No cheap-jack bugged-eyed monsters', was ignored and in the show's second serial story its eponymous hero, Dr Who, encountered his first Dalek, as cheap-jack and as bug-eyed a BEM as had ever been created. Verity Lambert, *Dr Who*'s producer, saved the Daleks by convincing Newman they were merely post-nuclear holocaust humans who needed some help getting around.

The Drama Group, under Newman, was no stranger to controversy. One Potter play, *Brimstone and Treacle*, was kept off the air for eleven years because of a scene where a traumatised young woman has pleasurable sex with the Devil, and the overt political agenda of much of the output outraged middling taste and opinion on an almost constant basis. But, at Carlton Greene's BBC, shielded by the Pilkington Report's endorsement, this was, almost uniquely in its history, not seen as an automatically bad thing. In other parts of the BBC, irreverence was also stirring. The old radio Talks department had metamorphosed into TV Current Affairs, a genre of programming deemed to be midway between the news and documentary. This was responsible for *Panorama* and, when programming had been introduced in 1956 to fill the slot between 6 and 7 p.m. (which had been deliberately left empty to allow parents to get their children to bed – the so-called 'Toddler's Truce'), Current Affairs was chosen to programme it. *Tonight*, with an eclectic mixture of trivia and comment, brought a new informality to non-fictional production. Performers on camera, for example, would pick up the phone to talk to the gallery (as the BBC called control boxes) when things went wrong.

Successfully arguing for the late night Saturday slot, Alasdair Milne (later to be Director General) and Donald Baverstock, *Tonight*'s creators, assigned Ned Sherrin to produce something newsy and light. The result was the satirical *That Was the Week That Was*, plugging into the world of Oxbridge satire exemplified by the hit stage revue, *Beyond the Fringe*. Such a tone had never before been heard on television. A savage political attack on Tory leader Alec Douglas-Home, for example, finished with presenter David Frost, naturally abrasive and given to a somewhat curious over-emphatic delivery, telling the camera: 'And so, there is a choice for the electorate; on the one hand Lord Home – and on the other Mr Harold Wilson. Dull Alec versus Smart Alec.'[17] Six hundred outraged viewers phoned in to express their displeasure. Another 300 wrote. 'Auntie' had thrown off her corsets, if only for the moment. *That Was the Week That Was* was prematurely cancelled in December 1963 on the specious grounds that 1964 was an election year. Its post-election successor, *Not So Much a Programme More a Way of Life*, suffered the same fate with even less overt explanation in 1965.

The Pilkington Report's carte blanche for the BBC suggested that it be given a second television channel, colour and local radio. Yet in the 1960s, as in the late 1940s, the problem was that money was required to expand services before the higher revenues (from increased licence fees) accrued to pay for them. The BBC was happy to have a second channel, to leave its first freer to compete with ITV, but the black and white TV licence fee remained the same although television output jumped 50 per cent. Taking the lead in pushing for colour, for which a fee-hike was agreed, meant that the BBC asked the government for a favour, since

365

increasing the licence was always unpopular; whereas had the demand been left to ITV, the BBC would have needed to be rescued on competitive grounds. BBC2 began in 1964, colour TV transmissions and the first local radio station (in Leicester) in 1967. By 1970, the Corporation was, unsurprisingly, in the red, threatening it with a hidden, but potentially heightened, dependency on the political process.

All over Europe, television expanded, increasingly at the expense of the original public broadcast channels. UK commercial local radio stations had been licensed after 1972. Italy followed suit, allowing both commercial local radio and television in 1976. The TV stations that emerged were to be the building blocks from which Silvio Berlusconi assembled three national commercial networks. In France, a second channel was added in 1964 and a regionally based third channel in 1973. In 1982 the first channel, TF1, was completely privatised while France 2 and 3 remained uncommercial state broadcasters. In Britain, another commercially funded service, Channel 4, owned by the licensing authority itself joined ITV.[18] Two more commercial French channels, including one funded on a pay-per-view basis, were also created. By the end of that decade, no Western European country preserved ad-free television. All the Western European countries but Austria, Ireland and Switzerland were now copying Italy and Britain in running dual systems. The exceptions had allowed commercials on the state system; but, still, only Luxembourg had a purely commercial system. In the USA, Australia and Canada, where there were also dual systems, the public broadcasters, always attenuated in America, were increasingly under pressure.

'Multiple systems operators'

Television's technology was also changing. Quickest of the advances to penetrate the home was the domestic videotape cassette, developed by the Japanese. They had shrunk the 2-inch wide tape used by broadcasters, which had seriously impacted on the organisation of TV production and scheduling from the late 1950s on, to half an inch, encasing it in a plastic box, a 'videocassette', which word entered the language by the mid-1970s. The videocassette used the television cathode ray tube of the domestic receiver to display its signal and it broke the tyranny of the TV broadcasting scheduler, allowing for 'time-shifting' and personal archiving. It also enabled a new stream of programming via rented or purchased pre-recorded cassettes, largely, initially, of feature films or pornography. Ten per cent of Americans rented movies in 1979; four years later, it was 70 per cent. This success was, as ever, not merely a function of the technology. Hollywood, alarmed by the videocassette player's recording capability, had sued Sony, then only a hardware manufacturer, for facilitating copyright infringement. In October 1981, the court threw the case out, saving the studios from themselves because, over the next two decades, the US video sales and rental market would become three times more valuable than the domestic box office.

The law and regulation were similarly crucial to other media technologies in the United States: cable, for example. The Supreme Court, conscious of the discrepancy in signal provision between urban and rural America, had affirmed cable operators' right to rebroadcast TV signals in defiance of copyright, but the FCC, acting for their primary clients the broadcasting licensees, had moved in the opposite direction. FCC hostility could not dent cable's steady growth: 850,000 mainly rural homes served by 800 'Ma 'n' Pa' providers by the end of the 1950s became 5.9 million subscribers on 2,750 systems, many owned by the same 'multiple systems operators'. Two decades later, more than one in ten television households were cabled. In the early 1980s FCC cable regulations, and the controls exercised over cable systems by municipal governments, were both either relaxed or removed.

All of this had been accomplished with almost no original programming but on 4 November 1972, 365 subscribers in Wilkes-Barre, in the centre of Pennsylvania's depressed anthracite coal industry, the heartland of cable television, had seen the very first transmission of a new

367

original service, Home Box Office – HBO. For an extra fee over and above the basic cable charge that first night subscribers received a hockey game and the feature film, *Sometime a Great Nation*, uninterrupted by commercials. The idea did not prosper until the FCC agreed in 1974 to license domestic satellite TV transmissions, which it had previously refused to do, essentially because it was protecting AT&T's long-line co-axial activities, then worth some $75 million a year. Without satellite transmission, HBO's owner, Time Inc, could not have assembled an economically viable subscriber base; but with the two transponders the FCC allowed it to lease on Westar, the first domestic communications satellite, it could. The live transmission of the Ali–Frazier heavyweight title fight in the Philippines ('The Thrilla from Manila' as the bout was billed) to the 'head-ends' of cable systems, demonstrated that a fee-paying, national audience could be reassembled. By 1975, HBO was in nearly 300,000 homes and the $1.3 million a year it was costing Time to lease the transponders was well justified. Eight years later, with a schedule of recent features, sport, a degree of sexual explicitness forbidden the networks and, perhaps above all, no advertisements, it had twelve million subscribers and, on occasion, achieved a bigger audience than any of the three terrestrial networks.

Others also did well from the satellite. Ted Turner, for example, was to float a media empire on the back of a minor Atlanta TV station which he rebroadcast nationally via satellite to small cable systems desperate to fill their channels. Buying programming as a local station and selling advertising as a national one was the clue to WTBS's financial success. It enabled him to buy the MGM film library – *Gone with the Wind*, *The Wizard of Oz*, *Citizen Kane* – and to found a cable-news service, CNN, in 1980. By the early 1980s, there were four domestic satellites carrying at least 40 services, although most were in effect unprofitable 'loss leaders' designed to enhance cable's attractiveness.

Elsewhere, the same drive for increasing channel choice underpinned cable. To take an extreme European example, TV in Belgium followed radio in importing signals from the surrounding countries and over 80 per cent of homes received their television via a wire. Canada, similarly, was heavily cabled, in its case to obtain desirable American network television. Importation of distant or even foreign signals, improving reception or, to a lesser extent, providing specialised channels was the driver allowing cable to curtail the dominance of broadcast television. Most dramatically in the United States, the terrestrial networks' audience share fell inexorably from 93 per cent in 1975 to just over 50 per cent by the end of the century.

This disguises the fact that less had changed than might have been thought. For one thing, the absolute number of TV households in the United States had increased during this period by over 20 million so network advertising revenues as a whole had fallen less precipitously than had audience share. In fact, terrestrial television remained profitable enough for Rupert Murdoch, closed out of cable growth in America, to create a conventional broadcast network, Fox TV, during this period.[19] The American cable industry, in effect, denied the broadcasters the benefits due to them from having an ever-growing population to serve, but it did not destroy them.

It could not, because it did not have, nor could it ever earn, the revenues to do so. Each of the American networks earned as much individually as the 30 or so major nationally distributed advertising-supported cable services did collectively and, therefore, no basic cable channel managed to mount a successful challenge to the networks in the twentieth century. Basic cable was (and is) only possible because of endless repeats, most 'off-network', spun as 'convenience scheduling' but driven by these revenue realities. With 45 per cent of the nation wired by 1985, cable secured a mere 5 per cent of TV's advertising take. Cable, of course, had a further $7,420 million to spend from basic subscriptions, but those revenues had to sustain a vastly more expensive distribution system than the masts – the 'sticks' – that the broadcasters use. The cable operators, closely controlled by the municipalities which licensed them to erect (or bury) their wires and constantly badgered by an FCC eager to protect free-to-air broadcasters, achieved their best moment for dominance in the Reagan era. The 1984 Cable Communications Act gave the industry carte blanche as broad as Pilkington's to the BBC in the

1960s. It removed municipal control and hobbled the FCC and the broadcasters but all the cable industry managed to accomplish was to become such a by-word for poor service and uncontrolled rate hikes that it had to be re-regulated, over President Bush Snr's veto, a decade later by a Congress whose postbags contained more letters of complaint about its doings than on any other subject.

The bottom line was that the cable channels have almost totally failed to alter the established genres and forms of TV broadcasting, never mind create new ones. The 24-hour news channels, for example, repeat a traditional news bulletin every half-hour – its contents remaining almost entirely unchanged hour after hour. That the 24-hours news channels could clear down for major events merely echoed network procedures – President Kennedy's assassination in 1963 was the first time the American broadcasters had responded to an event in this way.[20] Only shopping and sex were, as it were, new. Otherwise, the 'changed' TV landscape has actually meant little alteration of the programming scenery.

Hostile broadcasters, nevertheless, might well have been overstating the case by describing the cable channels as '48 times the usual rubbish'. For one thing, not all the additional channels were 'rubbish'. True community access where a real community still existed and voices within it could be cultivated to use the medium, or channels cablecasting governmental assemblies and meetings at every level, were socially valuable and the subject of much experimentation. The subscription channels' lack of ads and their more adult programming – when this was not mere titillation – was an advance which eventually was to produce a level of programme sophistication never seen on the networks. Of course, one could also claim that the rubbish, which certainly predominated, was anyway far from usual. Dr Johnson had once complained to Sheridan that he was an unusual fool: 'Such stupidity, Sherry, is not in nature. You must be at pains to study it.' Unquestionably it was no common lack of creativity that generated hours of people selling exercise machines or carpets; 'phantom train' images which lasted, not as they had on film in the last years of the nineteenth century, for a minute, but for hour after hour through the night; amateur chat programmes of stultifying banality; off-network shows of little worth but great (in TV terms) antiquity, all end-lessly, endlessly, repeated. Somebody must indeed have been at pains studying how to transmit such tat.

This is not a matter of a supposed lost 'Golden Age' and an implication that the past offered consistently richer TV pickings would be hard to sustain. Any sense that the medium was more creative in its first decades must be primarily attributed to its immaturity. Having discovered a rich range of effective formulae across all genres, but being limited culturally by millennia of performance traditions and centuries of non-fiction communication forms, a certain repetitiveness and sense of tiredness was bound to grow through time. Compensatory searches by producers betting their all on cheap outrage to revive jaded audiences' palates increase the power of an argument that the medium is 'dumbing down'; yet without a doubt television's significance in its audiences' lives remains, even though people are very slowly reducing the time they give it. Whether it dumbed the medium down or not, cable TV's 'revolution' certainly turned out to involve less than its hyped billing actually delivered.

Nevertheless, the technological enchanter would not let go. On 28 April 1981, Sony unveiled its latest wonder, production-line High Definition Television (HDTV) equipment in Tokyo. On hand to bless the range was Francis Ford Coppola, who announced, a tad prematurely, that he would never again make a movie on film. The Sony system, which produced an analogue signal with 1,125 lines resolution, the electronic equivalent of 35mm, on a 16:9 tube, was being unveiled as a substitute for celluloid because it had already failed to convince the world's broadcasters that it should be a new TV standard. It was to be no more successful as a film substitute, but it did have an impact on broadcast television's technological future. It kick-started a fundamental R&D programme into using digital pulse coding to modulate a signal. Hype around yet another technology-based revolution in the way we use TV began, blithely ignoring how fundamentally unrevolutionary cable was turning out to be. Like Jehovah's Witnesses, who have never been deterred when their predictions of Armageddon prove false, technicist witnesses began trumpeting predictions of yet another technological 'rupture': 'being digital' was going to change everything.

Sources

Albert Bandura, Dorothea Ross and Sheila A. Ross (1961), 'Transmission of Aggression Through Imitation of Aggressive Model', *Journal of Abnormal and Social Psychology* 63.

Asa Briggs (1995), *The History of Broadcasting in the United Kingdom*, Oxford: Oxford University Press.

Les Brown (1992), *Encyclopaedia of Television*, Detroit: Gale Research.

John Cain (1992), *The BBC: 70 Years of Broadcasting*, London: BBC.

Harry Castleman and Walter J. Podrazik (1982), *Watching TV: Four Decades of American Television*, New York: McGraw Hill.

John Corner (ed.) (1991), *Popular Television in Britain*, London: British Film Institute.

John Corner and Sylvia Harvey (1996), *Television Times*, London: Arnold.

Geoffrey Hare (1997), 'The Broadcasting Media', in J. Flower (ed.), *France Today*, London: Hodder & Stoughton.

Hilde Himmelweit *et al.* (1958), *Television and the Child: An Empirical Study of the Effect of Television on the Young*, Oxford: Oxford University Press.

Timothy Hollins (1984), *Beyond Broadcasting: Into the Cable Age*, London: British Film Institute.

Stuart Lang (1991), 'Banging in Some Reality: The Original *Z-Cars*' in J. Corner (ed.), *Popular Television in Britain*, London: British Film Institute.

Alex McNeil (1980), *Total Television*, Harmondsworth: Penguin.

Howard Newcomb (ed.) (1997), *Encyclopaedia of Television*, Chicago: Fitzroy Dearborn.

Denis Norden, Sybil Harper and Norma Gilbert (1985), *Coming to You Live!: Behind the Scenes Memories of Forties and Fifties Television*, London: Methuen.

Ned Sherrin (1983), *A Small Thing – Like An Earthquake*, London: Weidenfeld & Nicolson.

Anthony Smith and Richard Patterson (1998), *Television: An International History*, Oxford: Oxford University Press.

A. M. Sperber (1986), *Murrow: His Life and Times*, New York: Freundlich Books.

Tise Vahimagi (1994), *British Television*, Oxford: Oxford University Press.

Jan Wieten, Graham Murdock and Peter Dahlgren (eds) (2000), *Television Across Europe*, London: Sage.

CONVERGENCE

Epilogue

'FREE EXPRESSION IS IN VERY DEEP TROUBLE': MEDIA TO 1991 AND BEYOND

'The digital microchip is the Gothic Cathedral of our time'

> Tired of watching TV? With the artful programming of tele-computers, you could spend the day interacting with Henry Kissinger, Kim Basinger or Billy Graham. . . . You could take a fully interactive course in physics or computer science with the world's most exciting professors. . . . You could have a fully interactive workday without commuting to the office or run a global corporation. You could watch your child play baseball at a high school across the country, view the Super Bowl from any point in the stadium that you choose. . . . All on a powerful high resolution display.

Behind this smokescreen of promised wonders, envisioned in the early 1990s by minor US Republican speechwriter George Gilder, lies a hostility to the existing world of liberal free expression. 'The digital microchip' was for Gilder 'the Gothic Cathedral of our time . . . It will transform business, education and art. It can renew our entire culture.' Yet whose idea of a purposeful activity embraced chats with 'virtual' conservative politicians and Baptist preachers? Who was 'tired of TV'? Who felt the 'entire culture' needed renewing? Who else but Gilder and those of like mind? His intervention made him momentarily a player in the deepening American *Kulturkampf* of the millennium's last decades, a sustained conservative war on liberal expression which was part of a wider political divisiveness.

Such technicist excitement over electronics had begun in earnest with 'robot brains' in the 1950s, swelled into a supposed 'information revolution' thereafter and climaxed in the 'dot.com' stock market bubble at the end of the 1990s. Throughout this half-century, the hype was dependent on a fundamental misunderstanding of the digital, grounded in a basic loss of its history and an imperfect sense of physics. The binary had been integral to some advanced mathematics since the nineteenth century. The crucial mathematical formulae to determine digitising sampling rates for signals of different complexities – sound, say, as against vision – was published in the 1920s. The first actual device to sample a sound wave digitally was constructed and patented by a telephone engineer, A. H. Reeve, in 1938. By 1940, John Atanasoff had built a digital calculator to solve linear algebraic equations. Solid-state electronics had an equally long development time: from the first demonstrations of semi-conductor materials in the 1870s; through the theoretical physics behind the transistor in 1920s; to transistors themselves in 1948; and to the first marketable general integrated solid-state circuit – an oscillator – four years later, designed by Jack Kilbey at Texas Instruments. Gilder's 'digital microchip' was itself 25 years old by the time he was writing, having been perfected by Marcian (Ted) Hoff at Intel in 1969. That these technologists – Kilbey, Hoff and many others – who had a hand in its development remain as anonymous as any medieval ecclesiastical architect is crucial to the oxymoronic idea that a fundamentally transformative 'digital revolution' is under way.

Digital microchips are in essence merely processors of electrical currents that have been created by the various input devices of a computer or modulated by light or sound through the transducing agency of camera chip or microphone. These signals are sampled and encoded into a digitised stream of electronic presences and absences, like the Morse telegraph, but this does not mean, on its face, that when they are decoded, they differ *of themselves* from signals modulated in other ways – to the eye they look like images and to the ear they sound like sounds. It is also more or less irrelevant that, in their journey from keyboard, mouse (etc.), camera and mike to the eye or ear, encoding renders such signals identical electronically speaking – for all that this is spun as an extremely significant phenomenon known as 'convergence'. At one level, a converged world of wonderful machines – telephones that are cameras, computers that are televisions, radios that are 'ipods' – was made possible by digitisation (and is to hand 'in the metal'); but what functions in reality might in the long term usefully go together and with what social consequences has yet to be determined. Putting all these machines in the same box, however small and elegant, cannot mean that much since such functions, because of the human senso-rium – eyes v. ears – if for no other reason, must remain discrete. Nor is it true that a multiplicity of channels or the ease with which images can be meshed together *requires* digitisation, although in digital such pro-liferation and special effects can be accomplished efficiently.

'Convergence' was not just a matter of nifty devices (or even one extremely nifty device – the 'comradtelcam-pod', say), hundreds of channels and fancy special effects. Technological convergence, it was claimed, was making inevitable the rise of international media con-glomerates operating across a range of previously discrete industries, from publishing through recorded music to broadcasting to movie pro-duction. This rhetoric implicitly downplayed the usual logic of capital concentration as a cause. One box plausibly implied, or so it was held, one supplier of signals to that box. Rupert Murdoch was, by this light, as powerless a victim of a particular technological 'reality' as the least-resistant early adopter of digital's newest gizmos. Such an ideologically significant rationale, especially at a time of neo-liberal deregulation, is not only naïve in economic and political terms; the 'convergence' con-cept even at the technological level is somewhat asinine. It is no more profound than suggesting all writing 'converges', whether done by pen, pencil or brush, types, typewriter or word processor: it does – but, to use what William Labov once called in another context the 'withering interjection', 'so what?' That people can listen to their radio over their digital television – so what? That they can make telephone calls on their computers – so what? The reality is that the change-over to digi-tal is far more comparable to the move from analogue amplitude

377

modulation to analogue frequency modulation in radio 40 years ago than it is, say, to the slightly earlier post-war shift from radio to television.

Gilder's vision, although inherently a veiled shill for late capital, was shared by liberal or radical technicists as well as those across the political spectrum who were hostile to, rather than celebratory of, the supposed power of digital technology. For all technicists, pro or anti, misunderstanding of the significance of the digital is simply grounded in a failure to distinguish necessary from sufficient means. The capacity of digital modulation systems and the increasing power of computers and the networks that connect them to provide the necessary infrastructure to sustain Gilder's vision is insufficient of itself to overcome any social or cultural factors set against it. These remain vast: humans are gregarious, including the CEOs of 'global corporations', and while commuting may be stressful, it is less damaging for most people than is solitary confinement, even if that is voluntarily assumed as home-based work. (This has been a main reason for the extreme slowness in the development of videophones as an alternative to face-to-face meetings over the last 80 years.) Children might be assuaged by the thought that Mom and Dad are watching them at bat on some high-def TV screens but surely they would prefer them to be sitting in the bleachers. Most of the views of the Super Bowl are, in terms of representing a game's progress, more or less of equal worth. That a thing can, or might, be done is less than no reason to believe it will be done. Technological capacity is not the main determinant.

Indeed, the development of digital television, along lines presumably still making Gilder 'tired', is as much a creature of his own neo-liberal economic laisser-faire ideology as it is a consequence of any microchip – or perhaps more so. Mass communication systems demand compatibility because without it they cannot service a mass. Ignoring this, neo-liberal laisser-faire technicism argues that technological 'standards' for mass communications, imposed even with the agreement of the players, inhibit market forces and should therefore be avoided. In consequence, and in contrast to the introduction of radio or television, digital media are being diffused with a high degree of chaos – 18 different formats, six at high-definition level (over 1,000 horizontal lines of resolution or its equivalent), four wide-screen. There are twelve different professional video recording standards. The confusion has been made bearable thanks only to the computer's ability to translate between incompatible encoding systems.[1] Even the compression format produced by the International Standards Organisation's Motion Picture Expert Group (MPEG) itself went through three formulations in its first decade. This sort of technological incoherence is attributed to the unprecedented speed-up of technological change; but that speed-up is more apparent than real. It is far more the result of a change in attitude and process; what would have previously remained in the lab while interested parties argued about it in a forum created by government, today gets rushed to market as quickly as possible and computing is left to sort out the mess. For instance, further (and total) audience fragmentation through computerised automated individual recording systems threatens the economic basis of the 'million-dollar-an-hour' rule – how much must be spent on programming to meet audience expectations; but it is on the market. Its potential effect can be contained because the same computing power can register the audience, however fragmented, reassembling it for advertisers or subscription billing. Computing power also enables faux-digital TVs with 19:6 screens, which are actually analogue devices producing distorted wide-screen images at the edge of acceptability, to receive digital signals – and, in effect, ignore the fact that they are digital. The right, sacred to neo-liberals, to sell such devices trumps everything, even if doing this inhibits the supposedly transformative 'digital change-over'.

Digitisation, as long as it was combined with computer image-compression, was necessary to the next stage of satellite transmission, direct broadcasting to the home; but it was not sufficient of itself to cause the establishment of this as a third platform for domestic television. In the 1970s the use of domestic satellites to send analogue signals to the cable industry and, eventually, also feed the broadcasting networks via large 4.5-metre dishes, had produced a significant rural phenomenon in

America as home owners started to erect receivers on their lands, 'stealing' cable signals and eavesdropping on network material. Politically cable operators had failed to control the spread of these TVRO (Television Receive-Only) antennae because, at least in theory, the receivers were in districts not served by cable and, within a decade of their being given FCC approval on this basis in 1976, more than a million were in place across the countryside. However, the same legislation that freed the cable operators from municipal control in the 1980s also allowed providers such as HBO signal encryption for the first time, so they could begin to collect subscriptions from the free-booting private dish owners.

The military had been shrinking the diameter of the receiving dish for battleground use throughout the 1970s, using ever higher-powered satellites to transmit to them. Irrespective of the state of the technology, the FCC remained loath to license a civilian service broadcasting directly to small 1-metre dishes on domestic roofs from space as this would admit another competitor to terrestrial broadcasting in addition to cable. It was not until the 1984 Act, balancing the advantages cable gained that year, that direct broadcasting via satellite (DBS) was introduced in the USA but the FCC and its terrestrial broadcasting clients need not have worried. Between cable and the VCR, DBS, at least initially, had little impact. In Britain, where cable had yet to take root, DBS flourished. In 1986, the commercial TV licensing authority allowed the inauguration of two services. One, Rupert Murdoch's Sky Television, rapidly absorbed the other. Within a decade one in five British households were paying Murdoch for television in addition to paying their BBC licence fee and the cumulative audience for all the new channels had reached 11.4 per cent. DBS was introduced in West Germany in 1987 and was equally successful. By 1996, 200 transponders were servicing a Europe-wide market.

Digital signals require about three times the bandwidth of analogue, 20 kilohertz instead of 6.5, but they nevertheless permit a proliferation of satellite-borne signals because they are easier to compress through computing power – a rare example of an immediately obvious convergence advantage between television and computing. Compression also facilitates conversion into analogue, permitting the necessary degree of compatibility with existing (and faux-digital wide-screen) home receivers. Interactivity – 'down-stream' responsiveness to viewer inputting – was also greatly enhanced by digital encoding. These two factors – DBS and interactivity – sustained the digital TV research programme inadvertently initiated by Sony in 1981.

What difference this would really make to programming was lost in the hubbub. Seized by technicist enthusiasm and its attendant technological purblindedness, some politicians in Britain decided that there was a 'race' under way to 'turn off' analogue signals, as if the digital really did offer a vision of a needed cultural 'renewal'. Multi-channel TV was no longer cable's unique selling point but digital DBS has brought as little that is fundamentally new as cable did; and that little scarcely depends on digital signal encoding – sex workers soliciting expensive telephone calls, for example. Interactively accessing at will discrete inset images – say on a news channel – is certainly an advance, if not exactly of a fundamental nature. In the 1990s, much talk was heard arguing that enhanced interactivity along such lines would allow viewers to intervene to condition a narrative, choosing different plot options to build individualised stories – as if narrativity, so essential a human construction that some believe it to be at the heart of our ability to acquire language, needed 'improving' in this way. Unlike the technicists propounding this vision, people in general seemed to understand the difference between creation and consumption and apparently valued the active pleasures of decoding stories too much to want to write or produce them instead.

Both DBS and cable have left terrestrial primetime surprisingly unchanged. For half a century, American primetime, dominated by three networks, has almost always consisted of between 70 and 80 slots. Each new season around a third of these are filled with fresh offerings in well-established genres and all but three or four are soon cancelled, not lasting into the following season. This pattern was as true of 2000 as it was of 1960. A third of the top 20 shows in the new millennium were cop series; and, although basic cable was by now achieving audiences close in size to those of the networks, a third of its 'hits' were cop series too. The new thing was the graphic depiction of the aftermath of violence (aided by computer-generated imaging (CGI) but not dependent on it), a sort of pornography of the forensic. The rest of the new had even less to do with the digital. The fad for 'reality' voyeuristic programming, for instance, relied on a surveillance technology that has existed for more than 30 years. The most notable change was that half a dozen programmes featured openly gay people, unthinkable in earlier decades, but this was a consequence of the struggle for gay rights: technology had nothing to do with it. Digitised TV primetime 'will become my time', warbled Nicholas Negroponte, an architect who had talked MIT into establishing a Media Lab[2] and another technicist of Gilder's persuasion. But to what end? We are still addicted to cop shows and voyeurism. In the US, analogue was supposed to be 'turned off' as a modulation system for signal distribution in 2002. It wasn't. In Britain, the 'turn-off' has been delayed until 2012, but it does not really matter much because culturally, the 'race' to digital is a race to nowhere.

'Films in the future'

In 1998, for the first time, at the annual celebration of film that is the televised Oscar ceremonies, the images seen on the screens during the presentations in the Kodak Theatre were, paradoxically, not 'stored' on celluloid. Digital laser projectors, patented by Texas Instruments (TI), were used. Celluloid's last protection, its superiority to electronic imaging as a display technology, disappeared before the eyes of Hollywood's assembled great and good. The following year, Pixel, a company founded on CGI, released *Toy Story II*, a sequel to its phenomenally successful cartoon *Toy Story* (1995). Ever since *Tron* in 1982, with a plot that takes place inside a computer, cameraless effects were finding their way into mainstream live-action pictures, often without the audience realising. CGI created armies and crowds, complex superimpositions and, more obviously, the impossible antics of the action blockbusters that spoke to the audience-dominant demographic of young people. All electronic digital effects, however, were transferred by laser printing to celluloid, and film remained the distribution medium even for *Toy Story*, a movie whose production was entirely cameraless. Its sequel was the first 'film' to be not only made in the computer but projected directly from the computer hard drive as well.

It is entirely possible, albeit somewhat cynical, to suggest that the TI system is not the end of the matter simply because the projector that produces images of a luminosity and definition to match film on cinema-sized screens is an electro-mechanical device. Electro-mechanical devices, as the histories of both the television and the computer itself reveal, tend to be way-stations en route to fully electronic solutions. The TI machine, created by Larry Hornbeck, who had begun work on optical signal processing at Texas Instruments in 1977, traces its origins to the Eidophor projector of 1939 and other large-screen television display systems produced in the 1970s. Hornbeck's 1987 solution was to attach a 'reflective digital light switch', a microscopic hinged mirror, to every pixel in the digital image, all 1.2 million of them. TI tests support a claim that the hinges will work for 20 years, which would involve 450 billion contacts between moving parts. The company is a long way from having to stand by this as it has installed only 150 such projectors worldwide.

The subservience of the technological to the social is well illustrated by the 'end' of film. *Toy Story II*'s very title speaks to continuity of content. It was well received and widely considered superior to the initial film. On the other hand, *Star Wars Episode II: Attack of the Clones*, the first live-action film to be shot, as well as released, digitally was the least successful of the series. Being entirely digital clearly meant as much to the creativity of the team making this *Star Wars* 'prequel' as having the first Hollywood soundtrack recorded on audiotape meant to the *Son of Cochise* crew in 1962. The hype is of a brave new world of digital production and distribution, a democratisation of cinema. The reality is quite other; it is, indeed, an attack of the clones. As celluloid slowly disappears, mainstream film expression in the West is threatened with

383

infantilisation. Three-quarters of a century ago, minds were exercised as to the potential of cinema as a means of expression. Eisenstein thought that 'films in the future . . . will have to do with philosophy'. Richter wrote, 'To varnish our lives with entertaining stories is too petty a task for this mighty technology, too petty if it is to grow to artistic maturity'. Instead, since *Star Wars* (1977) we have had computers controlling the movement of cameras across models of space ships; or 'bullet time' in *The Matrix* (1999), where actors in the shot move at different speeds thanks to complex computer manipulation of 120 still-camera images reassembled to give Kung-fu fighting a new twist. The technology has become ever mightier, mainstream cinema ever more petty.

'You can't be frivolous in hot metal'

The move from traditional movable type has had parallel limited effect on content. It has also been a slow process. Lithography and photography were both melded with the high-speed press in the second half of the nineteenth century. By 1852, Fox Talbot himself had patented a steel etching system for converting photographs into a printable form, and a steam-driven lithographic press dates from 1865. High-speed photography-based 'rotogravure' presses had been brought to market in 1889 but the real breakthrough occurred in 1905 when simultaneously several printers independently perfected a system for transferring – offsetting – full-page, half-tone photographs as well as text on to a rubber 'blanket'. At a less than revolutionary pace, over the next half-century, offset printing, on electric-driven presses, replaced traditional direct printing from plates and types almost everywhere.

Newspapers remained largely untouched by this change-over until composing itself, which had been the last area to be mechanised in the nineteenth century, was transformed by the computer in the 1960s and 1970s. Computers, children of the Cold War, developed for and dedicated to nuclear science, were nearly as slow to arrive in the world of print as they had been in the world of film and broadcasting. It was not until the 1960s that IBM produced a machine, the 360 series, on a scale usable in medium-sized organisations of all kinds, including the business of typesetting. In the 15 years after 1963, the number of hot-metal Linotype machines in American newspaper offices declined from 11,175 to 1,158 while the number of computer-based photocomposition machines, computers and video terminals increased by at least the same factor. The history of these technologies – offset's centuries and computing's decades of development – typically being ignored, melding them looked revolutionary in the first years of the 1970s. By 1974, hot-metal had gone from the offices of industry leaders such as the *Los Angeles Times*. Composing, and subsequent processes, for instance stereotyping, no longer required distinct equipment and skills. It was now all done – from writing the copy through subediting to page design – at computer terminals; and then offset for printing.

Needless to say, printers, aristocrats of skilled labour who had been organised into unions for centuries, resisted. Their hostility was quite rational. The new technology allowed papers to lose up to a third of their employees while cutting production time by two-thirds and increasing the number of pages. As early as 1947, the International Typographical Union, America's oldest institution of organised labour, had struck against the owners of the Chicago papers over the introduction of a proto-photocomposing system, which enabled a journalist's typewritten copy to go straight to photoengraving without being reset. The printers were out for 22 months. When the London *Times* management sought to introduce new technology in 1978, an ensuing strike closed the paper for 11½ months and cost management upwards of £60 million.

In Britain the balance of power was about to change. In 1979 a radical Tory government was elected under Margaret Thatcher and anti-union legislation followed. In 1985, Rupert Murdoch confirmed that this had broken the power of the printers' 'chapels' by moving all his London operations out of Fleet Street overnight to a new plant to the east of the city in Wapping. Murdoch, the Oxford-educated scion of a respected but quite minor Australian newspaper baron, had parleyed his patrimony, a small chain of papers in Adelaide, into a dominant position, first in Sydney and then in London. The union struck, but Murdoch simply left his workers behind. The Wapping move cost the printers some 6,000 jobs; but electricians could now mind the presses. Murdoch recruited his secretly, with the backing of their right-wing union, 81 miles from London in Southampton. He lost only one day's production.

Management was not merely seized by an ideological hostility to the heart of trade unionism. The truth was that in the developed world in the second half of the twentieth century newspapers were dying, albeit very slowly. For example, by the 1970s, their post-Second World War share of the American advertising market was reduced by a quarter. Total circulation of the British national dailies prior to 'Wapping' had been shrinking – two million copies a day lost between 1950 and 1970. By 1975, just over 14 million copies were being sold. National 'Sundays' sales had shrunk by a third in the same period; local papers by a fifth. It required a certain amount of what Liebling once called 'sporting blood' to gamble the considerable capital outlays involved in removing hot metal against savings which would, unless dramatic midnight flits figured in the business plan, only be achieved after expensive struggles with the workforce. But the prize was great: the change-over cost Murdoch £67 million, for instance, but in the following year his UK profits increased by 40 per cent, some £33 million more than he had made under the old system. Fleet Street's collective ability to walk away from its expensive production workers was funded by the rise in the fortunes of the news agency Reuters in which the press barons were major shareholders. Focusing this firm on financial information rather than general news had increased its profitability more than fifty-fold in the 1970s. The business of printing beside the Fleet river (bricked over by 1800 and now nothing more than a storm sewer) was at an end, nearly half a millennium after Wynkyn de Worde had begun it there at 'the sign of the sun' opposite Shoe Lane in 1501.

With computerised composing and offset printing, more photographs of better quality, many in full colour, as well as larger vivid graphics became commonplace in newspapers. In America especially, additional 'sections' appeared, ever more stuffed with advertising leaflets. District editions with special pages for specific suburban zones were possible. Otherwise, despite the upheaval in production practice, content remained essentially unchanged. Circulations were at best barely stabilised. In the five years post-'Wapping', British tabloid sales still declined by eight per cent. Overall the UK national daily figure is 20 per cent down since 1990. Most worrying of all, there are a third fewer readers aged under 24. Despite this, the press can still be profitable. Its falling sales and ageing demographic are being compensated for by increases in advertising rates. In the last half-century, UK advertising expenditure as a whole has grown from £102 million to over £10,000 million as consumerism has become ever more central to the economic system. In 2000, newspapers' share was still over 40 per cent of that. (Magazines took a further 15 per cent.)

Advertising had itself become big business by the late nineteenth century. By 1900, for example, T. B. Browne, Britain's biggest agency, had over 200 employees in four offices, including Paris. Whole-page newspaper adverts were not unknown and the *Daily Mail* carried one as its front page as early as 1902. The advertising industry's total annual revenues were more than £10 million by then; but circulation posed a problem. Ever since the removal of the stamp duties there had been a question mark over how many copies a title sold and, by the turn of the twentieth century, agencies were demanding 'statements of circulation' from publications before they would do business. In America, this problem was solved in 1914 when the press and the advertising industry established the Audit Bureau of Circulations to produce agreed figures, a solution which the British eventually copied in 1931.

Despite the flow of advertising money, the press remains threatened by shrinking circulation. In Britain, the contemporary excesses of the most down-market titles, the 'Red-Top' tabloids, can be attributed less to new technology or even to increasingly relaxed, less deferential mores than to this seemingly irreversible situation. The headline 'FREDDIE STARR ATE MY HAMSTER', the *Sun*'s splash weeks after the 1985 flit to Wapping, was editor Kelvin Mackenzie's masterpiece, a glorious addition to the canon of great British journalism; or its epitaph. The story, anyway apparently untrue, was three years old and it was peddled to Mackenzie by comedian Starr's PR man – but it caught the eye, lodged in public consciousness and helped propel the *Sun* further on its way to having Britain's biggest circulation, yet it could just as well symbolise a species of rigor mortis. The *Sun* itself was born of a paper, the *Daily Herald*, founded by the trade unions and massively successful in the 1930s; but, in 1964, by now in private ownership, it had been killed off. It was managing to lose £1 million a year on a circulation of 1.25 million. This readership, larger than that of all but three American newspapers today, was, to the mind of British advertisers, not worth having – too old, too northern, too male and, above all, too poor. The nineteenth-century worry that advertisers would come to control editorial in detail has never quite come to pass but, in the 100 years since display advertisements first appeared on the front page, advertising has exerted – as in the case of the *Daily Herald* – an underlying influence.

To prevent a medium speaking only to and for those with money to spend on advertised products and services is the central problem of market-driven organs of opinion and information in a representative democracy. The same underlying long-term decline as in Britain, especially among more popular papers, has been echoed all over the First World. For example, by 1980 in Paris, 31 post-Second World War papers had been reduced to nine; Germany's 255 had shrunk to 121; Denmark's 150 to 45. In essence, the French masses stopped reading papers; the Italians, post-war, once more failed to start to do so. Almost every American city has been reduced to one title. Manhattan still has three dailies;[3] a century ago there were 14. The protection of what was seen as a necessary diversity of political views in newspapers after the Second World War, especially in continental Europe, moved Italy, France, Austria, Sweden, Finland and Norway to use tax money, in contrast to that notion of the separation of powers enshrined in America's First Amendment, to ensure that as full a range of those political opinions as the state deems legitimate was reflected at the news kiosk. Elsewhere, reduced postage rates and other tax breaks have masked a lesser measure of official subvention. Even in countries where no overt role is played by the government, the principle that the press be owned by diverse entities, even if these all turn out to be press barons, is acknowledged and no industry attracts closer attention from anti-monopoly regulatory bodies.

On the afternoon of 15 September 1982 before a tent on the lawn below the Capitol, President Ronald Reagan, House Speaker 'Tip' O'Neill and the Senate Majority Leader Howard Baker were the guests of Al Neuharth, the flamboyant CEO and chairman of Gannett, America's largest newspaper chain, at the debut of 'The Nation's Newspaper'. That day *USA Today* was published only in greater Washington and sold 150,000 copies but soon, at a cost of some $50 million, it was being printed at 30 separate plants across the nation, the first true national newspaper. It took about three and a half minutes for Gannett's computers in Washington to send a black and white page to these presses via the ATS 2 domestic satellite and around 26 minutes to transmit a full-colour page. After printing, 380 trucks then delivered copies to around 80,000 subscribers and 120,000 newsracks, specially designed to look like pavement TVs. Today, *USA Today* has America's largest sale, at just over two million copies.

As early as 1964, Arthur C. Clarke, who had envisioned stationary communication satellites in 1945, had correctly predicted: 'One of the first countries to benefit [from the satellites] will be, rather ironically, the United States, which has never possessed a really national newspaper.'[4] Nobody had been in too much of a rush to test this. The *New York Times* was gingerly expanding its market using remote printing, city by city. It discovered a reasonable demand, but no call for dropping local New York content, almost certainly because buyers were led by expatriate New Yorkers. *USA Today*, Gannett's eighty-ninth title, was an experiment of a different magnitude, an attempt to think through what a national popular paper for the whole nation might be like. Yet although *USA Today* gave an unprecedented full-colour page to its weather forecast, it was still just a weather forecast. Its two pages of 'briefs', one from each of the 50 states of the Union, was as much a monument to the arbitrary nature of news judgement as it was to information. Gannett had worked out that *USA Today*'s primary readership would have to come from the 850,000 Americans who were then boarding planes each day, or the one and quarter million who found themselves in a hotel room. Neuharth intuited that a tit-bit from home is what they needed.

For the press as a whole, satellites meant as little to content as did offset and computing. Such changes as mark the contemporary newspaper in fact had occurred before the major move to new technology during the 1980s. For example, the London *Sunday Times* introduced a new feature, 'Insight', promising 'News in a New Dimension' in 1963. The brainchild of Clive Irving, it involved, in essence, transferring the contextualising business of the American weekly news magazines, *Time* and *Newsweek*, to a newspaper. The classic 1960s British sex scandal, the Profumo affair, with a cast including a Soviet diplomat, an osteopath, a cabinet minister, call-girls and other louche players, was 'Insight's' first major chance to demonstrate the viability of this idea. Thereafter, it developed a capacity to make its own headlines. Its exposé of a London slum landlord, Peter Rachman, gave a new word to English, 'Rachmanism'. Its persistent investigation of the drug Thalidomide, which caused foetal deformities, finished up with the judges of the European Court of Human Rights castigating the British bench for being too ready to injunct publication on behalf of Distillers' Company, who manufactured the drug.

The acme of twentieth-century investigative journalism began, in the *Washington Post* of 18 June 1972, as baldly as Sam Pecke's report on the beheading of Charles I 333 years earlier:

> Five men, one of whom said he is a former employee of the Central Intelligence Agency, were arrested at 2:30 a.m. yesterday in what authorities described as an elaborate plot to bug the offices of the Democratic National Committee here.

The follow-up report a day later named the 'former employee' as James

McCord and his employers as the Republican Committee to Re-elect President Nixon (CREEP). This story carried the by-line of *Post* staff reporters, Bob Woodward and Carl Bernstein. These two were to spend the next 26 months assiduously pursuing the connection between the break-in at the offices in the Watergate apartment block and the Oval Office in the White House. As with 'Insight', this classic demonstration of the press's fundamental function in a representative democracy, 'guarding' the 'guardians', had nothing to do with the technology of journalism and everything to do with management's expensive decision to pay its reporters to spend far more time researching than writing. Woodward and Bernstein's dogged reporting of the investigatory process contributed much to re-elected Nixon's forced resignation, the first by a serving president, on 8 August 1974.

That content, as ever, was more affected by editorial mind-set than by machinery can also been seen in the turn to non-fiction by a number of authors, including Truman Capote and Joan Didion, who began publishing long novelistic accounts of specific news stories from the late 1960s on – serial killers were a favourite. So was coverage of rock and roll and the rest of the emerging counter-culture, such as in Tom Wolfe's 1968 book, *The Electric Kool-Aid Acid Test*, with its stream of consciousness and heavily personal point of view. There was a commitment to literary writing, which had become unusual in reporting in English over the previous century, although it had always been found in continental Europe, where journalism at its best was held to bear a responsibility to the written language. Also, although most writers practising what Wolfe was to call 'New Journalism' were less experimental than he had been, they did tend to write themselves into their stories in a totally new way. Joe Eszterhas for *Rolling Stone* in July 1972:

> the next few days I wore the same get-up, exaggerating the effect, walking around with a fat Special Corona 77 cigar sticking out of my mouth. I sought out townspeople in the most razorbacked bars in town, buying them beer and malt liquor and getting them to talk . . . I told them I was from a

magazine in San Francisco and forgot to say which one. When I was finished talking to the townspeople I drove back to my motel and washed my hair and changed . . .

Rolling Stone, founded in 1967, was one of a slough of new publications reflecting the social ferment of the times, although this alternative press can be dated back to the appearance during the previous decade of oppositional papers such as the *Village Voice* in New York. As such titles established themselves, their perceived growing respectability spawned ever more excessive rivals. In 1965, with the *Voice*'s weekly circulation at 80,000, the *East Village Other* began. In London, the fount of the alternative press was the anti-nuclear movement and its paper, *Peace News*. Titles redolent of Britain's radical newspaper tradition – *Black Dwarf, Red Mole*, the *Leveller* – were soon grouped with publications more concerned with drugs, sex and rock'n'roll than with revolutionary politics – the magazine *Oz* and its sister weekly paper *Ink*, the listing magazine *Time Out*, the *International Times* (*It*).

This was the one area of the press where technology did have some immediate impact. Offset printing allowed the ceaseless underground editorial search for cheap outrage to produce, on occasion, typography of such flamboyance that it was all but illegible. Barry Miles, one of *It*'s founders, regretted the serious air of the paper's first ten hot-lead issues in late 1966, attributing it to the old technology – 'You can't be frivolous in hot metal', he claimed, a major flaw given his ambitions. Nevertheless, his end of the 'underground's' assault on bourgeois values was embedded far more in a certain liberal, romantic idealism – hippiness, flower power – than in advanced capitalism's extremely expensive offset press technology.

The next time yellow ink appeared on purple paper in the name of a 'revolution' was in 1993 in *Wired* magazine; but it was not offset so much as telecomputers and satellite signals – designated 'the information superhighway' or 'cyberspace' – which were deemed to constitute the technology foundation of a new freedom. *Wired*, apart from being quintessentially out of date by its own lights (it was on paper), took a view of the world very different from the one being propounded in the 1960s. Then the 'Underground's' iconic London image was the young Australian founder of *Oz*, Richard Neville, who had posed as the dandy epitome of cool with his mini-skirted girlfriend, Louise Ferrier, draped on a chaise longue before him. Instead, *Wired* deployed a raft of middle-aged right-wing technicist suits – Gilder, Negroponte *et al.* – flush with the fire of neo-liberal economics, to talk the talk. Despite its own materiality and the fact that it did not initially even notice the presence of the internet, it made the imminent death of the newspaper one of its articles of faith. Nicholas Negroponte not only wanted to give up on TV as we know it; he was also quick to suggest that the *New York Times* and the *Boston Globe* would soon be replaced by the *Daily Me*, simply because computerised data banks would allow home terminals to gather individually tailored news items. Given that few people ever read the entire contents of a paper, this clearly made a lot of sense to Negroponte, *Wired* and even, for a time, the newspaper industry itself. The problem is that this vision ignores the foundation of the social value of the press; this is, exactly, the creation of *shared* agendas for an otherwise atomised, individualised society. That not all of their content is read by all of their readers is acceptable wastage, given this broader collectivising function, one performed by all mass media. The individual newspaper is a contradiction in terms – it is, in essence, a letter and it has existed for millennia.

The technicists were far too seized with enthusiasm to be distracted by any insights that queried their vision. Cyberspace was widely seen as incorporeal and uncontrollable, perhaps because the protocols which created the internet were the product of the original end users – nuclear research labs at the heart of the military-industrial complex – and not imposed by the Pentagon, to which the hardware actually belonged. Nevertheless, the spine of the system was sufficiently corporeal to have cost the American taxpayer five million 1970s dollars to build. It is also, should society ever actually become concerned enough to spend the money to do this, controllable through the machinery – expensive, electronic boxes – held at the network's nodal points such as national gateways. The net can be turned on and off (or fail) just like any other electrical or electronic network. The same computing power that drives it can be deployed to control it and its contents.

In 1995, the spine was handed over by the US government to three of the extremely corporeal 'Baby Bells' – the companies created after the federal authorities finally managed to break up the AT&T monopoly. Even this very real transfer of property was unnoticed, or if noticed, treated with an insouciance even *It* and *Oz* would have been hard-pressed to match:

> Once upon a time there was a wide area network called the Internet. A network unscathed by the capitalist Fortune 500 companies and the like. Then somebody decided to deregulate the Internet and hand it over to the 'big boys' in the telecommunications industry . . . The Internet Liberation Front is a small, underground organisation of computer security experts. We are capable of penetrating virtually any network linked to the Internet – *any* network. . . . Just a friendly warning, Corporate America . . .

Corporate America took no notice. Instead, it set about indulging itself in a 'dot.com' revolution, a species of market hysteria perhaps best explained by merely noting its proximity to the millennium. The Internet Liberation Front got lost in cyberspace.

In the later 1990s, journalism, far from disappearing, was revealed as a still necessary filtering and agenda-setting process. The industry, ignoring the threat of the *Daily Me*, currently co-exists with new technology in a number of ways. Over 90 per cent of American journalists, for example, use the searchable electronic archives, databases and news sources of the net in their work. The archives include sites established by mainstream media themselves which transfer – 'shovel' – original print or broadcast contents on to the net. These have allowed many papers to abandon the expensive and labour-intensive business of keeping physical archives of clippings – 'morgues'. Journalists also use 'comment sites' such as the reactionary, propagandistic Drudge Report which by their partisanship echo the first English Civil War newspapers, having no trace of nineteenth-century notions of objectivity about them.

The possibility of electronic editions being more than mere 'shovelling' has thus far yielded little innovation in content and, apart from allowing hyperlinking back into the archive, the basic form of journalism has remained as untouched by these advances as it was by the disappearance of hot metal. Early studies show no fresh approaches, for example, to such stories as the American presidential campaigns of 2000 and 2004. Nevertheless, during the second decade of such activity some evidence began to emerge of a preference for the electronic among a minority of readers. For instance, nine per cent of the *Austin* (Texas) *Statesman–American*'s readership took the paper on line, a high percentage of them the missing young, but too many people were still sitting at the breakfast table or commuting to work with the old-fashioned paper version clutched in their hands for this to catch on. Nine million people worldwide were reportedly 'visiting' the *Guardian* website, the British press's most successful electronic offering, by 2004. The only problem was that on-line advertising revenues, despite exponential rises year on year in the UK, were still in their entirety less than one-tenth of what the old-fashioned press alone was earning. The on-line version of the *Guardian* was (for the moment at least) free unlike the hardcopy being bought by 400,000 people for ready cash. The value of fancy electronic accessibility is anyway unproven. Reading a newspaper is what newspaper readers do; mining information in any form, including delving into the vast polders of records held in the data banks of cyberspace, is what journalists do. The *Daily Me* remains an oxymoron; even Mr Drudge pretends to be addressing a public and not a personal agenda.

'What we obtain too cheap, we esteem too lightly'

By its two hundredth birthday on 15 December 1991, the First Amendment to the Constitution of the United States had become a shibboleth. A survey conducted on behalf of the American Society of Newspaper Editors revealed: 'Americans rate free speech as their second most valued precious First Amendment right and regard a free press highly – in the abstract.' Questioned in detail, more than two-thirds of the 2,500 respondents would not afford the media automatic protection to editorialise during a political campaign, cover the sexual behaviour of politicians, publish graphic photographs or report on security matters without prior government approval. More than one in five Americans thought that there should be no legal protection to criticise political leaders or the military. Supporters of the First Amendment can perhaps take comfort that some 40 per cent of those questioned defended the right to burn the flag as justified expression of opinion, despite the fact that the survey was conducted during the first Gulf War. Nevertheless, overall, those surveyed 'displayed an alarming willingness to remove legal protection from forms of free expression they merely disagreed with or found offensive'; and the pollsters concluded that 'it is apparent that free expression is in very deep trouble'.

As Tom Paine had written, slightly more than two centuries earlier: 'What we obtain too cheap, we esteem too lightly.' For the West, there is little or no sense that we have 'obtained' free expression and the rest of the Enlightenment's cluster of fundamental rights cheaply or, indeed, at any price at all. They are simply 'there' and, 50 years after the defeat of totalitarianism in the West and some years since its fall in Eastern Europe, the struggles that secured those releases are sufficiently forgotten for these rights to be subjected to fundamental criticism and dismissal. It becomes respectable for repressive opinion once more to question their very validity as concepts; or, at best, to demand that 'responsibilities', beyond those required in general by civil society, 'pay' in some way for such rights. It is not just free expression that is 'in very deep trouble'; rights in general are being recast as 'entitlements' and

then denied as nothing more than 'politically correct' – a phrase transformed in weaselly fashion by the anti-liberals into a term of abuse.
Meanwhile this effort, perhaps inadvertently, has been comforted, if not
overtly supported, elsewhere in the contemporary marketplace of ideas
by post-modernist thinking which has, with some justice given the elitism, paternalism, hypocrisy and materialism of eighteenth-century
liberalism, been undercutting the Enlightenment.

It is widely held on all sides that the place of modern media in society is too changed for the application of a seventeenth- or
eighteenth-century vision of press freedom – or rather, a twentieth-century version of what that vision was – to be applicable. Such levels of
press freedom as were attained in the nineteenth century might have
been partial and inadequate but they represented a degree of liberty not
achieved by the newer mass media in the twentieth century. Beyond its
extension from person to press, the universality of free expression was
not established. It remains largely not established today. In Britain, for
instance, Walpole's stage-censorship regime was removed only after
over two and half centuries, during which the theatre had become,
safely perhaps, a minority elitist institution. The cinema has yet to be
relieved of its certification system, although what its categories implied
has been constantly relaxed. Radio and television also proved to be too
popular for such liberties and the current era of electronic abundance,
which reduces any individual content provider's reach by virtue of channel and platform proliferation, has yet to do quite as much for
broadcasting.

Instead of a right, duly limited by law, newer media are being allowed,
in the words of the new British Communications Act of 2003, something
less – 'an *appropriate* level of freedom of expression' (emphasis added), as
determined by statutory bureaucratic structures beyond the courts. Such
a situation would not be acceptable if applied to the press or stage, but a
slough of reasons is usually given to justify why, in a liberal society, supposedly committed to free expression, differences of treatment between
media can be justified. The influence of non-print mass-communication
systems is deemed so vast that they cannot be allowed to function with-

out special extra control. Yet, it is not an absolute given that, for example, the newer media are more 'influential', for all that they are certainly more pervasive. Given the small size and disproportionate power of the literate population in the modern but pre-industrialised past, the 12.5 million British newspapers that were officially stamped annually in, say, the 1770s represented a considerable level of penetration. Paine's *Common Sense* went through 25 editions in 1776 and must have been known to every American, revolted or loyal. And what modern Fleet Street figure, with the possible exception of Rupert Murdoch, exercises the influence – the 'tyranny' even – that a John Thaddeus Delane possessed in the nineteenth century? The rise in the British population and, more particularly, the exponential growth in the size of the electorate, renders any simple assertion as to the increase in media power more vexed than 'common sense' would allow.

It is in any case no argument at all to abridge the principle of media free expression just because media are deemed to be influential as, logically, so to do is in effect to make free expression contingent upon its having no influence; and this is without prejudice to the possibility that media 'influence', in the West at least, is by no means so clearly demonstrated that it can be used as a justification in the first place. After all, nearly a century of media industry and sociological effort has failed to prove this in any remotely clear-cut fashion. Modern media penetration is beside the point.

Specific control is also (to use Clarke's phrase of 1695) 'very needless', because of physical scarcity in the broadcasting spectrum. This was never entirely convincing even in the age of analogue modulation and is now a complete nonsense given the proliferation of platforms and channels. In Europe, for example, the 1948 Convention on Human Rights specifically allowed for a state to require 'the licensing of broadcasting, television or cinema entertainments', which has been held to cover content control despite the Convention at the same time guaranteeing 'everyone . . . the right to freedom of expression' – that is, 'freedom to hold opinions and to receive and impart information and ideas without interference by public authority'. Only once, in 1990, have the judges at the European Court of Human Rights pointed out this contradiction, and then only *en passant*. The technological misunderstandings of the late 1940s should long since have been corrected and other justifications for 'very needless' curtailments of free expression – the spurious 'contract' broadcasters are supposed to have with the viewer not to be offensive (at least without warning!) and so avoid being an 'unwanted guest' in the home – should be dismissed for the cant they are.[5] Free expression can be proved to exist only when it is offensive, and should that paradox be forgotten then the right of free expression is seriously endangered.

The range of permitted expression, especially when it deals with sex and violence, has been so expanded at least in some media as to butt up constantly against the limits of freedom, classically expressed as doing no measurable social harm. In a world awash with pornography, telephoto lenses and audio bugging devices, where indeed anything seems to go, there would seem to be no basis for concern for media liberty; yet behind this flood the basics of free expression, as a concept receiving widespread support, are being eroded. There is, as American public opinion surveys or the current British Communication Act show, little appetite to support any general extension of press freedom to new media. Quite clearly, Alexander Hamilton's best guarantee of free speech – 'the general spirit of the people' – can no longer be taken for granted.

The people have been distracted, if not bamboozled, by the hyperbole surrounding media technologies for the last 50 years. It is time to flee the enchantments of technology and the seductive rhetoric of the technicists as well as the ignorances of politicians and put the right of free expression – and its sister right of access to information – on a new foundation, one that accepts their centrality to a democratic society. Free expression should not be abridged by assumptions about the supposed 'power' and pervasiveness of different media. Technology should have nothing to do with it as a principle; but this most assuredly does not mean a libertarian end of media control. It merely means that the media – new, old and to come – like all individual citizens, should stand equal before the law.

We may not be quite the shivering, ill-equipped, defeated soldiers Tom Paine found on the banks of the Hudson that Christmastide over 200 years ago – but the future we face is just as uncertain. Despite our tolerance and our permissiveness, the forces of illiberalism are massing outwith and within our midst. They force us once more to defend our freedoms. A battle to rejustify rights generally and reaffirm a media-blind right of free expression must now be joined. Indeed (in Paine's words): 'These are the times to try men's [and women's] souls'.

As ever.

High Barnet and Caenby, Christmas 2004

Sources

John Cassidy (2002), *Dot.Con*, Harmondsworth: Penguin.

James Curran and Jean Seaton (2003), *Power without Responsibility*, London: Routledge.

Nigel Fountain (1988), *Underground: The Alternative London Press 1966–1974*, London: Comedia/Routledge.

Nicholas Garnham (2000), *Emancipation, the Media, and Modernity*, Oxford: Oxford University Press.

George Gilder (1992), *Life After Television: The Coming Transformation of the Media and American Life*, New York: Norton.

John Gray (1986), *Liberalism*, Buckingham: Open University Press.

Dan Harries (ed.) (2002), *The New Media Book*, London: British Film Institute.

Groppera Radio and Others (European Court of Human Rights 14/1988/158/124)

Philip Hayward and Tana Wollen (1993), *Future Visions: New Technologies of the Screen*, London: British Film Institute.

Michael Leapman (1992), *Treacherous Estate*, London: Hodder & Stoughton.

Marshall McLuhan (1964), *Understanding Media: The Extensions of Man*, London: Routledge & Kegan Paul.

Denis McQuail (2003), *Media Accountability and Freedom of Publication*, Oxford: Oxford University Press.

Nicolas Negroponte (1996), *Being Digital*, New York: Vintage.

Roy Porter (2001), *The Enlightenment*, London: Macmillan.

Peter Pritchard (1987), *The Making of McPaper: The Inside Story of USA Today*, Kansas City: Andrew, McMeel and Parker.

Colin Seymour-Ure (1991), *The British Press and Broadcasting since 1945*, Oxford: Blackwell.

Anthony Smith (1980), *Goodbye, Gutenberg: The Newspaper Revolution of the 1980s*, Oxford: Oxford University Press.

Raymond Williams (1976), *Keywords*, New York: Oxford University Press.

Raymond Williams (1981), *Culture*, London: Fontana.

Raymond Williams (1983), *Culture and Society*, New York: Columbia University Press.

Brian Winston (1986), *Misunderstanding Media*, Cambridge, Mass.: Harvard University Press.

Brian Winston (1998), *Media, Technology and Society: A History from the Telegraph to the Internet*, London: Routledge.

Brian Winston (2000), *Lies, Damn Lies and Documentaries*, London: British Film Institute.

Benjamin Wooley (1992), *Virtual Worlds*, Oxford: Blackwell.

Robert Wyatt *et al.* (1991), *Free Expression and the American Public*, Murfreesboro, Tennessee: Middle State University.

NOTES

PROLOGUE I 'THE LIBERTY TO KNOW': PRINT FROM 1455

1 On the good side, though, that same century witnessed agriculture advances producing a diet in which meat figured heavily for the first time for all classes – all but the very poorest – at least on the 200 some days a year the Church permitted meat-eating.

2 Centuries before, the emperors Otto and Charlemagne had secured for Aachen, their capital, the Virgin's cloak, Jesus's swaddling clothes, the loincloth he wore on the cross and the cloth upon which had rested the head of John the Baptist.

3 Also in 1437, Ennel zur eisenen Tür, a patrician's daughter, sued Gutenberg for breach of promise. In another year he paid the Strasbourg authorities tax on 2,000 bottles of wine. He does not seem to have been the solidest of citizens.

4 He became Cardinal Cusenius. He was, in effect, an early humanist with an interest in mathematics and astronomy. He had collected Greek manuscripts of religious writings when on a papal mission to Constantinople in 1437.

5 Today's usual print run for paperback academic books in English is also around 2,000.

6 The last edition of the *Index* appeared 407 years later in 1966.

7 The contemporary Frankfurt book fair is a revival of the Renaissance original.

1 'TAKING OFF VIZARDS AND VAILES AND DISGUISES': NEWSPAPERS FROM 1566

1 Broadcast news can therefore be said to start here too.

2 As Rudyard Kipling was to characterise the heart of the business.

3 Legal process was much more a matter of accessing the mind of God, at that time considered the only reliable source of truth, than assessing the

credibility of witnesses, a far more difficult and complicated task. Hence trial by ordeal or battle.

4 *Messe* = fair.

5 The title 'Intelligencer' reflects the continental term *Intelligenzblatt* and has a slightly official air, as does the paper's subtitle 'to prevent mis-information'. An *Intelligenzblatt*, though, was actually a publication consisting of advertisements.

6 So termed for Cardinal Mazarin, the King's unpopular chief minister.

7 Many autocracies to the East also licensed such an activity, as a state monopoly in an *Intellegenzblatt* and the already closely controlled *Zeitung*s were not then allowed to carry any commercial announcements.

2 'CONGRESS SHALL MAKE NO LAW': JOURNALISM FROM 1702

1 It was to last until 1921.

2 This means they were marked confusingly e.g. 'March 18 N.S.' in the fashion of the new euro-style Gregorian calendar (which ran eleven days behind the Julian one with which the British persisted until 1752).

3 Cross country speed could be as much as 160 kilometres a day but was usually more like 40. The Thurn und Taxis service in the Hapsburg realms, which dates from 1516, set a speed of 6 kilometres an hour through the mountains and 8–10 on the level. It was not quick but it was regular. France also had a similar centrally directed public postal system, in place since 1480. Northern Europe, including England and Scotland, lagged behind.

4 See p. 212. The *Gentleman's Magazine* ceased publication in 1907. Both the *Tatler* and the *Spectator* still exist but the run of their publication has not been unbroken.

5 Supporters of William and Mary against James II were Whigs, so named after an obscure term of abuse given to Scottish Presbyterian rebels in the 1640s. The old pro-James Royalists, defeated in the Glorious Revolution, had acquired the name Tory, from the Irish *t'Úraidhe* for outlaw, during the rows over the succession in 1679.

6 Grubb Street, next to the Barbican in London, had been the home of professional hacks from the 1630s. It has now been renamed, presumably in a spirit of literary as well as civic improvement, Milton Street.

7 Which had acquired this title in the year of Joseph's accession having been previously called *Weiner Zeitung*.

8 *La libre communication des pensées et des opinions est un des droits les plus précieux de l'homme. Tout citoyen peut parler, écrire, imprimer librement, sauf à répondre l'abus de cette liberté dans les cas prévus par la loi.*

9 Given the centrality of the *Commentaries* to the creation of a civil society in the colonies, that 1980s American car bumper-sticker which asserted that 'God, guts and guns made America' would have done better, historically speaking, to have read 'God, guts and Blackstone etc. etc.'.

10 Although Locke had originally suggested 'estates' or property as the third of these objectives and Jefferson had taken it upon himself to substitute the more radical 'pursuit of happiness'.

11 As in London, female succession was not uncommon.

12 These anti-Federalists metamorphosed into the Democratic Party.

3 'HERE'S THE PAPERS, HERE'S THE PAPERS!': JOURNALISM FROM 1836

1 The term 'scoop' in the UK dates from 1884.

2 A word which would not exist until the next century.

3 Mayhew was one of the founders of the satirical weekly magazine *Punch*, on a French model. Although its name connoted the irrelevantly comic world of *La Commedia dell'arte*, 'Punch hangs the devil' (to use a phrase of editor Mark Lawson, writing in the first editorial) indicated the rather sharper intention of the publication. Initially it was not just funny cartoons; for instance, it carried Thomas Hood's biting radical poem, 'The Song of the Shirt'. Mayhew's London reports and biographies have remained in print as *London Labour and London Poor*, an early classic of British sociology.

4 As he was always quick to point out, Greeley did not originate this phrase. It comes from John Soule, a journalist of Terre Haute, Indiana.

5 The end crowns the work.

6 'Gordon Bennett', as a slang expression of wonder, relates to this son, a prominent sportsman and profligate, who eventually conducted the business of the *Herald* from Europe, living aboard his yacht *Lysystrata* in the Mediterranean. Under him, the paper lost its dominant position in the New York market to Pulitzer but it is not perhaps inappropriate that the name survives in the title of an international newspaper published in Paris.

7 The publicity got *Around the World in the 90 Days* reissued and reprinted ten times.

8 Richard Outcault's cartoon character 'The Yellow Kid' first appeared in the *World* in 1894. He was a two-toothed, slum-dwelling wordless toddler in a nightshirt who communicated via messages which appeared by magic on his shirt-front. Outcault was poached from Pulitzer by William Hearst in 1896 but Pulitzer hired another cartoonist, George Luks, to continue drawing the Kid. The court (of course) ruled that both strips could run, whereby the

World and the *Journal* became 'The Yellow Kid Papers', whence 'The Yellow Papers', whence 'Yellow Journalism' until finally 'the yellow press'. Some dispute this account of the origin of the term.

9 No other 'strangers' were allowed to do this, and still are not without the prior approval of the Sergeant-at-Arms.

10 The parliamentary privilege of immunity from defamation was extended to Hansard only after the firm had been prosecuted for libel in 1836 for a report printed by order of Parliament. Hansard became the brand for all official reporting across the British Commonwealth.

11 He took the concept of the fourth Estate from Burke.

12 They were not allowed out of the gallery into parts of Westminster reserved for the MPs until the end of the century. The establishment of a 'lobby' did not occur until the inter-war years of the twentieth century.

13 This claim occasioned William Hazlitt to say of *The Times*, that 'prodigious prosing paper . . . seems to be written as well as printed by a steam-engine'.

14 The technology had been created from elements that had existed for more than half a century before Morse (and Cooke and Whetstone and a number of others) to service the new steam railways, alongside whose tracks the first wires ran, rather than the press.

15 Bennett introduced the sensible business practice of obtaining money before he would run any advertisement.

16 Not true. See *Le Petit Journal* below.

17 Hirlap = newspaper.

18 'Tabloid' was a neologism registered as part of a trade mark by the pharmaceutical manufacturers Wellcome in 1884 to describes its compact, compressed pills.

19 Who was not, actually, above pointing out to him on occasion that his papers were pursuing political lines unacceptable to her – which should have told him something.

20 See p. 156 *et seq*.

21 She went on, rather unexpectedly, to marry one of the century's most influential English economists, John Maynard Keynes.

22 The illegitimate Henry Stanley — born in Denby, Wales, raised in a workhouse, naturalised American, renaturalised British, elected MP — was also knighted but for services to exploration rather than journalism.

23 N.S.B. = The National Socialist Party, the Dutch Nazis.

PROLOGUE II 'LEAL SOVVENIR': IMAGING FROM 1413

1 This raises the possibility that it was this device that prompted Brunelleschi into conceiving the Baptistery painting, making the camera the source of the Western perspective system.
2 Or, perhaps more accurately, he rediscovered this phenomenon since Pliny, writing in the 1st century AD, hints at it.
3 The plate is now in the University of Texas at Austin, barely discernible in the low light which ensures its preservation. Looking at it one feels, perhaps, like Wedgwood must have felt peering at his photograms.
4 See p. 228.
5 Now the University of Westminster.
6 Even with the help of the camera, it still took him more than 23 years to complete the painting of the convention.
7 Unless they also read the newspapers. See p. 119.

4 'WHO KNOWS NOT HER NAME': THEATRE FROM 1513

1 Although, in Roman times, Seneca's texts were almost certainly 'closet plays' – that is, were written to be read as literature rather than as scripts for production – and were therefore themselves somewhat 'theoretical' as performed dramas.
2 However, there were limits to this passion for emulating the ancients. In the Roman imperial age, the stage degenerated. A single performer, the pantomimus, seized control, unbalancing the older ensemble playing of the Republican stage. Actresses, who had been no part of Republican theatre, were allowed complete nudity and the Emperor Domitian – whose wife had a notorious affair with a pantomimus – even sanctioned the use of condemned prisoners actually to be killed on stage, in what we might today call 'snuff' plays.
3 The source of this account is George Harrison's twentieth-century pastiche.
4 It was to be a century and more before musicians in England and Germany, led by court instrumentalists, made a similar move into the public realm, establishing 'rooms' for ticketed musical performances which were, in the course of the eighteenth century, to become custom-built concert halls.
5 For instance, the powerful *Arte della Lana* had controlled the wool industry in medieval Florence.
6 Show girls became its main attraction only after the First World War.
7 The players here were not allowed dialogue so turned to monologue; and, when that provoked an ordinance forbidding speaking, to singing. When, in turn, they were not allowed to sing, they mimed the action and got the

audience to sing the words which were displayed on placards. Finally, in 1595, the objections were brushed aside and a Théâtre de la Foire was built, peopled by players in part from the Hôtel de Bourgogne.

8 He was also imprisoned for killing a fellow actor in a duel. Duelling was already illegal and Jonson, always a quarrelsome and prickly man, had been lucky to escape execution.

9 A succession of aristocratic ladies liked Kynaston enough as a male for him to enjoy a brief side-career as a kept toy-boy.

10 An actress and singer who appears to have been a very particular friend of the diarist, but not, it would seem, of Mrs Pepys.

11 The title then denoted maturity, not marital state.

12 In late twentieth century British tabloid parlance, surely a 'stunna'. As for the painting, while undress and languor, suggestive of post-coital repose, were to become commonplace in the pin-up, having a child to share the frame did not. In the Lely portrait, though, Nell is accompanied by a tod-dler. This curly-headed Cupid stands at the side of her couch threatening to pull away the sliver of drapery protecting her modesty. He is actually the Duke of St Albans, one of the two children she bore the King. Nell's figure, however, shows no signs of motherhood.

5 'SO MUCH FOR STAGE FEELING': STAGE AND SCREEN FROM 1737

1 Cave's magazine had a circulation of 10,000 at this time.

2 One of a group of female Restoration dramatists around Aphra Benn.

3 The oldest ballet in the repertoire, *La Fille mal gardé*, dates from 1789, choreographed by his pupil, Jean Dauberval.

4 On the other hand, on the continent, waiters were also on hand to serve drinks during performances.

5 'Vaudeville', which could possibly be a corruption of 'voix de ville', was ini-tially used in the late sixteenth century to describe satirical ballads and, later, light satirical plays with songs put on at popular Parisian theatres. As in the unpatented London houses, spoken drama was forbidden but music was permitted.

6 He was no angel. He once killed a fellow actor in a green room fight over a wig but, although indicted for murder, the charge was reduced to manslaughter and there is no record of him going to prison.

7 A tragic Shylock would not be seen until after the twentieth-century Holocaust.

8 In 1776 Garrick passed Drury Lane to Richard Sheridan, who, among other things, was a playwright (the only one of the period apart from Goldsmith whose work is still in the repertoire) as well as a politician. Two

years later Sheridan decided he was no manager and handed the theatre on to Kemble, a somewhat idiosyncratic leading actor. The star of Kemble's company was his sister, Sarah Siddons.

9 This was not the last time Chesterfield was to be at odds with Walpole and in 1742 he engineered the putsch against Sir Robert that brought his tenure to an end.

10 Sachs, a cobbler – which indeed he was by trade – and master singer, is a major character in Wagner's *Meistersinger von Nürnberg*, his theatrical activities are not, however, in evidence in the opera. The real Sachs's secular comedies included a set of stock characters mixing the usual (unfaithful wife, jealous husband) with the new (Catholic Priest).

11 However, the greatest playwright in German of the early nineteenth century remained unperformed in his own day. Georg Büchner, dead of typhoid at 24, published *Danton's Death* in 1835 but it was not staged until 1903. *Wozzeck*, unfinished at his death in 1837, was not discovered for decades and remained unstaged until 1913.

12 Although projectors were known in the East in antiquity, it seems probable that the modern technology was independently developed in the West and thence taken to the East, unlike printing (which might have gone the other way) and the *camera obscura* (which certainly did).

13 Some of the British Blondes' repertoire – *Aladdin and the Forty Thieves*, *Sinbad* – lost its erotic frisson, if not its cross-dressing ambiguities and *double-entrendre* scripts, to become the British Christmas children's pantomime.

14 This is, of course, not the case with works for the lyric stage or, indeed, the concert hall.

15 Not least because wearing the kilt in public had been forbidden by law in 1747.

16 Although Kean's respectability had led to command performances at Windsor Castle and earned him the revived title 'Master of the Revels', this was still not quite enough for the scholar to allow his name to be revealed.

17 He wore the leotard under shorts. The song was written by George Leybourne.

18 This line of development, which produced the first dictation machines in the early decades of the twentieth century, was to lead back into the mass media via audio-tape in the 1950s.

19 The most interesting film was *Electrocuting an Elephant* which recorded the death of a dangerous circus animal using direct electric current ('invented' by rival Teslar) – in order to advertise the curious claim that Edison's AC alternative current produced 'safer' electricity.

20 Based on a novel by George du Maurier in which the sinister Svengali turns the artist's model Trilby into an opera star.

21 It remained the largest car producer, for instance, until overtaken by the United States in 1906.

22 They have been revived in something like their most developed form in recent sophisticated theme park rides – high-tech versions of the old Hale's Tours involving journeys into space or through the body or chases with cartoon characters, in small 30/40-seat cinemas in the shape of hydraulically driven rocking (and swooping, twisting) capsules.

23 Actually the worst nineteenth-century theatrical riot had little to do with the theatre, although it was occasioned by a performance. In 1849, the American star Edwin Forrest's supporters decided to rerun the War of Independence. They fought a pitched battle in Astor Place, New York with fans of a visiting English star, William Macready (whose Hamlet Forrest had hissed when he visited London earlier). Nativist hostility (behind the façade of support for a popular star) was pitched against the Anglophilia of New York's *haute bourgeoisie* (for expressing an alien taste for high culture) and, when the army had cleared the square, 22 lay dead.

24 *S'il n'y avait pas de Pologne, il n'y aurait pas de Polonais!*

6 'GIVE THE PUBLIC WHAT WE THINK THEY NEED': RADIO FROM 1906

1 For example, it had spurned an elegant proto-telegraph built by Francis Ronalds in 1816: 'The war being at an end, and money scarce, the old [semaphore] system was sufficient for the country', thereby dooming Ronalds to be a footnote in communications history.

2 Berliner had become rich because he had designed a variant on the Edison telephone mouthpiece. Locked in a desperate patent battle with Edison in the late 1870s, Bell had hired Berliner to build, to order, a telephone mouthpiece which did not use carbon (and so went round Edison's patent) but which worked just as well. Berliner did it in six weeks in 1877. This early incident convinced Bell and his backers of the value of structured R&D, a positively twentieth-century managerial view that was to lead eventually in 1923 to the establishment of the Bell Labs.

3 In later years, he elaborated a complex legend about how he alone stayed on the air transmitting to the *Titanic* after President Taft had ordered silence from the shore. In fact, he was one of a number of Marconi shore-station operators who caught a morse echo of the disaster unfolding on the North Atlantic on the night of 14 April 1912.

4 There has never been a woman chair.

5 Mutual, the most nearly successful of these potential rivals, was a large group of smaller stations which provided 'network' programming on a

cooperative basis. *The Lone Ranger* (and *The Shadow*) were its most famous shows. Founded in 1934, it was viable by 1938 and hung on till 1999.

6 Four years after its successful transfer to television, where it yet runs (p. 411).

7 It was, however, already a corporation by the time of this remark.

8 The Savoy Orpheans, the first hit dance band to be heard regularly on the air, was a twelve-piece ensemble of mainly American musicians. It broadcast via OBs from the Savoy Hotel just behind the first BBC headquarters at Savoy Hill by the Thames in London.

9 Wilton had debuted as a melodrama villain in 1903 and his radio shows ran until 1952.

10 Although he did manage to influence the Canadians away from commercialism while there.

11 Marketed in Britain by Ludwig Blatner, the builder of Elstree film studios.

7 'AMERICAN SHOTS': CINEMA FROM 1925

1 A classic example of what 1960s media guru Marshall McLuhan called 'driving into the future with our eyes firmly fixed on the rear-view mirror'.

2 Although born in Missouri, White was to move to France when her popularity ebbed in 1923/4. She died there in 1938.

3 Originally this stick was a split bat carried by the Harlequin in *La commedia dell'arte* but the Americans had come to use its name as a term to describe the physicality of the comic acrobatic vaudeville sketch.

4 Music, sound effects and even spoken commentaries had been part of all nineteenth-century spectacles. All this was transferred to the cinema. The initial cue sheets issued with films became ever more complex, with symphonic accompaniment becoming of itself a mark of cultural legitimacy, or at least pretension. By reinforcing contrast, the cheapest film shows could only afford a piano-player.

5 Their missing voices, though, could be – and were – recorded but film and gramophone disk were not yet effectively married, although it was being tried.

6 The films caused a scandal and confirmed her as a star but Brooks went back to the States where her unwillingness to bow to studio discipline, which was why she went to Berlin in the first place, soon stifled her.

7 Pommer went to America in 1924 with Lang to open their epic, *Siegfried's Death*. The myth is that their first sight of the Manhattan skyline inspired Lang's vision of *Metropolis*.

8 Gunsmoke can be seen at the side of the frame and, in a recently unearthed off-cut, the shot continues panning to show Buñuel himself, costumed à la Hemingway as the great white hunter, wielding the pistol.

9 Three years after panchromatic became as cheap as orthocromatic, Hollywood was still conducting endless 'experiments' with it.

10 This is where Ludwig Blattner, the founder of Elstree Studios in England, got the steel-tape recorders he successfully marketed to the BBC's 'Empire' service. The BASF tape was used to record speeches by the Nazi leadership and allow for high-quality 'canned' music broadcasts. The patents for it and the audiotape machine in which it was used were seized by the victorious Americans in 1945.

11 Normal 35mm sound film has an 'Academy' aspect ratio of 1.37:1.

12 Zooms became standard for 16mm news and documentary filming in the 1960s.

13 The term, Executive Producer, was coined by one of his rivals, David Selznick, at RKO in 1931.

8 'SEE IT NOW': TELEVISION FROM 1954

1 The Japanese were also active in TV research. Hidetugu Yagi had presented the design of the standard 'H' receiving antenna to an international radio engineering conference in New York in 1927. Nippon Hoso Kyokai (NHK) also began experimental TV transmissions in 1937 using RCA derived technology.

2 'Eidophor' means 'image-bearer'.

3 The British called these 'chat shows', a rare example of metropolitan English usage being more vivid than that of America.

4 Radio, though, had, somewhat curiously, coped with ventriloquism. An American ventriloquist, Edgar Bergen, had been a radio star with his dummy 'Charlie McCarthy' as had Peter Brough and his doll 'Archie' in Britain. Neither was as successful on TV although Charlie McCarthy's appearance on NBC's pioneering TV show *Hour Glass* in November 1946 was one of the first times the new medium captured a star of the old.

5 A young writer named Woody Allen was also involved.

6 *The Guiding Light* was the only soap to transfer successfully to TV, in June 1952. In 1956, when *The Guiding Light* was killed off on the radio, both *As the World Turns* and *The Edge of Night* began as new soaps on TV on the same day, 2 April. By 1960, all the radio soaps were gone. On TV, *The Guiding Light* and *As the World Turns* both persisted to the millennium and beyond. *The Edge of Night*, though, only lasted 28 years.

7 More time honoured, of course, was the equal unreality of Rod Steiger's plaint that he was 'just an ugly little guy!'

8 All references herein to ratings and industrial research must be read in this light.

9 In fact, it persisted even longer so that, after the advent of effective video-tape editing in the late 1960s, it was seen, especially at the BBC, as still saving costs, now in the form of expensive time in the video editing suite.

10 Pabst's 1931 classic, *Kameradschaft*, about a mining disaster, had an enormous, realistic set of a coalmine gallery which was widely regarded as one of the greatest ever built for a film.

11 These others had been chaired by a viscount, a lord and a major general.

12 It returned to the BBC in 1994 and continued until 2003.

13 Rakoff failed to bring Jack Palance, who had originally played the lead in the American production, over and so had to cast a British unknown, Sean Connery.

14 They used the same accents in the next parts of the trilogy, *Oh Lena My Lena* and *A Little Winter Love*.

15 It survives because Kodak and Dumont had introduced an effective tele-recording system that January.

16 Day, knighted in 1981, with his trademark spotted bow-ties, unfortunately became a caricature of the establishment figures he initially so skillfully confronted.

17 David Frost received his knighthood in 1993 and was still on screen in the new millennium, having become, like Sir Robin Day, something of a caricature of his former self.

18 In Wales, Channel 4 is S4C, a Welsh-language service.

19 The terrestrial Fox TV network is based on the Metromedia group of stations, which was the county's biggest group of independents. Metromedia itself was built on the remains of fourth DuMont network which had started in 1942 and failed in 1958, having been less successful with television than Mutual had been with the radio. Allen Dumont was an electrical engineer who had assisted de Forest in the 1920s.

20 The failure that day to maintain normal standards of editorial care by, for example, transmitting material straight from the developing labs without any journalist having seen it first, has also become a norm.

EPILOGUE 'FREE EXPRESSION IS IN VERY DEEP TROUBLE': MEDIA TO 1991 AND BEYOND

1 This is still an inefficient waste of computing power and calls, at least among engineers, for a more rational response – a traditional sort of 'standard' – were to be increasingly heard in the new millennium.

2 Over the previous quarter of a century, the Media Lab's only widely diffused technology has been the development of the ubiquitous white-light hologram to be found on credit cards and the like. All its more significant

projects, despite the millions lavished upon them by the computing and communications industries, have failed to bear even this much fruit.

3 The *Post*, the *Times*, the *News*. There are also the *Wall Street Journal* and *Newsday* published on Long Island.

4 Clarke's more general technicist prediction of cross-border publications printed via satellite, on the other hand, has never really happened except for specialised readerships – the financial press for example, or publications to serve diasporas. The Arabic press has taken particular advantage of this. Nevertheless, his technicist concept that the International Satellite Communications treaty of 1971 was 'the first draft of the articles of Federation of the United States of Earth' – seems totally off-beam three decades on. Al-Qaida's apparent use of the satellite phone alone is rebuttal enough.

5 In Britain, broadcasters frequently say of the regulatory regime that it keeps them 'honest' which, as it presupposes them actually to be 'honest' – that is, truth-telling paragons of inoffensive objectivities – is grounds enough for smelling a rat or two.

INDEX

Related titles from Routledge

Power without Responsibility
Sixth Edition

James Curran & Jean Seaton

'This is a useful and timely book'
Richard Hoggart, Times Educational Supplement

'In a fast-changing media scene this book is nothing less
than indispensable'
Julian Petley, Brunel University

'*Power without Responsibility*, the best guide to the
British media'
Nick Cohen, The New Statesman

Power without Responsibility is a classic, authoritative and engaged
introduction to the history, sociology, theory and politics of media
and communication studies. Written in a lively and accessible style,
it is regarded as the standard book on the British media. This new
edition has been substantially revised to bring it up-to-date with
new developments in the media industry. Its three new chapters
describe the battle for the soul of the internet, the impact of the
internet on society and the rise of new media in Britain. In
addition, it examines the recuperation of the BBC, how
international and European regulation is changing the British
media and why Britain has the least trusted press in Europe.

Hb: 0-415-24389-0
Pb: 0-415-24390-4

Available at all good bookshops
For ordering and further information please visit:
www.routledge.com

Related titles from Routledge

Media and Power

James Curran

Media and Power addresses three key questions about the relationship between media and society.

- How much power do the media have?
- Who really controls the media?
- What is the relationship between media and power in society?

In this major new book, James Curran reviews the different answers which have been given, before advancing original interpretations in a series of ground-breaking essays.

Media and Power also provides a guided tour of the major debates in media studies. What part did the media play in the making of modern society? How did 'new media' change society in the past? Will radical media research recover from its mid-life crisis? What are the limitations of the US-based model of 'communications' research? Is globalization disempowering national electorates or bringing into being a new, progressive global politics? Is public service television the dying product of the nation in an age of globalization? What can be learned from the 'third way' tradition of European media policy?

Curran's response to these questions provides both a clear introduction to media research and an innovative analysis of media power, written by one of the field's leading scholars.

Hb: 0-415-07739-7
Pb: 0-415-07740-0

Available at all good bookshops
For ordering and further information please visit:
www.routledge.com